Lifelong Learning in Europe

National Patterns and Challenges

Edited by

Ellu Saar

Tallinn University, Estonia

Odd Bjørn Ure

Fafo, Norway

John Holford

University of Nottingham, UK

Edward Elgar

Cheltenham, UK • Northampton, MA, USA

Published by
Edward Elgar Publishing Limited
The Lypiatts
15 Lansdown Road
Cheltenham
Glos GL50 2JA
UK

Edward Elgar Publishing, Inc.
William Pratt House
9 Dewey Court
Northampton
Massachusetts 01060
USA

A catalogue record for this book
is available from the British Library

Library of Congress Control Number: 2012955988

This book is available electronically in the ElgarOnline.com
Social and Political Science Subject Collection, E-ISBN 978 0 85793 736 0

MIX
Paper from
responsible sources
FSC
www.fsc.org
FSC® C013056

ISBN 978 0 85793 735 3

Typeset by Servis Filmsetting Ltd, Stockport, Cheshire
Printed and bound in Great Britain by T.J. International Ltd, Padstow

Contents

Contributors

Bjørg Eva Aaslid is a researcher at SINTEF Technology and Society, Department of Health Research, Group of Work and Health in Oslo, Norway. Aaslid was a research assistant at the Fafo Institute for Labour and Social Research, on the EU Sixth Framework Project, 'Towards a Lifelong Learning Society in Europe: The Contribution of the Education System' (LLL2010). Her research areas are: school development, quality in education, lifelong learning, learning environment and work environment in the educational sector.

Szilvia Altorjai is a sociologist conducting her PhD research at the Institute for Social and Economic Research, University of Essex. Her research interests include labour markets, education, human capital transferability, over-qualification and migration.

Saida Ayupova is a freelance writer and international affairs specialist. She has conducted research on the socio-political relation between European integration and freedom of the media in the Balkan region. Within the LLL2010 project she was responsible for processing and analysing interview data to create an overview of the state of formal adult education in Hungary.

Ellen Boeren started her research career at HIVA (Research Institute for Work and Society) at the University of Leuven, Belgium. She successfully defended her PhD thesis 'Participation in adult education: a bounded agency approach' in 2011. She is interested in lifelong learning policies, motivational aspects of adult learning, European comparative research and survey methodologies. She is currently employed as a Chancellor's Fellow at the Moray School of Education, University of Edinburgh, UK.

Pepka Boyadjieva is a Professor at the Institute for the Study of Societies and Knowledge and member of the General Assembly of the Bulgarian Academy of Sciences. She is also Honorary Professor of Sociology of Education, University of Nottingham. Boyadjieva was leader of the Bulgarian team of the LLL2010 project. Her research areas are higher education and social justice, university models, educational inequalities and social modernization. She is an editorial correspondent of the

International Journal of Lifelong Education, a member of the editorial board of the *Journal of Social Science Education* and a member of the editorial board of the ISA's SSIS series Sage Studies in International Sociology Books.

Paul Downes is Director of the Educational Disadvantage Centre and Senior Lecturer in Education (Psychology) at St Patrick's College, Dublin City University, Ireland. His areas of research interest include lifelong learning, early school leaving, phenomenology, psychoanalysis, developmental psychology and structuralism. He has been a member of various Expert Advisory Groups to the European Commission, including the Network of Experts on the Social Aspects of Education and Training (NESET).

Leta Dromantienė is a Professor in the Social Policy Department and Dean of the Social Policy Faculty at Mykolas Romeris University, Vilnius, Lithuania. She was national coordinator of the LLL2010 project. Her research areas are social cohesion, social policy, educational management and lifelong learning. She is editor-in-chief of the editorial board of *Social Work* and a member of the editorial board of *Social Studies*.

Galin Gornev is a Professor at the Institute for the Study of Societies and Knowledge of the Bulgarian Academy of Sciences in Sofia. He served as a Bulgarian representative and a member of the Standing Committee on the Social Sciences (SCSS) of the European Science Foundation (2005–2011). His research interests are in the fields of human agency and social structure, science and society, social conflicts and disturbances in communication, and transition to a hydrogen society.

Günter Hefler is Senior Researcher and Project Manager at 3s Unternehmensberatung GmbH in Vienna, Austria. Within the LLL2010 project, he was responsible for the cross-country comparative synthesis of findings of subproject 4 studying the role of formal adult education in small and medium-sized enterprises. His areas of research include comparative studies on lifelong learning and continuing vocational training, workplace learning, and adult learning and development.

John Holford is Robert Peers Professor of Adult Education and Director of the Centre for Research in Higher, Adult and Vocational Education at the University of Nottingham, UK. His main current research interest is in lifelong learning policy, especially in Europe, in adult learning of citizenship, and in the history of adult education. He is Editor of the *International Journal of Lifelong Education*, and a convenor of the Policy

Studies Network for the European Society for Research in the Education of Adults.

Angela Ivančič is a part-time researcher at the Institute for Developmental and Strategic Analysis (IRSA) in Ljubljana, Slovenia and a contracted Assistant Professor at the Faculty for Social Sciences, Ljubljana University. Her current research interest involves the study of socio-cultural dimensions of knowledge creation and transfer in a comparative perspective.

Anisya Khokhlova is an Associate Professor at the Faculty of Sociology, St Petersburg State University, Russia. The field of her scientific interests covers cultural studies, urban studies and the sociology of everyday life. As a participant in the LLL2010 project, she was primarily involved in the collection and analysis of qualitative data.

Vladimir Kozlovskiy is a Professor at the Department of Sociology, St Petersburg State University, Russia, and a researcher at the Sociological Institute of Russian Academy of Sciences. His research areas are civilizational analyses and modernities, history of Russian sociology, modernization of Russian society, social communication, labour migration and educational institutes. He is editor-in-chief of the *Journal of Sociology and Social Anthropology*.

Liutauras Labanauskas is a researcher at the Institute of Sociology of the Lithuanian Social Research Centre, and a post-doctoral research fellow at the Centre for Social Anthropology at Vytautas Magnus University, Kaunas, Lithuania. He was responsible for administrative and research support for the LLL2010 project. His research interests include lifelong learning, knowledge transfer, migration and development, national identity and social cohesion.

Jörg Markowitsch is founder and Senior Partner of 3s Unternehmensberatung GmbH in Vienna, Austria. As former Head of Department for Continuing Education Research and Educational Management at the Danube University Krems he led the Austrian research team of the LLL2010 project. He is a member of various scientific boards and EU expert groups. His areas of research include comparative studies in vocational education and training, lifelong learning and European educational policy.

Catherine Maunsell is Senior Lecturer in Education (Psychology) and Human Development at St Patrick's College, Drumcondra (SPD), a college of Dublin City University (DCU) and coordinator of SPD's collaborative partnership with DCU on the BSc Psychology, Ireland. She is currently chairperson of the Advisory Group of the Educational

Disadvantage Centre EDC and has recently been Acting Director of the Centre. She was joint Irish coordinator with Dr Paul Downes in the LLL2010 project and is currently Irish coordinator of the Grundtvig RISE Learning Partnership on prison education and the Grundtvig Network research on adult education and social inclusion titled 'OED: Outreach Empowerment and Diversity' with the European Association for the Education of Adults (EAEA).

Valentina Milenkova is a Professor at the Sociology Department, South-West University, Blagoevgrad, Bulgaria, where she teaches the courses 'Sociology of Education' and 'Social Stratification and Inequalities'. Milenkova's main interests are equal education opportunities, ethnic minorities and lifelong learning. She is a member of the editorial board of the e-journal *Problems of Postmodernity*.

Agata Mleczko is a former Research Fellow at the University of Nottingham, UK and presently an associate of the Centre for Migration Studies at the University of Adam Mickiewicz in Poznań, Poland. Her research interests are focused on social capital in the migration setting, education of immigrants and parental involvement in schools.

Diana Nenkova is a sociologist at the the Department of Knowledge-based Society, Institute for the Study of Societies and Knowledge, Bulgaria. Her main interests are in the sociology of science and education.

Ides Nicaise has a background in economics and is head of the unit 'Education and Lifelong Learning' at HIVA (Research Institute for Work and Society), a multidisciplinary research institute of the University of Leuven, Belgium. He specialized in social policy, more precisely the relationships between education, labour market policy and social inclusion (in rich as well as developing countries). He also teaches 'Education and Society' and 'Economics of Education and Training' in the Department of Education Sciences at the same university.

Kristina Petkova is a Professor at the Institute for the Study of Societies and Knowledge, Bulgarian Academy of Sciences. She is co-editor of the main Bulgarian sociological journal *Sociological Problems*. Petkova is a member of the European Association of Social Psychology Science. She has been a team leader in different national representative and international cross-cultural studies. Her research interests are related to attitudes and attitude-behaviour consistency, lifelong learning, social stereotypes and social cohesion, and public understanding of science.

Marko Radovan is an Assistant Professor in Didactics of Adult Education at the Faculty of Arts, University of Ljubljana, Slovenia.

He has participated in many international and national research projects dealing with adult participation in education and learning. His research interests are participation in education, motivation to learn, didactics of adult learning and e-learning. He is also a member of the editorial board of the *Andragogic Perspectives*, a Slovenian journal on adult education.

Stephanie Rammel is Austrian National Contact Point for Socio-Economic Sciences and the Humanities in the 7th EU Framework Programme at the Austrian Research Promotion Agency FFG. From 2007 to 2011 she was a researcher at Danube University Krems. Her research in the LLL2010 project focuses on participants in adult education and on social and institutional barriers to social inclusion. She is a sociologist and political scientist, specializing in gender and diversity research.

Sheila Riddell is Director of the Centre for Research in Education Inclusion and Diversity at the Moray House School of Education, University of Edinburgh, UK. Her research interests are in the broad field of equality and social inclusion, with particular reference to gender, social class and disability in education, training, employment and social care. She has published extensively in these areas and sits on policy advisory committees on disability and equal rights in the UK.

Paul Ringler is a sociologist at the SORA Institute for Social Research and Consulting, Vienna, Austria, working on social scientific projects at the national and EU level. He worked as a researcher on LLL2010's comparative report on participation in formal adult education in Europe. He specializes in quantitative data collection and analysis. His research areas include transition from education to the job market, adult education, adult literacy and new forms of communication.

Péter Róbert is Professor of Sociology at the Szechenyi Istvan University in Gyor, Hungary. He is also Senior Researcher at the Institute for Political Science of the Hungarian Academy of Sciences. He has participated in the LLL2010 project representing the TARKI Social Research Institute. His research fields include social stratification and mobility, educational inequalities and life course analysis, school to work transition as well as political participation, behaviour, values and attitudes. His current project is running the European Social Survey in Hungary.

Triin Roosalu is a sociologist at the Institute of International and Social Studies, Tallinn University, Estonia. Her main research interests lie in sociology of education, employment and working life in comparative perspective. She was a member of the coordinating team of the LLL2010 project and held a personal grant to carry out the national Primus programme project 'Adults acquiring higher education: reconciliating studies with work and life'. She co-edited (with V. Kozlovskiy and R. Vöörmann) *Learning in Transition: Policies and Practices of Lifelong Learning in Post-Socialist Countries* (2010). In 2012, she was elected to the drafting committee for the global International Social Survey Programme survey of 2015 on work and employment.

Eve-Liis Roosmaa is a researcher, lecturer and graduate student in sociology at the Institute of International and Social Studies, Tallinn University, Estonia. She was a member of the coordinating team of the LLL2010 project. Her main fields of study are education, the labour market and lifelong learning, mostly in a comparative perspective. She has participated in various national and international research projects, which address the inequality issues regarding adult education and lifelong learning.

Ellu Saar is a Professor at the Institute of International and Social Studies, Tallinn University, Estonia. She coordinated the LLL2010 project. Her research areas are social stratification and mobility, educational inequalities and life course studies. She is an editor of *Studies of Transition States and Societies*, a member of the editorial board of *European Sociological Review* and a member of the Steering Committee of the European Consortium of Sociological Research.

Meilutė Taljūnaitė is a Professor at the Institute of Sociology of the Lithuanian Social Research Centre, and a Professor at the Lithuanian University of Educational Sciences. She was national coordinator of the LLL2010 project. Her research interests include EU citizenship and European social integration, gender policy, migration, national identity, inequalities and social cohesion. She is a a member of the editorial board and chief editor of *Filosofija, Sociologija* and a member of the Helsinki Group on Women and Science of the European Commission.

Auni Tamm is a project assistant at the Institute of International and Social Studies Tallinn University, Estonia, where she is currently working on her PhD thesis. Her research interests are connected to issues of lifelong learning, continuing education and background career choices.

Odd Bjørn Ure works as an independent researcher in his own company CONSULTUR. Studies & Analyses. He was a researcher at the Fafo Institute for Labour and Social Research in Norway during the contractual period of LLL2010. Ure has a cand. polit. degree from the University of Bergen, Norway, and has held several posts in the field of research strategy and educational policy, with an emphasis on vocational training. When serving as Visiting Scientist at the Institute for Prospective Technological Studies in Seville, Spain, he particularly covered online access to lifelong learning resources. Ure now primarily works for the EU Lifelong Learning Programme.

Maria Veits is a sociologist, independent researcher and curator based in St Petersburg, Russia. She is a co-founder of the Creative Association of Curators TOK, an organization that realizes multidisciplinary projects in the fields of contemporary art and social sciences. Among other projects organized by TOK, such as public and visual exhibitions, lectures, publications and other initiatives aimed at knowledge production, Maria is currently a curator and sociologist of the project Design Platform. Its mission is to apply socially integrated innovative design practices to the social sector, including educational organizations, for the improvement and transformation of the learning environment.

Rein Vöörmann is a Senior Researcher and Chair of the Department of Social Stratification, Institute of International and Social Studies, Tallinn University, Estonia. His current research addresses social stratification in Estonia against the backdrop of other post-socialist countries, social inequalities and gender segregation. He is a member of the editorial board of *Studies of Transition States and Societies*, and a member of the Steering Committee of the SHARE – ESTONIA.

Elisabet Weedon is Deputy Director of the Centre for Research in Education Inclusion and Diversity at the Moray House School of Education, University of Edinburgh, UK. Her main research interests are in the area of adult learning and equality in education. She is currently involved in projects on inclusion in education and educational experiences and outcomes for Muslim pupils in England and Scotland.

Thushari Welikala is a Research Fellow in Participatory Research at Liverpool Hope University, UK. Before joining Hope University, she worked at the University of Nottingham, UK, as a Senior Research Fellow. She has contributed to a number of research projects funded by major funding bodies: the Liverhulme Trust, British Academy, Higher Education Academy and Leadership Foundation for Higher Education. Her main research interests are in the internationalization of higher education and the mediation of culture in higher education teaching and learning. She is the principal investigator of a project funded by the Higher Education Academy and the UK Council for International Student Affairs on internationalisation.

Irena Žemaitaitytė is a Professor at the Faculty of Social Policy, Mykolas Romeris University, Lithuania. Her research areas are adult education, professional training, non-formal adult education and third-age education. She is a member of the editorial board of *Societal Studies* and a member of the European Society for Research on the Education of Adults.

Foreword

In the wake of the European Union's (EU) Lisbon Strategy to become 'the most competitive and dynamic knowledge-based economy in the world' by 2010, the 'lifelong learning' (LLL) concept has gained substantially in importance. Lifelong Learning even became the central keyword for the EU's Education and Training programmes in the 2007–2013 period.

It is worthwhile to recall that the research project 'Towards a Lifelong Learning Society in Europe: The Contribution of the Education System' (LLL2010), on which this volume builds, responded to a call for proposals (drafted in 2002–2003) on 'Promoting the knowledge society through lifelong learning':

> Research capacities on various key aspects of lifelong learning should be integrated in order to compare the various discourses, improve conceptual clarity, better understand trends in lifelong learning policies and practices in Europe as well as their implications for the creation of a European knowledge society, for social cohesion, inequalities and quality of life.

While the socio-economic and policy context has changed substantially since the start of the project, key issues regarding 'inclusive growth' remain as essential as before for Europe's future prosperity and well-being, and the project has connected its research findings to these new and evolving realities.

Since its very conception, the LLL2010 consortium has taken an ambitious and holistic approach to analyse the 'lifelong learning' concept comprehensively. While limiting itself to formal adult education, the team has integrated researchers and institutions from a wide range of countries and academic disciplines across Europe, making best use of a broad range of quantitative and qualitative research methods.

The project has identified, in a structured way, barriers and obstacles to fuller implementation of LLL strategies at various levels:

- macro level: policies at national and EU levels;
- meso level: institutions – small and medium-sized enterprises (SMEs) and schools; and
- micro level: individuals – adult learners, trainers, managers, etc.

Connecting and integrating these research levels, the project has invested substantially in developing some new typologies, for example for formal adult education systems, for adult learners in SMEs, and so on. With its focus on formal adult education, an original and relatively under-researched topic, the LLL2010 project has provided an additional angle to qualify and refine the traditional typologies of European welfare states.

It has in particular provided some deeper insights into the 'newer' EU member states in Central and Eastern Europe on which the availability and analysis of data has been more limited. That the project has been coordinated by an organization from such a country adds to the institution and capacity building that EU programmes seek to contribute to.

An important focus of the project design and analysis was placed on social inclusion. The research design has allowed the LLL2010 researchers to explore the learning practices (aspirations and difficulties) of adult learners from less advanced socio-economic groups; in turn, this allows policy-makers to design strategies and adapt polices to address these issues. Moreover, the project has also made a valuable exploratory contribution in studying adult education policies and strategies in prisons in the countries concerned.

This volume summarizes the knowledge accumulated during almost a decade of preparation and cooperation. It constitutes a valuable contribution to the academic and policy communities, and opens up avenues for future developments. On a personal note, I would like to thank all those involved in this effort for their cooperation, commitment and perseverance on this pan-European comparative journey.

*Marc Goffart,European Commission Scientific Officer**

NOTE

* This contribution is written in the name of the author and does not reflect the opinion of the European Commission as an institution.

Preface

In March 2000, the then 15 European leaders committed the European Union (EU) to become by 2010 'the most dynamic and competitive knowledge based economy in the world, capable of sustainable economic growth with more and better jobs and greater social cohesion, and respect for the environment'. The research project sustaining this book started in 2005, five years after the formulation of the 2010 goals. The Lisbon strategy, as it has come to be known, was a comprehensive but interdependent series of reforms which have significant implications for a whole range of social policies, including policies for learning. As part of the Lisbon strategy, the European Union set the goal of raising the number of adults participating in lifelong learning to 12.5 per cent by 2010. However, the proportion of learning adults in Europe differs widely across countries. This book is dedicated to identifying the reasons behind these differences and to studying the policies and practices related to adults' participation in and access to lifelong learning in a number of European countries.

The research focused on the contribution of the education systems to the process of making lifelong learning a reality and its role as a potential agency of social integration in 13 European countries: Austria, Belgium, Bulgaria, the Czech Republic, England, Estonia, Hungary, Ireland, Lithuania, Norway, Russia, Scotland and Slovenia. We addressed several pivotal problems. Are there differences in terms of lifelong learning between EU countries and, if so, do these depend on country-specific institutions? To what extent may lifelong learning in reality (as opposed to merely rhetoric) be allocated a residual role in national policy-making? What are the barriers to lifelong learning and how can these be overcome? How could employers, especially small and medium-sized enterprises (SMEs), promote the participation of adults in lifelong learning? Which are the main obstacles for SMEs to invest in lifelong learning? How can educational institutions promote the access of adults to the education system? Are schools and universities ready to change their admission policies and become institutions of lifelong learning?

The above questions were scrutinized in five subprojects all reported in this volume, which is one of two compilations of the research stemming from the international research project 'Towards a Lifelong Learning

Society in Europe: The Contribution of the Education System' (LLL2010), financed by the European Union's 6th Framework Research Programme. The first volume, entitled *Lifelong Learning in Europe: Equity and Efficiency in Balance*, was published by Policy Press in 2012. The strategic objectives of the project, now terminated, included the following: (1) achieving a better understanding of the tensions between a knowledge-based society, lifelong learning and social inclusion in the context of EU enlargement and globalization; (2) analysing the role that education systems play in the enhancement of lifelong learning – and in particular, the role that institutions play at micro, meso and macro levels; (3) providing an analysis, based on evidence, of the adequacy of lifelong learning policies for different social groups (especially the socially excluded). Any further information about the project can be found at http://LLL2010.tlu.ee.

An important goal of the LLL2010 project was to create and utilize an international research network that collectively pursued specific, substantive and methodological analyses of lifelong learning. This volume depended on the contributors to this volume of experts working in their respective countries. Our gratitude goes to all participants of the project (see the List of Contributors) for their enthusiastic, professional and supportive teamwork during the project.

We would like to thank all the authors for their collegiality, support and patience during the project. In Tallinn, our gratitude goes to Eve-Liis Roosmaa, Triin Roosalu and Epp Reiska for technical assistance and to Marcus Denton for the language editing. We would also like to thank the project review team, Dragana Avramov, Jacky Brine, Philipp Grollmann and Hanna Shapiro, who all helped us to improve the final outcome. We have highly appreciated the assistance from Tim Williams, Emily Neukomm and Jennifer Wilcox at Edward Elgar Publishing when preparing for the publication of this volume. Finally, we would like to thank our contacts, Marc Goffart and Angelos Agalianos, from the European Commission for their patience and continued help.

Ellu Saar
Odd Bjørn Ure
John Holford

Introduction

Ellu Saar, Odd Bjørn Ure and John Holford

This book is designed to provide an illuminating account of the nature of contemporary lifelong learning (LLL) in Europe. The institutional and social context to lifelong learning, as well as path-dependency of its development, is the cornerstone of the approach this book takes. The chapters also study the complex relationships between perspectives at the European level and the lifelong learning policies and practices within European countries. The book contains country chapters written by authors from the respective countries, who best know and can meaningfully explain the context. Based on prior cooperation by the authors who jointly carried out the research agenda within a European Union (EU) project that explored policy and practice in 13 countries, the book covers not only established Western EU member states (Austria, Belgium, the United Kingdom, Ireland), but a spectrum of newer EU member states of post-socialist Central and Eastern Europe (Bulgaria, the Czech Republic, Estonia, Hungary, Lithuania, Slovenia) as well as non-members of the EU (Norway, Russia). Different political, economic and cultural backgrounds of the participating countries allowed the research teams to compare various concepts and practices of lifelong learning adopted in these countries.

As the research was carried out between 2005 and 2011, the chapters in this book are all based on up-to-date empirical investigations. Largely, the chapters address lifelong learning policies, the participation of adults in formal learning, their access to learning, perceived obstacles to participation and perceived individual demand for learning opportunities.

The first section in this introductory chapter explores the importance of a formal education system in lifelong learning. The second section describes the research project LLL2010 and the data on which the book draws. The third section describes the structure of the book. The remaining sections discuss the themes and theoretical perspectives developed throughout the chapters written by various country teams.

LIFELONG LEARNING IN THE FORMAL EDUCATION SYSTEM

The 'life-wide' dimension of LLL refers to the fact that learning takes place in a variety of environments and is not only confined to the formal education system (Green 2002). As the EU Memorandum on Lifelong Learning from 2000 mentioned, 'the "life-wide" dimension brings the complementarity of formal, non-formal and informal learning into sharper focus' (CEC 2000). The lifelong aspect raises questions about the structure and interrelationship between different sectors of the education system. A crucial prerequisite for lifelong education is a system that promotes smooth progression with no dead ends. Mechanisms for transition from school to work, and repeated later transitions between work and education, are highlighted.

During the implementation of the EU 'Education and Training 2010' work programme, now replaced by the strategic framework for European cooperation in education and training (ET 2020), several European Commission interim reports (e.g. CEC 2003) on the follow-up of the objectives in the member states, pointed to a situation in which efforts are made in all the European countries to adapt the education and training systems to the knowledge-driven society and economy. However, the reforms undertaken are not up to the challenges and their current pace will not enable the EU to attain the objectives. As in national policy-making, there is a tendency to formulate objectives to the point of displaying optimistic visions. The present book reveals some structural constraints in reaching policy objectives, such as the fact that the qualities people need to develop through learning are changing. Learning to learn, critical thinking and self-management have been traditionally the focus of higher education but not of secondary or basic education (Jarvis 2001). The rapid changes in the qualification demands of the labour market cannot be met unless basic qualifications as a minimum are available. This furthermore may lead to social exclusion of those with less basic skills. There is evidence that a higher level of initial education leads to greater participation in training.

Results from the International Adult Literacy Survey indicated that employers seldom contribute to the general education of workers with limited literacy skills (OECD 2000b). Thus, the public sector has the task of providing the foundation for lifelong learning for a large segment of the adult population. The challenge posed to the formal education system by lifelong learning lies primarily in giving individuals a stable foundation for lifelong learning. Lifelong learning presupposes that compulsory schooling achieves the goal of individuals developing their own unique characteristics and, in this context, refers to the broadening of upper secondary education. In addition, the education system has the important task of promoting equality through the recruitment and participation of everyone in lifelong learning, and in making the importance of social background less dominant. Adult education is one way of reducing existing education gaps.

Many adults have not had any possibility to enter secondary or higher education earlier in their lives, or they have dropped out, but yet are capable as adults to continue their studies in the education system. Despite much greater recognition that the education system is fundamental to lifelong learning, rather than a separate set of provisions that precedes it, there is as yet little evidence that schools now fundamentally rethink their role in meeting this challenge. However the contribution from the formal education system in implementing lifelong learning is important for several reasons.

Firstly, age matters in the sense that adults' propensity to engage in systematic learning activities diminishes over the years (OECD 2001). Enrolment rates in formal education of those aged 30 years and over are rather limited and vary significantly from country to country. One issue this raises is how well education systems respond to the population shrinkage of younger generations and the commensurate expansion of the older generations. This fact highlights the importance of adult education as the focus of policies, particularly in the fight against low levels of adult literacy, which represents a major hurdle to the successful achievement of lifelong learning. The International Adult Literacy Survey found that from one-quarter to over one-half of the adult population do not have the suitable minimum skills level deemed necessary for coping with the demands of modern life and work (OECD 2000b).

Secondly, informal as well as formal learning tends to concentrate on adults who are already qualified and enjoy relatively high professional status. Individuals who acquire more schooling are also more likely to receive post-school training, while those with minimal education find it extremely difficult to make up this deficiency in human capital once they enter the labour market. The strong link between education level and the level of training suggests that the strategy for strengthening schooling is a potent means of encouraging participation in lifelong learning. This underlines the more general challenge of establishing effective systems of basic educational preparation for all. Without integrating schooling fully within a lifelong strategy, recurrent education would stumble over these critical intra-generational inequalities.

Thirdly, with the main exception of the Scandinavian countries, general education tends to be conspicuously absent from the much-expanded adult education and training programmes, whether public or enterprise-based. Adult education almost became synonymous with continuing professional or vocational education. Already in the Organisation for Economic Co-operation and Development (OECD) report *Human Resources in the New Economy: Challenges and Opportunities for Education and Training* (OECD 2000a), it was mentioned that 'the traditional concept of an occupation with its clear set of technical skills is rapidly losing currency. Workers need a broad mix of technical and general skills, which will enable them to change direction or specialise as the need arises'.

Fourthly, formal adult education has an institutionalized social character (Meyer 1970), which involves transitions, not only from work to school and back to work, but also between institutionalized categories of personnel (Hefler 2012, p. 17).

GENERAL DESCRIPTION OF THE PROJECT

This book is based on the results of the research project 'Towards a Lifelong Learning Society in Europe: The Contribution of the Education System' (Lifelong Learning 2010, or LLL2010), that the team of researchers across 13 countries carried out during 2005–2011 with co-funding from the European Commission under the 6th Framework Programme. The project focuses on the contribution of the education systems to the process of making lifelong learning a reality and its role as a potential agency of social integration.

The project's innovative approach of multilevel institutional analysis had the following three principal points of departure. Firstly, we assumed that lifelong learning is functioning within the broader economic, social and cultural systems in which it is embedded. Country-specific and historically developed institutional systems shape the opportunities as well as the incentives for lifelong learning, and therefore it is likely that there is no universal lifelong learning system across the countries. Secondly, all subsystems strongly interact. This means that the differences between lifelong learning systems are systematic. The systems could therefore be classified along a number of dimensions of institutional variation, and may be grouped into types of systems with common characteristics. Thirdly, these institutional 'packages' and subsystems yield strikingly different outcomes of analogous political reforms and thus become the main mechanisms for promotion of the so-called Europeanization of the societies and their country-specific policies. This in turn means that solutions are path-dependent and changes are institutionally bounded.

Following the outlined basic principles, the key questions about participation in lifelong learning have been approached in this project as being subject to influence from three analytical levels: national policies on the macro level; institutional factors and actors on the meso level; and strategies of relevant individual actors on the micro level. Given the novelty of such a systematic approach in cross-country comparisons, there was a clear lack of any data that could enable the team to answer the questions of relevance to this type of approach.

During the project, the team designed and carried out a number of innovative empirical studies with regard to macro, meso and micro levels. These studies enabled the project to systematically take into account, and compare, the macro-structural factors and national policies, as well as meso-level institutional factors and actors' motivation and actions at the micro level. All of these were considered to influence the role that educational systems have in promoting lifelong learning. The project was structured into five subprojects, which were arranged on the basis of the specific research questions each addressed, and which thus helped to achieve the objectives of the whole project. There were four original research projects initiated by the research consortium to collect comparable data. Subproject 1 comprised policy analysis of lifelong learning policies (LLP) at the national as well as EU level, based on data collected in 2006. Subproject 3, in 2007, consisted of a survey of adult learners in formal education (ALiFE), which covered both learners and the formal education institutions they were engaged in. Subproject 4, in 2008, consisted of case studies on formal learning practices in small and medium-sized enterprises (SME-LLL) that shape access to lifelong learning of the employees. Subproject 5, in 2009, collected interviews with other stakeholders in adult education (SAE). Additionally, the team analysed representative lifelong learning. Subproject 2 comprised analyses of data from Eurostat's 2007 Adult Education Survey (AES) and an ad hoc module on lifelong learning within the 2003 European Labour Force Survey (LFS), which sought to answer specific research questions deriving from the team's novel conceptual approach.

The proposed methodology enabled the team to address different dimensions of the subject of research. The research covered three levels as well as different aspects:

1. Macro level:
   - Macro-structural aspect, to describe how country-specific institutions influence the supply and demand for lifelong learning.
   - Policy aspect, to describe different lifelong learning concepts fixed at the EU level as well as national policy documents, to analyse national policy measures focusing on lifelong learning policies, to identify the barriers to a coordinated focus across

different policy fields, and the concrete initiatives and public sector policies implemented at each level of the education system.

2. Meso level:
   - Schools and universities, to analyse the role of schools in meeting the lifelong learning challenge, to promote the access of adults to the education system.
   - Small and medium-sized enterprises (SMEs), to analyse the more fruitful approaches to improving the financial incentives for SMEs to invest in adult general education, and the demand of SMEs for more educated employees.
3. Micro level:
   - Adult population, to analyse participation and access of adults to formal learning. We analysed the data of Eurostat's Adult Education Survey and an ad hoc module on lifelong learning of the European Labour Force Survey.
   - Adult learners, to analyse the motivation of adults participating in formal learning, the expectations and attitudes towards LLL, obstacles to access and support received, determinants of choice behaviour, evaluation of ongoing training, and so on. We carried out a survey of adults studying in the formal education system (at the basic, secondary and tertiary levels).

The project's general methodology presented many important characteristics. Firstly, an international comparison. The research included European countries at different points of the continuum in relation to the access of adults to formal education. Some countries (mostly post-socialist countries) are very much at the starting point of the continuum with very few adults participating in formal education; while in other countries, such as Norway and the United Kingdom (UK), full adult participation in education – certainly in further education institutions – is the norm. Some countries, therefore, have a lot of catching up to do if they are to make lifelong learning in formal education a possibility. The countries of comparison were selected for the purpose of having a well-presented range of institutional settings.

Secondly, the project employed an approach combining quantitative and qualitative analysis: the project combined large-scale statistical and sociological studies, documentary and policy studies and qualitative studies (interviews and focus group interviews). And thirdly, it had a multidisciplinary approach: the teams involved in the project comprised of researchers from many disciplines (sociology, economics, political sciences, history, psychology, the educational sciences).

OVERVIEW OF THE BOOK

As mentioned above, the point of departure for the research project in this book was to scrutinize formal adult education within a lifelong learning (LLL) perspective. The team realized very quickly that the notions of adult education, as well as formal education and their antonym, non-formal education, had to be profoundly revisited – and even revised. Likewise, the notion of lifelong learning and the extent to which national education and training systems have embarked on lifelong learning trajectories instead of only paying tribute to LLL slogans, became a critical issue. Chapter 1 starts with an investigation of national LLL policies from the European perspective, in which the EU policy framework is at the centre.

Chapter 2 follows by discussing typologies of LLL systems along the wide range of education and training practices, which for good or perhaps opportunistic reasons are assigned to lifelong learning. The third chapter in Part I of the book proposes a comparative framework of formal adult education based on a typology particularly emphasizing the composition of the organizational populations providing one type of formal adult education. This composition encompasses organizations belonging to different organizational fields, notably liberal adult education, management training, trade unions and initial vocational education. The proposed framework partly builds on observations accruing from the Adult Education Survey carried out at a national and cross-national level. Subsequently, the notion of organizational fields is applied to the Austrian educational system in one of the 12 country chapters constituting the second part of the book. In Part II, the national teams sum up key findings from their domestic research carried out during the five-year project period.

EU AND NATIONAL-LEVEL POLICIES: HUMAN CAPITAL VERSUS SOCIAL CAPITAL PERSPECTIVES

In the policies of the European Union, lifelong learning has been a means of achieving both competitiveness and social cohesion in an increasingly knowledge-based and globalized economy. The concept and practice of lifelong learning in Europe has developed in close connection with wider political, economic and social forces. This is true at both EU and national levels. Early research on this topic strongly suggested that Europe's diversity was deeply important, and 'a single model of lifelong learning' across the EU was unlikely to be achieved (Holford et al. 2008).

In lifelong learning, economic and social concerns have often been in tension (Holford 2006). Lifelong education as conceptualized in the 1970s had a strong humanistic dimension; when lifelong learning re-emerged in the 1990s, the emphasis was firmly on economic performance, individual and societal (Field 2006). The EU's approach to lifelong learning after 2000 evolved in many ways along lines set in the 1990s. The key themes continued to be competitiveness and social inclusion. Two themes emerge clearly in both Lisbon and Europ. 2020 strategies: on the one hand, competitiveness and growth; on the other, social cohesion and inclusion, strongly linked to employment. Europe's policies for lifelong learning over the past decade have been formulated within this context. As widely noted, the emphasis of lifelong learning policies internationally has been strongly 'economistic' since their emergence in the early 1990s.

As in EU policies, there is a general trend across the countries of lifelong learning policies focusing on labour market issues. Several country chapters report biased policies because LLL is predominantly following a narrow employability agenda. Chapter 4 on Scotland investigates these two perspectives by looking into the LLL discourses from the angle of social inclusion. Recent policies are moving away from LLL as a means of achieving social capital in terms of personal development and social inclusion. Young people are increasingly targeted because they are – from a human capital perspective – more salvageable in a labour market context. The redistribution discourse is therefore evident in Scotland, although the target groups for this redistribution continue to be under consideration, while there is a shift away from older people, who are generally more reluctant learners but who stand to gain if provided with learning in a nurturing environment. The authors find no evidence for the moral underclass discourse, meaning that the individual is expected to take responsibility for engaging in learning, with the assumption that such personal initiative would encourage norms and values conducive to social inclusion. The social integrationist discourse considers LLL to have a vital role in terms of upskilling, reskilling and in providing essential skills for entering the labour market. This discourse is present in Scotland and now centres on the working-age adult population. The country team points out that the three discourses are not mutually exclusive: the redistribution of the opportunity to participate in learning may, for example, enable an individual to achieve a qualification for entry into the labour market.

POLICY LEARNING AND BORROWING

One diagnosis in Chapter 1 on national LLL policies in the European perspective is that lifelong learning strategies are often exercises in policy learning. Those countries borrowing tools and concepts for domestic policy-making are not only the new member states trying to learn to catch up with 'best practices' heralded by the EU. The old member states also have, albeit often reluctantly, plunged into exercises of mutual policy learning and the open method of policy coordination.

In Chapter 10, judging from the available data on developments in adult education, the country team argues that during the preparation period before becoming an EU member, Slovenia benefited from EU policies in the field of lifelong learning and employment. Good practices from some European countries also contributed to the development of more coherent systems, which facilitated participation in formal and non-formal adult education. At a declarative level, Slovenia has adopted the concept of lifelong learning as defined by the EU. However, lifelong learning is understood narrowly, as education of adults – predominantly the non-formal part. One sign of this is that education of adults is not treated as complementary to youth education, with its own requirements. Also, structures and institutions of the education system directly affecting participation in adult education have not experienced changes which could ease the access of adults to formal education. This particularly applies to the most deprived groups.

Chapter 14 on Lithuania looks back at the first years after independence from the Soviet system and concludes that the education system evolved from a highly ideological and domestic, to a more open 'internationalizing' system, culminating in EU membership in 2004. In the early 1990s, during Lithuania's 'Singing Revolution' movement for independence, education reform was subject to public debate, which could sustain the nation-building process as well as fostering economic and political stability. By mid-1992, the Lithuanian government announced that 'the education system is based on European cultural values', and set out fundamental guidelines for the reform of the education system. A next step was the discussions in mid-2001 on the EU Memorandum on Lifelong Learning, introducing new terms and concepts in Lithuanian policy documents and into the general academic discourse. Following the gradual implementation of these education policies and strategies, a system of formal and non-formal adult education providers was formed, with shared responsibilities between the main organizers. The Lithuanian country team concludes that the efforts to improve participation in lifelong learning have so far proven to be insufficient, mainly because too little importance is attached to adults' access to higher education.

Whilst Bulgaria after 2007 was extremely sensitive to all initiatives coming from international and especially European organizations, the assimilation of these initiatives has often assumed the character not of learning and harmonization, but of borrowing, imitation and copying (see Chapter 12). In this way, certain elements quite distant in nature from Bulgarian post-communist reality were introduced and artificially implanted, thereby generating distorted and ineffective social practices. The Bulgarian country team holds that contemporary LLL policy is subordinated to employment policy and LLL is predominantly subsumed under vocational education and training.

TYPOLOGIES OF LIFELONG LEARNING

The macro-level structural and institutional environment can only be captured if we take account of the wide definition of LLL: both as a realm of policy-making with its subsectors, and also accounting for LLL as a social field subject to scientific enquiry. The authors of the chapter 'Lifelong learning systems: overview and extension of different typologies' (Chapter 2) approach LLL from these two angles by discussing typologies being produced to analyse welfare state systems, skill formation systems and theories on varieties of capitalism.

Existing analyses clearly demonstrate large differences in how institutional factors impact participation in LLL across European countries (Saar and Helemäe 2008; Roosmaa and Saar 2010). In countries with different skill formation systems, the same combination of labour market institutions and education systems yields divergent patterns of participation in LLL. This means that variations in links between education systems, labour market institutions and participation opportunities reflect the embeddedness of LLL in 'packages' of mutually interdependent and coherent institutions.

The authors claim that typologies help researchers and policy-makers in escaping from assumptions of a single economic trajectory for market economies and for their LLL systems. Furthermore, as with the much more widespread conceptualization of education systems, researchers need to look for demarcations of those institutions that constitute emerging or already established LLL systems. Bearing in mind that the constituting subsystems of LLL are analysed as societal fields in this book, the work of typologization becomes more than a neat dissection of these fields into smaller parts. Instead, the efforts reflect transformations of Europe's educational systems.

Existing typologies are often developed from particular educational and labour market perspectives. The varieties of capitalism typologies are more complex because they use the unique skill sets distinctive of national economies to provide an explanation of the relationship between skill formation, adult learning, the labour market and the nature of the welfare state. These typologies need revision however. The authors demonstrate this by particularly looking into post-socialist countries, where the structural and public policy frameworks can only be captured by more finely tuned analytical tools, such as the additional distinction 'dependent market economies'.

TYPOLOGY OF POST-SOVIET VERSUS POST-SOCIALIST COUNTRIES

The additional typology emerges from the presence of Lithuania, Estonia and Russia among the country chapters. The possibility of comparing these post-Soviet countries with other post-socialist countries, such as Bulgaria, Slovenia and Hungary, have nurtured thoughts on whether the centralized Soviet education system ironed out specific conditions for the transformation of adult education practices into something that fed into the European LLL discourse that all countries later were offered. This is discussed in the chapter on Estonia (Chapter 15), which points out that the country's changes came within the framework of the dissolution of not only the socialist system but also the Soviet state.

The chapter on Russia (Chapter 13) delves more into the Soviet heritage, while pointing out that the formal education system remains a product of the Soviet plan system and is unable to adapt to and meet the demands of the nascent capitalist labour market. Recent reforms to modernize formal education have mainly touched upon the formal aspect, while the core problems persist. Examples are the lack of available funds hampering a modernization of education programmes and equipment. There is also a deficiency of qualified and motivated teaching staff, especially in vocational education. The Russian country team maintains that the largest obstacle in bridging the gap between the formal education system and the labour market is the inability to effectively use the positive heritage of the Soviet education system. Below, we will return to this danger of eradicating too many educational institutions during the transition to more democratic systems.

TRIAD OF FORMAL, NON-FORMAL AND INFORMAL LEARNING

By the mid-1970s, the 'formal, non-formal and informal' triad of learning was firmly established. Informal education was defined as the lifelong process by which every person acquires and accumulates knowledge, skills, attitudes and insights from daily experiences and exposure to the environment. Formal education is often relegated to the highly institutionalized, chronologically graded and hierarchically structured 'education system'. Non-formal education is understood as any organized, systematic, educational activity carried out externally to the framework of the formal system to provide selected types of learning to particular subgroups in the population (Coombs and Ahmed 1974, p. 8). These two authors point out that there are no definitive or clear-cut boundaries between these three modes of education. They are overlapping, and interactions between them occur. Moreover, the offer and inclusiveness of non-formal education affect the field of formal adult education and lifelong learning in any given society. The authors therefore point out that elements from formal, non-formal and informal education should be synthesized and strong links developed between them, in order for systems of lifelong education to evolve.

Chapter 6 on Ireland makes the theoretical point that LLL should encompass both socio-personal and institutional processes. One approach is to forge links between the sectors of community education, primary, secondary, further and higher education in order to enable individuals who have experienced educational disadvantage to continue their education. In this context, the significance of non-formal education is that when it is present in the local community, it can reach out to those who had to leave school early and who have been marginalized by the mainstream education system. The institutional form of such non-formal education can be community LLL centres. During the last decade community building has been one of six priority areas of the Irish state's educational policies, but has been confronted with several constraints, notably inadequate resourcing, isolation from other educational sectors and lack of research support. Theoretically, community LLL centres represent what the Irish country team calls 'community capital'; in other words a combination of cultural and social capital embodying collective resources for the entire community. This brings us back to the human capital perspective versus social capital perspective evoked above.

In contemporary Russia (Chapter 13), non-formal and informal learning is basically split from the further education system. LLL is understood as the interconnection between the labour market and adult education, be it formal or non-formal. There are few interfaces between the system of education and the labour market by means of graduate placements in enterprises, patronage of enterprises over educational institutions or internship systems. Overall, non-formal educational experiences are not recognized by formal education institutions and the Russian government hesitates in strengthening the legal basis of adult education. There is thus a clear need for moving towards building bridges between the formal and non-formal learning settings.

Chapter 7 on Flanders (in Belgium) shows that non-formal education per se is not a panacea for social inclusion in adult education, because vulnerable groups of learners participate less in non-formal than in formal learning. The relatively low propensity of adults to attend learning activities may come from the discouraging effect on low achievers of a stratified initial education system. The traditional inequalities in participation by gender, age, citizenship, labour market status and level of education are stronger in non-formal than in formal education. Non-formal education is dominated by vocational aspects. Highly educated adults therefore participate more in non-formal courses, mostly organized in the private sector and focused on job skills or in-company training. Unemployed adults have the highest participation rates in formal adult education. The Flemish government has taken these trends seriously and recent legislation has aimed to streamline and strengthen formal adult education, while stimulating 'life-wide' learning and the socio-cultural development of the population. This does not, however, rule out that the Flemish lifelong learning policy also aims at a smoother functioning of the labour market.

ADULT FORMAL LEARNING

By the mid-1970s, non-formal education was ideologically constructed as an alternative to formal education. Formal adult education remained the underdefined counterpart of the newly introduced, broadly discussed concept of non-formal adult education (see Colletta 1996; Tuijnman and Boström 2002). Representatives of new institutionalism, such as Richard Scott and John W. Meyer (1994), put formal and non-formal education on the same level, comparing them for their particularities instead of taking non-formal as a remedy for the shortcomings of formal education.

The authors of Chapter 3, 'Seven types of formal adult education and their organizational fields: Towards a comparative framework', contribute to a theoretical foundation of formal adult education by applying arguments developed within organizational institutionalism on institutional effects of education (Meyer and Rowan 1977, 2006; Meyer 1977). They argue that formal adult education has an institutionalized social charter (Meyer 1970), which promises that 'taking steps' on the educational ladder results in eligibility to move up on established career ladder (see also Hefler 2012). According to them, formal adult education imitates initial education's categories, symbolic and belief systems and demonstrates cognitive isomorphism, but it also expands the scope of education as an institution by providing social categories, symbolic orders and beliefs not available within initial education (Hefler 2012, p. 60). The concept of formal adult education provides a new bracket, which summarizes various educational activities under a new heading. Institutionally separated fields of education are addressed as a new (at least statistical) unity of analysis.

Moving then to the typologization of formal learning, Chapter 9 on Austria offers a typology focusing on the adult population. According to a diversification of formal education into seven organizational fields, varying from basic skills programmes to continuing professional training, the authors call for a transgression of traditional 'demarcation lines', allowing to take account of formal adult education, non-formal firm-based training, liberal and civic adult education. This perspective enables an analysis of institutional logics and ongoing processes of importance in the development of a national qualifications framework in Austria. The chapter highlights the social acceptance of educational programmes and their resulting qualifications, instead of the traditional approach of grouping actors along institutional similarities or grouping of qualifications along types of programmes. One consequence of the present restricted view is that adult-education providers still play a minor role in part-time *Fachhochschule* degree courses or university training courses, not yet perceived as adult education by relevant administrators, policy-makers, the participants and the wider public.

PATH-DEPENDENCY, THE POWER OF STRUCTURES AND INSTITUTIONAL AGENCY

A central theme in social sciences is individual and institutional agency, including the influence of institutional structures on policy and practice. Several chapters in this book analyse the interaction between structural factors and individuals' dispositions in the field of LLL. These analyses provide insight into agency mechanisms, for example how various actors – such as interest groups – promote or resist transformations of education and training systems, possibly in the direction of a nascent national framework for LLL.

This process in Norway (Chapter 8) leads to educational practices gradually forming patterns pointing towards the existence of building blocks of a lifelong learning system. A low level of stratification of students, and a low degree of compartmentalization between education trajectories, are proof of attempts to install practices that fall under an LLL paradigm. Departing from the assumption that LLL can be understood as an 'organizational field', composed of actors with their identities and roles, the chapter on Norway discusses the role that institutions exercise within this field. The analysis reveals LLL practices that partly fall into patterns pointing to systemic elements, embracing institutional and motivational aspects mediated through institutional strategies. The institutions exercise a certain freedom in defining their own LLL strategies, for example in terms of recruiting students from backgrounds of social exclusion. However, this leeway is less frequently used in higher education institutions, which are more independent from the local or central government, than in institutions at the upper secondary level. It therefore turns out that institutional strategies, being more ambitious than mirroring minimum requirements and mainstream public policy, do matter.

Institutional agency in Estonian adult education (Chapter 15) should be understood against the background of the population arriving to the 1990s transition period with a high educational level and sound labour market experiences. These assets were quite evenly distributed among the population but Estonia inherited from the Soviet period a poorly diversified formal adult education system, which only functioned when the State Power was crucial in the process of lifelong learning. Later, this low diversification, combined with marketization and liberalization of education, brought about a sharp increase in inequality of participation because individuals suddenly became responsible for their own education.

Eager to adopt the EU *acquis communautaire* in matters of education and training, Bulgarian institutional transition (Chapter 12) featured conflicts between the social agents of externally imposed modernization on the one hand and, on the other, the endogenous way of life. The outcome of these conflicts partly depends on national self-esteem and social integration in the recipient societies. As a whole, societies characterized by stronger integration and self-esteem are more likely to follow a creative pattern of modernization, while those weakly integrated and with lower self-esteem tend to follow a pattern of passive imitation and (self)-alienation, which predominates in Bulgaria and several other post-socialist countries.

CHANGE AND SOCIAL FIELDS

When analysing change and path dependency in LLL, the country teams build on earlier contributions to organizational sociology, for example Crozier and Friedberg (1977), who emphasized that change implies collective creation during which members of a collective learn together. This paves the way for new social practices of conflict and cooperation, while allowing for forms of collective action that simultaneously create and express a new structuration of one or several social fields (Crozier and Friedberg 1977, p. 35).

Pierre Bourdieu considers education as one field among others, in the sense of being 'structured spaces of positions (or posts) whose properties depend on their position within these spaces and which can be analysed independently of the characteristics of their occupants (which are partly determined by them)' (Bourdieu 1993, p. 72). Within fields, struggles take place between individuals over resources, stakes and access.

The limits of a field are defined by the limits of efficacy of a particular form of capital (Bourdieu and Wasquant 1992, p. 101). Bourdieu distinguishes between different societal fields (e.g., economy, education, arts, mass media and politics). Although these fields may both overlap and be composed of diverse subfields, they are characterized by distinct norms, values and rationalities. Bourdieu conceptualizes fields as arenas for competition with their 'rules of the game' modified by powerful actors. It is important to notice, however, that the success of actors in one field cannot easily be translated into other fields.

Institutional fields are relatively autonomous arenas, each with their own gravitational logic; in other words, zones in which particular forms of capital have efficacy in the pursuit of what is at stake in the game (Bourdieu and Wasquant 1992, pp. 97–101). The logic of a field is overwhelmingly defined by its distributive possibilities between groups of people differentially positioned within it; the stances and strategies these positions afford; and the conditions of access of these positions as well as the capitals they command. Adult learners fit easily into these theoretical categories and several country chapters deal with the distribution of access to learning possibilities, and even more systematic support structures for LLL. The fact that empirical material fits to a theoretical framework is however no guarantee of the theories' explanatory power.

This brings us to some critiques of Bourdieu; notably for grounding institutional fields primarily in the struggles of agents and groups, not the purposes of organizations. Almost all of Bourdieu's discussion of fields is pitched at the level of individual actors who find themselves in fields where they act. His concept of field thus focuses mostly on individuals gaining position and power and not on collective actors who work to build and then hold their group together in the face of struggle in a broader field (Fligstein and McAdam 2011).

DiMaggio and Powell (1983) appropriate and adapt the concept of field from Bourdieu, emphasizing its relational features. Their perspective is meso-sociological. They consider organizations as being deeply shaped by other organizations. The basic units are organizational fields and any organization is embedded in a distinct setting of organizations (Greenwood and Hinings 1996, pp. 1026–1027). DiMaggio and Powell (1983) identify three forces driving organizations in fields toward similar outcomes: coercive, normative isomorphism and mimetic. Coercion results from regulatory agencies; normative isomorphism is based upon professional associations, consulting firms and educational institutions; and mimicry stems from the ongoing observations of peers, competitors and collaborators. All organizations are exposed to rather specific influences. DiMaggio and Powell (1983) argue that fields develop alongside: increased interaction between similar organizations; the emergence of sharply defined interorganizational structures of domination and patterns of coalition; an increase in the information load with which organizations in a field must contend; and the development of mutual awareness among participants in a set of organizations.

Other proponents of new institutionalism assumed differentiations of organized context, such as Scott and Meyer (1991) who developed the concept of societal sectors. Sectors were conceptualized as functional domains that are composed of diverse organizations as well as corresponding non-organizational features, such as meaning and belief systems or governance structures and other 'rules of the game'. Scott (1991) also emphasizes characteristic features of organizational fields. The 'field approach' is characterized by the assumption that organizational fields mediate between a single organization and broader social contexts (Hasse 2008); or in the words of McAdam and Scott:

> The concept of field identifies an arena – a system of actors, actions, and relations – whose participants take one another into account as they carry out interrelated activities. Rather than focusing on a single organization or movement, or even a single type of organization or movement (population), it allows us to view these actors in context. (McAdam and Scott 2005, 10)

Many authors have criticized the new concept of institutional field for underestimating the role of power in the structuring of fields (Fligstein 2001; Emirbayer and Johnson 2008). The questions of why, and in whose interest, fields exist are rarely addressed in institutional theory, and the power to pursue interests is insufficiently accounted for. Fligstein and McAdam (2011) therefore propose the concept of 'strategic action field', which is a meso-level social order where actors (who can be individual or collective) interact with knowledge of one another under a set of common understandings about the purpose of the field, the relationship in the field (including who has power and why), and the field's rules. They emphasize that this concept combines the new institutional field concept with underlying processes determining who gets what.

MODELS OF PARTICIPATION IN LLL

Moving to socio-psychological theories that inform research on lifelong learning, the chain-of-response model developed by Cross (1981) aimed to explain what instigates some people to participate in adult learning and others not to do it. The model starts with a person's self-perception and attitudes toward education. From this mainly psychological angle, the model moves on to more external factors such as opportunities and barriers. The next step is formed by the expectations and the values attached to participation. According to the model, factors such as life transitions, information, opportunities and barriers further influence whether or not an individual participates in adult education. In the end, the importance of barriers depends on how strong an interest the individual has in learning. The emphasis in the model is on psychological and environmental variables.

The 'expectancy-valence' of Rubenson (1976) also starts from the interaction between the individual and his environment. The valence in the model refers to the importance of the likely outcomes of participation, and the expectancy refers to the likelihood of achieving outcomes. Rubenson refers to Lewin's field theory (see Lewin 1997) and proposes components defining the life space of an individual at a given time. On a personal level previous educational experience, individual needs and personal characteristics play a role. The most important environmental factors are the individual's own welfare, the standards of a person's reference group and the availability of educational opportunities. However, according to field theory these factors should be included among the conditions creating motivation and not as a barrier at a particular moment, when motivation is already established.

Darkenwald and Merriam (1982) develop the psychosocial interaction model emphasizing the importance of social environment factors and of socio-economic status of the individual for later participation in adult education. The background characteristics and the social environment of the childhood strongly influence the school career and later socio-economic status. Socio-economic status has a positive effect on participation as well as on the perceived value and usefulness of participating in education. The last factor influencing participation according to this model is the barriers, which are negatively correlated with participation stimuli.

Common to these models is the importance of psychological aspects. This means that these models belong to the school of socio-psychological interactionism (see also Boeren et al. 2010; Hefler 2012). These models remain one-sided, because with emphasis on the individual, structural components are pushed into the background. Environmental factors are often described only in relation to the individual's life situation. The factors of the educational institutions and on the broader country level are mostly absent.

Historical and organizational institutionalism approaches (Scott and Meyer 1994) have rarely been used to explain the participation of adults but instead examine cross-sectional or country differences (Hefler 2011, p. 107). Institutional approaches explain participation by the emergence of beliefs in societies that education is a means for achieving legitimate goals. This belief becomes institutionalized on coercive, normative and cognitive levels.

The bounded agency model, developed by Rubenson and Desjardins (2009), suggests that broader structural conditions and targeted policy measures impact on participation. Structural conditions play an important role in forming circumstances faced by individuals and limit the feasible alternatives to choose from. Decisions to take part in adult learning activities are affected by government measures and initiatives as well as by individual choice. Studies of participation, Rubenson and Desjardins (2009) argue, need to use a 'bounded agency' approach and include the role of various agents in society. Structural and institutional contexts can also affect individual consciousness, while the system of dispositions is a result of social experiences, collective memories and ways of thinking.

This model is helpful for modelling the interference between micro, meso and macro contexts, as it provides a theory for how to express any change on the meso and macro levels on the individual basis. Authors of several country chapters have used this model to explain participation in lifelong learning.

REFERENCES

Boeren, Ellen, Ides Nicaise and Herman Baert (2010), 'Theoretical Models of Participation in Adult Education: The Need for an Integrated Model', *International Journal of Lifelong Education*, **29** (1), 45–61.

Bourdieu, Pierre (1993), 'Some Properties of Fields', in *Sociology in Question*, London: Sage, pp. 72–77.

Bourdieu, Pierre and Loic J.D. Wacquant (1992), *An Invitation to Reflexive Sociology*, Chicago, IL: University of Chicago Press.

Colletta, Nat J. (1996), 'Formal, Informal and Nonformal Education', in Albert C. Tuijnman (ed.), *The International Encyclopedia of Adult Education and Training*, Oxford: Pergamon Press, pp. 22–27.

Commission of the European Communities (CEC) (2000), *A Memorandum on Lifelong Learning*, Brussels.

Commission of the European Communities (CEC) (2003), *Education and Training 2010. The Success of the Lisbon Strategy Hinges on Urgent Reforms. Interim*

Report on the Implementation of the Detailed Work Programme on the Follow-Up of the Objectives of Education and Training Systems in Europe, Brussels.
Coombs, Philip H. and Manzoor Ahmed (1974), *Attacking Rural Poverty: How Nonformal Education Can Help*, Baltimore, MD: John Hopkins University Press.
Cross, K. Patricia (1981), *Adults as Learners*, San Fransisco, CA: Jossey-Bass.
Crozier, Michel and Erhard Friedberg (1977), *L'acteur et le système. Les contraintes de l'action collective*, Paris: Editions du Seuil.
Darkenwald, Gordon G. and Sharan B. Merriam (1982), *Adult Education: Foundations to Practice*, New York: Harper & Row.
DiMaggio, Paul J. and Walter W. Powell (1983), 'The Iron Cage Revisited: Institutional Isomorphism and Collective Rationality in Organizational Fields', *American Sociological Review*, **48** (2), 63–82.
Emirbayer, Mustafa and Victoria Johnson (2008), 'Bourdieu and Organizational Analysis', *Theory and Society*, **37** (1), 1–44.
Field, John (2006), *Lifelong Learning and the New Educational Order, 2nd edition*, Stoke on Trent: Trentham Books.
Fligstein, Neil (2001), 'Social Skill and the Theory of Fields', *Sociological Theory*, **40** (2), 397–405.
Fligstein, Neil and Doug McAdam (2011), 'Toward a General Theory of Strategic Action Field', *Sociological Theory*, **29** (1), 1–26.
Green, Andy (2002), 'The Many Faces of Lifelong Learning: Recent Education Policy Trends in Europe', *Journal of Education Policy*, **17** (6), 611–626.
Greenwood, Royston and C.R. Hinings (1996), 'Understanding Radical Organizational Change: Bringing Together the Old and New Institutionalism', *Academy of Management Review*, **21** (4), 1022–1054.
Hasse, Raimund (2008), 'Systems Theory, Societal Contexts, and Organizational Heterogeneity', in Kerstin Sahlin-Andersson, Royston Greenwood, Christine Oliver and Roy Suddaby (eds), *Handbook of Orgainational Institutionalism*, London: Sage, pp. 539–559.
Hefler, Günter (2012), *Taking Steps: Formal Adult Education in Private and Organizational Life*, Vienna: Lit-Verlag.
Holford, John (2006), 'The Role of Lifelong Learning in Building Citizenship: European Union Approaches in the Light of British and Colonial Experience', *International Journal of Lifelong Education*, **25** (3), 321–332.
Holford, John, Sheila Riddell, Elisabet Weedon, Judit Litjens and Guy Hannan (2008), *Patterns of Lifelong Learning: Policy and Practice in an Expanding Europe*, Vienna: Lit Verlag.
Jarvis, Peter (2001), 'The Changing Educational Scene', in Peter Jarvis (ed.), *The Age of Learning*, London: Kogan Page.
Lewin, Kurt (1997), *Resolving Social Conflicts: Field Theory in Social Sciences*, Washington, DC: American Psychological Association.
McAdam, Doug and Willaim Richard Scott (2005), 'Social Movements and Organizations', in Gerald Davis, Doug McAdam, William Richard Scott, John Mayer and Nathan Zald (eds), *Social Movements and Organization Theory*, New York: Cambridge University Press, pp. 4–40.
Meyer, Heinz-Dieter and Brian Rowan (eds) (2006), *The New Institutionalism in Education*, New York: State University of New York Press.
Meyer, John W. (1970), 'The Charter: Conditions of Diffuse Socialization in Schools', in W. Richard Scott (ed.), *Social Processes and Social Structures: An*

Introduction to Sociology, New York, USA and London, UK: Holt, Rinehart & Winston, pp. 564–578.
Meyer, John W. (1977), 'The Effects of Education as an Institution', *American Journal of Sociology*, **83** (1), 55–77.
Meyer, John W. and Brian Rowan (1977), 'Institutionalized Organizations: Formal Structures as Myth and Ceremony', *American Journal of Sociology*, **83** (2), 340–363.
OECD (2000a), *Human Resources in the New Economy: Challenges and Opportunities for Education and Training*, Paris: OECD.
OECD (2000b), *Literacy in the Information Age. Final Report from the International Adult Literarcy Survey*, Paris: OECD.
OECD (2001), *Beyond Rhetoric: Adult Learning Policies and Practices*, Paris: OECD.
Roosmaa, Eve-Liis and Ellu Saar (2010), 'Participating in Non-Formal Learning: Patterns of Inequality in EU-15 and the New EU-8 Member Countries', *Journal of Education and Work*, **23** (3), 179–206.
Rubenson, Kjell (1976), *Participation in Recurrent Education*, Paris: Centre for Educational Research and Innovations.
Rubenson, Kjell and Richard Desjardins (2009), 'The Impact of Welfare State Regimes on Constraints to Participation in Adult Education: A Bounded Agency Model', *Adult Education Quarterly*, **59** (3), 187–207.
Saar, Ellu and Jelena Helemäe (2008), 'Estonia on the Backdrop of the European Union States: Country-Specific Institutional Context and Lifelong Learning', *Studies for Learning Society*, **1**, 7–16.
Scott, Richard W. (1991), 'The Organizations of Environments; Network, Cultural, and Historical Elements', in John W. Meyer and Richard W. Scott (eds), *Organizational Environments: Ritual and Rationality*, Newbury Park, CA: Sage, pp. 155–175.
Scott, Richard W. and John W. Meyer (1991), 'The Organization of Societal Sectors', in John W. Meyer and Richard W. Scott (eds), *Organizational Environments: Ritual and Rationality*, Newbury Park, CA: Sage, pp. 129–153.
Scott, Richard W. and John W. Meyer (1994), 'The Rise of Training Programs in Firms and Agencies: An Institutional Perspective', in Richard W. Scott and John W. Meyer (eds), *Institutional Environments and Organizations. Structural Complexity and Individualism*, Thousand Oaks, CA: Sage, pp. 228–254.
Tuijnman, Albert and Ann-Kristin Boström (2002), 'Changing Notions of Lifelong Education and Lifelong Learning', *International Review of Education*, **48**, pp. 93–110.

PART I

Conceptual considerations

1. Lifelong learning: national policies from the European perspective

John Holford and Agata Mleczko

INTRODUCTION

Two decades ago, an influential article lauded the European Union (EU) as 'the most successful example of institutionalized international policy co-ordination in the modern world' (Moravcsik 1993, p. 473). A few years earlier, in 1988, Jacques Delors – then President of the European Commission – had claimed that about 80 per cent of the socio-economic legislation in EU member states stemmed from the EU's treaties, policies and legislation (Wallace et al. 2005, p. 3). Since then, the EU has grown – from 12 member states and 350 million people, to 27 member states comprising over 500 million people. The hubris which accompanied this growth was of a piece with the so-called 'end of history': the collapse of the Communist governments of Central and Eastern Europe and the apparently inexorable onward march of globalized markets. By the time the European Council met at Lisbon[1] in early 2000, the EU's optimism embraced not only continued expansion, but a new currency (plans for the euro were far advanced), a new constitution, and 'a new strategic goal . . . to become the most competitive and dynamic knowledge-based economy in the world capable of sustainable economic growth with more and better jobs and greater social cohesion' by 2010 (CEC 2000).

In Greek tragedy, nemesis succeeds hubris; for Europe, the decade after Lisbon brought neither dynamism nor competitiveness:

> The ink had scarcely dried on the agreement before the worldwide stock market bubble imploded, the epicentre of which was the collapse of the overvalued prices of American dot.com and telecom shares amid evidence of financial and corporate malpractice. Scepticism mounted about the potential of the knowledge economy. The US suffered two years of economic slowdown and recession and the European economy followed suit. (High Level Group 2004, p. 9)

And this was only the beginning. In 2005 the voters of France and The Netherlands – two of the EU's original six founding states, signatories to the Treaty of Rome – rejected the Constitutional Treaty. In 2008, United States (US) and European banks brought the global financial system to the edge of oblivion; the price of their rescue by governments and central banks proved in due course to be the Western economic crisis of 2010 and 2011. This, of course, had particularly serious implications for a number of EU member states, led by Greece, and for the 'eurozone' as a whole.

From the early 1990s, the EU became a strong advocate of lifelong learning – among international organizations, perhaps the strongest. (It remains to be seen whether, having waxed with Europe's hubris, lifelong learning will now share in its economic nemesis – early signs are not encouraging.) As we shall see in this chapter, lifelong learning became a much-vaunted weapon in the armoury of European economic and social development, and there is now a considerable literature on the EU's lifelong learning policies (e.g., Dale and Robertson 2009; Holford et al. 2008; Holford and Mohorčič Špolar 2012; Pépin 2006). These have tended to emphasize the evolution and purpose of policy. To simplify greatly, their focus has been on the evolution of the key themes of EU policy: that lifelong learning should contribute to economic competitiveness on the one hand, and to social cohesion, inclusion and citizenship on the other. This emphasis is probably natural. In EU terms, lifelong learning is not just a child of hubris: more prosaically, it is a product of the European Commission's development of an educational bureaucracy in the late 1980s and early 1990s – formally speaking, a directorate-general for education came into being only in 1995, though in practice this was the culmination of growth over the previous decade or so (Holford and Mohorčič Špolar 2012; Pépin 2006).

The purpose of this chapter, and indeed of this entire book, however, is to explore how lifelong learning has developed and taken root across the various countries that comprise Europe. In part, this is an examination of the impact of EU policy. The relationship between the EU and its member states is a complex one. From one perspective, its main function is to shape the activities of member states. There are many variations on this theme. To the political right in Britain, it is a 'superstate' (Campbell 2010). Manuel Barroso (quoted in Charter 2007) famously compared the EU 'to the organisation of empires': 'We have the dimension of empire', he said (though in contrast to empires which were made 'with force' and 'a centre imposing diktat', EU members had 'fully decided to work together and to pool their sovereignty'). Dale and Robertson (2009) see the EU as an institution educating and disciplining its member states in the interests of capitalist globalization: to understand the role of Europe in education, Dale argues, we must dispense with 'methodologically nationalist and statist assumptions' (Dale 2009, p. 32).

These perspectives are in line with Jacques Delors's assertion that 80 per cent of member states' social legislation stemmed from the EU. Conversely, however, Wallace et al. suggest that some 80 per cent of the concerns of national policy-makers' daily lives are probably 'framed by domestic concerns' (2010, p. 9). As a 'policy arena', they suggest, the EU

> rests on a kind of amalgam of . . . two levels of governance. Country-defined policy demands and policy capabilities are set in a shared European framework to generate collective regimes, most of which are then implemented back in the countries concerned. . . . [However,] how those European regimes operate varies a good deal between one EU member state and another. In other words, the EU policy process . . . has differentiated outcomes, with significance variations between countries. (Wallace et al. 2010, p. 9)

To understand EU policy processes, they continue, it is 'just as important' to understand national institutional settings as EU-level institutions (pp. 9–10). This chapter emphasizes the EU level; the aim of the book is to explore the intersections between this and the national.

EUROPE AND ITS NATIONS

Based on an investigation of lifelong learning policies, one of the earliest 'outputs' of the 'Towards a Lifelong Learning Society in Europe: The Contribution of the Education System' (LLL2010) project (Holford et al. 2008) drew attention to the importance of national context. This early research strongly suggested that Europe's diversity was deeply important, and 'a single model of lifelong learning' across the EU was unlikely to be achieved. European policy was important, it argued, and had an impact at national level. But countries would very likely 'pick and choose' between different EU priorities – influenced by their national institutional, political, social, and ideological contexts (Holford et al. 2008). The present book develops this theme by taking the analysis beyond the level of policy. The project has examined lifelong learning in 13 countries – most, though not all, are EU member states. Although the LLL2010 project did not take a historical approach, an earlier publication drew attention to some of the countries' characteristics, and did so with an eye to history. Drawn from Northern, Eastern and Central Europe, their histories include periods of convergence and divergence – especially during the twentieth century:

> To take but three examples: in 1914 Ireland, Scotland and England formed parts of the United Kingdom; Hungary, Slovenia, and Austria formed part of the Austro-Hungarian Empire; while Estonia and Lithuania formed part of the

> Russian Empire. Today all are independent countries.[2] During the twentieth century, however, their histories have varied: Estonia and Lithuania enjoyed a brief period of independence between the two world wars, but were absorbed into the USSR in 1939; Hungary became independent from 1918, though it fell under German rule during the Second World War and into the Soviet 'sphere of influence' after 1945; Slovenia became an integral part of Yugoslavia; Austria remained independent after 1918, apart from a period of absorption into 'greater Germany'. Although educational policy and practice are not simply a product of history, we cannot make sense of the diversity of how lifelong learning has been understood and operationalized without an awareness of the diversity – but also the commonalities – of these national histories. (Holford et al. 2008)

As we have seen, the EU's enthusiasm for lifelong learning coincided with its rapid expansion. Many of the new member states of the 1990s and 2000s lay to the east of the former 'iron curtain', or to the south, around the Mediterranean. Their incorporation into the EU was widely seen as a consolidation of 'Western values': democracy and human rights, free markets and good governance. The EU would play this consolidating role, of course, precisely to the extent that it was successful in shaping or reshaping the practices and institutions of these countries. This did not imply that it would intervene in detail, or in an oppressive way, in the activities of member states, although it clearly meant establishing parameters for acceptable policy, legislation and political behaviour. A favoured EU term for this is 'policy learning' – a concept central to the Open Method of Coordination and to the 'Lisbon process' – although these methods do not apply solely to new member states.

The LLL2010 project provided an opportunity to explore the intersection between EU policies in lifelong learning and the activities of new member states in particular. The countries represented in the research team, and investigated by it, included a significant number from those newer EU member states that had, until around 1990, been governed for several decades by Communist Party-led regimes.

EU POLICIES ON LIFELONG LEARNING

Origins and Development

The European Union is the direct descendant of the European Common Market and the European Economic Community. While it has grown and changed in many ways, in important respects its character today reflects its origins. The principal focus of both the Common Market and the EEC was economic: the strengthening of economic ties, internal free trade and a free market. Education was nowhere on the agenda; indeed Blitz has suggested that education was a 'taboo' topic in European-level discussions until the 1970s (Blitz 2003, p.4). In the early 1970s, however, the Community began tentatively to discuss some educational issues. The results were modest: the education ministers adopted a non-binding and decidedly uncontroversial resolution in 1971 'to provide the population as a whole with the opportunities for general education, vocational training and lifelong learning' (Blitz 2003, p. 5), while in 1974 – influenced perhaps by the first enlargement – they agreed to encourage cooperation in various priority sectors, while preserving 'the originality of educational traditions and policies in each country' (CEC 1979, p. 2).

This approach – cooperation amid diversity – has continued to mark the development of educational policies and activities by the European Union and its predecessor institutions. Rhetorical assertions of the importance of education provided a basis for incremental development by civil servants; as Blitz argues, 'co-operation generated further co-operation and new ideas about the role of education in the Community' (2003, p. 15). This process continued, and gathered momentum, during the 1980s, initially with legal judgments permitting the development of an educational role by the Commission, but critically toward the end of the decade by the *de facto* formation of a Directorate-General in the Commission with responsibility for education and training.

The Treaty of Maastricht (Treaty on European Union 1992) represented a new turn in European unity, with the formation of the European Union; and unlike Community and Common Market, the EU had explicit, if limited, legal authority in education. It could make 'a contribution to education and training of quality and to the flowering of the cultures of the Member States' (Article G). This general aim was limited – in particular, it was subject to the principle of subsidiarity[3] – but there were also a number of very specific areas of legitimate Community activity set out, such as: developing a 'European dimension' in education and strengthening language teaching; encouraging student and teacher mobility and recognition of qualifications; promoting cooperation between educational bodies; exchanging 'information and experience' on common educational issues; encouraging youth exchanges and 'exchanges of socio- educational instructors'; and encouraging distance education (Article G). Following Maastricht, member states could no longer object on principle to the Commission taking initiatives in education. However, schooling rather than post-compulsory or 'lifelong' education, and the 'European dimension', were clearly at the forefront of the Treaty-makers' minds.

The development of the Directorate-General (and various quasi-independent agencies to support educational policy-making and programme delivery, such as Cedefop[4] and the European Training Foundation) in the mid-1990s coincided with a marked shift in international educational thinking. In the early 1990s, lifelong learning re-emerged onto the stage after a decade or so in the policy background. As many commentators have pointed out, it re-emerged in a strongly economistic form, associated with the perceived shift toward a 'knowledge economy'. But more importantly, from the perspective of EU policy development, it was taken up as central to Europe's economic policies, especially in the white paper *Growth, Competitiveness, Employment* (CEC 1993). Education – albeit dressed up as 'lifelong learning' – was now seen as central to the economic success of the European project. This was taken up in educational policy-making, notably in the white paper *Teaching and Learning: Towards a Learning Society* (CEC 1995), and in a rash of lesser policy documents during the later 1990s. By 2000, lifelong learning had become a distinctive feature of EU education policy – an organizing theme, linking policies in education with other areas (notably economic policy and social exclusion), and identifying various programmes to strengthen citizens' identification with Europe and the EU.

As we have seen, the Lisbon strategy, first enunciated in 2000, aimed to turn the EU into 'the most competitive and dynamic knowledge-based economy in the world capable of sustainable economic growth with more and better jobs and greater social cohesion' by 2010 (CEC 2000). In pursuit of this, it encouraged Europe's education and training systems 'to adapt both to the demands of the knowledge society and to the need for an improved level and quality of employment'. Adults (or more specifically, 'unemployed adults' and employed people 'at risk of seeing their skills overtaken by rapid change') were given a central role (CEC 2000). Other objectives, also in line with Maastricht specifications, related to lifelong learning: 'a substantial annual increase in per capita investment in human resources'; a European framework for 'new basic skills to be provided through lifelong learning' (information technology skills, foreign languages, technological culture, entrepreneurship and social skills); more elaborated mechanisms for 'mobility of students, teachers and training and research staff' through Community programmes (Socrates, Leonardo, Youth); and greater transparency and mutual recognition of qualifications (CEC 2000).

The EU's approach to lifelong learning after 2000, therefore, evolved in many ways along lines set in the 1990s. The key themes continued to be competitiveness and social inclusion. Yet a focus on the overarching policy aims may overlook a number of important developments. The most commonly noted of these are at the level of detail, particularly in methodologies of policy development and implementation. We turn to these below;

they are important. However, behind these lay significant strengthening of the legal status of education in the European Union. This came in two main forms. Firstly, in 2000, the European Parliament, the Council and the Commission 'proclaim[ed]' the 'Charter of Fundamental Rights of the European Union' (Charter of Fundamental Rights 2000). 'Everyone has the right to education and to have access to vocational and continuing training', this asserted (Article 14). Intended for inclusion in the ill-fated EU Constitutional Treaty, the Charter's legal status remained unclear through most of the following decade. It was, however, incorporated into the Treaty of Lisbon (signed in December 2007, which came into force on 1 December 2009) as having 'the same legal value as the Treaties' (Article 6.1). The Lisbon Treaty also specified that:

> In defining and implementing its policies and activities, the Union shall take into account requirements linked to the promotion of a high level of employment, the guarantee of adequate social protection, the fight against social exclusion, and a high level of education, training and protection of human health. (Article 9)

Imprecisely, to be sure, this gave legal – arguably constitutional – underpinning to advocates of education in the Commission and elsewhere. In specification of detailed areas of educational activity, the Lisbon Treaty was almost identical to Maastricht. EU action should 'be aimed at':

- developing the European dimension in education, particularly through the teaching and dissemination of the languages of the Member States;
- encouraging mobility of students and teachers, by encouraging inter alia, the academic recognition of diplomas and periods of study;
- promoting cooperation between educational establishments;
- developing exchanges of information and experience on issues common to the education systems of the Member States;
- encouraging the development of youth exchanges and of exchanges of socio-educational instructors, and encouraging the participation of young people in democratic life in Europe;
- encouraging the development of distance education, . . . (Treaty on European Union 2010, Article 165.2)

However, the Treaty also gave legal force to a policy development process to help in 'achievement of the[se] objectives'. The European Parliament and the Council were empowered to 'adopt incentive measures' (excluding harmonization of member states' laws and regulations), while the Commission could make proposals to the Council, which could in turn 'adopt recommendations' (Article 165.4).

In reality, these features of the Lisbon Treaty provided little more than legal dressing for methodologies of policy development and implementation practices which had evolved over the previous decade or so. This approach, often labelled 'soft governance' (Lawn 2006; Trubeck and Trubeck 2005), sought to establish common standards and practices across the EU through persuasion rather than statutory enforcement. Three initiatives, which serve to illustrate the EU's approach to developing a common framework in education and training, also show how it has done so through 'soft governance'. Now, therefore, we look successively at the EU's development of indicators and benchmarks; its encouragement of national lifelong learning strategies; and its encouragement of a European Qualifications Framework (EQF).

Benchmarks and Indicators

The Lisbon strategy covered the full range of EU policy and activities; one of its key elements was the so-called 'Open Method of Coordination' (OMC). The OMC had evolved during the 1990s, especially in employment policy, but was now given a formal role in social and economic policy development generally (Hantrais 2007). This has had profound importance for the EU's role as an actor in education and lifelong learning. Two elements of the OMC have been critical for lifelong learning. Although subsidiarity was restated, the Lisbon approach emphasized agreement on timetables and goals, indicators and benchmarks, and 'monitoring, evaluation and peer review' (CEC 2000). Monitoring was both of the Commission's activities and of the EU's progress, and the latter implied – despite the emphasis on subsidiarity – an increasing intervention in member states' policy and performance. European guidelines were to be 'translated' into national policies 'by setting specific targets and adopting measures', and by ensuring that monitoring, evaluation and peer review were 'organised as mutual learning processes' (CEC 2000).

Benchmarks were, in the words of the EU Council (European Council 2003), 'reference levels of European average performance . . . which will be used as one of the tools for monitoring the implementation of the "Detailed work programme on the follow-up of the objectives of education and training systems in Europe"'. Indicators were to provide accurate measurement of the EU's, and member states', progress against the benchmarks. Indicators were to be 'all based on valid and comparable data' (CEC DG-EAC 2003).

Indicators and benchmarks have provided a powerful mechanism by which the EU, through its Commission, has sought to influence the activities of member states. Countries' performance is measured. Those falling short of benchmarks are liable to be named (perhaps even shamed): labelled as needing to 'catch up' or as 'falling further behind'. They find themselves under pressure to address problems, and to adopt measures from other countries which are seen as 'good practice'. Of course, member states are not all equally susceptible to such influence. In Slovakia, Bulgaria or Poland, for instance, the EU's influence is more marked; while in the United Kingdom (UK), France and Germany national influences are to the fore in the rhetoric of policy-making.

Arguably, the machinery of indicators and rankings pushes more 'obedient' countries towards greater dependency on Commission suggestions. Dale and Robertson (2009), for instance, see the OMC as providing the EU with a mechanism to control and discipline member states in the interests of neoliberal globalization. Others have argued for seeing the OMC as an area of contestation, rather than as inevitably a transmission belt for the neoliberal. Holford (2008) has examined attempts to maintain social and 'citizenship' priorities within the Lisbon structure of indicators and benchmarks. Lee et al. see the OMC's significance principally as facilitating 'policy learning':

> The OMC cast the Commission in a positive light by demonstrating a democratic approach to constructing EU educational and training policy, allowing the Commission to relax from its burden of regaining technocratic legitimacy. Furthermore, the OMC enabled the Commission to be exposed to, learn from, internalise, and adopt the best practices or models of lifelong learning from others. This . . . was a major form of the Commission's institutional learning. Within this context, on the threshold of 2000, the Commission's lifelong learning discourse boiled down to the two equally significant aims of lifelong learning: active citizenship and employability. Thus . . . the OMC, as a wide-ranging consultation process, has been a crucial element of the formulation of the EU's lifelong learning policy since 2000. (Lee et al. 2008, p. 456)

Whatever its significance and effect, the Lisbon strategy has involved a marked increase in the volume, detail and specificity of policy-formulation in lifelong learning, and a greater intervention in the educational policies of member states.

Lifelong Learning Strategies

A second exercise in 'soft governance' has been the EU's encouragement of national 'lifelong learning strategies'. By a series of European Council decisions (2000, 2002, 2004), member states undertook to 'develop and implement coherent and comprehensive LLL strategies' by 2006 (CEC DG-EAC 2009, p. 103). Lifelong learning strategies would, as the Commission saw it, operationalize European policies at the national level. They would be drawn up by member states through a process involving 'all relevant players, in particular the social partners, civil society, local and regional authorities'; they would nevertheless reflect the Commission's 'principles and building blocks', setting national 'targets for an increase in investment in human resources, including lifelong learning' in each country (European Council Resolution 27 June 2002). Strategies would therefore be a mechanism by which European objectives would be translated, in a democratic and inclusive way, into the policies and practices not only of member states, but also of public and private sector agencies and social partners. 'To enhance their relevance and impact, and to motivate individuals to participate in learning, a greater involvement of stakeholders and better cooperation with policy sectors beyond education and training is needed' (European Council 2010). Lifelong learning strategies were, therefore, exercises in policy learning.

As a mechanism, however, lifelong learning strategies have been a somewhat qualified success. A 2009 Commission survey suggested that while the 'vast majority' of countries had 'progressed' in education and training, 'the coherence and comprehensiveness as well as concrete implementation of LLL policies remained for the majority of them a challenge' (CEC DG-EAC 2009, p. 103). At that time, seven countries[5] had adopted, and were implementing, a single 'broadly comprehensive and coherent' strategy document which 'is of high relevance for policy-making, covers all levels of education and is based on analysis, accompanied by specific objectives, embedded in legislative regulations with an associated budget, supported by a roadmap having performance targets and support by stakeholders' (CEC DG-EAC 2009, p. 103).

Most, however, fell significantly short of this. Lithuania, Latvia and Slovakia had adopted a document focussed on a specific target group or sector, rather than covering the 'full spectrum' of lifelong learning. Germany's provided little more than 'an analytical framework', while the Hungarian strategy's 'relevance . . . across sectors' needed 'to be improved'. In 12 countries[6] where policies and sectoral strategies covering all key areas of lifelong learning were being implemented, these were not 'underpinned by a single LLL strategy document'. Poland and Romania were 'still in the process of developing a single strategy document' (CEC DG-EAC 2009, p. 103). The Commission also complained that 'very little information' was provided on adequate budget allocation for effective implementation, and that 'only a few countries' (the Czech Republic, Latvia, Slovakia) reported the approval of detailed implementation plans. Many strategies were of a 'relatively short-term nature', with 'a planning-horizon of 3 to 5 years and . . . a single legislative period', and there was 'little documentation' of the 'evidence base' used to develop strategies, and to measure their progress and 'impact on national policy-making across sectors' (CEC DG-EAC 2009, p. 104). Overall, the European Council concluded in 2010 that 'implementation and further development of lifelong learning strategies remains a critical challenge' (European Council 2010).

The European Qualifications Framework

The European Qualifications Framework (EQF), formally adopted in 2008, provides a further example of the EU's approach to reshaping lifelong learning within member states. The rationale for national qualifications frameworks has been widely discussed (e.g., Allais et al. 2009; Cedefop 2010; Lauder 2011; Young 2003, 2008); the EQF follows a rationale and structure similar to the qualifications frameworks adopted in, for example, Scotland and New Zealand. It was designed as:

> a common European reference framework which links countries' qualifications systems together, acting as a translation device to make qualifications more readable and understandable across different countries and systems in Europe. It has two principal aims: to promote citizens' mobility between countries and to facilitate their lifelong learning. (CEC DG-EAC 2008, p. 3)

Its function, however, is not to substitute for national qualifications frameworks, but to encourage them: the EQF is 'a translation device' to make qualifications more readable and understandable to employers, individuals and institutions by 'providing a bridge across countries and sectors, covering general education, vocational training and higher education and facilitating the validation of non-formal and informal learning' (CEC DG-EAC 2009, p. 13).

While formally adherence to the EQF is voluntary (member states were 'invited . . . to relate their national qualifications systems or frameworks to the EQF by 2010 and to develop national qualifications frameworks, where appropriate'; CEC DG-EAC 2009, p. 107), in practice countries which do not engage with the EQF tend to be isolated from the principal directions of European policy development. The Commission's review of progress towards the Lisbon objectives in education and training in 2009 concluded that EQF had 'triggered or strengthened the development of an NQF based on learning outcomes' in many countries. Such a framework was already in operation in four countries,[7] but was 'a high priority . . . in virtually all' (CEC DG-EAC 2009, p. 107). A Cedefop report on development of national qualifications frameworks in the 27 EU member states, candidate countries (Croatia and Turkey) and in Iceland and Norway (Cedefop 2010) concluded that all aimed to develop and introduce a national qualifications framework (NQF) for lifelong learning 'responding to the EQF' (Cedefop 2010, p. 1). While there were 'differences in specific objectives and in design features' reflecting national systems, it was 'generally accepted' that they should be built on explicit qualifications levels, level descriptors, and a learning outcomes approach. While the EU encouraged countries to engage a 'broad range of stakeholders' from education, training and employment in planning and implementing NQFs, Cedefop described discussions about how vocational and higher education should relate as 'sometimes tense' (Cedefop 2010, p. 2), while the involvement of stakeholders varied 'significantly' between countries. It warned countries not to 'establish "pro forma" frameworks only loosely connected to the existing [national] systems and practices': if 'a significant number' did so, this 'could undermine the overall positive developments which currently can be observed' (Cedefop 2010, p. 2).

A deeply political enterprise, the European Union has long sought depoliticization in its working methods. Its procedures claim to be technical and 'transparent'. To this end, the Commission has established extensive mechanisms for collecting, sorting, sifting and weighing a seemingly endless volume of data: indices of participation, frameworks for qualifications, benchmarks of performance. Generic agencies such as Eurostat provide a statistical evidence base across the entire range of European policy areas and activities, education included. These are complemented by more specialist bodies. Eurydice 'provides information on and analyses of European education systems and policies' and is comprised '37 national units based in all 33 countries participating in the EU's Lifelong Learning programme' (Eurydice 2009). The Centre for Research on Lifelong Learning (CRELL), established in 2005 within the Commission's Joint Research Centre at Ispra in Italy, provides expertise in 'indicator-based evaluation and monitoring of education and training systems' drawing on expertise across 'economics, econometrics, education, social sciences and statistics' (CRELL 2011). The Directorate General for Education and Culture has its own unit for 'Analysis and Studies': preparing the 2011 version of *Progress towards the Common European Objectives in Education and Training: Indicators and Benchmarks* drew on nine of its staff, as well as 13 from CRELL, ten from Eurostat, three from Eurydice and one from the European Agency for development in special needs education (CEC DG-EAC 2011, p. 2). These agencies, underpinning the apparatus of measurement and comparison, are the unsung heroes of European 'soft power' in education.

THE EU'S AIMS IN LIFELONG LEARNING

'We have the dimension of empire,' said Manuel Barroso. One dimension of empires, at least in their early years, is growth; as we have seen, the European Union grew very fast over the decade or so around the millennium: from 12 member states and 350 million people in 1994 to 27 member states and over 500 millions by 2007. But while growth is common to all empires, another dimension is shared only by those that survive: organization – the management and control of people, institutions and territory. Historically, empires have often worked through highly devolved authority structures: the nineteenth century revolution in communications, for instance, did little to dent the British empire's reliance on its district officers, the 'men on the spot', and on 'indirect rule'. From this perspective, the EU's principle of subsidiarity may appear practical good fortune as well as constitutional necessity. However, devolution can go only so far in any common enterprise: it must be matched by coordination and common purpose.

Thus far, this chapter has focused on the evolution and nature of coordination in education. We must now consider common purpose. Many empires have found that growth and success provide purpose enough while they last; but as the EU is currently finding, they seldom do.

Competitiveness and Cohesion

The EU has long sought to balance economic success with social welfare. As we have seen, in 2000 the Lisbon strategy set a strategic goal for the EU: 'to become the most competitive and dynamic knowledge-based economy in the world capable of sustainable economic growth with more and better jobs and greater social cohesion' by 2010 (CEC 2000). The aims of the 'Europe 2020' strategy, which effectively replaced the Lisbon goals in 2010, are in many respects similar:

- Smart growth – developing an economy based on knowledge and innovation.
- Sustainable growth – promoting a more resource-efficient, greener and more competitive economy.
- Inclusive growth – fostering a high-employment economy delivering economic, social and territorial cohesion. (CEC 2010, p. 8)

Two themes emerge clearly in both the Lisbon and Europe 2020 strategies: on the one hand, competitiveness and growth, founded on a vibrant knowledge economy; on the other, social cohesion and inclusion, strongly linked to employment. Europe's policies for lifelong learning over the past decade have been formulated within this context. As widely noted, the emphasis of lifelong learning policies internationally has been strongly 'economistic' since their emergence in the early 1990s. The European Union has followed this trend, which chimed with its origins as an 'economic community' committed to an internal free market. As argued elsewhere, however, the EU was unusual among international organizations in maintaining a clear non-economic strand in its approach (Holford and Mohorčič Špolar 2012). This can be seen as early as its 1995 white paper, *Teaching and Learning: Towards a Learning Society* (CEC 1995), the five key objectives of which for building a learning society included combating social exclusion and developing proficiency in three Community languages. In the mid-1990s, economic aims in lifelong learning began to be complemented by programmes with clear social and cultural objectives (Dehmel 2006). The trans-European dimensions of programmes such as Socrates, Leonardo da Vinci and Erasmus (exchanges of teachers and students across EU member states and the like) contributed to building European identity, and non-economic aims continued to be emphasized through the later 1990s, often in the language of active citizenship and social inclusion. (This also reflected Commission concerns about disengagement between Europe and its citizens.) For example, a 'Community action programme' was approved in 2004 'to promote active European citizenship (civic participation)'. It aimed, *inter alia*:

- to bring citizens closer to the European Union and its institutions and to encourage them to engage more frequently with its institutions;
- to involve citizens closely in reflection and discussion on the construction of the European Union;
- to intensify links and exchanges between citizens from the countries participating in the programme, notably by way of town twinning arrangements; and
- to stimulate initiatives by the bodies engaged in the promotion of active and participatory citizenship. (European Council 2004)

In lifelong learning, economic and social concerns have often been in tension (Holford 2006). In the EU, this is made more complex by the legal context. The EU's founding treaties provided the Union with a strongly economic rationale. In comparison, the social dimension is more weakly underpinned constitutionally. European citizenship, as legally defined, has been described as 'anaemic' (Follesdal 2001, p. 314): it confers few rights, requires few duties, and is conferred not by the EU itself, but indirectly by virtue of the nationality laws of member states.[8] And the writ of the EU, and its Commission, to develop policy in any area of education or lifelong learning is quite tightly constrained by the treaties and the principle of subsidiarity. Those within the Commission and beyond who wish to develop its educational role have long made a virtue of blurring the boundaries between the Union's economic and social objectives.

Some have identified a shift in the rhetoric and content of EU educational policy in the wake of the Kok report (High Level Group 2004) and the so-called 'crisis' of the Lisbon strategy (Robertson 2008), with a downplaying of social concerns and a renewed emphasis on economic competitiveness. Although this can be overstated, and contrary tendencies have been noted (Holford 2008), the direction of movement seems clear. This is apparent in the Europe 2020 strategy, under which priorities for education and lifelong learning have been narrowed, and incorporated into a National Reform Programme for each member state. On the basis of these, the Commission makes proposals, which are negotiated with the government concerned. Many, of course, are principally focussed on economic policy; however, they also cover issues of education and training. For instance, for 2011–2012 the Commission 'recommended' that the UK government:

> Take steps by 2012 to ensure that a higher share of young people enter the labour market with adequate skills and to improve the employability of 18 to 24-year-olds who left education or training without qualifications. Address skill shortages by increasing the numbers attaining intermediate skills, in line with labour market needs. (European Council 2011a)

For Slovenia the recommendations included:

> Set up a system to forecast skills and competencies needed to achieve a responsive labour market. Evaluate the effectiveness of the public employment service, notably on career guidance and counselling services, to improve the matching of skills with labour market needs. (European Council 2011b)

For Hungary the recommendations included:

> Take steps to strengthen the capacity of the Public Employment Service and other providers to increase the quality and effectiveness of training, job search assistance and individualised services . . . In consultation with stakeholders, introduce tailor-made programmes, for the low-skilled and other particularly disadvantaged groups. (European Council 2011c)

For Estonia the recommendations included:

> While implementing the education system reform, give priority to measures improving the availability of pre-school education, and enhance the quality and availability of professional education. Focus education outcomes more on labour market needs, and provide opportunities for low-skilled workers to take part in lifelong learning. (European Council 2011d)

For Bulgaria the recommendations included: 'Advance the educational reform by adopting a Law on Pre-School and School Education and a new Higher Education Act by mid 2012' (European Council 2011e). The Europe 2020 strategy seems, therefore, to have strengthened the policy salience of lifelong learning within the EU, and the national reform programme process suggests a stronger apparatus of 'soft power'; but at the price of a further privileging of economic purpose in European lifelong learning policy.

Education as International Relations?

While commentators have typically focussed on how 'cohesion' and 'competitiveness' have fared in recent EU lifelong learning policies, Dale (2009) has suggested that education plays a political as well as social and economic role in the 'European project'. The EU, he argues, has 'more than economic ambitions . . . seeing its project spreading wider and deeper than short-term collective economic benefit' (Dale 2009, p. 28). This 'distinct "Europe-centred" project' aims 'to "thicken" the discourses and institutions of Europe, irrespective of economic competition' (Dale 2009, p. 27). He sees the Lisbon goals as less about responding to global competition, and more concerned with competing with specified competitors (the US, Japan and so forth). On this view, the European Higher Education Area, the Bologna Process and related projects are 'ambitious global strategies' (Robertson 2009, p. 77). Bologna is not just a means of achieving uniformity across Europe; it seeks to transform higher education globally in the European image and the European interest. 'While for a long time Europe has legitimated its activities by presenting itself as a civilising rather than imperialising presence, its more explicit economic and transnational interests open it up to charges of modern-day colonialism and imperialism' (Robertson 2009, p. 78). Similar arguments could doubtless be developed in other sectors of education and training: the European Training Foundation, for instance, works with '30 partner countries' across South-Eastern Europe, North Africa and Central Asia 'to help transition and developing countries to harness the potential of their human capital through the reform of education, training and labour market systems in the context of the EU's external relations policy' (European Training Foundation 2012). Its work includes training and retraining to facilitate 'adaptation to industrial changes', encouraging 'vocational integration and reintegration into the labour market', 'stimulating cooperation' between educational establishments and firms, and 'designing, introducing and implementing reforms in education and training systems in order to develop employability and labour market relevance' (European Training Foundation 2012).

Dale and Robertson see such developments as part of a 'hegemonic project' of 'constructing Europe, economically, politically, culturally', which involves reconstructing governance. European education policy should, they argue, be seen in this light; as implicated in the spread of neoliberal globalization, a key feature of which is 'harnessing the apparatuses of the state to its own purposes in place of the decommodifying and 'market-taming' role the state had under social democracy' (Dale 2009, p. 29). The EU, in their view, is principally a mechanism that educates and disciplines nation-states to this end; and the EU's lifelong learning policies and educational governance mechanisms play their part. Soft power, from this perspective, is the EU's preferred mode of behaviour in external and international relations, as well as in its internal affairs. There is indeed a case that if the EU is to find 'advantage' in a competitive world – and amid the crisis of the euro, Europe's competitive advantages do not seem numerous – it may well lie in governance expertise; and that the technologies it has developed in the educational realm have their part to play.

NOTES

1. Confusingly, Portugal's enchanting capital was the backdrop for – and thus lends its name to – several of the policy developments described in this chapter. We shall therefore encounter the Lisbon Council (the meeting of the European Council held at Lisbon in March 2000), and 'Lisbon goals', 'Lisbon objectives' and the 'Lisbon strategy' and 'Lisbon process' (policy goals, a process for setting them and a strategy for achieving them set for the EU at that meeting). In addition, but wholly distinct, we shall also encounter the Lisbon Treaty (the Treaty amending the EU's foundational treaties signed at Lisbon in December 2007).
2. Apart from England and Scotland, which form part of the United Kingdom: Scotland has a substantial element of devolved decision-making, with its own parliament and government; England is governed by the UK parliament.
3. 'Under the principle of subsidiarity, in areas which do not fall within its exclusive competence, the [European] Union shall act only if and in so far as the objectives of the proposed action cannot be sufficiently achieved by the Member States, either at central level or at regional and local level, but can rather, by reason of the scale or effects of the proposed action, be better achieved at Union level' (Treaty on European Union 1992, Article 5).
4. The European Centre for the Development of Vocational Training.
5. The Czech Republic, Denmark, Estonia, Finland, Lithuania, Slovenia and Scotland (UK). Austria was 'at an advanced stage in developing such a strategy' (CEC DG-EAC 2009, p. 103).
6. Flanders (Belgium), Spain, France, Ireland, Iceland, Luxemburg, The Netherlands, Norway, Portugal, Sweden, England (UK).
7. Ireland, France, Malta, the United Kingdom.
8. European Citizenship comprises: freedom of movement and residence within the Union; the right to vote and stand for election in local government and European Parliament elections in one's country of residence; the right to diplomatic and consular protection from authorities of any member state; and the right to access the European Ombudsman (Preuss et al. 2003, p. 5).

REFERENCES

Allais, Stephanie, David Raffe, Rob Strathdee, Leesa Wheelahan and Michael Young (2009), *Learning from the First Qualifications Frameworks*, Geneva: International Labour Office.

Blitz, Brad (2003), 'From Monnet to Delors: Educational Co-operation in the European Union', *Contemporary European History*, **12** (2), 1–16.

Campbell, Jacob (2010), *Democracy and the European Superstate*, London: Bruges Group. Available at http://www.brugesgroup.com/mediacentre/comment.live?article=14077 (accessed 24 August 2011).

Cedefop (European Centre for the Development of Vocational Training) (2010), 'The Development of National Qualifications Frameworks in Europe', Working Paper No. 8, Luxembourg: Publications Office of the European Union.

Centre for Research on Lifelong Learning (CRELL) (2011), 'CRELL website'. Available at: http://crell.jrc.ec.europa.eu/ (accessed 15 November 2011).

Charter, David (2007), 'Call for Vote on "Europe Empire"', *The Times*, 11 July. Available at: http://www.timesonline.co.uk/tol/news/world/europe/article2056576.ece (accessed 24 August 2011).

Charter of Fundamental Rights (2000), 'Charter of Fundamental Rights of the European Union (2000/C 364/01)', *Official Journal of the European Communities*, C 364/1, 18 December.

Commission of the European Communities (CEC) (1979), *The European Community and Education* (European File 18/79, October). Luxembourg: Office for Official Publications of the European Communities. Available at: http://aei.pitt.edu/14348/1/Eur_File_18–79.PDF (accessed 17 January 2013).

Commission of the European Communities (CEC) (1993), *Growth, Competitiveness, Employment: The Challenges and Ways Forward into the 21st Century – White Paper*, Luxembourg: Office for Official Publications of the European Communities.

Commission of the European Communities (CEC) (1995), *Teaching and Learning: Towards a Learning Society*, Luxembourg: Office for Official Publications of the European Communities.

Commission of the European Communities (CEC) (2000), *Lisbon European Council 23 and 24 March 2000. Presidency Conclusions*. Available at: http://www.europarl.europa.eu/summits/lis1_en.htm#a (accessed 19 July 2011).

Commission of the European Communities (CEC) (2010), *Europe 2020: A Strategy for Smart, Sustainable and Inclusive Growth*, Communication from the Commission, Brussels, COM(2010) 2020.

Commission of the European Communities, Directorate General for Education and Culture (CEC DG-EAC) (2003), Standing Group on Indicators and Benchmarks, *Final List of Indicators to Support the Implementation of the Work Programme on the Future Objectives of the Education and Training Systems: Results of the Consultation of the Working Groups*, July.

Commission of the European Communities, Directorate General for Education and Culture (CEC DG-EAC) (2008), *The European Qualifications Framework for Lifelong Learning (EQF)*, Luxembourg: Office for Official Publications of the European Communities.

Commission of the European Communities, Directorate General for Education and Culture (CEC DG-EAC) (2009), *Key Competences for a Changing World.*

Progress towards the Lisbon Objectives in Education and Training. Analysis of Implementation at the European and National Levels, Commission staff working document, Accompanying document to the Communication from the Commission to the European Parliament, the Council, the European Economic and Social Committee and the Committee of the Regions, SEC(2009) 1598, COM(2009) 640, Brussels.

Commission of the European Communities, Directorate General for Education and Culture (CEC DG-EAC) (2011), *Progress towards the Common European Objectives in Education and Training. Indicators and Benchmarks 2010/2011*, Commission staff working document (based on document SEC(2011)526).

Dale, Roger (2009), 'Contexts, Constraints and Resources in the Development of European Education Space and European Education Policy', in Roger Dale and Susan Robertson (eds), *Globalisation and Europeanisation in Education*, Didcot: Symposium Books, pp. 23–43.

Dale, Roger and Susan Robertson (eds) (2009), *Globalisation and Europeanisation in Education*, Didcot: Symposium Books.

Dehmel, Alexandra (2006), 'Making a European Area of Lifelong Learning a Reality? Some Critical Reflections on the European Union's Lifelong Learning Policies', *Comparative Education*, **42** (1), 49–62.

European Council (2000), 'Lisbon European Council, 23 and 24 March 2000. Presidency Conclusions'. Available at: http://www.europarl.europa.eu/summits/lis1_en.htm (accessed 17 January 2013).

European Council (2002), 'Council Resolution of 27 June 2002 on lifelong learning (C 163/01)', *Official Journal of the European Communities*, 9 July.

European Council (2003), 'Council Conclusions on Reference Levels of European Average Performance in Education and Training (Benchmarks)', Outcome of Proceedings of the Council on 5 and 6 May, 8981/03, Brussels, 7 May.

European Council (2004), 'Council Decision of 26 January 2004 establishing a Community action programme to promote active European citizenship (civic participation) (2004/100/EC)', *Official Journal of the European Union*, 4 February.

European Council (2010), '2010 Joint Progress Report of the Council and the Commission on the implementation of the "Education and Training 2010 Work Programme"', *Official Journal of the European Union*, C 117/1, 6 May.

European Council (2011a), 'Council Recommendation of 12 July 2011 on the National Reform Programme 2011 of the United Kingdom and delivering a Council opinion on the updated Convergence Programme of the United Kingdom, 2011–2014', *Official Journal of the European Union*, C 217/04, 23 July.

European Council (2011b), 'Council Recommendation of 12 July 2011 on the National Reform Programme 2011 of Slovenia and delivering a Council opinion on the updated Stability Programme of Slovenia, 2011–2014', *Official Journal of the European Union*, C 217/01), 23 July.

European Council (2011c), 'Council Recommendation of 12 July 2011 on the National Reform Programme 2011 of Hungary and delivering a Council Opinion on the updated convergence programme of Hungary, 2011–2015', *Official Journal of the European Union*, C 209/03, 15 July.

European Council (2011d), 'Council Recommendation of 12 July 2011 on the National Reform Programme 2011 of Estonia and delivering a Council opinion

on the Stability Programme of Estonia, 2011–2015', *Official Journal of the European Union*, C 213/02, 12 July.
European Council (2011e), 'Council Recommendation of 12 July 2011 on the National Reform Programme 2011 of Bulgaria and delivering a Council Opinion on the updated convergence programme of Bulgaria, 2011–2014', *Official Journal of the European Union*, C 209/02, 15 July.
European Training Foundation (2012), 'European Training Foundation website'. Available at: http://www.etf.europa.eu/web.nsf/pages/home (accessed 30 January 2012).
Eurydice (2009), 'Eurydice website'. Available at: http://eacea.ec.europa.eu/education/eurydice/index_en.php (accessed 15 November 2011).
Follesdal, Andreas (2001), 'Union Citizenship: Unpacking the Beast of Burden', *Law and Philosophy*, **20**, 313–343.
Hantrais, Linda (2007), *Social Policy in the European Union*, 3rd edn, Basingstoke: Palgrave Macmillan.
High Level Group (2004), *Facing the Challenge. The Lisbon Strategy for Growth and Employment. Report from the High Level Group chaired by Wim Kok*, Luxembourg: Office for Official Publications of the European Communities.
Holford, John (2006), 'The Role of Lifelong Learning in Building Citizenship: European Union Approaches in the Light of British and Colonial Experience', *International Journal of Lifelong Education*, **25** (3), 321–332.
Holford, John (2008), 'Hard Measures for Soft Stuff: Citizenship Indicators and Educational Policy under the Lisbon Strategy', *European Educational Research Journal*, **7** (3), 331–343.
Holford, John, Sheila Riddell, Elisabet Weedon, Judit Litjens and Guy Hannan (2008), *Patterns of Lifelong Learning: Policy and Practice in an Expanding Europe*, Vienna: Lit Verlag.
Holford, John and Vida Mohorčič Špolar (2012), 'Neoliberal and Inclusive Themes in European Lifelong Learning Policy', in Sheila Riddell, Jörg Markowitsch and Elisabet Weedon (eds), *Lifelong Learning in Europe: Equity and Efficiency in the Balance*, Bristol: Policy Press, pp. 39–61.
Lauder, Hugh (2011), 'Education, Economic Globalisation and National Qualifications Frameworks', *Journal of Education and Work*, **24** (3–4), 213–221.
Lawn, Martin (2006), 'Soft Governance and the Learning Spaces of Europe', *Comparative European Politics*, **4**, 272–288.
Lee, Moosung, Tryggvi Thayer and Na'im Madyun (2008), 'The Evolution of the European Union's Lifelong Learning Policies: An Institutional Learning Perspective', *Comparative Education*, **44** (4), 445–463.
Moravcsik, Andrew (1993), 'Preferences and Power in the European Community: A Liberal Intergovernmentalist Approach', *Journal of Common Market Studies*, **31** (4), 473–524.
Pépin, Luce (2006), *The History of European Cooperation in Education and Training. Europe in the Making – An Example*, Luxembourg: Office of Official Publications of the European Communities.
Preuss, Ulrich K., Michelle Everson, Mathias Koenig-Archibugi and Edwidge Lefebvre (2003), 'Traditions of Citizenship in the European Union', *Citizenship Studies*, **7** (2), 3–14.
Robertson, Susan L. (2008), 'The Bologna Process Goes Global: A Model, Market, Mobility, Brain Power or State Building Strategy?' Invitational paper to ANPED's Annual Conference, October, Brazil. Available at: http://www.bris.

ac.uk/education/people/academicStaff/edslr/publications/31slr (accessed 19 July 2011).

Robertson, Susan (2009), 'Europe, Competitiveness and Higher Education: an Evolving Project', in Robert Dale and Susan Robertson (eds), *Globalisation and Europeanisation in Education*, Didcot: Symposium Books, pp. 65–83.

Treaty of Lisbon (2007), 'Treaty of Lisbon Amending the Treaty on European Union and the Treaty Establishing the European Community', signed at Lisbon, 13 December 2007, *Official Journal of the European Union*, C 306, 17 December.

Treaty on European Union (1992), *Treaty on European Union* (The Treaty of Maastricht), *Official Journal of the European Communities*, C 191, 29 July.

Treaty on European Union (2010), 'Consolidated Version of the Treaty on European Union', *Official Journal of the European Union*, C 83/01, 30 March.

Trubeck, David M. and Louise G. Trubeck (2005), 'Hard and Soft Law in the Construction of Social Europe: The Role of the Open Method of Co-ordination', *European Law Journal*, **11** (3), 343–364.

Wallace, Helen, Mark A. Pollack, and Alasdair R. Young (eds) (2010), *Policy-Making in the European Union*, 6th edn, Oxford: Oxford University Press.

Wallace, Helen, William Wallace and Mark A. Pollack (eds) (2005), *Policy-Making in the European Union*, 5th edn, Oxford: Oxford University Press.

Young, Michael (2003), 'National Qualifications Frameworks as a Global Phenomenon: A Comparative Perspective', *Journal of Education and Work*, **16** (3), 223–237.

Young, Michael (2008), 'Towards a European Qualifications Framework: Some Cautionary Observations', *Journal of European Industrial Training*, **32** (2–3), 128–137.

2. Lifelong learning systems: overview and extension of different typologies

Ellu Saar and Odd Bjørn Ure

INTRODUCTION

From the outset, the project partners summarizing their findings in the present book looked for systemic elements in their national education, training and labour market structures that could point to the emergence of national lifelong learning systems. Albeit some countries show few signs of a (public) lifelong learning discourse (Holford et al. 2008), some dimensions of lifelong learning (LLL) are present at a system level, therefore paving the way for a discussion of lifelong learning typologies.

Ericson (1982) claims that wherever the education system emerges, it basically distributes two distinct types of goods. The first consists of knowledge, skills and certain values; the second consists of symbolic grades, diplomas, transcripts, letters of recommendation and so on (see also Bills 2003). The second kind of goods acts as the common coinage or medium of exchange that connects separate educational institutions; as Ericson (1982, p. 309) explains: '[w]ithout them, there can be no education system as such'. Ericson holds that a general theory of the educational system needs to 'yield some kind of standards for judging which social institutions belong to the educational system and which stand outside it' (1982, p. 299). In this chapter, we argue that beyond a general theory of LLL systems, there is a need for multiple typologies in order to escape assumptions of a single economic trajectory for market economies and for their LLL systems. Equally, as for the conceptualization of education systems, we need to look for demarcations of which institutions form parts of the systems. By following this research direction, LLL becomes less of a fluid concept or even slogan, particularly because it will then lead to theorization of how institutions beyond the traditional education systems are being mobilized for the purpose of LLL.

Several authors have mentioned problems regarding the development of typologies, for example of education and training systems, of skill formation systems, of transition systems and so on. They indicate that almost all of these typologies have to struggle with the level of abstraction, namely the need to move beyond national specificities and to generate conceptual models, which fit a number of countries (Ashton et al. 2000; Raffe 2008). However, the elaboration of these typologies is relevant for theoretical and policy interests. The typologies emphasize the interrelationships between different social and economic institutions (for example, initial education and training systems, labour market and industrial relations systems, welfare state systems, production systems etc.). Three distinct purposes in policy analysis could be distinguished (see also Raffe 2008): the first purpose is to compare the effectiveness of alternative institutional arrangements or policy interventions; the second purpose is to identify types of systems within which different interventions might be effective; because policies do not always work in every system, the third purpose is to help policy-makers to understand their own systems' logic for which specific policies must be designed.

Various institutions belonging to the European Union (EU) are already intervening in LLL for these purposes. The open method of policy coordination (OMC) in moving towards the 2010 objectives, now updated to 2020, makes use of: country classifications; several services of the European Commission propose mutual policy learning activities for the member states during which country clusters emerge spontaneously or even haphazardly; Calls for Proposals instigating mutual policy learning are launched by the European Commission and guides of good practice are produced for all areas of LLL.

The policy implication of the present book for these ongoing EU activities primarily rests on utilizing sound typologies to demonstrate the limits of comparability and possible hurdles in the uptake of experiences gained in other contexts (cf. Arrowsmith et al. 2004; Stuart and Greenwood 2006), which is especially relevant when different typologies are applied. Whereas countries may be compared according to the dimensions of one specific typology, they may not be comparable along the dimensions of another typology. This may hurt the pride of ambitious LLL nations but sound research in LLL might illustrate why certain comparisons do not produce practicable knowledge. When communicating the practicability of refined LLL typologies in the different policy contexts outlined above, the balance between simplicity and abstraction needs careful consideration. Furthermore, typologies should not be communicated as a panacea for all problems that LLL policy-making is faced with. There have been a number of attempts to develop typologies of education, training and skill formation systems, many of which have emanated from particular disciplines, namely education, industrial relations, labour market studies, economics and political sciences (Ashton et al. 2000). Several recent works have recognized the importance of an interdisciplinary approach, which combines theoretical assumptions and moves towards a much broader perspective (cf. Lauder et al. 2008).

An additional problem is that much of the research has been based on a limited number and range of countries, mostly large countries such as the United Kingdom (UK), Japan, the United States of America (USA), Germany and France. Central and Eastern European (CEE) countries either have not received any attention or they are classified as one type, which was partly due to the lack of comparative data, partially because of fundamentally different characters of the systems. Although Green (2006) indicates that it is too early to identify different models in the transformation states of CEE countries, we try to classify these countries using previously developed typologies.

This chapter discusses how various dimensions are combined to produce different typologies of education and training systems, lifelong learning and skill formation systems, notably by leaning on theories on the varieties of capitalism. The chapter builds on earlier attempts to develop a conceptual framework for the comparative analysis of education and skill formation systems. Following a critical review of these previous approaches, the chapter tries to explain LLL systems in order to improve existing typologies based on the varieties of capitalism approach because this approach captures more labour market dimensions of vital importance for the understanding of lifelong learning.

We start with a brief look at typologies developed from particular disciplines (educational or labour market perspectives). Skill formation typologies, as opposed to education and training systems typologies, can also account for labour market structures. The varieties of capitalism typologies aim at explaining the relationship between skill formation, lifelong learning, the labour market and the nature of the welfare state. We will finally account for the most clear-cut institutionalist perspectives on skill formation, often with a sharp eye for historical change and continuity.

TYPOLOGIES DEVELOPED FROM EDUCATIONAL PERSPECTIVES

In a seminal work on the social origins of educational systems, Margaret Archer (1979) analyses how education systems develop and change by looking into centralized education systems (France, Russia during the Soviet period) versus decentralized systems (England, Denmark), concluding that the change mechanisms differ between the two systems. In spite of certain convergence among these typologies, 'to stress convergence is to emphasize the growth of progressive segmentation in the centralized system and of progressive systematisation in the decentralized system' (Archer 1979, p. 785). The term 'systematization' is used in conjunction with 'unification', which 'involves the incorporation or development of diverse establishments, activities and personnel under a central, national and specifically educational framework of administration' (Archer 1979, p. 72). Archer uses both 'systematization' and 'unification' to describe the emergence of education systems. She maintains that the pairing of unification with systematization develops conjointly with the pairing of differentiation and specialization, 'but the latter remains the weaker pair as it was upon the emergence of the system. It is this pair which has to do the accommodation, has to take second place and has to accept the precedence of the first pair' (Archer 1979, p. 189).

'Differentiation' relates to the multiplicity of services sought from education by the various sections of society. The pressure they exert engenders and sustains a high overall degree of differentiation, which enables theorizing of how organized interests influence and are influenced by the education system. Archer proceeds by summing up that:

> the co-ordination of parts and levels only helps in the negative sense of removing obstacles to multiple goal attainment. In itself it does nothing to ensure that education does serve a variety of demands and service a plurality of institutional operations . . . The concept of *specialization* refers to a range of internal changes rather to any single one. (Archer 1979, p. 76)

Much research from educational perspectives has focused on the identification of different models of education provision. Furth (1985) distinguished the education and training systems according to post-compulsory vocational training arrangements. He identified three models of educational provision: the schooling model, which integrated most forms of provision within the formal educational system (typical for the USA, Canada and Japan); the dual model which was characterized by a strong and developed apprenticeship system (typical for Germany, Austria and Switzerland); and the mixed model where greater importance is assigned to the non-formal sector, typical of the UK. This typology is closely connected with differentiation of countries based on the organization of vocational training (Blossfeld and Stockmann 1998–99; Shavit and Müller 1998). They separate the following types: (1) 'theoretical' vocational training, mainly in schools (the Netherlands, Sweden); (2) a dual system that includes both school training and gaining work experience at the workplace (Germany, Denmark); and (3) on-the-job training (the US, the UK, Italy, Spain[1]).

Green (1991) distinguished between the employer-led model, which provides a work-based system of training (Germany); the education-led system which provides both general and vocational training in different institutions (France, Italy); and the education-led system which provides general and vocational training within the same institution (Sweden).

In the beginning of the privatization and restructuring processes in CEE countries, employers largely withdrew from the provision of training opportunities as they were unable to maintain provision of training infrastructure (Saar et al. 2008), which led to the dismantling of well-established links between schools and enterprises. Elements of enterprise-based apprentice training are now found in the Czech Republic, Slovenia and Hungary, whereas in the rest of the CEE countries vocational education is mostly carried out under the auspices of schools (Kogan 2008). In CEE countries training is less occupation-specific, but relates to broader occupational areas, and in some countries (e.g. Poland and Slovakia) school-based vocational education is combined with a much smaller-scale apprenticeship system.

Allmendinger (1989) introduces a widely used typology of education systems, which focuses on two dimensions: standardization and stratification. Müller and Shavit (1998) added the degree of occupational specificity. Standardization denotes 'the degree to which the quality of education meets the same standards nationwide' (Allmendinger 1989, p.46) and therefore coincides with Archer's notion of systematization. The concept of stratification refers to the extent and form of tracking in the education system. Occupational specificity relates to the extent to which training fosters specific occupational competences rather than more general knowledge (see also Müller and Jacob 2008). An additional dimension is the extent to which there are direct links between the education system and employers (cf. Archer's point about differentiation). All these aspects are not distinct but are closely connected with each other (see Breen 2005).

In highly standardized systems, educational credentials send clear and reliable signals to employers about the quality of education and skills of a potential worker. In a majority of European countries the general education system is rather standardized, yet any differences are revealed in the vocational education systems. Primarily in German-language countries, standardization is considered especially important for vocational schools, because if there are established professional standards issued to school graduates, the employers can rely on school-leaving certificates when hiring their labour force. Employers can then be confident that those new workers will meet their expectations. We assume that standardization would have a twofold impact on LLL opportunities. Firstly, standardization will form the basis for achieving adequate job–person matches. Secondly, from the employers' viewpoint there is less need to develop intra-firm career structures or to promote additional training for workers because recruitment from the external labour market becomes a more viable option (Müller and Gangl 2003). Nevertheless, standardization would help to make educational paths more flexible and to facilitate a return to the education system.

Inequality in further learning participation is linked to the education system via the extent to which initial education and further education are complements or substitutes (Wolbers 2005). The stratification of the education system is responsible for whether they are complements or substitutes, to the extent to which general education and vocational training are separated into distinctive tracks and the rigidity of the boundaries between those different tracks. Comprehensive school systems with more emphasis on general skills are defined as those of low stratification (for example, the US, Sweden, Ireland and the UK) in which specific skills are primarily obtained, after the initial education, in on-the-job training. In this case, participation in non-formal learning is considered to be a form of compensation for the deficiencies of initial education (Crouch et al. 1999; Brunello 2001). In a highly stratified education system (Germany, Austria, Switzerland), each educational track is designed to specialize in awarding rather narrowly defined, occupationally relevant credentials. In this case, the specific skills are obtained in initial (vocational) education, and there is no need to compensate for the lack of specific skills, that is, to participate in non-formal learning. However, Bassanini et al. (2007) indicated that it is an open question as to whether a more comprehensive system is conductive to higher participation in non-formal education than a more stratified one. If vocational schools in stratified systems produce highly specialized skills that become rapidly obsolete in the conditions of technical progress, additional training might be required to update existing skills.

Occupational specificity of the education system directly affects the expected training costs of employees. In some cases, vocational schools are simply a way of providing education for pupils of low abilities and have a limited success in teaching occupationally useful skills; for example, Italy and France (Breen 2005). In post-war Sweden the vocational system was reformed (Olofsson 2007) with a view to impart 'transferable vocational skills under broad headings . . . whilst avoiding specialization' (Müller and Shavit 1998, p. 5). Since 2008, trials with apprentice schemes have however been reintroduced and there are signs that they will become a more permanent feature of the Swedish system.[2] In German-speaking countries, vocational education is quite specific and there are often clear institutional links between vocational training and employers (cf. Thelen 2004).

Although the organization of education systems in CEE countries into different tracks resembles the highly stratified arrangement of German-speaking countries, weak links between the educational system and the labour market in some CEE countries (e.g. in the Baltic countries) make such systems more similar to moderately stratified systems, found for example in France and the UK (Saar 2005).

TYPOLOGIES OF EDUCATION AND LIFELONG LEARNING SYSTEMS DEVELOPED FROM LABOUR MARKET PERSPECTIVES

Another major source of research has emanated from the study of labour market structure and organization. The approach focuses on the interdependence between the educational, organizational and industrial relation spheres (Ashton et al. 2000).

While, according to human capital theory, low participation in adult education results from employers' reluctance to invest in employees' portable skills (Becker 1975), empirical evidence has not provided much support for this suggestion. The most often offered explanations for the inadequacy of the human capital theory is the imperfection of the labour market due to its segmentation and the role of the labour market institutions. The central idea of theories of labour market segmentation is that the labour market is composed of 'non-competing groups'. Boundaries between these groups are created by institutional rules; these rules are established by labour market institutions, such as collective agreements between trade unions and employers' associations, sometimes supported by government intervention or legislation (Kerr 1954).

A basic difference in models of skill acquisition can be found between occupational and internal models or between qualificational and organizational labour markets (Marsden 1986, 1990; Maurice and Sellier 1979; Maurice et al. 1986). The key issue is the linkage between training provided by the education system and skills recognized in the labour market. In a system of organizational space, education is academic or general in character, with specific occupational skills learned on the job. The career pattern subsequently depends to a large extent on the on-the-job training acquired (Doeringer and Piore 1971). Additional training allows workers to obtain the necessary skills for making internal upward moves in a given company. The intensity of additional training is expected to be high in a system of organizational space. In qualificational space, education is closely tied to job requirements and more importance is placed on diploma requirements and certificates (Maurice et al. 1986). Access to skilled jobs is reserved for those workers who have the specific skills needed for these jobs. In qualificational space, the education system produces workers with occupation-specific skills (in other words, vocational education dominates). Education systems with a high degree of occupational specificity support the prevalence of occupationally segmented labour markets, while intra-firm labour market structures prevail in countries with little occupation-related training in the education system (Shavit and Müller 1998). The acquired skills are transferable across firms and are recognized by employers. The main body of research has been concerned with France (a typical internal labour market – ILM – country) and Germany (typical occupational labour market – OLM – country).

Based on previous studies one would expect Austria, Denmark, Switzerland, Germany and the Netherlands, in the capacity of countries with extensive systems of vocational training, to lean towards the OLM patterns, whereas the remaining Western European countries should form the contrasting ILM pole. Research suggests that the category of ILM countries is very heterogeneous (Müller and Gangl 2003). The position of the UK along the ILM–OLM axis has been an issue of some debate, because some authors (see Kerckhoff 1995) argue that the institutional context in the UK is close to OLM, while others (Soskice 1993) do not agree with this statement. Except for Marsden's (1990) result of classifying Italy alongside the French ILM model, there has been little systematic evidence for Southern European countries. Gangl (2001) argues that Southern European countries do not fit into the ILM–OLM dichotomy. The Southern European pattern combines elements present in both ILM (strong impact of experience on unemployment) and OLM arrangements (strong effect of education on labour market outcomes). Research on Southern European countries has demonstrated the need to allow for family-related factors (Raffe 2008).

Similarly, as for the Southern European countries, it is difficult to find the exact placement for the location of CEE countries along the ILM–OLM axis. According to previous studies, Slovenia (and perhaps the Czech Republic) has an education–labour market link of the OLM kind, and employment protection legislation (EPL) is relatively strong, at least in Slovenia (see Gebel 2008). Hungary used to be a typical OLM country but has moved to ILM in the last two decades (Róbert and Bukodi 2006), and Poland can be relatively close to Hungary in terms of institutional conditions. Employment policies and protection legislation can be weak in the more liberal Baltic countries where education and the labour market link is of the ILM kind (Eamets and Masso 2005). Preliminary analysis by Helemäe and Saar (2011) indicates that the Estonian institutional regime, following the major changes in the 1990s, is more similar to that found in liberal countries (e.g. the UK, Ireland) where there are much fewer institutionalized connections between education, training and the labour market. The liberal institutional regimes are potentially more open to competition between people with different levels and types of educational qualification for the same occupational positions; that is, there is less segmentation within the labour market (Helemäe and Saar 2011). Results of cluster analysis conducted by Gangl (2001) indicate that the UK and Ireland belong to the ILM cluster together with France and Belgium. On the other hand, some features of the Baltic states, particularly a strong insider–outsider logic that decreases labour market flexibility in Estonia (Saar and Täht 2005), are close to Southern European countries.

Combining education and labour market perspectives, Rainbird (1992) distinguishes features of three models: (1) the market model, which is characterized by dependence on the labour market and limited institutionalization of training (e.g. the UK, Italy); (2) the educational model, which is subdivided to a state-regulated system where training is provided through the education system (France); and (3) the organized partner model, characterized by the dual system (Germany).

TYPOLOGIES BASED ON THE ROLE OF STATE, FORMAL EDUCATION SYSTEM AND LABOUR MARKET

Green (1999), working from the educationalist perspective, stresses the modes of articulation between central governments, education systems, labour markets and firms as the basis of typology. Green (1999) separates five primary models of education and training systems (ETSs) within Western Europe and East Asia (see Table 2.1). The 'Japanese' model is also termed as the 'state developmentalist' model, in which ETSs are generally highly centralized and place strong emphasis on the development of group cohesion and conformism. In the Japanese model, general secondary education predominates over vocational secondary education. Standard-based qualifications are not important in recruitment since recruitment is based on recommendations, company assessment tests and the reputation of the institution. Green (1999) contrasts Japan with the German ETS, which is organized on a regional basis and dominated by the dual system that differentiates young people into various tracks leading to occupational positions. Varieties of the dual system are found, for example, in Austria, Belgium, the Netherlands and Switzerland.

France has provided the basis for the other dominant ETS tradition within continental Europe, and Green (1999) claims that this model applies throughout the 'Latin rim' states. The French model is characterized by strong centralization (cf. Margaret Archer on its genesis), alongside comprehensive systems of compulsory schooling and school-based systems of

Table 2.1 Typology of education and training systems

	Japanese model	German model	French model	Swedish model	UK model
Countries	Japan, South Korea, Taiwan, Singapore	Germany, Austria, Switzerland, the Netherlands, Czech Rep., Slovak Rep., Hungary, Slovenia	France, the 'Latin rim' states, Bulgaria, Romania	Sweden, other Nordic countries	England, Wales, Baltic countries
The role of the state	Government of the market providing investment and strategic leadership	State intervention to regulate labour markets and coordinate the roles of the social partners	State centred concepts of political membership	Social democratic state, active labour market measures for unemployed and redeployed adults	
Management–labour relations	Paternalistic form of organizations; lifetime employment, seniority wages, compliant single company unions	Large sectoral unions; cooperation and compromise; relatively high levels of 'trust'; strong traditions of social partnership	Widespread sectoral agreements between unions and employers		
Labour market structure	Internal labour market	Occupational labour market	Internal labour market	Internal labour market	Mixture of occupational and internal labour markets

Table 2.1 (continued)

	Japanese model	German model	French model	Swedish model	UK model
Characteristic features of skills formation	Cultivation of specific technical skills less important; in-company training	Standards-based occupational qualifications act as the crucial exchange mechanism	Externally assessed, state-validated certificates play quite an important role	Strong traditions of liberal adult education	
Education and training system: general organization and principles	Generally highly centralized; strong emphasis on the development of group cohesion and conformism	ETS is organized on a regional basis	Strong central control; emphasis on civic education	Substantial devolution of control during the last decade to the local or municipal levels; strong emphasis on equality and social solidarity	Limited state control in education: in recent years introducing competitive, quasi-market relations into education and training
Compulsory education	Comprehensive	Different tracks leading to different occupational destinations	Comprehensive systems of compulsory schooling	Comprehensive schools	
Secondary schools	General secondary schools predominate over vocational secondary schools	Vocational secondary schools predominate; dual system of apprentice training	School-based systems of upper secondary education with only a residual apprentice system	Predominantly school-based with the dominant institution being the comprehensive secondary school;	A 'mixed system' compromising both school-based and work-based elements: more differentiated than

				the apprenticeship is either essentially school-led (Sweden) or dual (Denmark, Norway)	the more integrated upper secondary systems
Adult education and training		Less developed, participation comparatively low	Less developed, participation comparatively low	Prevalent, often subsidized by the state	Relatively widespread, unevenly distributed
Relationships between firms and ETS	Standards-based qualifications are not important; recruitment is based on recommendations, company assessment tests and the reputation of the institution	Strong company commitment to training	Qualifications play an important role in job recruitment and promotion and pay levels; many firms are unable to deliver extensive in-company training		
Skill formation: level of skills		Intermediate level of skills	Intermediate level of skills	High aggregate level of skills	Moderate aggregate level of skills
Skill formation: skill polarization		Quite evenly distributed	Signs of skill polarization	More evenly distributed	High level of skill polarization

Source: Based on Green (1999, 2006).

upper secondary education with only a residual apprentice system. The Swedish model, shared to some degree by the other Nordic countries, is comprehensive; the post-compulsory phase is school-based. The apprenticeship is essentially school-led. There is a strong emphasis on equality and social cohesion. The ETS in England and Wales, based on liberal, individualist philosophy, has limited state control and institutional autonomy. Quasi-market relations in education dominate. Initial post-compulsory education has been categorized as a 'mixed system' (OECD 1985). Green observed in 1999 that during the foregoing 15 years the system had shifted towards being predominantly school-based.

In another paper, Green (2006) identifies four models of lifelong learning (see Table 2.1), which are largely based on his earlier typology. Green concentrates on Western EU member states, indicating that it is still too early to identify different models in the transformation states of CEE countries. Green uses three dimensions of LLL outcomes: the overall output of skills for the labour market; the distribution of these skills; and the rates of participation in adult learning. The LLL systems in the Anglo-Saxon model tend to produce moderate aggregate levels of skills with a high degree of skill polarization. The LLL systems provide quite good opportunities for adult learning but the opportunities are closely linked to students' initial levels of education. The LLL systems in core European countries produce aggregate levels of skills with rather narrower distribution. In France and Mediterranean states adult education and training provision is less developed than in Northern European countries and levels of participation are generally comparatively low. In the German-speaking countries the majority of the workforce is qualified at intermediate levels (Brown at al. 2001). Labour market regimes and the strong apprenticeship system create strong barriers to employment for the unqualified. The Nordic countries produce high aggregate levels and narrow distribution of skills. The participation of adults in learning is high, which is partly related to active labour market measures as well as to state-funded general adult education (see also Rubenson 2006).

Earlier analyses indicate that in CEE countries geographically and historically closer to Germany and Austria (e.g. the Czech and Slovak Republics, Slovenia, Hungary) vocationally oriented education has maintained its dominance over more general education (Strietska-Ilina 2001). Kogan and Unt (2005), for example, show a clear strengthening of the dual system in Slovenia during the 1990s (see also Ivančič 2000). The emerging institutional structure of the education system in these countries is approaching the model of the German-speaking countries, particularly that of Austria (Kotásek 1996). The skill level is intermediate and skills are quite evenly distributed. Participation of adults in training is quite high (except in Hungary) and inequality in participation is of medium level (see Roosmaa and Saar 2010). The three Baltic States (Estonia, Lithuania, Latvia) have been influenced by both the German and the Soviet education traditions. Since regaining independence in the early 1990s, upper secondary schools in the Baltic countries have even stronger emphasis on general education (Helemäe and Saar 2000). Comprehensive secondary education in the Baltic states also includes elements of school-based vocational education. Signs of marketization and liberalization in education, such as introduction of fees at the university level (Kogan et al. 2008), bring these countries closer to the Anglo-Saxon model. Participation of adults in further training is quite high but rather unevenly distributed. Kogan (2008) indicates that Bulgaria and Romania constitute a separate group of countries marked by significant Soviet influence. The system of secondary education in these countries combines both general and vocational elements. According to Kostova (2008), the number of companies providing practical training is rather limited and these companies are usually established through foreign investments. Masson (2004) mentions that despite reforms, major structural problems have made it difficult to modernize education systems. Bulgaria and Romania seem to be quite close to other Southern European countries in this respect. However, we do not think that it is justified to classify these countries as following the French model, because they have no widespread sectoral agreements between unions and employers, nor internal labour markets.

TYPOLOGY OF SKILL FORMATION SYSTEMS

With skill formation typologies there is a move away from a focus on the supply of skills through initial training towards a greater appreciation of the impact of labour market and economic institutions on the generation of skills and on the source of pressure on employers to train. Different skill formation systems tend to follow the skills requirements of the national economies (cf. Culpepper and Thelen 2008). One early contribution comes from Lazonick and O'Sullivan (1994), who emphasize the historic foundations of skill formation. For example, in Germany the evolution of advanced machine building has had a prolonged success in export markets, supported by sophisticated vocational training institutions at all levels as well as by networks of small and large enterprises. Lazonick and O'Sullivan compare the origin and transformations in skill formation in three other countries (the UK, USA and Japan) and relate the competitive advantages of nations to the nature of corresponding skill formation systems.

In the policy discourse and in practical life, LLL has an employability dimension that can be explored by looking at labour markets and the role of employers in generating the demand of skills. According to Crouch (2004), there are three sources of skill investment: the individual, the state (at local, national or regional level) and firms (either singly or in associations). The particular configurations of these three mechanisms constitute a skill formation system. Recent work stresses the need to focus on relationships between central governments, education systems, labour markets and firms.

Ashton et al. (2000) assume that the relationships central to an understanding of the process of skill formation are those between the state, in the form of the political elite and the state apparatus; the education and training systems which deliver skills; capital in the form of employers through whom the demand for skills arise; and workers in the form of employees and their organizations which influence the supply of skills. These provide the basic groups which in specific cultural contexts form the institutions through which skills are formed. The authors distinguish between four models: the market model, the corporatist model, the developmental state model and the neo-market model, but only two of these are characteristic to Western European countries (see Table 2.2).

In the case of the market model – for example the UK, USA and Canada – economies are characterized by a 'low skills equilibrium' (Finegold and Soskice 1988). The system of industrial relations operates with a relatively high degree of autonomy. Within the context of a culture of individualism, training is the responsibility of either the employer or the individual. Education and training has been left a high degree of autonomy in relation to the demands of the employers. The result is that in-company training is the dominant form of skill formation outside the professions (Ashton et al. 2000). The coordination of the supply and demand for skills operates through the market. Government programmes are primarily focused on the unemployed.

Germany, Austria, Switzerland, the Netherlands and Denmark provide examples of the corporatist model. Their governments are heavily involved with employers and unions in regulating not only the training system but also the employment relationship and social welfare arrangements. Governments also developed a centralized system of control over the education system to ensure an adequate supply of skills for the labour market. With support from labour organizations, governments have therefore encouraged the growth of high levels of initial training, either in the form of the apprenticeship system or as strong provision of school-based vocational education. Coordination of the demand for the supply of skills is undertaken through a broader institutional framework. This model

Table 2.2 Typology of skill formation systems

	Market model	Corporatist model	Developmental state model	Neo-market model
Countries	The UK, USA, Canada etc.	Germany, Austria, Switzerland, Denmark etc.	Japan, Singapore, South Korea	Chile, Mexico, Brazil
Key societal characteristics	Large social inequalities	Low degree of inequality	Economic security provided by the family, relatively egalitarian distribution of income	Large social inequalities
Production system	Low-value-added industries with a few higher-value-added industries	High-value-added industries	Mostly low-value-added industries; more recently the shift in direction of higher-value-added forms of production	Low-value-added industries with a few higher-value-added industries associated with foreign capital
Management–labour relations	The dominance of capital; only the professions sustained a strong control over training and entry to the occupation	Strong labour movement; strong control over training; trust between capital and labour	Unions remain defensive and focused almost exclusively on wage bargaining	Relatively strong labour organizations; increasing power of capital relative to labour
Form of interaction between the state and market	A relatively high degree of autonomy in relations to the state	The state is more heavily involved with both employers and unions	An important role of the state in relation to labour	The privatization of major industries reduced the power of the state
Main principles of skill formation	Training is seen as the responsibility of either the employer or the individual	Governments, with support from labour, have encouraged the growth of high levels of initial training	Leading role of the state	The state has relinquished control over the delivery of training to the market

Table 2.2 (continued)

	Market model	Corporatist model	Developmental state model	Neo-market model
Skill formation system	In-company training	Use of Education and Training System (ETS) to provide the appropriate skills	ES and training controlled by the state	Foreign capital, private providers
Vocational training system	Support the immediate needs of employers	Stronger impact on the employers' demand for skills, creating pressure on employers to sustain higher-value-added forms of production	Different	Support the immediate needs of employers
Coordination of supply and demand	Through the market, slow	Agreements between the state, capital and labour; a 'tighter fit' between demand and supply	State	Market
The role of the state	Training of the unemployed, maintaining the employability of marginal workers operating in low-cost forms of production	Beyond the provision of training for the unemployed	Upgrading the skills of the employed	Training of the unemployed, maintaining the employability of marginal workers operating in low-cost forms of production

Source: Ashton et al. (2010).

ensures that a high proportion of the labour force is provided with an intermediate level of skills.

The other two models are represented by countries from Asia and South America. In countries exhibiting the developmental state model (South Korea, Taiwan, Singapore), the need for utilizing their advantage (cheap labour) in the world markets led to the initial development of low-skilled, low-value-added forms of production. Confucian culture has created very high demand for education. Governments have controlled this demand. The state has also played a leading role in the field of training.

Characteristic to the neo-market model is the shift of the locus of control over the process of skill formation from the state, industry and labour to the hands of foreign capital. Control over the education system is decentralized. The coordination of the demand for and supply of skills is left largely to market forces. The state intervenes in the delivery of training in the case of market failures, mainly for the unemployed.

CEE countries are very difficult to classify according to these four types. Research on these countries has shown that typologies also need to take into account market liberalism and labour market flexibility (Saar et al. 2008). Baltic countries seem to have some characteristic features common with the market (the dominance of capital and coordination of the supply and demand is taking place through the market) as well as neo-market models (important role of foreign capital). The Visegrad countries (the Czech Republic, Hungary, Poland and Slovakia) combine elements present in corporatist and neo-market models.

VARIETIES OF CAPITALISM APPROACH

Recently, the trend has been towards comprehensive approaches that view institutional contexts as multidimensional and highly interactive. Institutional systems are then viewed as interdependent; they complement each other and are therefore best understood as country-specific institutional 'packages' (Blossfeld 2003).

The employer-centred 'varieties of welfare capitalism' approach seeks out 'institutional complementarities' between different production regimes, industrial relations, education institutions and social protection systems (Hall and Soskice 2001). According to Hall and Soskice (2001, p. 18): 'The point about institutional complementarities suggests that nations with a particular type of coordination in one sphere of the economy should tend to develop complementary practices in other spheres as well.' Rather than grouping countries under a single regime, this perspective seeks to develop multidimensional models of institutional structures that are country-specific.

The varieties of capitalism approach draws a distinction between two modes of coordination. In the first, firms coordinate their activities primarily via hierarchies and competitive market arrangements, the equilibrium outcomes of firm behaviour usually being given by demand and supply conditions in competitive markets. In the second, firms depend more heavily on non-market relationships to coordinate their endeavours with other actors and to construct their core competences. In contrast to the first mode, the equilibrium on which firms coordinate in the second mode is most often the result of strategic interaction among firms and other actors. Hall and Soskice (2001) suggest that nations with a particular type of coordination in one sphere of the economy should tend to develop complementary practices in other spheres as well.

The balance between these two types of coordination varies across welfare production regimes. At one end of the spectrum there are liberal market economies (LMEs) where relations between firms and other actors are coordinated primarily by competitive markets. At the other end there are coordinated market economies (CMEs) where firms typically engage in more strategic interaction with trade unions, suppliers of finance and other actors. According to varieties of capitalism approach, the important institutional settings that contribute to different mechanisms of functioning in CMEs versus LMEs are financial systems, systems of industrial relations, education and training systems and inter-company relations. Specific features of these institutions have certain implications for the types of innovations firms prefer and types of skills they rely on. In this literature, industrial relations are among the important spheres in which firms must develop relationships to resolve coordination problems central to their competence (Hall and Soskice 2001). In the sphere of industrial relations, wage and productivity levels that condition the success of the firm and rates of unemployment or inflation in the economy as a whole are at stake. Vocational training and education is another important sphere of coordination for firms that face the problem of securing a workforce with suitable skills, while workers face the problem of deciding how much to invest in which skills. The outcomes of this coordination problem affect not only the fortunes of individual companies and workers, but also the skill levels and competitiveness of the overall economy.

It has been argued that such institutional complementarities helps to explain differences between LMEs and CMEs in the level and composition of skills of their workforces, as well as differences in market strategies of their firms. Two alternative roads to competitiveness have been followed in Europe: a 'low road' based on a low-wage, low-skill, low-involvement and low-quality equilibrium, and a 'high road' entailing high wages, high skills, high cooperation and high product quality (Soskice 1993; Berger and Dore

1996; Crouch and Streeck 1997; Regini 2000). Economically developed countries distinguished by varieties of capitalism approach are identified as coordinated market economies (CMEs) (cf. Hall and Soskice 2001) and might also be characterized as 'high road' competition economies, while those identified as liberal market economies (LME) rather follow the 'low road' of competition.[3]

Although there are variations among them, the USA, the UK, Ireland, Canada, Australia and New Zealand are generally identified by this approach as liberal market economies. Germany provides a good example of a coordinated market economy. Austria, Sweden, Norway, Finland, Denmark, Belgium, the Netherlands and Switzerland are also identified as belonging to this type (Hall and Gingerich 2004; Hall and Thelen 2009). Hall and Soskice (2001) have termed Southern European countries as those that do not fall easily into the categories of liberal, coordinated or mixed market economies. These political economies have been characterized by high level of strategic coordination secured largely by the actions of the relatively interventionist state (Schmidt 2002).

Some recent research critical of this approach has shown that institutional arrangements may be more loosely coupled within national innovation and production systems, allowing not only for incoherences at the national level, but also for the creation of autonomous subsystems at the sectoral or local level. These subsystems may establish their own governance structures, diverging from the national model (Crouch et al. 2009). National systems may also be in competition with both supranational regulatory regimes and internationally available services (Deeg and Jackson 2007).

SKILL FORMATION IN DIFFERENT TYPES OF POLITICAL ECONOMIES

According to the framework developed by Estevez-Abe et al. (2001) within the 'varieties of capitalism' approach, the creation of incentives for firms and workers to invest in a certain type of skills is the key mechanism underlying the logics of skill formation regimes. Just as in human capital theory (Becker 1975), an important distinction is made between the development of general (portable) skills versus specific (non-portable) skills. The main idea of this approach is that certain institutional packages should be in place to encourage firms to invest in general skills while encouraging workers to invest in specific (non-portable) skills.[4] Within the institutional packages, three distinct types of protection of investments have been identified: employment protection, unemployment protection and wage protection (Estevez-Abe et al. 2001). The welfare state is seen as a complementary institution, with firms relying heavily on non-market relationships to coordinate and sustain their businesses. The varieties of capitalism approach seeks to explain how the production and social protection systems are interlinked.

LMEs and CMEs differ in the ways they protect investments in specific skills. In CMEs, firms follow product market strategies that depend heavily on firm and industry-specific skills. In this environment, unemployment security and the promise of employment are of great importance, being incentives for workers to invest specific skills in either firm or industry, or in both. The more successful these firms are, the greater their demand for specific skills and, consequently, the greater the need for all three types of investment protection. Firms are prepared to invest in training because they can expect workers' loyalty for a sufficient length of time. The logic of this specific skills regime is characteristic for CME.

By contrast, the logic of the general skills regime is characteristic of the LMEs, which are more fluid and provide economic actors with greater opportunities to move their resources around in search of higher returns. Thus, economic actors are encouraged to acquire exchangeable assets, of which general skills form a key element. The institutional framework of LMEs, not structured by any of the three types of investment protection, does not create any incentive for firms or their employees to invest in either industry- or firm-specific skills. Individuals and firms therefore hardly invest in training and the LME relies on the general skills regime.

Estevez-Abe et al. (2001) developed their approach primarily to explain initial skill formation, but it is also helpful for understanding countries' peculiarities in terms of patterns of participation in further training. If applied to further training, one could say that there are in LMEs fewer incentives for employers and workers to invest in intensive further training. In other words, the total demand for work-related LLL in these countries should be more differentiated (i.e. shifted to low skills, but to very high skills as well). To the contrary, in CMEs most firms pursue a specific skills strategy.

As countries within the coordinated category reveal substantial differences in terms of the welfare regimes (conservative versus social democratic versus familistic regime, see Table 2.3), differences in the welfare regimes may be reflected in how training opportunities are distributed. Within these welfare production regimes, education and labour market institutions are considered to be of crucial importance for initial training and, one might also expect, for further and continuing training.

POST-SOCIALIST COUNTRIES AND THE VARIETIES OF CAPITALISM APPROACH

Some studies claim a convergence of post-socialist countries on the CME type (Lane 2005). Others argue a convergence on the LME type (Cernat 2002), while a third group mentions the rise of a hybrid variety of capitalism that combines features of both types (Iankova 2002). However, many researchers remain convinced that the region's institutional configurations are truly unique (Stark and Bruszt 1998; Bohle and Greskovits 2007a; Nölke and Vliegenthart 2009). During the post-socialist reconstruction, governments and other institutional actors in CEE countries have been presented with various powerful exogenous models (Crouch et al. 2009), meaning that the 'varieties of capitalism' approach does not capture the dynamics of the economic systems in countries undergoing transformations. The 'varieties of capitalism approach' entails an exclusion of the central characteristics of the region, its external dependency from multinational firms as well as from international organizations such as the World Bank, the International Monetary Fund and so on. These exogenous forces do not simply offer ideas for consideration; they offer important inducements to compliance. Nölke and Vliegenthart (2009) identify a special type of capitalism: a dependent market economy (DME), which emerges in Hungary, Poland, the Czech Republic and the Slovak Republic. This type of capitalism has comparative advantages due to skilled but cheap labour, the transfer of technological innovations within transnational enterprises and the provision of capital via foreign, direct investments. Transnational corporations will not accept costly institutions, such as comprehensive collective agreements, because they require low labour costs. Corporations are not driven by a necessity to invest heavily in innovation and in skills relevant for innovative activities because they prefer to import technologies. The DME model differs from the CME model in the sense that in the case of DME, public vocational training occurs outside of corporate domains, that is, little training is provided at the workplace. The DME countries are used as platforms for semi-standardized goods. For that purpose, the existing skills of employees are adequate and investments to upgrade skills would endanger these countries' cost advantages. Nölke and Vliegenthart (2009, p. 678) mention that there is no need for an LME-type of general-skill education combined with massive research and development expenditures, or for a CME-type system of comprehensive vocational training.

Bohle and Greskovits (2007a) distinguish between three variants of transnational capitalism emerging in Central-Eastern Europe: a neoliberal type in the Baltic States, an embedded neoliberal type in the Visegrad states and a neo-corporatist type in Slovenia. There is some overlap between the

Table 2.3 Varieties of capitalism approach and its extension

	Liberal market economy	Coordinated market economy	Dependent market economy
Economic governance	Limited business coordination, antitrust laws	Strong business associations, intercompany networks	Hierarchy within transnational corporations
Corporate governance	External control/dispersed shareholders	Internal control/concentrated shareholders	Control by headquarters of transnational enterprises
Industrial relations	Market based Few collective agreements Decentralized bargaining Trade unions and employer associations are weak; low-cost hiring and firing	Corporatist Sector-wide and even national agreements Coordinated bargaining Statutory worker representation Strong trade unions and employer associations; employee cooperation in firms and wage moderation	Company-level collective agreements Decentralized bargaining Trade unions and employer associations are weak
Education and training system	General competences Initially employers invest little in human capital	Industry and/or company-specific competences Initially employers invest in human capital	Limited expenditures for further qualification
Transfer of innovations	Based on markets and formal contracts	Important role of joint ventures and business associations	Intra-firm transfer within transnational enterprise

Welfare state	Liberal	Social democratic	Conservative, familistic	Neoliberal	Embedded neoliberal
Labour market policies	Minimal income protection	Generous income protection Strongly developed active labour market policy	Good income protection Medium developed active labour market policy	Minimal income protection Less developed active labour market policy	Medium income protection Medium developed active labour market policy
Countries	United States, the United Kingdom, Ireland, Canada, Australia, New Zealand	Sweden, Norway, Finland, Denmark	Germany, Austria, Belgium, the Netherlands, Switzerland, Italy, Greece, Spain, Portugal, Slovenia	Baltic countries	Hungary, the Czech Rep., Poland, the Slovak Rep.

Sources: Based on Hall and Soskice (2001), Estevez-Abe et al. (2001), Esping-Andersen (1990, 1999), Ebbinghaus and Manow (2003), Bohle and Greskovits (2007a), Nölke and Vliegenthart (2009).

two classifications. The Visegrad countries fit in the DME type, while the Baltic States seem to be a drastic and liberal example of DME. Exports from the Baltics are based on labour-intensive traditional industries and services which are controlled by highly mobile transnational corporations. These corporations, rather than significantly investing in local facilities, usually subcontract production, meaning that there is no need to train employees. The cutbacks in government spending on education and the liberalization of educational policies have diversified the general educational system. The Baltic states are distinguished 'by radically liberalized markets, a thoroughly reformed market-supporting institutional framework, and are the least generous welfare states among the new EU members' (Bohle and Greskovits 2007b, p. 106). Only Slovenia seems to be close to the CME type (see also Feldmann 2006; Buchen 2007; Adam et al. 2009), featuring a strong role of the state and specific corporatist elements. Adam et al. (2009, p. 79) indicate that in the case of Slovenia, we can speak of a 'corporatist welfare state'.

Thus, in the framework of the varieties of welfare capitalism and its extension to post-socialist countries, the human capital approach is used to explain specificity of certain types of skill formation regimes through their 'embeddedness' into the institutional framework of different types of political economies.[5] The investments into skill formation is deemed to depend on protection by the labour market institutions, while both the labour market institutions and education system are parts of more general country-specific institutional 'packages'. This approach extends the conventional analyses of skill formation by placing firms and their strategies at the heart of an understanding not only of skill formation, but also of its relationship to different types of labour market and welfare regimes.[6] This extended typology based on the varieties of capitalism approach is characterizing the main institutional context where formal adult education operates.

INSTITUTIONALIST PERSPECTIVES ON SKILL FORMATION

A classification of research works that are relevant for lifelong learning is somewhat arbitrary. This element of arbitrariness is rooted in the nature of scientific discovery, populated by scholars who adjust to contributions from their fellows and even change, or at least modify, their previous opinions over time. More than representing paradigms whose defenders may stick to them even after they are refuted (cf. Kuhn 1970), the perspectives outlined on the preceding pages sometimes converge. We have har-

Table 2.4 The logic of three major forms of employment systems

Attribute	Vocationalism	Professionalism	Managerialism
Affiliated unit	Industrial trade union	Professional association	Firm (or company union)
Training	'On-the-job'	Postgraduate education	Universities
Intra-generational mobility (career)	Intra-occupational	Intra-occupational	Intra-firm
Country example	Germany	France United States	Japan

Source: Adapted from Fligstein and Byrkjeflot (1996, p. 11).

vested from institutional perspectives, for example heralded by Ericson and Archer, before addressing these perspectives in a separate section.

Well-known contributors to this perspective, such as Richard Scott and John Meyer (1994), have analysed the US education system in similar terms as those suggested by Archer (1979). The complementarity is particularly strong when they apply the notions of fragmentation, centralization and bureaucratization in an organizational analysis of the US system (see Chapters 7–9 in Scott and Mayer 1994).

One example of a comparative, institutional analysis is provided by Fligstein and Byrkjeflot (1996) who claim that employment relations have a unique social origin that can only be studied historically. They use Germany, France, the USA and Japan as examples, holding that the path to industrialization for these nations had profound effects on the system of employment that emerged (Fligstein and Byrkjeflot 1996, p. 31). The influence from institutionalist perspectives is founded on their understanding of the process of institutionalization which 'suggests why systems of employment relations can last for long periods of time' (Fligstein and Byrkjeflot 1996, p. 39). These relations are embedded in larger social arrangements, including states and educational systems (see Table 2.4).

Another comparative analysis written from an institutionalist perspective is provided by Kathleen Thelen (2004). The subtitle of her book reads '*The Political Economy of Skills in Germany, Britain, the US and Japan*' and refers to the varieties of capitalism tradition which covers multiple approaches. The political economy tradition, which she explicitly builds on, is labelled with an ambitious heritage combining numerous disciplines, notably history, political sciences and economy. Her book offers more of a methodology for comparison than a cross-country typology. Thelen's central thesis is that national trajectories for skill formation and workplace-based training depend on differences in the 'coalitional alignments' among employers in skill-intensive industries, traditional artisans and early trade unions. Her analysis of institutional arrangements governing skill formation delves into the past (in the German case, back to the 1870s), implying that her work is much concerned with institutional evolution and change that she analyses together with institutional reproduction. By this means, the importance of subtle and smaller scale changes comes to the fore, that is, not only big changes at critical junctures involving major transformations also affecting the education system are visible. The argument for studying institutional evolution is that changes considered of minor importance by contemporary observers can be more determinant when assessed and related to similar occurrences over a longer time span. Thelen's works therefore illustrate path-dependency perspectives and are inscribed in historical sociology (cf. Mahoney 2000; Thelen and Steinmo 1992).

A very recent contribution along the same train of thought carries the title *The Political Economy of Collective Skill Formation* (Busemeyer and Trampusch 2012). Their central thesis is that collective skill formation systems are determined by the specific shape of cleavages and their representation via intermediary associations within the employers' and trade unions' camps:

> respectively, by the overall balance of power between business and labour, and by the dynamic of partisan competition and state structures. Thus, different 'settings' in these institutional variables during specific periods of time can explain the emergence of different trajectories within the group of collective skill formation systems. (p. 27)

In the concluding chapter of this book, Wolfgang Streeck (2012) illustrates that research on skill formation can be paved with discrepancies, such as his refutation of the general/specific skills set that structures major contributions to the varieties of capitalism approach. Streeck is highly critical of this approach which, according to him, reflects a misunderstanding of what skills are and how they are acquired. The misunderstanding 'is rooted in an uncritical reception of human capital theory, as well as in a rationalist misconception of the relationship between politics and the economy, or between social structures and economic pressures for efficiency'. Streeck's position is that:

> general skills need not always be high, and high skills not always broad or portable; that specific skills are not necessarily low, and low skills not always immobile; and that occupational skills in some countries may be as high and broad as academic skills in others, and far from firm or even industry-specific. (Streeck 2012, p. 317)

In spite of these conflicting appreciations of skill formation and of the varied paths on which more and less developed market (capitalist) economies have embarked, the authors cited in this chapter tend to converge on one point: skill formation displays national variations that do not point towards a single national model; nor do ongoing processes of globalization and Europeanization automatically wipe out these singularities. For these reasons, we apply the 'varieties of capitalism' label with some liberty in this chapter and compare contributions not written under this heading or belonging to this specific research community.[7]

CONCLUSIONS

Many country typologies of relevance for research on LLL are determined by one single or two main factors. As these can vary depending on their disciplinary origin and perspective, recent research has tended to develop different typologies by grouping countries in dissimilar ways. Such tendency points to a research standard consisting of specifying which criteria are used as the basis of any typology. Another issue is the heterogeneity of systems. The dimension approach assumes that the system can be placed at a single point along each dimension, whereas the systems in place are very diverse. Such typologies tend to reduce differences between cases which are seen to be within the same group, whilst simultaneously increasing the differences between groups. The main objective has been to present national cases precisely so that they fit neatly into a homogeneous, internally isomorphic type (Crouch and Farrell 2004). Typologies have appeared to be useful while most comparisons covered few countries, but studies of a larger number of countries have found that many cross-national variations remain unexplained by any available typology.

An additional problem is that country typologies fail to explain the substantial differences within a country. By classifying countries according to simple distinctions, typologies risk overshadowing the actual social mechanisms at a subnational level, for example in some industries or regions. This has implication for LLL policy-making, as outlined in Federighi (2007).

Previous research has mainly focused on a limited number of countries. Most authors concentrated only on typical examples. As researchers have compared more countries, they have tended to reject dichotomies or simple typologies developed from comparisons of a small number of Western European and North American countries (see also Gallie 2007; Raffe 2008). Most CEE countries continue to be underrepresented in comparative research on LLL systems. Attempts to classify these countries according to typologies developed for Western countries are not very successful due to their path-dependent development. Moreover, the institutional and structural dimensions of LLL systems have often been measured in an arbitrary and unreliable way. The problem is connected with poor measurements of policy, institutional and structural dimensions other than the socio-economic ones.

The challenge is to move beyond descriptions of changes in LLL systems in order to explain them, thus challenging the assumption that institutional configurations are relatively stable (see Hillmert 2008). When developing a new framework and typology we should move forward by taking continuity and change more seriously, and analyse the underlying tensions in the LLL systems. The next chapter in this book reveals that some tensions occur when voluntaristic policies collide with historic and institutional patterns. For this reason, path-dependency retrospectives should scrutinize whether a historic event tends to trigger a subsequent sequence that follows a relatively deterministic pattern, be it self-reinforcing or reactive sequences (cf. Mahoney 2000, p. 535). However, in order to avoid deterministic and lock-in perspectives in LLL research, a guiding principle should be to look for changing patterns. The new framework and typology suggested in this book aim to better capture developments and, consequently, to nurture policy-making.

We argue that the most fruitful general framework to live up to this challenge should combine the varieties of capitalism approach together with institutional perspectives and its extension to CEE countries. More than the existing literature, this extension has to account for variations within contemporary societies and for connections between them. The undeniable disagreements between these theoretical approaches and perspectives underline a need for further research and debate in the scientific community. The country teams laying out their conclusions in the present book have combined national and international insights in order to better capture developments in lifelong learning, with repercussions for the scientific community as well as for policy-making.

NOTES

1. The appropriateness of classifying Spanish vocational education and training in this way does not comply with recent national reforms; see for example Souto-Otero and Ure (2012).
2. http://www.nationellalarlingskommitten.se/default.asp
3. However, analysis indicates that even very liberal states and welfare systems (for example, the US) could produce high-quality jobs (in the sense of tenure, paid vocation, parental leave etc.) for the substantial part of the working population by weak enforcement, market pressure and institutional processes on the level of the economic field (see Dobbin and Sutton 1998).

4. For a fierce critique of the divide between general and specific skills and of rational choice theories such as the one proposed by Gary Becker, see Wolfgang Streeck (2012).
5. It has been argued that the varieties of capitalism approach has failed to recognize the emergence of significant changes in transnational corporations' (TNCs') use of skills (Ashton et al. 2010; Lauder et al. 2008). TNCs have been increasingly reducing their dependence on the national business systems from which they originated. We can see this in terms of their ability to manage corporate skill formation, as they are able to source high-skilled labour from different national locations and speed up the process of work-related learning, making them less reliant on any individual country for their supply of labour (Ashton et al. 2010, p. 847).
6. Aiginger and Guger (2006) argue that the education system and institutions of the knowledge economy are playing an increasingly important role in the new European socio-economic model. The typology of countries suggested by Aiginger and Guger draws heavily on the Esping–Anderson model and, despite emphasizing the importance of education and lifelong learning, strongly reflects traditional economic indicators such as annual growth, gross domestic product (GDP) per capita, employment rates and unemployment rates. It includes the following groupings:

   - Nordic Model (e.g. Denmark, Finland, Netherlands, Sweden, Norway);
   - Continental Model (e.g. Germany, France, Italy, Belgium, Austria);
   - Anglo-Saxon Model (e.g. Ireland, United Kingdom);
   - Mediterranean Model (e.g. Greece, Portugal, Spain);
   - Catching-up Model (e.g. Czech Republic, Hungary).

   This typology reduces post-socialist differences to relative backwardness of these countries, indicating that these countries are perpetually deemed to be 'catching-up' in both material and institutional terms (see also Stenning and Hörschelmann 2008).
7. Cf. also Peer Hull Kristensen and Kari Lilja (2011) who try to cross the divides between varieties of capitalism, national business system, welfare state analysis and political economy.

REFERENCES

Adam, Frane, Primož Kristan and Matevž Tomšič (2009), 'Varieties of Capitalism in Eastern Europe (with Special Emphasis on Estonia and Slovenia)', *Communist and Post-Communist Studies*, **42** (2), 65–81.

Aiginger, Karl and Alois Guge (2006), 'The European Socioeconomic Model', in Anthony Giddens, Patrick Diamond and Roger Liddle (eds), *Global Europe, Social Europe*, Cambridge: Polity Press, pp. 124–150.

Allmendinger, Jutta (1989), 'Educational Systems and Labour Market Outcomes', *European Sociological Review*, **5** (3), 231–250.

Archer, Margaret S. (1979), *Social Origins of Educational Systems*, London: Sage.

Arrowsmith, James, Keith Sisson and Paul Marginson (2004), 'What can "Benchmarking" Offer the Open Method of Co-ordination', *Journal of European Public Policy*, **11** (2), 311–328.

Ashton, David, Philip Brown and Hugh Lauder (2010), 'Skill Webs and International Human Resource Management: Lessons from a Study of the Global Skill Strategies of Transnational Companies', *International Journal of Human Resource Management*, **21** (6), 836–850.

Ashton, David, Johnny Sung and Jill Turbin (2000), 'Towards a Framework for the

Comparative Analysis of National Systems of Skill Formation', *International Journal of Training and Development*, **4** (1), 8–25.

Bassanini, Andrea, Alison Booth, Giorgio Brunello, Maria De Paole and Edwin Leuven (2007), 'Workplace Training in Europe', in Giorgio Brunello, Pietro Garibaldi and Etienne Wasmer (eds), *Education and Training in Europe*, Oxford: Oxford University Press, pp. 143–329.

Becker, Gary (1975), *Human Capital*, 2nd edn, New York: Columbia University.

Berger, Suzanne and Ronald Dore (eds) (1996), *National Diversity and Global Capitalism*, Ithaca, NY: Cornell University Press.

Bills, David (2003), 'Credentials, Signals, and Sreens: Explaining the Relationship between Schooling and Job Assignment', *Review of Educational Research*, **73**, 441–469.

Blossfeld, Hans-Peter (2003), 'Globalization, Social Inequality and the Role of Country-specific Institutions: Open Research Questions in a Learning Society', in Pedro Conceicao, Manuel V. Heitor and Bengt-Ake Lundvall (eds), *Towards a Learning Society: Innovation and Competence Building with Social Cohesion for Europe*, Aldershot, UK and Brookfield, VT, USA: Edward Elgar, pp. 303–324.

Blossfeld, Hans-Peter and Reinhard Stockmann (1998–99), *Globalization and Chances in Vocational Training Systems in Developing and Advanced Industrial Societies*, New York: Sharpe.

Bohle, Dorothee and Béla Greskovits (2007a), 'Neoliberalism, Embedded Neoliberalism and Neocorporatism: Towards Transitional Capitalism in Central-Eastern Europe', *West European Politics*, **30** (3), 443–466.

Bohle, Dorothee and Béla Greskovits (2007b), 'The State, Internationalization, and Capitalist Diversity in Eastern Europe', *Competition and Change*, **11** (2), 90–115.

Breen, Richard (2005), 'Explaining Cross-national Variation in Youth Unemployment', *European Sociological Review*, **21** (2), 125–134.

Brown, Philip, Andy Green and Hugh Lauder (2001), *High Skills: Globalisation, Competitiveness and Skill Formation*, Oxford: Oxford University Press.

Brunello, Giuseppe (2001), 'On the Complementarity between Education and Training in Europe', IZA Discussion Paper No. 309.

Buchen, Clemens (2007), 'Estonia and Slovenia as Antipodes', in David Lane and Martin Myant (eds), *Varieties of Capitalism in Post-communist Countries*, Basingstoke: Palgrave, pp. 65–89.

Busemeyer, Marius R. and Christine Trampusch (eds) (2012), *The Political Economy of Collective Skill Formation*, Oxford: Oxford University Press.

Cernat, Lucian (2002), 'Institutions and Economic Growth: Which Model of Capitalism for Central and Eastern Europe?' *Journal of Institutional Innovation, Development, and Transition*, **6**, 18–34.

Crouch, Colin (2004), 'Skill Formation Systems', in Stephen Ackroyd, Rosemary Batt, Paul Thompson and Pamela S. Tolbert (eds), *Oxford Handbook of Work and Organizations*, Oxford: Oxford University Press, pp. 95–114.

Crouch, Colin and Henry Farrell (2004), 'Breaking the Path of Institutional Development? Alternatives to the New Determinism', *Rationality and Society*, **16** (5), 5–43.

Crouch, Colin, David Finegold and Mari Sako (1999), *Are Skills the Answer – The Political Economy of Skill Creation in Advanced Industrial Countries*, Oxford: Oxford University Press.

Crouch, Colin, Martin Schröder and Helmut Voelzkow (2009), 'Regional and Sectoral Varieties of Capitalism', *Economy and Society*, **38** (4), 654–678.

Crouch, Colin and Wolfgang Streeck (eds) (1997), *Political Economy and Modern Capitalism: Mapping Convergence and Diversity*, London: Sage.

Culpepper, Pepper D. and Kathleen Thelen (2008), 'Institutions and Collective Actors in the Provision of Training: Historical and Cross-National Comparisons', in Karl Ulrich Mayer and Heike Solga (eds), *Skill Formation. Interdisciplinary and Cross-National Perspectives*, Cambridge: Cambridge University Press, pp. 21–49.

Deeg, Richard and Gregory Jackson (2007), 'The State of the Art: Towards a More Dynamic Theory of Capitalist Variety', *Socio-Economic Review*, **5** (1), 149–179.

Dobbin, Frank and John R. Sutton (1998), 'The Strength of a Weak State: The Rights Revolution and the Rise of Human Resources Management Divisions', *American Journal of Sociology*, **104** (2), 441–476.

Doeringer, Peter and Michael Piore (1971), *Internal Labor Markets and Manpower Analysis*, Lexington, MA: Heath.

Eamets, Raul and Jaan Masso (2005), 'The Paradox of the Baltic States: Labour Market Flexibility but Protected Workers', *European Journal of Industrial Relations*, **11** (1), 71–90.

Ebbinghaus, Bernard and Philip Manow (eds) (2003), *Comparing Welfare Capitalism. Social Policy and Political Economy in Europe, Japan and the USA*, London: Routledge.

Ericson, David P. (1982), 'The Possibility of a General Theory of the Educational System', in Margaret Scotford Archer (ed.), *The Sociology of Educational Expansion*, Thousand Oaks, CA: Sage, pp. 293–313.

Esping-Andersen, Gosta (1990), *The Three Worlds of Welfare Capitalism*, Cambridge: Policy Press.

Esping-Andersen, Gosta (1999), *Social Foundations of Postindustrial Economies*, Oxford: Oxford University Press.

Estevez-Abe, Margarita, Torben Iversen and David Soskice (2001), 'Social Protection and the Formation of Skills: A Reinterpretation of the Welfare State', in Peter A. Hall and David Soskice (eds), *Varieties of Capitalism: The Institutional Foundations of Comparative Advantage*, Oxford: Oxford University Press, pp. 145–183.

Federighi, Paolo (ed.) (2007), *Learning among Regional Governments. Quality of Policy Learning and Policy Transfer in Regional Lifelong Learning Policies*, Bielefeld: W. Bertelsmann Verlag.

Feldmann, Magnus (2006), 'Emerging Varieties of Capitalism in Transition Countries: Industrial Relations and Wage Bargaining in Estonia and Slovenia', *Comparative Political Studies*, **39** (7), 829–854.

Finegold, David and David Soskice (1988), 'The Failure of Training in Britain: Analysis and Prescriptions', *Oxford Review of Economic Policy*, **4** (3), 21–51.

Fligstein, Neil and Haldor Byrkjeflot (1996), 'The Logic of Employment Systems', LOS-senter paper (notat 9601), University of Bergen.

Furth, D. (1985), *Education and Training after Basic Schooling*, Paris: OECD.

Gallie, Duncan (2007), 'Production Regimes and the Quality of Employment in Europe', *Annual Review of Sociology*, **33**, 85–104.

Gangl, Markus (2001), 'European Patterns of Labour Market Entry. A Dichotomy of Occupatonalized Systems vs. Non-occupational Systems?' *European Societies*, **3** (4), 471–494.

Gebel, Michael (2008), 'Labour Markets in Central and Eastern Europe', in Irena Kogan, Michael Gebel and Clemens Noelke (eds), *Europe Enlarged. A Handbook*

of Education, Labour and Welfare Regimes in Central and Eastern Europe, Bristol: Policy Press, pp. 35–62.
Green, Andy (1991), 'The Reform of Post-16 Education and Training and the Lessons from Europe', *Journal of Education Policy*, **6** (3), 327–339.
Green, Andy (1999), 'Education and Globalization in Europe and East Asia: Convergent and Divergent Trends', *Journal of Education Policy*, **14** (1), 55–71.
Green, Andy (2006), 'Models of Lifelong Learning and the "Knowledge Society"', *Compare*, **36** (3), 307–325.
Hall, Peter A. and Daniel W. Gingerich (2004), 'Varieties of Capitalism and Institutional Complementarities in the Macroeconomy', Max-Planck-Institut für Gesellschaftsforschung Discussion Paper 04/5.
Hall, Peter A. and David Soskice (2001), 'An Introduction to Varieties of Capitalism', in Peter A. Hall and David Soskice (eds), *Varieties of Capitalism: The Institutional Foundations of Comparative Advantage*, Oxford: Oxford University Press, pp. 1–69.
Hall, Peter A. and Kathleen Thelen (2009), 'Institutional Change in Varieties of Capitalism', *Socio-Economic Review*, **7** (1), 7–34.
Helemäe, Jelena and Ellu Saar (2000), 'Linkages between the Education System and Labour Market: Estonia against the Backdrop of EU Countries', in Raivo Vetik (ed.), *Estonian Human Development Report*, Tallinn: TPU RASI, pp. 85–99.
Helemäe, Jelena and Ellu Saar (2011), 'Institutional and Ideological Foundations of Marketization', in Ellu Saar (ed.), *Towards A Normal Stratification Order: Actual and Perceived Social Stratification in Post-Socialist Estonia*, Frankfurt: Peter Lang, pp. 33–60.
Hillmert, Steffen (2008), 'When Traditions Change and Virtue Become Obstacles', in Karl Ulrich Mayer and Heike Solga (eds), *Skill Formation: Interdisciplinary and Cross-National Perspectives*, Cambridge: Cambridge University Press, pp. 50–83.
Holford, John, Sheila Riddell, Elisabet Weedon, Judit Litjens and Gary Hannan (2008), *Patterns of Lifelong Learning: Policy and Practice in an Expanding Europe*, Vienna: Lit Verlag.
Hull Kristensen, Peer and Kari Lilja (2011), *Nordic Capitalisms and Globalization: New Forms of Economic Organization and Welfare Institutions*, Oxford: Oxford University Press.
Iankova, Elena A. (2002), *Eastern European Capitalism in the Making*, Cambridge: Cambridge University Press.
Ivančič, Angela (2000), 'Education and Shifts between Labour-Market States in the Transition from the Socialist to the Market Economy: The Slovenian Case', *European Sociological Review*, **16** (4), 403–425.
Kerckhoff, Alan C. (1995), 'Institutional Arrangements and Stratification Processes in Industrial Societies', *Annual Review of Sociology*, **15** (1), 323–347.
Kerr, Clark (1954), 'The Balkanization of Labor Markets', in Wright E. Bakke (ed.), *Labor Mobility and Economic Opportunity*, Cambridge, MA: MIT Press, pp. 92–110.
Kogan, Irena (2008), 'Education Systems of Central and Eastern European Countries', in Irena Kogan, Michael Gebel and Clemens Noelke (eds), *Europe Enlarged: A Handbook of Education, Labour and Welfare Regimes in Central and Eastern Europe*, Bristol: Policy Press, pp. 7–34.
Kogan, Irena, Michael Gebel and Clemens Noelke (eds) (2008), *Europe Enlarged:*

A Handbook of Education, Labour and Welfare Regimes in Central and Eastern Europe, Bristol: Policy Press.
Kogan, Irena and Marge Unt (2005), 'Transition from School to Work in Transition Economies', *European Societies*, **7** (2), 219–253.
Kostova, Dobrinka (2008), 'Bulgaria', in Irena Kogan, Michael Gebel and Clemens Noelke (eds), *Europe Enlarged: A Handbook of Education, Labour and Welfare Regimes in Central and Eastern Europe*, Bristol: Policy Press, pp. 97–122.
Kotasek, Jiří (1996), 'Structure and Organization of Secondary Education in Central and Eastern Europe', *European Journal of Education*, **31** (1), 25–42.
Kuhn, Thomas S. (1970), *The structure of scientific revolutions*, 2nd edn, Chicago, IL: University of Chicago.
Lane, David (2005), 'Emerging Varieties of Capitalism in Former State Socialist Societies', *Competition and Change*, **9** (3), 227–247.
Lauder, Hugh, Philip Brown and David Ashton (2008), 'Globalisation, Skill Formation and the Varieties of Capitalism Approach', *New Political Economy*, **13** (1), 19–35.
Lazonick, William and Mary O'Sullivan (1994), *Skill Formation in Wealthy Nations: Organizational Evolution and Economic Consequences*, STEP-report 23, Nordic Institute for Studies in Innovation, Research and Education, Oslo.
Mahoney, John (2000), 'Path Dependence in Historical Sociology', *Theory and Society*, **29** (4), 507–548.
Marsden, David (1986), *The End of Economic Man? Custom and Competition in Labour Markets*, Brighton: Wheatsheaf.
Marsden, David (1990), 'Institutions and Labour Mobility: Occupational and Internal Labour Markets in Britain, France, Italy and West Germany', in Renato Brunetta and Carlo Dell'Aringa (eds), *Labour Relations and Economic Performance*, Houndmills: Macmillan, pp. 414–438.
Masson, Jean-Raymond (2004), 'Implementation of the Lisbon Objectives by the Acceding and Candidate Countries', *Vocational Training*, **33**, 7–22.
Maurice, Marc and Francois Sellier (1979), 'Societal Analysis of Industrial Relations: A Comparison between France and West Germany', *British Journal of Industrial Relations*, **17** (3), 322–336.
Maurice, Marc, Francois Sellier, Jean-Jacques Silvestre and Arthur Goldhammer (1986), *The Social Foundations of Industrial Power: A Comparison of France and Germany*, Cambridge, MA: MIT Press.
Müller, Walter and Markus Gangl (2003), 'The Transition from School to Work: A European Perspective', in Walter Müller and Markus Gangl (eds), *Transitions from Education to Work in Europe: The Integration of Youth into EU Labour Markets*, Oxford: Oxford University Press, pp. 1–22.
Müller, Walter and Marita Jacob (2008), 'Qualifications and the Returns to Training Across the Life Course', in Karl Ulrich Mayer and Heike Solga (eds), *Skill Formation: Interdisciplinary and Cross-National Perspectives*, Cambridge: Cambridge University Press, pp. 126–172.
Müller, Walter and Yossi Shavit (1998), 'The Institutional Embeddedness of the Stratification Process: A Comparative Study of Qualifications and Occupations in Thirteen Countries', in Yossi Shavit and Walter Müller (eds), *From School to Work: A Comparative Study of Educational Qualifications and Occupational Destinations*, Oxford: Clarendon Press, pp. 1–48.
Nölke, Andreas and Arjan Vliegenthart (2009), 'Enlarging the Varieties of

Capitalism: The Emergence of Dependent Market Economies in East Central Europe', *World Politics*, **61** (4), 670–702.
OECD (1985), *Education and Training beyond Basic Schooling*, Paris: OECD.
Olofsson, Jonas (ed.) (2007), *Utbildningsvägen – vart leder den?* Stockholm: SNS Förlag.
Raffe, David (2008), 'The Concept of Transition System', *Journal of Education and Work*, **21** (4), 277–296.
Rainbird, Helen (1992), 'Comparative Perspectives on Training: Britain, France and Germany', in Michael Gold (ed.), *Europe: The Social Dimension*, London: Macmillan Press, pp. 184–202.
Regini, Marino (2000), 'Between Deregulation and Social Pacts: The Responses of European Economies to Globalization', *Politics and Society*, **28** (1), 5–33.
Róbert, Péter and Erzebet Bukodi (2006), 'The Effects of the Globalization Process on the Transition to Adulthood in Hungary', in Hans-Peter Blossfeld, Erik Klijzing, Melinda Mills, and Karin Kurz (eds), *Globalization, Uncertainty and Youth in Society*, London: Routledge, pp. 177–213.
Roosmaa, Eve-Liis and Ellu Saar (2010), 'Participating in Non-Formal Learning: Patterns of Inequality in EU-15 and the New EU-8 Member Countries', *Journal of Education and Work*, **23** (3), 179–206.
Rubenson, Kjell (2006), 'The Nordic Model of Lifelong Learning', *Compare*, **36** (3), 327–341.
Saar, Ellu (2005), 'New Entrants on the Estonian Labour Market: A Comparison with the EU Countries', *European Societies*, **7** (4), 547–580.
Saar, Ellu and Kadri Täht (2005), 'Men's Late Careers and Career Exits in Estonia', *Trames*, **9** (3), 228–258.
Saar, Ellu, Marge Unt and Irena Kogan (2008), 'Transition from Educational System to Labour Market in the European Union: A Comparison between New and Old Members', *International Journal of Comparative Sociology*, **49** (1), 31–59.
Scott, Richard W. and John W. Meyer (eds) (1994), *Institutional Environments and Organizations – Structural Complexity and Individualism*, Thousand Oaks, CA: Sage.
Schmidt, Vivien A. (2002), *The Futures of European Capitalism*, Oxford: Oxford University Press.
Shavit, Yossi and Walter Müller (eds) (1998), *From School to Work. A Comparative Study of Educational Qualifications and Occupational Destinations*, Oxford: Clarendon Press.
Soskice, David (1993), 'Social Skills from Mass Higher Education: Rethinking the Company-Based Initial Training Paradigm', *Oxford Review of Economic Policy*, **9** (1), 101–113.
Souto-Otero, Manuel and Odd Bjørn Ure (2012), 'The Coherence of Vocational Education and Training in Norway and Spain: National Traditions and the Reshaping of VET Governance in Hybrid VET Systems', *Compare*, **42** (1), 91–111.
Stark, David and Laszlo Bruszt (1998), *Postsocialist Pathways: Transforming Politics and Property in East Central Europe*, Cambridge: Cambridge University Press.
Stenning, Alison and Kathrin Hörschelmann (2008), 'History, Geography and Difference in the Post-socialist World: Or, Do We Still Need Post-Socialism?' *Antipode*, **40** (2), 312–335.

Streeck, Wolfgang (2012), 'Skills and Politics: General and Specific', in Marius R. Busemeyer and Christine Trampusch (eds), *The Political Economy of Collective Skill Formation*, Oxford: Oxford University Press, pp. 317–359.

Strietska-Ilina, Olga (2001), 'Research on Vocational Education and Training at the Crossroads of Transition in Central and Eastern Europe', in Pascaline Descy and Manfred Tessaring (eds), *Training in Europe. Second Report on Vocational Training Research in Europ. 2000: Background Report*, Vol. 3, Cedefop Reference series, Luxembourg: Office for Official Publications of the European Communities, pp. 209–311.

Stuart, Mark and Ian Greenwood (2006), 'National and European Policies for Lifelong Learning: An Assessment of Developments within the Context of the European Employment Strategy', in Michael Kuhn and Ronald G. Sultana (eds), *Homo Sapiens Europaeus? Creating the European Learning Citizen*, New York: Peter Lang, pp. 131–148.

Thelen, Kathleen (2004), *How Institutions Evolve: The Political Economy of Skills in Germany, Britain, the United States and Japan*, Cambridge: Cambridge University Press.

Thelen, Kathleen and Sven Steinmo (1992), 'Historical Institutionalism in Comparative Politics', in Sven Steinmo, Kathleen Thelen and Frank Longstreth (eds), *Structuring Politics*, Cambridge: Cambridge University Press, pp. 1–32.

Wolbers, Maarten H.J. (2005), 'Initial and Further Education: Substitutes or Complements? Differences in Continuing Education and Training over the Life-Course of European Workers', *International Review of Education*, **51** (5–6), 459–478.

3. Seven types of formal adult education and their organizational fields: towards a comparative framework

Günter Hefler and Jörg Markowitsch

INTRODUCTION: 'FORMAL ADULT EDUCATION' AS AN OXYMORON

Within research and policy analysis on lifelong learning (LLL), formal adult education pursues a double life. While the concept of formal adult education remains a poorly understood oxymoron, it has become firmly established as a category within statistics on lifelong learning. However, difficulties immediately arise with the interpretation of statistical data. What do we actually know, when according to the Adult Education Survey (2005–2007) participation in formal adult education is 'high' in the United Kingdom (UK) (15 per cent), 'moderate' in Austria and Estonia (4 per cent) and 'low' in Bulgaria and Hungary (2 per cent)?

In English, 'formal education' is typically used as a synonym for 'initial education' (UNESCO 1979; 1997, p. 47). When childhood and, much later, adolescence were constructed within European societies (Ariès 1962; Kamens 1985), being in school became the defining criteria for childhood and youth, and adulthood began with the end of initial education. Adults returning to 'school' literally lose their adult status, becoming 'students among students'.

Against this background, early twentieth-century 'liberal' adult education could define itself in clear opposition to initial, formal (and vocational) education: the modern nation-state, having gained control and systematized education late in the nineteenth century (Ringer 1979; Müller et al. 1987), was not prepared to weaken its power to classify citizens by allowing new parties to provide educational credentials (Meyer and Rowan 1978; Ramirez and Rubinson 1979). The opposition between state-controlled formal education and offers of non-formal adult education from agencies of the wider society remained firm until the second half of the twentieth century; formal adult education was not allowed any reasonable ground beyond 'second-chance education'.

This divide still endures: the frequently cited definition of 'formal adult education' by the United Nations Educational, Scientific and Cultural Organization (UNESCO) (1979) avoids linking 'formal learning' to the (initial) 'education system'. However, beginning in the 1960s and through highly different pathways, European states' control over formal education of adults became weaker and began to allow for more civil activity and new types of programmes and providers. In a contra-movement, nation-states expanded their control over non-formal education, making funding conditional and pressing towards a formalization of the non-formal sector (Parkes 1990; Ure 2006). Consequently, the formal–non-formal opposition started to erode.

Participation of adults in 'education provided in the system of schools, colleges, universities and other formal educational institutions that normally constitutes a continuous "ladder" of full-time education for children and young people' (Eurostat 2006, p. 13) has been measured since nation-states started to compile information available in educational organizations' registers. A joint activity by UNESCO, the Organisation for Economic Co-operation and Development (OECD) and Eurostat brings together national register data on formal adult education to form 'UOE', a standardized global collection of educational data. Thus, when UNESCO started working towards compiling comprehensive statistics of adult education in the early 1970s (UNESCO 1975), formal education was regarded as the 'easy' part, more or less completed by the register statistics. 'Non-formal' adult education – a term introduced as a new umbrella concept between 1968 and 1974 by researchers affiliated with UNESCO (Rogers 2004) – was painfully missed by classifications and statistical information (Chu 1996).

In the late 1970s newly introduced large scale surveys on 'non-formal' adult education began to cover, as a minor aspect, the formal education of adults. However, the line seemed clear cut between 'participation in non-formal education' and 'being a pupil or student' within the education system. Educational reforms starting in the 1970s began to blur the clear formal–non-formal distinction. Recently, formal adult education has been redefined in order to try to cover reforms in educational systems: for example, introducing credit-based qualifications and national qualification frameworks. However, as more educational activities became classified as formal, the institutional dimensions of the formal–non-formal division, originally central to the definition, have been overshadowed and are rarely addressed any more.

In this chapter, we seek to contribute to an adequate theoretical foundation of formal adult education by applying arguments developed within organizational institutionalism (Greenwood et al. 2008) on institutional effects of education (Meyer 1970, 1977; Meyer and Rowan 1977, 1978; Meyer and Rowan 2006; Meyer et al. 2005). Furthermore, we will provide a new typology of formal adult education present in European societies. In the final section, we discuss how our proposals may be helpful for gaining a fresh start within comparative research on formal adult education.

THE CURRENT STATE OF DEFINING AND MEASURING FORMAL ADULT EDUCATION

For comparative research and policy monitoring on formal adult education in Europe, three sources exist: the UNESCO, OECD and Eurostat (UOE) statistics, the Labour Force Survey (LFS; specifically, the 2003 ad hoc module on lifelong learning) and the Adult Education Survey (AES). We highlight here only the most striking commonalities and differences in the definitions applied (for more details, see Hefler 2013).

All approaches define the formal quality of a programme in relation to the state-controlled initial education system, that is to say the system of state-recognized formal qualification. In each state, authorities (partly bound by laws) define which type of organization, programme or qualification is or is not part of the education system and consequently within the scope of formal adult education. Reflecting the vast differences in educational systems, the unified definition of formal adult education leads, therefore, to highly different sets of activities labelled as formal. In formal adult education, the single most important reason why data mainly represent different compositions of educational activities and less overall levels of performance is that credit-based qualifications can have a more extended presence (e.g. England, Scotland and Ireland) or a more restricted presence (e.g. Austria, Bulgaria and Estonia).

The three definitions differ in the extent to which they absorb on a societal level the newly defined formal educational activities. The AES definition covers by formal education any provision that contributes to acquiring qualifications stated within a national qualification framework. The UOE definition, however, clearly restricts the concept of formal education to any educational programme representing at least a six-month workload of full-time education (UNESCO et al. 2010). Shorter courses are excluded, despite providing credits useful for acquiring qualifications. Thus, when considering participation in formal adult education, the UOE and LFS

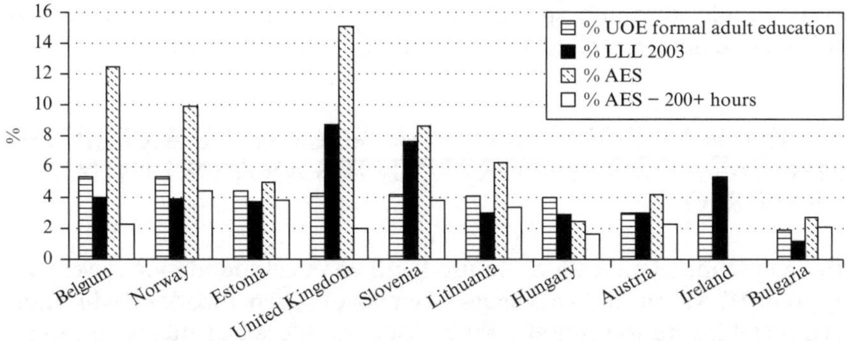

Sources: LFS (2003), UOE (2007), AES (2005–2007), authors' calculations.

Figure 3.1 Three measures of formal adult education

note moderate differences between countries; however, the AES reflects the availability of credit-based education and thus reports that countries have striking differences. However, the effect disappears as soon as one only compares participation in longer formal programmes (with more than 200 hours a year) (see Figure 3.1).

The three data sources represent a historical and institutional account for formal education. At its core, the register-based UOE data represent the state-controlled educational systems, as developed in the late nineteenth century, that lead to qualifications with clear-cut categories of personnel pursuing 'low', 'medium' or 'elite' education. For UOE, and despite its ongoing adaptations, the particular institutional status of formal adult education has remained visible. The LFS approach is more closely attached to the UOE mapping than AES. Finally, the AES definition clearly represents the attempt to expand the concept of formal adult education to cover any activity leading to qualifications. They abandon the more traditional link to the educational system, its qualifications and its institutional consequences. While formal courses identified by AES have much more heterogeneous lengths, UOE definitions are better at indicating the homogeneity and resemblance to the model of schooling as a multi-year, full-time endeavour leading not only to a qualification, but also to a particular step on the educational ladder.

However, in our view, any reasonable definition of formal adult education has, from the very beginning, included institutional qualities that justified the formal–non-formal distinction, although going unnoticed because of the reference to the 'system of schools, colleges and universities'. Clarity can be regained by articulating exactly the institutional qualities that make formal adult education special and worth the scrutiny of research and policy on lifelong learning. This is the task of our next section.

A NEW WAY FORWARD: THE 'SOCIAL CHARTER' OF EDUCATIONAL OPPORTUNITIES AS A DEFINING CRITERION

To analyse initial education, we use the theoretical foundation developed by John W. Meyer and colleagues (see above). Their theory of education as a social institution is useful for considering the social effects on formal adult education (for a detailed discussion, see Hefler 2013).

While non-formal programmes typically do not, formal adult education generates the symbolic or institutional effects of graduation to provide membership in a particular category of personnel or, in other words, 'charters' (Meyer 1970) for sets of social positions, irrespective of individual learning achievements; formal programmes could be understood best by referring exactly to these institutionalized effects. Credentials achieved in formal adult education have their value, because their acceptance is institutionalized in the wider society or types of occupational career. While any learning could provide practical, technical tools for making personal progress, only formal adult education provides institutionalized guarantees for their social recognition. Formal adult education allows – as defining criteria – opportunities to take steps on an institutionalized educational ladder, reinforced or even created by an educational programme. Beyond any proof for learning or socialization effects, formal adult education guarantees an institutionalized effect that symbolically transforms the learner – in the eyes of the world – into a different kind of person, with new rights, possibilities, obligations and liabilities.

In any society, the initial-education system shapes both a specific 'educational ladder' and the institutional effects attached to the membership categories created by the education system. Formal adult education clearly builds on established institutionalized modes and remains therefore in the shadow of the initial system. It cannot but participate in institutional processes shaped by initial education. Therefore, programmes of formal adult education acquire their charter by applying institutional rules present in the initial-education system or – to use organizational institutionalism terminology – by isomorphic processes.

However, formal adult education also expands the categories and sources of legitimacy available in initial education. By linking itself to professional fields or particular economic sectors, it benefits from their legitimacies and creates the 'social charter' for its programmes. Moreover, organizations in formal adult education, catering for a particular type of education (for example, Master of Business Administration programmes), develop particular sources of legitimacy as an organizational field in their own right, setting standards and defining their borders to their fields. For securing the charter of a programme, isomorphism with the most legitimate players in the organizational field becomes both required and sufficient.

The link to the educational ladder has always been part of the definition of formal adult education. Applying the criteria, whether or not a programme (or the qualification achieved) charters its graduates to particular (advanced) positions, allows for a counterweight to a more arbitrary definition of formal adult education. Because the institutional effects do not result from a programme's learning or socialization effects, defining criteria clearly could not be the programme's content, length, provider, and so on. However, they may play an indispensable role for establishing the legitimacy of programmes (for example, a participant's total workload). How programmes connect institutionally to the world of work takes centre stage for actually explaining the social charter of programmes: programmes with the very same content could meet or fail the criterion for formal adult education, depending on their embeddedness in and linkage to particular career patterns.

Of course, when crossing country borders, the institutional value of qualifications depends on membership category and classification of types of personnel. A programme's charter could be universal within one society (being an academic) or specific to one type of organizational, occupational or professional field, but without much significance outside these contexts. Steps could be upward to a higher social position or also sideways, changing or expanding positions without actually improving one's overall social status. One person's formal adult education, which clearly follows the logic of a particular career trajectory, may be without institutional value for another person who has not embarked on that career path.

DIMENSIONS OF A NEW TYPOLOGY OF FORMAL ADULT EDUCATION

We propose a new typology of formal adult education that focuses on organizational fields arising around a particular issue – the use of formal adult education for a specific cause – and the isomorphic processes applied to secure a social charter for programmes and their certificates.

To our knowledge, no typology for formal adult education exists; however, many typologies are available within research on adult education. Classifications for isolated dimensions – for example, on programme content or providers, participant groups or orientation – often lead to poor results despite outstanding efforts. Therefore, despite the abundant typologies, discontent with existing ones prevails.

One promising way out is a more socio-historical approach referring to whole social sectors. This approach would classify them according to their typical provider organizations, typical programmes, sources of funding, professional groups, *raison d'être*, values and instruction patterns, main competitors and links to other fields of adult education. Focussing on existing social arenas would allow the study of their rise, progress, crisis, decline or reinvention. Tuijmann's typology of adult education providers (1996) offers an example for such an approach. Our approach follows the idea of a socio-historical approach. However, we apply the conceptual framework developed within organizational institutionalism for crafting a more systematic framework useful for single-country studies as well as cross-country comparison.

Because the areas of institutional life that provide formal adult education often do not fit into already established social sectors or organizational fields, one could also refer to them as hybrid fields, emerging around the issue of providing a type of formal adult education with a particular cause. Hybridization is thereby a frequently studied institutional process (Pedersen and Dobbin 2006; Sahlin and Wedlin 2008). 'Hybrid' refers to the fact that various institutional elements are borrowed from other fields which newly entering organizations come from or also belong to. For example, when trade unions start to deliver basic education, they bring particular approaches and ideologies that become candidates for becoming part of the institutional infrastructure of the 'new' hybrid field of formal basic education. Organizational (hybrid) fields may be coherent, yet may also consist of poorly coordinated, highly independent subfields, which empirical research would properly prefer to address as distinct organizational fields. However, even if comparable subfields – for example, organized around independent funding sources – have little mutual perception, all subfields deliver services that potentially replace each other and therefore compete for funding and legitimacy.

According to Paul DiMaggio and Walther Powell's seminal paper (DiMaggio and Powell 1991), institutional life takes place within organizational fields:

> By organizational field we mean those organizations that, in the aggregate, constitute a recognized area of institutional life: key suppliers, resource and product consumers, regulator agencies, and other organizations that produce similar services or products . . . The virtue of this unit of analysis is that it directs our attention not simply to competing firms . . . as to the totality of relevant actors. (DiMaggio and Powell 1991, pp. 64–65)

Richard Scott inserts the terminology taken from organizational ecology (Baum and Shipilov 2006) of 'organizational population' for any organizations competing to provide a particular service, and 'organizational set' for other organizations crucial for institutional life; for example, regulatory authorities, organizations administering public (co-)funding, collective-interest organizations or customers (Scott 2008). Our typology places particular importance on the composition of the organizational populations providing one type of formal adult education out of organizations, coming from and belonging to different organizational fields (e.g. liberal adult education; management training, trade unions, initial vocational education etc.) (for more details, see Hefler 2013).

To identify an organizational field as an area of institutional life, DiMaggio and Powell require a minimum and steady increase of interaction between all parties resulting in a reciprocal awareness of demonstrated behaviours and the development of minimal infrastructures for managing information observed within the interaction processes. As a result of the strongly increasing interaction between the members of a field, structures of dominance, subordination and exclusion develop, compounding institutional processes with power relations. Most importantly, organizational fields replace the vague and general notion of 'organizational environment': particular organizations share and interact with their particular organizational fields as environments, as they become relevant for them. Therefore, any potential institutional influence, coming from outside the organization (e.g. a management fad or new regulation), becomes filtered and translated by the organizational field and its particular established institutional order.

Within organizational (hybrid) fields of formal adult education, the social charters of programmes are crafted by coercive, mimetic and normative isomorphic processes (DiMaggio and Powell 1991). As also revealed in research on private elementary, higher secondary and tertiary education (Scott and Meyer 1994a; Davies et al. 2006; Levy 2006), organizations within formal adult education must acquire institutional legitimacy in order to provide recognized credentials. For organizations providing formal adult education, three main options are available:

- They could participate in the institutional legitimacy of initial education.
- They could participate in the social legitimacy of occupational and professional fields and, to a lesser extent, the economic sectors (understood as organizational fields) for which they prepare their participants.
- They could model themselves according to the most legitimate organizations established in a particular field of formal adult

> education. However, this strategy requires a considerable development of the (hybrid) field which is strong enough to produce and safeguard its own legitimacy.

The three strategies are not exclusive in general terms; they may occasionally conflict and may be pursued simultaneously by a single organization.

Growth and dynamics within organizational fields are driven by various institutional processes that come from inside and outside the organizational fields. We increase our understanding of the particular profile of each type of formal adult education when we reflect on the nature of the most likely institutional drivers.

It is important to stress that the typology – summarized in Table 3.1 – addresses ongoing institutional processes, not their immediate outcomes (for example, particular programmes of formal adult education). Thus, headings do not stand for types of programmes, but for organizational fields. Consequently, characteristics of types of formal adult education could be highly different between countries and between different moments of time within one country. The typology is meant, therefore, more as a research framework to explain the emergence and social significance of programmes than as a classification of educational programmes. In the following section, we characterize briefly each of these fields by focussing on how the institutional qualities of formal status are achieved, how the organizational populations and sets are composed and how institutional processes feed the expansion of the fields.

SEVEN TYPES OF FORMAL ADULT EDUCATION AND THEIR ORGANIZATIONAL FIELDS

Basic Skills and Remedy Programmes

Formal programmes are increasingly used to overcome the risk of social exclusion due to low literacy skills, including low official-language skills for native speakers of another language. Programmes providing basic skills exist in most countries. Programmes run over several months or years, with highly variable numbers of teaching units per week. The target groups are typically adults with comparatively low levels of formal schooling, who have never attained or have lost skills usually delivered by compulsory schooling. However, while some countries follow the UOE recommendation to classify these programmes as formal, many others see the related courses as non-formal.

This indecisiveness also reflects comparatively weak isomorphic links of

Table 3.1 *Overview of seven types of formal adult education and their related (hybrid) organization fields*

	(1) Core issue(s) supported by formal adult education	(2) Isomorphic process mainly oriented towards	(3) Organizational population – fields of adult education	Aspects of organizational set (selection)		(6) Typical ISCED level	Examples
				(4) Founding sources	(5) Main participation groups:		
I Basic skills programmes	a) overcoming exclusion and stigmatization by low literacy; b) providing access to credit-based qualifications c) integrating migrants	Initial education system	Typically heterogeneous, highly different between countries; liberal adult education; trade unions; general education, providers linked to active labour market policies	– local municipalities – welfare-to-work agencies – public employment policy	– people in routine jobs (having lost literacy) – unemployed – formally low qualified – migrants	1–2 (however, often embedded in 3)	– basic literacy, numeracy and IT skills – languages courses
II Second-chance education	a) providing access to higher education b) access to higher secondary vocational qualifications (terminal)	Initial education system	Typically more homogenous; general education, vocational education, higher education (bridging courses); more rarely, adult education, active labour market policies	– educational authorities – public employment services – public co-funding agencies for LLL – households	– young adults (18–24) – adults in early mid-career (well-established) – migrants (well educated abroad)	3a, b 4a, b 5a, b	– evening gymnasium – access course for higher education

Table 3.1 (continued)

	(1) Core issue(s) supported by formal adult education	(2) Isomorphic process mainly oriented towards	(3) Organizational population – fields of adult education	Aspects of organizational set (selection)		(6) Typical ISCED level	Examples
				(4) Founding sources	(5) Main participation groups:		
III Higher education programmes	a) providing membership among graduates b) vocational specialization at tertiary level	Initial education system	Exclusively higher education institutions (state-run/ private)	– educational authorities different between countries – households	– young adults (18-24) – adults in early mid-career (well-established)	5a, 5b	– part-time programmes in HE
IV (Re)-training	a) re-entering the labour market b) changing to the non-disadvantaged core segment of the labour market	Occupational fields and their initial vocational education Organizational fields (fields employing disadvantaged groups e.g. temporary work agencies)	Typically heterogeneous, active labour market policy, vocational education, adult education, on-the-job/off-the-job training,	– public employment services – municipalities – joint employer–employee organiza-tions	– (long-term) unemployed (including mature 50+); low-qualified individuals (with outdated skills etc.)	3b	– retraining for another occupation
V Customized vocational programmes	a) broadening validity for securing shared	Organizational fields (employment)	Mainly management training,	– employers' organiza-tions	– mid-career employees and skilled	3b 4b 5b	– customized program-mes

	commitments/ contributions of employer employees b) internal career patterns	for acceptance; initial education system and professional fields (for minimal requirements)	vocational education, higher education professional education, various combinations	– public agencies for business promotion – public co-funding agencies for LLL	blue-collar workers (core segment)		in mechatronics (ISCED 3b, 4)
VI Continuing higher education	occupational/ professional specialization	Autonomous field of continuing higher education; initial education system; alternatively, organizational fields (sectors)/ professional fields	Mainly management training, higher education, professional education	– households – employers' organizations	– mid-career employees with higher education/ higher secondary education	5a, b 6	– Master in Marketing – MBA
VII Continuing Professional Education (CPE)	a) access to professional-status groups b) professional specialization	Professional fields and autonomous field of CPE; initial education (minimal requirements)	The particular fields of higher education and management training	– households – employers	- mid-career employees with higher education; specific groups of skilled workers and semi-professionals	5a, b 6	– bar exams – certified programmes in psychotherapy – workmaster examination

these types of programmes to the institutional qualities of formal education. The claim that basic skills and remedial programmes are formal may be supported by one or more of the following possibilities: public funding for mandatory courses; individual rights or requirements to participate may be established for particular groups (for example, migrants or individuals receiving social aid); the course content may be mapped against the backdrop of primary and lower secondary education curricular and credits may be awarded that could help attain higher levels of education in subsequent programmes. Formal status is thereby both a requirement for public funding and the result of public funding; this makes 'basic adult education' a new area of state-supervised educational activity. However, providers are mostly private non-profit entities and mostly do not belong to the initial education system; instruction is not given by persons holding degrees comparable to those of teachers in traditional schools; programmes do not exactly follow any curriculum; and tests and examinations play a more subordinated role.

In any case, basic education typically has a weak formal charter. Any adult having left compulsory schooling is institutionally expected to hold some essential competences. Therefore, before a person participates, basic skill programmes could not simply award credentials to expand the given level of skills. Programmes often effectively expand participants' abilities and provide empowerment and social inclusion. However, institutions hardly support the transformation of achieved competences into social mobility. Consequently, the label 'formal' is not particularly justified, because any kind of non-formal provision could achieve comparable outcomes. The formal status of basic education seems fully justified only when developing basic skills results in credits that can be used to acquire higher levels of qualifications. In many countries, where basic education is regarded as formal (for example, Norway and Scotland), this is exactly the case.

Because of their positive effects, literacy programmes have traditionally been a key issue in various social movements of non-formal adult education. Programmes are typically labelled on International Standard Classification of Education (ISCED) levels 1 and 2. Various traditional organizations in liberal adult education or workers' education (trade unions) – together with more specialized non-profit organizations – form the core of the organizational populations. For-profit provision is rare. To avoid repeating negative experiences with previous schooling, styles of instruction are typically learner-centred. Personal interaction is encouraged among small groups of learners. The provision of basic skills requires considerable expertise and therefore professional development of specialized instructors; however, levels of professionalization of the field differ widely between countries. Organizational fields arise around one or a few public funding sources; their variations are likely to explain much of multilateral provision. Private financial contributions are negligible. Enterprises frequently cooperate in basic education programmes, because newly acquired communication skills add to productivity while participation typically does not result in demands for higher wages.

Greater public engagement in migration policies and welfare-to-work programmes, as well as the acceptance of a prevailing problem of adult illiteracy, has resulted in an increase in programmes. However, the programmes can have ambiguous institutional qualities. To add institutional value, basic-skills programmes can be combined with vocational elements essential for formal credentials. They can deliver credit points that lead to institutionally valuable qualifications. Programmes may even decide to hide their main purpose by using alternative headings, thus becoming more attractive to learners and avoiding the risk of negative symbolic effects for their participants who risk being potentially labelled as illiterate.

Second-Chance Education

The organizational (hybrid) field of 'second-chance education' arises around the tasks of allowing access to higher education or providing terminal higher-secondary vocational education. All countries have programmes that allow adults to acquire lower-secondary and higher-secondary educations. Traditionally, the term 'second-chance education' was reserved for programmes that provide access to higher education (Schleicher 1990). Today, the notion also covers other programmes and degrees, corresponding to initial education up to the ISCED 4b level and usually finished before the age of 19. Typical examples are 'evening gymnasiums', programmes that prepare for entrance permission to higher education or part-time vocational schools on a higher-secondary level. In most countries, numerous types of programmes and providers populate the field and compete for students. Modularized provision or availability of credit-based qualifications may add substantially to the institutional complexities.

This organizational field caters to comparatively large student populations, dominated by young adults (16–25 years old) enjoying a socially institutionalized, extended adolescence. For adolescents, second-chance education may be experienced more as a variation in 'initial-educational careers' than an overall distinct pattern. Second-chance education typically demonstrates a high level of regulative, normative and cognitive isomorphism with corresponding programmes and organizations in initial education. Consequently, differences between national education systems strongly shape the specific composition of the organizational field. Initial-education organizations may also provide adult education. Curricula are closely matched to the curricula of traditional students. Teachers often share the same professional background as their initial system counterparts: they may even work with both children and adults. The initial-education model typically has a uniform procedure to organize teaching and testing. Organizations focusing only on adults may be created that follow a curriculum comparable to the initial-education programme. However, important variants demonstrate significantly lower levels of isomorphism. Isomorphism may be reduced to curricula subject content and types of monitoring, while the providing organizations, styles of instruction and professional status of teachers may or may not follow prescribed patterns. Organization-bound programmes often show high levels of isomorphism, but various alternatives (preparation for external examinations, modularized programmes offered by various providers etc.) may demonstrate only limited isomorphism.

The 'charters' of programmes reflect their main purpose and the degree of isomorphism with initial education. Alternative access routes to higher education may have little institutional value beyond granting permission to enter higher education. However, competitive entrance procedures for higher education may limit the value of this institutionalized right. Any further charter effect is bound to later completion of the higher education programme. General programmes (e.g. evening gymnasiums) and vocational schools, which are highly isomorphic with initial education, offer a charter comparable to qualifications earned in initial education. However, the adult status may imply some penalization, reducing the value of the credentials. Alternative routes to vocational qualifications may even be highly devalued compared to their traditional counterparts and inherit less of the certificate's rights. This aspect would differ greatly between countries because of different educational organizations and the varying prestige of vocational education.

As an organizational hybrid field, second-chance education covers independent subfields that typically arise around particular governing and funding bodies. Educational opportunities more isomorphic to initial education are funded by the state and organized within the educational system, so that subfields are formed; for example, evening gymnasiums or part-time higher vocational schools. Authorities define members of the organizational populations. In sharp contrast, providers of alternative, less isomorphic pathways include various organizations such as liberal adult education or for-profit educational providers. Although alternative routes may have state (co-)funding, private sources provide substantial financial contributions that allow for the emergence of a demand-led market for educational services with weaker isomorphism to initial education that does not go beyond mastering codified requirements (for example, passing a set of examinations). However, competition for student populations will integrate various subfields into one organizational hybrid field structure. Student populations turn out to be highly volatile. For groups seeking access to higher education, programmes that require less effort ('loss of time') may be much more attractive than more in-depth programmes. Participants may willingly pay high fees for time-efficient private tutoring. More traditional schools for adults may lose clientele and thereby risk legitimacy necessary for their lump-sum, state funding. The availability of new programmes may revolutionize the organizational field within a few years.

The ongoing expansion of educational participation translates into paradoxical tendencies within second-chance education. The constantly increasing pressure to attain at least a higher-secondary-level certificate leads to expanding student populations. However, higher education has become both increasingly dominant and the natural goal for any second-chance education. The comparable weak 'charter' of many available qualifications reflects four decades of 'credential inflation' that significantly cuts into the legitimacy of terminal qualifications provided by the hybrid field. Second-chance education provides knowledge that risks becoming regarded only as something required for the examination day; life starts anew after entering higher education. The field could experience a crisis because of fading legitimacy and loss of institutional power of available vocational credentials. In this case, second-chance education would then become an ideal field for studying both 'institutional entrepreneurship' and processes of 'de-institutionalization' (Harney and Koch 2010).

Higher Education Programmes Accessible for Non-Traditional (Adult) Students

For adults, higher education provides membership among graduates – no matter if this still signals an elite position – and allows for a professional specialization. Higher education of adult students traditionally does not resort to 'adult education' but is regarded as a subfield covered by higher education policy and research. However, the space of higher education also forms the single most important organizational field for formal adult education, when one considers the number of participants and the goal sought by participants in 'second-chance education'.

Traditional universities owe their legitimacy, and power to determine valuable credentials, to their own institutional model: their position was institutionalized within society even before the rise of modern education systems. However, universities are entrenched in a dense network of coercive, normative and cognitive institutions. Moreover, by the late nineteenth century, state administration had fully integrated universities into educational bureaucracies in all European societies. Private universities are typically bound by strong regulations that add to isomorphic pressure within the organizational field. Consequently, to remain a degree programme on a predefined level, a set of criteria have to be met, no matter how ritualized the compliance may be. Virtually the same rules apply to adult-oriented programmes that lead to certificates with comparable institutional value.

The organizational field has become more complex with the rise of non-traditional universities catering to new groups of students or employers, which divert students from more prestigious 'old' universities. For organizational newcomers into the field of higher education, demonstrating high levels of isomorphism is a question of institutional life and death. Yet, typically, new organizations partially fail in becoming full universities so must distance themselves from the leading model in order to find their niche in a strongly and highly expanding market for prospective students and their graduates' prospective employers.

The tensions between 'old' and 'new' universities – such as the presence or absence of doctoral-level education on ISCED 6 – are highly significant for formal adult education within higher education. 'New' universities are more inclined (partly as their *raison d'etre*) to cater to non-traditional students, while 'old', elite organizations enjoy more discretion. Any deviation from the gold standard of university education intending to help adult students proceed at a more accelerated pace may be interpreted as devaluing credentials. When adult students become diverted to less prestigious types of organizations or programmes, the value of their credentials may be undisputed, yet clearly devalued, in comparison to all more prestigious educational tracks. As a result, explicitly serving adult students is risky and, to avoid marginalization, non-traditional students may even opt for the traditional full-time programmes.

Among higher educational institutions, we find organizations with and without programmes designed or even reserved for adult students. University systems differ widely to the extent that organizations compete for students, for public funding, for private tuition fees and for mere legitimacy. The most typical examples are part-time programmes that deliver the same curriculum as full-time studies, yet extended over longer periods, and provided mainly in evening hours. Moreover, some programmes are available only for adult students. In many higher education systems (following the German university model), employed adults could attend full-time programmes and, on an individual basis, lengthen the duration of their study. In other systems, adult students must complete full-time educational programmes within a predefined period.

Ongoing expansion of mass higher education towards universal higher education will certainly bring more adult students into higher education. Already, a viable field of research focuses on the consequences of shifting the overall composition of higher education students – making non-traditional students the majority – on the institutional foundations and the everyday operation of universities. An under-researched area involves the institutional processes that enhance or limit adult participation in formal adult education. Changes in the institutional and 'exchange' value of higher education credentials have been discussed since the late eighteenth century; however, our own vocabulary for describing 'credential inflation' and 'status competition' stems mainly from the 1970s. Newer concepts, reflecting an additional three decades of expansion, are still in short supply.

(Occupational) (Re)Training Programmes

These formal programmes help the (long-term) unemployed to re-enter the labour market or to overcome their marginalized position by entering the labour market core segments. All European countries have public employment services and related welfare institutions that initiate varied forms of occupational retraining programmes for workers who could not stay in their previous occupations. The programmes' governance and orientation vary over time and between countries. When programmes lead to acknowledged qualifications, they should be seen as formal adult education. Various countries follow this view, while others do not perceive retraining programmes as formal.

Occupational programmes take place in highly complex institutional environments that require securing sufficient isomorphism with the education system and particularly with the vocational tracks. The funding organizations such as employment services, public health agencies or local communities have a clear-cut purpose: bring beneficiaries of welfare payments back to work within their field's legal and normative requirements. Typically, they are allowed to provide support only for clearly defined eligible groups. Therefore, participants can be highly preselected and consist of multiple disadvantaged social strata. The legitimacy of the publicly funded intervention depends on re-employment of most participants. Programmes thereby directly involve organized interests in the world of work. Business-interest organizations must accept programmes for their technical and/or institutional outcomes. Trade unions have to accept that more skilled workers, whose training costs are strongly co-funded by public means, may have an impact on the employment prospects of members of their trades, both for those currently employed as well as those who are unemployed but not eligible for the programme. Challenges are further exacerbated by the multiple vulnerabilities and needs of the typical participant groups, often requiring professional support beyond mere instruction. Finally, participation is often *de facto* mandatory, undermining the voluntary-participation principle fundamental for adult education. Even when training organizations fail to meet their participant needs, they could not protest by simply walking away.

As a solution for complex, competing institutional claims, programmes may be defined as a temporary compromise established for a set period. Over the decades, a steady flow of temporary programmes may be introduced; this establishes a highly informal, institutional ordering of the possible and the impossible. Alternatively, new vocational-training organizations, typically under control of either or both employer interest organizations and trade unions, could cater to various groups and provide both formal programmes and short-term non-formal training. Within a particular country, one solution typically dominates; however, combinations of both approaches are also seen.

Although some isomorphic links to initial vocational education may be present, the previously described institutional compromise shapes the capacity of retraining programmes to provide qualifications. Frequently, we find second-tier qualifications: substandard credentials are awarded for meeting clearly reduced requirements. The qualifications often lack the institutional qualities expected and rarely help find employment on institutionalized grounds, beyond what has been technically learned by participation. While programmes deliver formal rights of specific qualifications (for example, entitlements for skilled workers set by binding collective agreements), they fail to deliver the positive evaluation expected from their educational credentials. In their symbolic strategies, they are limited to demonstrate effective transmission of skills. To fight against the consequences of negative stereotyping of their clientele, various placement services are usually offered, based on stable collaboration between educational providers and selected employers.

The organizational fields for (re)training programmes vary across countries. Public spending is high in many countries and – by comparison – among the most substantial for formal adult education altogether. Private contributions are negligible. When public retraining organizations are institutionalized, they may absorb most funds available, restricting the number of entrance competitors. However, when no permanent structures are developed, huge training markets may arise, attracting organizations with various backgrounds to compete for their part of the market. Training organizations related to the trade unions or to employer organizations are often preferred suppliers, because the social partner's interests are crucial for forging compromises. Vocational schools are partly involved for matters of legitimacy and expertise. Various non-profit organizations with strong backgrounds in social work are also often present. Yet, when substantial public funds are invested, the market could also attract for-profit providers from the field of training for enterprises, which have experience at organizing large-scale programmes. Modes of instruction vary with the institutional background of providers and the professional standards required for the instructors.

Occupational retraining programmes expand with rising levels of long-term unemployment and also with attempts by the pension system to reduce access to early retirement by extending occupational rehabilitation or work-to-welfare programmes seeking to reduce costs for communal welfare. Shifts away from specialized programmes happen periodically because of disappointment with results of large-scale retraining and the poor long-term labour market integration of participants. Moreover, the programmes' mandatory character threatens to discredit lifelong learning among the most vulnerable social groups, over-represented among participants of retraining programmes. However, creation of programmes can hardly be replaced by training vouchers, which typically do not fit opportunities available for the particular target groups.

Customized Vocational and Professional Programmes for Organizations

Formal adult education is used to improve the balance of the competing interests attached to company training of employees and their employers and to justify internal career patterns. Education providers may customize their programmes for employees of a single or a group of organizations. Alternatively, education providers can cooperate with companies by adding formal status to existing non-formal training programmes. In both cases, customization and restricting access to predefined participants do not necessarily conflict with symbolic requirements for formal education. Countries vary in their institutional frameworks that allow for tailored formal programmes. Moreover, the typical ways to secure formal status differ between countries.

Securing formal status of customized programmes requires a minimal level of isomorphism with initial programmes. Typically, the providing organizations belong to the legitimate organizations of initial education, for example, a higher secondary technical school or a university of applied science. Moreover, counterparts available in open programmes of formal education model the programmes' subjects, workload and duration. While the subject names may remain unchanged, the content may be completely adapted to the current needs of the participants and their employer. Where required, other bureaucratic rules may be applied to secure the formal status. When non-formal programmes are transformed into formal ones, providers look for appropriate matches among existing formal programmes. By increasing isomorphism between the non-formal programmes in question and comparable existing programmes, the former could be made eligible for certification by the educational provider. In case of formalization of existing programmes, the latter makes up a model for the search for a formal counterpart to match with; next, amendments and slight changes of company programme make the programme sufficiently similar, so that the educational organization could certify graduation.

The rise of customized formal programmes results from both educational entrepreneurs and trends within companies that lead to the establishment of internal training programmes, which closely follow formal education models. Traditionally, company-based educational programmes are non-formal; however, as Scott and Meyer observe (1994b), already in the 1980s in the United States, these company-based programmes had adopted typical forms and techniques of formal education for increasing their legitimacy. Companies arrange in various ways the certification of their programmes and generate organization-specific credentials, which claim to be recognized informally within certain industries. The hype of corporate universities early in the 1990s represents only the most visual development in the field (see Markowitsch and Jonach 2006; Dobbin et al. 1994).

Higher-secondary vocational schools and universities mainly provide customized programmes on their own initiative. By providing customized programmes, they typically deepen relationships with potential employers for their graduates and collect cutting-edge experience, which may enter curricula development for open programmes. Moreover, profit providers in the market for corporate training provision find it attractive to forge formalization opportunities for their customized educational programmes; they typically create networks with recognized educational organizations within formal education, which provide their authorization to compete in the market. Enterprises cover most of the fees for programmes, partly supported by available public co-funding schemes. Public funds available exclusively for supporting formal adult education in enterprises – with or without requirements to target particular groups – may also drive the expansion of the field: in extreme cases, some educational providers have the core business model of restlessly searching for companies prepared to receive free formal educational programmes for their employees.

The number of training programmes in enterprises may be more or less stable, yet demand seems to be increasing for certification of education.

Entrepreneurial activities of organizations within formal education are increasing as they seek to replace increasingly scarce public funds and to improve network relations with potential employers of graduates.

(Post-Tertiary) Continuing Higher Education

Continuing higher education supports vocational or professional specialization. Organizations entitled to provide higher education also typically have the right to provide continuing education programmes; their full control includes setting tuition fees, which usually cover full costs (or even allow for profits) and lead to high fees compared to regular studies. Programmes often require an academic degree or a number of years of occupational experience as an entrance requirement. The typically more flexible regulations for continuing higher education empower the organizations to develop market-oriented niche products. Thus, programmes also change quite often. Even in relatively small countries, several hundred different programmes are available within continuing higher education, yet the number of students per programme is low. Typically, programmes cater to adult students with some years of professional experiences. A particular organizational field is formed from formal programmes attached directly to occupational or professional groups that provide 'continuing professional education' (see the subsection on 'Continuing Professional Education Governed by Professional Bodies' below).

To secure legitimacy, the programmes' content and organization are combined with models known from non-formal management training. However, differences in local traditions greatly blur the borders. Successfully distributed international models for continuing higher education, such as the Master of Business Administration (Mazza et al. 2005), often inspire the search for other opportunities in higher continuing education. These models typically include small groups of learners, frequent personal interaction between teaching experts and students, and problem-based learning. Reflecting high tuition fees, the quality of their service typically exceeds that found in initial education.

The status of the organization (for example, a well-known, respectable 'full' university) adds much to any degree's potential value; this increases the horizontal stratification within higher education: participants or their employers may become attracted only for the symbolic value of the name of the organization, not by the programme content. Because of the comparatively weak legitimacy, a key step for a new programme is to establish links with the working world. Only by serving the participants' expectations established in various occupational fields and by meeting requirements of their employer organizations can programmes thrive in a highly competitive market.

In many countries nearly all higher education organizations enter the market. Specialized organizations might also be in place typically when universities establish legally independent for-profit entities. As a market, the field is particularly segmented by the programme content, which allows for submarkets including business education, technical education and cultural or health sector programmes. While higher-education organizations can use their state-funded infrastructure and personnel, private households or the participants' employers typically contribute most to the fees for continuing higher education. Some participants may be eligible for public co-funding of their fees with various schemes supporting participation in continuing training. Attracting enough participants to reach the breakeven level becomes the single most important criteria within the organizational field. Many advertised programmes never come into existence because of a lack of paying customers. Beyond state agencies with supervisory authority, monitoring includes local or international agencies that set and assess quality standards as well as various professional organizations and business-interest organizations engaged in particular subfields.

The strong expansion of continuing higher education seems to be mainly driven by status-competition and the formalization of eligibility criterion for access and promotion to increasingly specified career patterns. The labour markets for higher education graduates have become horizontally segmented by the formalization of continuing education programmes. The symbolic status of the providing organization and the programme content both add to the segmentation. However, the institutionalization of degrees earned in continuing higher education does not match the level of formal degrees typically forming the 'educational ladder'. While programmes may work well and provide considerably benefits for insiders already established with occupational career trajectories, the same programmes may add little to career progress for outsiders. Continuing higher education therefore risks becoming a sequel of the 'great training robbery' describing the expansion of higher education in the 1970s (Berg and Govelick 1973; Brown and Hesketh 2004).

Continuing Professional Education Governed by Professional Bodies

Access to professional-status groups or fields of particular professional expertise is bound to the provision of particular programmes in continuing professional education. Professions develop their own systems of continuing professional education; particular programmes prepare for officially recognized degrees that entitle graduates to a set of professional activities.

Professional or occupational associations provide, or at least control, programmes and claim the right to set, control and develop the standards for providing credentials. Typically, members of the professional groups belong to the examination boards. Thus, continuing professional education forms an important mechanism within the 'control of the production of producers' (Larson 1977, p. 49), which is at the heart of social closure required for controlling professional work. When leading to particular degrees and marking steps within professional careers, continuing professional education is typically understood as formal adult education within national systems. However, formal status for various professional programmes substantially differs within a country and in cross-country comparison. Since continuing professional education includes occupational or semi-professional (non-academic) and professional (academic) programmes, the programmes have highly diverse requirements and participants.

Examples for the non-academic level include preparing for 'craft-master' (*Meisterprüfung*) examination, real-estate management and preparing for bar exams or for becoming a psychotherapist of a particular school of therapy on an academic level. Other examples also clearly indicate that the social status of particular professions or occupations evolve over time and may differ between countries: an established profession in one country may be a subordinated, unregulated field in another country (for example, psychotherapy has become an independent profession with its particular formal education in most countries, while in France it is still a prerogative of physicians) (Strauß and Kohl 2009).

Continuing professional education gains its legitimacy mainly by its relation to the professions. Faith in the value of its credentials depends on the professions' ability to defend their areas of expertise against usurpation by competing professions and to regulate access to their own 'guild'. Programmes show a particular isomorphism with the regulative, normative and cognitive patterns of the various occupational or professional fields. Programmes within continuing professional education may be coopted by the initial education system: for example, the historic incorporation of the 'work master' (*Werkmeister*) in Germany or Austria within the education system. However, the impact of institutional models for 'good' education within higher education is certainly felt within the field of continuing professional education. Moreover, occupational schools and professional schools have become major providers for continuing professional education; they have merged the institutional logics of education and the profession. By balancing formal education requirements with institutional requirements from the professional field, the credentials can secure some value even outside their professional fields. However, as a rule, credentials earned within professional continuing education are fully acknowledged only within a particular profession. Although highly institutionalized within a particular profession, these credentials may lack any value outside the field.

Reflecting the strong linkage to various professional fields, the organizational field of continuing formal education is segmented into nearly unconnected subfields. Organizational populations for each subfield typically include professional associations and their educational organizations, higher-education organizations, non-profit organizations established in various occupational fields (e.g. mutual-welfare organizations) and for-profit organizations. Interaction and competition within each subfield is high: the single most important issue is for a programme to secure legitimacy as providing access to a particular professional (sub)field. Tuition fees of individual participants and their employers are the most important financial source. Typically, the same organization provides formal programmes (leading to a predefined step) and non-formal programmes that help satisfy requirements for compulsory continuing education as defined in various regulations. The organizational set will include regulators of the profession and organizations responsible for funding clients of the professions; for example, the social insurance agencies for all medical and paramedical occupations.

The strong expansion of continuing professional education reflects the expansion of professionalism as an important way of controlling work. However, traditional non-academic provision of skills such as the 'work-master' programmes could also lose ground. Specialization within professional fields is a major strategy to compete for particular sources of income. Balancing the costs and benefits for increasing educational requirements becomes a core tension within the professions. However, given the belief in the power of education, any perceived social problem – from misconduct in health care to poor counselling in financial services – results in calls for more and better continuing professional education.

CONCLUSIONS AND OUTLOOK

We started this chapter by pointing out two problems: the ambivalent conceptual status of formal adult education, and shortcomings in meaningfully interpreting available statistical accounts. For both issues, we have identified areas for future research.

Our institutional analysis has shown that the evolution of formal adult education has been shaped by the expansion or contraction in seven somewhat independent organizational fields. We see independent processes as composing the total of formal adult education. Moreover, countries' education systems change and these changes transform the very meaning of formal education and the link between qualifications and programmes. The statistical data collected for various countries are not comparable because they represent quite different educational activities; however, they are also not artefacts. By 'comparing the incomparable' (Maurice 2000), we become aware of different processes of institutional changes – typically prescribed on the global level, yet delivered locally in highly distinct fashions – going on or being blocked in various societies.

Processes, reflected by the data on formal adult education, include:

- more organizations becoming entitled to provide education regarded as formal (for example, organizations providing programmes to prepare for external examinations);
- more programmes being classified as formal by expanding applicable rules (for example, any provision within active labour market policy such as in Sweden and Norway, or any provision financed by the Ministry of Education, such as in Flanders, may be classified as formal);
- a broader range of qualifications becoming available on different educational levels, particularly within vocational education on the ISCED level 3 and post-secondary or post-tertiary level (ISECD 4, 5a, 5b);
- more programmes becoming available in modules;
- more qualifications being achieved on the basis of collecting credits, within or outside the formal education system and thus any course providing credits becomes a candidate for being reported as formal adult education; and
- more types of occupational or professional education having become or becoming represented in already established or currently introduced national qualifications frameworks (NQFs).

Countries differ considerably in how these developments become vital for their systems. Figure 3.2 provides a tool for clarification. We can suppose for all countries that at one point in history, typically after the systematization of the educational systems late in the nineteenth century, the concept of formal adult education equals the participation of adults in the newly systematized, state-controlled education system. We could use this as a zero point. This starting point has a comparatively high homogeneity of formal adult education in regards to curricula, workload, duration or providing organizations.

Finally, formal adult education becomes more differentiated along two basic dimensions. New organizations develop with the right to provide formal adult education. Examples include night schools for adults, or degree-awarding organizations run by public employment services. By

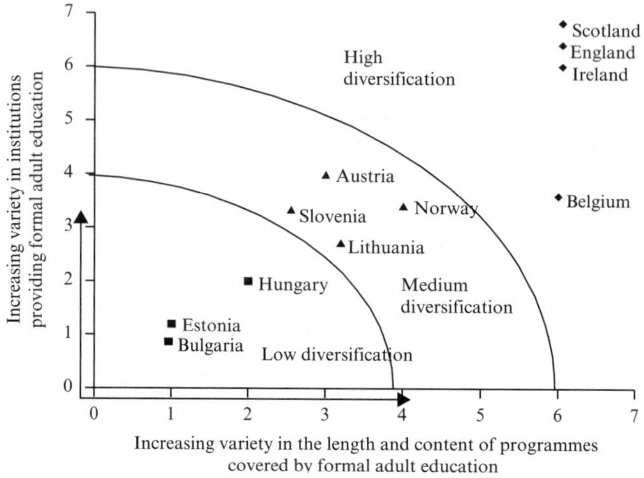

Figure 3.2 Grouping of countries according to the degree of diversification of the formal adult education system

various mechanisms, the number of organizations providing education regarded as formal could increase considerably, for example, by the availability of external examinations or by introducing credit-based qualifications. Countries differ clearly in their range of organizations involved in formal adult education. The number of programmes or courses that provide credits to acquire qualifications could outgrow the basic model of a formal qualification involving completion of a multi-year programme of full-time education. The programme content can become much more narrowly defined. Workload can be much more variable. When credit-based qualifications become available, even short courses potentially contribute to them and might be counted as formal. Countries differ clearly in the range (content and length) of available programmes regarded as formal.

Together, the range of organizations entitled to provide formal adult education and the range of programmes potentially labelled as formal add up to different levels of diversification among activities labelled as formal adult education. While we find countries with considerable low differentiation (Bulgaria, Estonia, Hungary and Russia), we find countries with medium variation (Slovenia, Lithuania, Austria and Norway) and considerable high variation (Scotland, England, Ireland and Belgium). High diversification is mainly introduced either by the existence of credit-based qualifications or rules that broadly give the 'formal' label to any courses offered by various important institutions. Medium diversification is, for example, achieved by differentiating between available qualifications pro-

Table 3.2 Provisional grouping of participating countries

		Understanding of formal adult education		
		'low diversification' clearly narrow (more than 70% +200 hours)	'medium diversification' medium range (40–70% more than +200 hours)	'high diversification' clearly broad (less than 40% more than 200 hours)
General activity in LLL	Low	Bulgaria Hungary		
	Moderate	Estonia	Lithuania	
	High		Austria Norway Slovenia	Belgium Ireland England Scotland

vided by an ever-increasing number of highly specialized organizations. In countries with low diversification, we find more restrictive control by educational authorities for the scarce good of acknowledged qualifications; this results in giving only the 'non-formal' label to various educational opportunities.

We must consider differences in the diversification of the perceived formal adult education in order to interpret statistics on formal adult education – particularly those provided by the Adult Education Survey. Figures reflect both overall participation levels in lifelong learning and the narrow or broad understanding of formal adult education that result in different pathways in control and reform of educational systems. Table 3.2 structures the countries participating in the LLL2010 project, according to these two dimensions. It becomes clear that differences in the meaning of 'formal adult education' result in the extraordinarily high variety of participation rates in formal adult education reported by the AES.

However, while the scheme helps us to avoid pitfalls in using statistical data, it tells us little about the actual meaning of low and high participation rates or the actual reasons behind the compositional effects represented in the data.

For further progress, we need better-justified criteria for including an educational activity within the concept of formal adult education. By focusing on the presence or absence of a 'social charter', we can meaningfully discern formal from non-formal adult education. Moreover, this allows for the argument that formal adult education is a social institution in its own right, providing particular social opportunities. Exploring the social charter of programmes and their institutional foundations also allows for a less arbitrary basis for classifying formal programmes as formal or non-formal.

Next, we need an account of the different issues addressed by formal adult education and the organizational fields that arise around these issues. Our typology aims at developing such an account. As we have demonstrated, formal adult education includes more fields than 'second-chance education' or 'higher education for non-traditional adults'. In all fields, the validity and social charter of credentials awarded is secured in a specific way that requires constant adaptation and evolution.

Each type of formal adult education has different dynamics of growth and contraction as well as access or exclusion of various social groups. As we have seen, fields of formal adult education are driven by their particular social and institutional processes: LLL policy often focuses not on simply expanding participation, but on fairly distributing benefits and burdens between employers and employees, participants and non-participants. However, only three out of seven fields of formal adult education cater to more disadvantaged groups; these fields all depend strongly on receiving public funds and applying regulative policies. When considering all types of formal adult education together, it matters if disadvantaged groups could participate only within 'basic skills and remedy' or retraining programmes, or find their way – typically via second-chance education – to higher education or continuing professional education. We are interested in understanding the extent that formal adult education actually succeeds in changing membership categories and ends a person's status as 'disadvantaged': a promise easily given, yet difficult to make a reality (Inbar and Sever 1989). By introducing our typology, we assert that a country's total participation in formal adult education results from the seven independent organizational fields. Any comparisons between countries or any study of participation of social groups within one country becomes fully fertile and useful for policy issues by responding to the existence of these rather independent fields of educational provision; our typology provides a framework for meeting this requirement.

REFERENCES

Ariès, Philippe (1962), *Centuries of Childhood*, London: Pimlico.

Baum, Joel A.C. and Andrew V. Shipilov (2006), 'Ecological Approaches to Organizations', in Stewart R. Clegg, Cynthia Hardy, Thomas B. Lawrence and Walter R. Nord (eds), *The Sage Handbook of Organization Studies*, 2nd edn, London: SAGE, pp. 55–110.

Berg, Ivar and Sherry Govelick (1973), *Education and Jobs: The Great Training Robbery*, Harmondsworth: Penguin Education.
Brown, Phillip and Anthony Hesketh (2004), *The Mismanagement of Talent: Employability and Jobs in the Knowledge Economy*, Oxford: Oxford University Press.
Chu, Shui-kee (1996), 'Statistics of Adult and Nonformal Education', in Albert C. Tuijnman (ed.), *The International Encyclopedia of Adult Education and Training*, Oxford: Pergamon Press, pp. 878–883.
Davies, Scott, Linda Quirke and Janice Aurini (2006), 'The New Institutionalism Goes to the Market: The Challenge of Rapid Growth in Private K-12 Education', in Heinz-Dieter Meyer and Brian Rowan (eds), *The New Institutionalism in Education*, New York: State University of New York Press, pp. 103–122.
DiMaggio, Paul J. and Walter W. Powell (1991), 'The Iron Cage Revisited: Institutional Isomorphism and Collective Rationality in Organizational Fields', in Walter W. Powell and Paul DiMaggio, J. (eds), *The New Institutionalism in Organizational Analysis*, Chicago, IL, USA and London, UK: University of Chicago Press, pp. 63–82.
Dobbin, Frank, John R. Sutton, John W. Meyer and Richard W. Scott (1994), 'Equal Opportunity Law and the Construction of Internal Labor Markets', in Richard W. Scott and John W. Meyer (eds), *Institutional Environments and Organizations: Structural Complexity and Individualism*, Thousand Oaks, CA: Sage, pp. 272–300.
Eurostat (2006), *Classification of Learning Activities: Manual*, Luxembourg: Office for Official Publications of the European Communities.
Greenwood, Royston, Christine Oliver, Kerstine Sahlin and Roy Suddaby (eds) (2008), *The Sage Handbook of Organizational Institutionalism*, Los Angeles, CA: Sage.
Harney, Klaus and Sascha Koch (2010), 'Steuerungsprobleme im Zweiten Bildungsweg. Eine empirische und organizationstheoretische Analyse des Phänomens der bildungssystemischen Funktionsüberlappung', in Karin Dollhausen, Timm C. Feld and Wolfgang Seitter (eds), *Erwachsenenpädagogische Organizationsforschung*, Wiesbaden: VS Verlag für Sozialwissenschaften, pp. 197–218.
Hefler, Günter (2013), *Taking Steps: Formal Adult Education in Private and Organizational Life*, Vienna: Lit-Verlag.
Inbar, Dan E. and Rita Sever (1989), 'The Importance of Making Promises: An Analysis of Second-Chance Policies', *Comparative Education Review*, **33** (2), 232–242.
Kamens, David H. (1985), 'Youth and the State: A Cross-National Analysis of the Changing Status of Adolescence', *Comparative Political Studies*, **18** (3), 3–36.
Larson, Magali Sarfatti (1977), *The Rise of Professionalism: A Sociological Analysis*, Berkeley, CA: University of California Press.
Levy, Daniel C. (2006), 'How Private Higher Education's Growth Challenges the New Institutionalism', in Heinz-Dieter Meyer and Brian Rowan (eds), *The New Institutionalism in Education*, New York: State University of New York Press, pp. 143–161.
Markowitsch, Jörg and Michaela Jonach (2006), *Anerkennung und Zertifizierung betrieblicher Aus- und Weiterbildungsleistungen im Kontext nationaler und internationaler Entwicklungen: Eine Überblicksexpertise*, Wien: BMWA.
Maurice, Marc (2000), 'The Paradoxes of Societal Analysis: A Review of the Past

and Prospects of the Future', in Marc Maurice and Arndt Sorge (eds), *Embedding Organizations: Societal Analysis of Actors, Organizations and Socio-Economic Context*, Amsterdam: John Benjamins, pp. 13–36.

Mazza, Carmelo, Kerstin Sahlin-Andersson and Jesper Strandgaard Pedersen (2005), 'European Constructions of an American Model: Developments of Four MBA Programmes', *Management Learning*, **36** (4), 471–491.

Meyer, Heinz-Dieter and Brian Rowan (eds) (2006), *The New Institutionalism in Education*, New York: State University of New York Press.

Meyer, John W. (1970), 'The Charter: Conditions of Diffuse Socialization in Schools', in W. Richard Scott (ed.), *Social Processes and Social Structures: an Introduction to Sociology*, New York, USA and London, UK: Holt, Rinehart & Winston, pp. 564–578.

Meyer, John W. (1977), 'The Effects of Education as an Institution', *American Journal of Sociology*, **83** (1), 55–77.

Meyer, John W. and Brian Rowan (1977), 'Institutionalized Organizations: Formal Structures as Myth and Ceremony', *American Journal of Sociology*, **83** (2), 340–363.

Meyer, John W. and Brian Rowan (1978), 'The Structure of Educational Organizations', in Marshall W. Meyer (ed.), *Environments and Organizations*, San Francisco, CA: Jossey-Bass, pp. 78–109.

Meyer, John W., Francisco O. Ramirez, David John Frank and Evan Schofer (2005), 'Higher Education as an Institution', in Patricia J. Gumport (ed.), *Sociology of Higher Education: Contributions and Their Contexts*, Baltimore, MD: Johns Hopkins University Press, pp. 187–221.

Müller, Detlef K., Fritz K. Ringer and Brian Simon (1987), *The Rise of the Modern Educational System: Structural Change and Social Reproduction 1870–1920*, Cambridge: Cambridge University Press.

Parkes, David (1990), 'Managing the Gaps: The Interpretation of Policy to Create Second Chance in the Further Education Systems of the United Kingdom', in Dan E. Inbar (ed.), *Second Chance in Education*, London: Falmer, pp. 215–226.

Pedersen, Jesper Strandgaard and Frank Dobbin (2006), 'In Search of Identity and Legitimation: Bridging Organizational Culture and Neoinstitutionalism', *American Behavioral Scientist*, **49** (7), 897–907.

Ramirez, Francisco O. and Richard Rubinson (1979), 'Creating Members: The Political Incorporation and Expansion of Public Education', in John W. Meyer and Michael T. Hannan (eds), *National Development and the World System: Educational, Economic and Political Change, 1950–1970*, Chicago, IL: University of Chicago Press, pp. 72–82.

Ringer, Fritz K. (1979), *Education and Society in Modern Europe*, Bloomington, IN: Indiana University Press.

Rogers, Alan (2004), 'Non-Formal Education: Flexible Schooling or Participatory Education?' CERC Studies in Comparative Education no. 15, Hong Kong: Hong Kong Comparative Education Research Centre (CERC), Faculty of Education, Hong Kong University.

Sahlin, Kerstin and Linda Wedlin (2008), 'Circulating Ideas: Imitation, Translation and Editing', in Royston Greenwood, Christine Oliver, Kerstine Sahlin and Roy Suddaby (eds), *The Sage Handbook of Organizational Institutionalism*, Los Angeles, CA: Sage, pp. 218–242.

Schleicher, Klaus (1990), 'Second Chance: Emancipation and/or Alienation:

The German Experience', in Dan E. Inbar (ed.), *Second Chance in Education*, London: Falmer, pp. 167–191.
Scott, W. Richard (2008), *Institutions and Organizations: Ideas and Interests*, London: Sage.
Scott, W. Richard and John W. Meyer (1994a), 'Environmental Linkages and Organizational Complexity: Public and Private Schools', in W. Richard Scott and John W. Meyer (eds), *Institutional Environments and Organizations: Structural Complexity and Individualism*, Thousand Oaks, CA: Sage, pp. 137–159.
Scott, W. Richard and John W. Meyer (1994b), 'The Rise of Training Programs in Firms and Agencies: an Institutional Perspective', in W. Richard Scott and John W. Meyer (eds), *Institutional Environments and Organizations: Structural Complexity and Individualism*, Thousand Oaks, CA: Sage, pp. 228–254.
Strauß, Bernhard and Steffi Kohl (2009), 'Entwicklung der Psychotherapie und der Psychotherapieausbildung in europäischen Ländern', *Psychotherapeut*, **54** (6), 457–463.
UNESCO (1975), *Manual for the Collection of Adult Education Statistics*, Paris: Office of Statistics.
UNESCO (1979), *Terminology of Adult Education*, Paris.
UNESCO (1997), *International Standard Classification of Education (ISCED 1997)*, Paris.
UNESCO, OECD and Eurostat (2010), *UOE Data Collection on Education Systems – Volume 1 – Manual Concepts, Definitions and Classifications*, Montreal, Paris and Luxembourg.
Ure, Odd Bjørn (2006), 'Lifelong Learning for Civic Employees and Employable Citizens?' in Michael Kuhn and Ronald, G. Sultana (eds), *Homo Sapiens Europæus: Creating the European Learning Citizen*, New York: Peter Lang, pp. 167–188.

PART II

Country studies

4. Has lifelong learning policy and practice in Scotland promoted social inclusion?

Elisabet Weedon and Sheila Riddell

INTRODUCTION

In this chapter we explore the extent to which lifelong learning (LLL) policy and practice promote social inclusion, and which are the main target groups of policy strategies. We draw on data from a 6th framework project entitled 'Towards a Lifelong Learning Society in Europe: the Contribution of the Education System' (LLL 2010), focusing on interview data from both managers of LLL provision and two government-related officials. Education has traditionally been seen as a means to social mobility in Scotland and as essential to a strong democracy and a meritocratic social system (Devine 1999). The extent to which education fulfils these expectations has been questioned by Scott and Mooney (2005), who feel that the presentation of Scotland as an egalitarian society is misplaced. Nonetheless, the egalitarian nature of the Scottish society is apparent in policy documents. Initially, the government's focus was on the compulsory education system, but during the second half of the twentieth century tertiary education increased in importance. However, in spite of the importance attached to education as a means to social mobility, persistent inequalities related to socio-economic background still exist in all sectors of education. The role of post-compulsory education in addressing such inequalities was noted in the late 1990s in the Green Paper *Opportunity Scotland* (Scottish Office 1998). This paper paved the way for the first LLL strategy, published in 2003 (Scottish Executive 2003), which claims that: 'Lifelong learning has an important and distinctive contribution to make to people's well-being, to a more inclusive society and to a vibrant and sustainable economy' (Scottish Executive 2003, p. 4).

The LLL strategy for 2003 was published after the formation of the Scottish Parliament in 1999. Whilst the Scottish education system has always differed from that of the rest of United Kingdom, devolution brought additional powers to the new government formed in 1999, leading to a number of changes in relation to education with new departments and key bodies changing or merging (Bryce and Humes 2008). Therefore, the formation of the Scottish Parliament is a reasonable starting point for exploring the Scottish LLL policy. In 2007, the newly elected Scottish Nationalist Party (SNP) published an updated LLL strategy *Skills for Scotland: A Lifelong Skills Strategy*. As the title implies, its focus was strongly on skills development, indicating a shift towards LLL as a means for economic growth. However, social justice remained high on the government agenda. Equal access and participation in skills and learning was seen as a means to tackling social exclusion, to ensure that 'those trapped by persistent disadvantage' benefited from continuous education (Scottish Government 2007a, p. 5).

LLL policies rest on the assumption that learning and obtaining qualifications lead to increased access to the labour market, which in turn provides a better standard of living and enhances social inclusion. However, the extent to which this applies equally to all, irrespective of earlier levels of education, is questionable. In this chapter we examine the perspectives of managers and government officials in relation to whether LLL provision is equitable and fair to all. We also examine the extent to which learning is accessible and available to all, or whether certain groups, such as younger people, are specifically targeted using particular measures.

In the next section, we provide a brief overview of the literature in relation to social capital development and social inclusion. We also give a brief account of the educational context in Scotland with a particular emphasis on social justice issues, followed by an overview of the LLL policy. Much policy discourse has emphasized the role of LLL in promoting social inclusion. To explore this claim Levitas (2005) developed a model of three types of discourses on social inclusion: redistributionist discourse (RED), moral underclass discourse (MUD) and social integrationist discourse (SID). We use this model to examine the policy in relation to the data gathered. We then outline our methodology, followed by the findings from the interviews.

The following questions are explored in this chapter:

- What are the main target groups for LLL policy measures and what do they reveal about social justice principles?
- To what extent are the different types of discourses developed by Levitas evident in Scottish LLL policy?

REVIEW OF LITERATURE AND POLICY

Social Inclusion, Exclusion and Policy Discourses

Although there is no single pan-European definition for either social inclusion or social exclusion, these concepts frequently occur in European social policy. In her analysis of social inclusion in the United Kingdom (UK), Levitas (2005) identifies three ideal-type discourses, which lead to different solutions being proposed for social inclusion. According to the redistribution discourse (RED), poverty, defined as household earnings below 60 per cent of the median household income, is considered to be a key factor in social inclusion. RED advocates redistribution of wealth, including, in the case of LLL, the redistribution of the opportunity to engage in learning to enhance employment opportunities and to increase income. This discourse advocates the state's role in enhancing opportunities through progressive taxation and social transfers. In terms of education, RED could lead to the redistribution of the opportunity to access education such as that witnessed in the widening access measures. The moral underclass discourse (MUD) differs from RED by holding individuals responsible for their values that prevent them from engaging in society effectively. According to MUD, individuals have to accept the social norms of the majority in order to be socially included. In terms of LLL, the individual would be expected to take responsibility for engaging in learning, with the assumption that such personal initiative would inculcate norms and values conducive to social inclusion. Finally, the social integrationist discourse (SID) considers integration with the labour market as the key to social inclusion. This discourse would advocate a vital role for LLL in terms of upskilling, reskilling and in providing essential skills for entering the labour market. None of these discourses are necessarily dominant, although they may appear, from time to time, in both LLL and social policy. In addition, these discourses are not necessarily mutually exclusive. For example, the redistribution of the opportunity to participate in learning may lead to an individual achieving a qualification enabling entry to the labour market.

Lifelong Learning

Field claims that the concept of LLL originates from the beginning of the twentieth century, although international events from the 1930s to the 1950s marginalized the importance of adult learners. The concept re-emerged in the 1970s and was fostered by organizations such as the United Nations Educational, Scientific and Cultural Organization (UNESCO) in humanistic terms and by the Organisation for Economic Co-operation and Development (OECD) in human capital terms (Field 2006). The European Union (EU) adopted the concept of lifelong education in the 1990s, with LLL forming the basis of the Lisbon strategy. Initially, this strategy emphasized the importance of human capital at the expense of social and personal development. Nevertheless, the final version of the strategy acknowledges all three aspects of lifelong education, although there is some disagreement over the extent to which human capital remains dominant within the EU policy (Holford et al. 2008).

The term 'lifelong learning' has been called into question by many in the academic community. Johnston describes the term as 'broad, imprecise and elastic' (Johnston 2000, cited in Rogers 2006, p. 125) and Boshier considers LLL to be 'human resource development in drag' (Boshier 1998, p. 4). However, Field (2006) argues that LLL as a term carries value for a number of reasons, one of them being that society has changed and that the way people nowadays have to acquire new skills and capacities throughout life is captured by the term. Field also notes that there is a danger of LLL becoming a mechanism for exclusion and social control and that the discourse of individual agency places a duty on learners to take responsibility for their own learning. Mills argues that what can be discerned is a marketization of learning with a focus on employability (Mills 2002). He suggests that the focus on the individual as a learner does not recognize learning as a social activity and reduces learning to what is useful for work. In addition, the individual agency discourse does not recognize the role of social class in attitudes to learning. The discourse fails to take into account that those already possessing high qualifications are the most likely to engage with learning, and that those with no qualifications are the least likely to do so. Hudson (2006) explored the relationship between inequality and the knowledge economy, claiming that the development of the knowledge economy is likely to increase inequality as changes in employment patterns lead to differences in income. This is due to the development of a highly skilled workforce serving the knowledge economy, a decline in skilled trades and an increase in unskilled labour. These concerns are also voiced by Hake in relation to the stress for autonomous learners who felt that the developing knowledge economy would 'sharpen the divisions between the socially included and excluded' (Hake 1999, p. 67).

Education and LLL in Scotland

School attendance is compulsory until the age of 16 and consists of a primary sector for pupils aged five to 12, and a secondary sector with lower secondary finishing at 16 and upper secondary continuing up to the age of 18. Formal post-compulsory education is provided by colleges or other institutions of higher education. There are 41 colleges, 19 universities, one dental school, two art colleges and one academy of music and drama in Scotland. Scottish universities offer International Standard Classification of Education (ISCED) level 5 and 6 courses at undergraduate and postgraduate level. Colleges include provision from basic courses at ISCED level 2 to undergraduate and some postgraduate courses at ISCED level 5. Non-formal learning is provided through Community Learning and Development Departments (CLDs) and voluntary organizations, mainly at ISCED levels 2 and 3. Private training providers also play an important role in delivering non-formal learning.

Although Scotland is committed to an education system that promotes equity and fairness for all, a recent OECD report on Scottish schools (OECD 2007) reveals that pupils from low socio-economic backgrounds were at a considerable disadvantage in relation to educational outcomes. The report states that within schools organizational and cultural factors, as well as the impact of social area deprivation, contributes to the educational disadvantage often overlooked in the context of performance across all pupils (OECD 2007, p. 141). The educational disadvantages are obscured by the fact that Scottish pupils do relatively well in the Programme for International Student Assessment (PISA) evaluations and a high proportion of school leavers go on to further or higher education. Eurostat figures (Eurostat 2010) show that the UK, including Scotland, has a relatively high proportion of 18–24-year-olds completing only lower secondary level education (Figure 4.1), indicating that a proportion of the population leaves school with low qualifications. The impact of social class on Scottish school leavers can also be seen in official statistics which state that nearly 10 per cent of school leavers from the most deprived decile leave with low to no qualifications, compared to 0.5 per cent from the least deprived decile (Scottish Government 2010b).

Social background continues to affect learners even in post-compulsory education. Students from the least deprived backgrounds (first quintile) are most likely to continue their studies in the most prestigious institutions, whilst those from the most deprived backgrounds (fifth quintile) are more likely to study in colleges or new universities (Figure 4.2).

Higher educational levels enable benefits such as access to better jobs and better salaries. In addition, adults with higher qualifications are far more likely to continue learning than adults with low to no qualifications, as can be seen from the 2005 *National Adult Learning Survey (NALS) Scotland Report* (Ormston et al. 2007). The report shows that 85 per cent

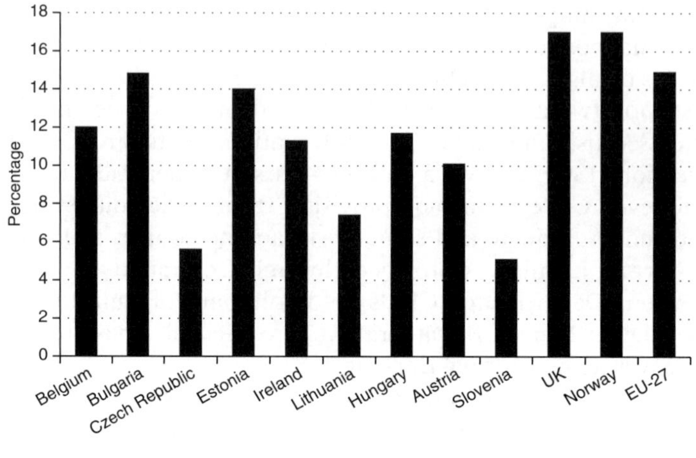

Source: Eurostat, 2010.

Figure 4.1 Proportion of population of 18–24-year-olds with at most lower secondary level (ISCED 1, 2, 3c), LLL2010 countries, 2008

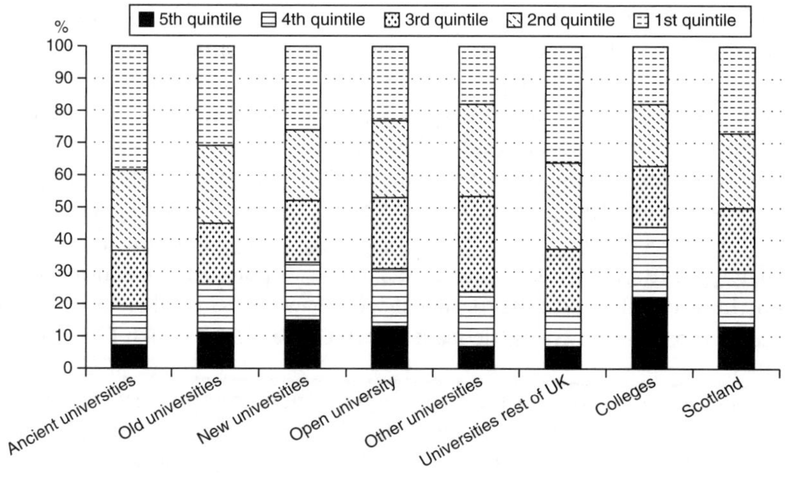

Note: 5th quintile is most deprived; 1st quintile is least deprived.

Source: Scottish Funding Council (2010).

Figure 4.2 Scottish-domiciled higher education students at UK universities and Scottish colleges in percentages by deprivation quintile, 2008–2009

Table 4.1 Percentages of highest qualification groups reporting different types of learning

	SVQ level 5 %	SVQ level 4 %	SVQ level 3 %	SVQ level 2 %	SVQ level 1 %	No qualifications %	Total %
Any learning	100	98	85	88	73	28	83
Taught learning	85	83	67	67	55	23	67
Self-directed learning	94	88	63	74	50	15	67
Vocational learning	98	92	73	83	59	22	74
Non-vocational learning	27	35	27	34	26	10	29

Source: Ormston, et al., 2005.

of those with Scottish Vocational Qualifications (SVQ) level 5 (ISCED level 5) had taken part in taught learning in the three years preceding the survey. Only 23 per cent of those with no qualifications (ISCED level 1–2) had taken part in taught learning (Table 4.1).

These statistics suggest that early educational disadvantage leads to fewer opportunities for further education, irrespective of whether this is following post-compulsory education or later in life. Policy-makers have been committed to work towards eradicating such disadvantage, which can be seen from the first LLL strategy produced by the Labour-led Scottish Executive. The strategy, published in 2003 and entitled *Life through Learning: Learning through Life* (Scottish Executive 2003), stated that 'lifelong learning policy in Scotland is about personal fulfilment and enterprise; employability and adaptability; active citizenship and social inclusion' (Scottish Executive 2003, p. 7). One of the five aims of the strategy was to enable opportunities for learning irrespective of an individual's background or current circumstances. One of the policy measures was the introduction of the Education Maintenance Allowance (EMA) for 16–19-year-olds, with the aim of encouraging young people from poorer households to stay in education. EMA provides an example of a measure of the RED discourse; however, EMA only covers non-advanced education and is not available to older disadvantaged learners. Measures such as enabling wider participation in higher education with additional support for students from low socio-economic backgrounds provide another example of measures in relation to RED.

In May 2007, the Scottish Nationalist Party minority administration was elected and one of its first actions was to produce an economic strategy and a skills development strategy for the current and future workforce in Scotland. SNP stressed the importance of the links between the economy and LLL. The national performance framework, *Scotland Performs* (Scottish Government 2007b), provides a set of 45 indicators; those relating to education stress the links with the labour market. *Skills for Scotland: A Lifelong Skills Strategy* (Scottish Government 2007a) strongly emphasizes developing skills and vocational education and provides a Scottish response to the UK-wide Leitch Review of skills (HM Treasury 2006). The Scottish skills strategy does not mention the previous LLL strategy, but it could be argued that its aims are similar to the earlier document with its stress on learners taking responsibility for their own development:

> We need successful learners, confident individuals, responsible citizens and effective contributors to build a smarter Scotland . . . We need individuals to take more ownership of their own development and a system that identifies people who need extra support and ensures that support is there. We need a system for developing skills that meets everybody's needs and aspirations and equips individuals with skills that are flexible enough to meet the needs of today and respond to the demands of tomorrow. (Scottish Government 2007a, p. 2)

Adult literacy and numeracy was causing concern in the 1990s, leading to the publication of the 2001 report on *Adult Literacy and Numeracy in Scotland* (Scottish Executive 2001). Additional funding was channelled through local authorities to CLDs and colleges to offer classes that would improve adult literacy and numeracy. The SNP administration retained the strategy on adult literacy but, arguably, put greater stress on its importance for the economy. Reduction of the number of people with low literacy and numeracy levels is one of the National Indicators in the Scotland Performs Framework on the grounds that 'if an individual has a weakness in these skills, they are less likely to make an effective contribution to Scotland's economy' (http://scotland.gov.uk/About/scotPerforms). Although the LLL skills strategy recognizes the benefits of learning for the individual, the main emphasis seems to be on enhancing an individual's contribution to the economy, showing the dominance of the social integration discourse (SID). The strategy also retained the focus on the 'More Choices More Chances' programme for 16–19-year-olds not in education, employment or training (Scottish Executive 2006). A key issue for this group is the link between unemployment and a lack of 'positive' destination when leaving school.

The focus of the skill strategy changed from post-compulsory education to inclusion of compulsory education, potentially placing greater emphasis on young people. This change has been noticeable over the years in further education colleges, which increasingly cater for learners under 16 years of age (Figure 4.3). We explored the increased focus on youth below in the

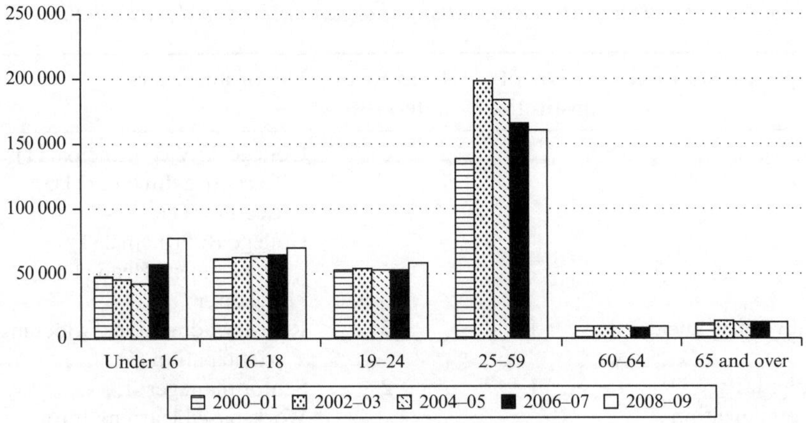

Source: SFC, Infact database.

Figure 4.3 Participation by age in further education colleges, 2001–2009 (headcount)

interviews with the managers. In October 2010, the government published a 'refreshed' skill strategy, referring to skills rather than LLL and having, arguably, an even stronger focus on skills development and measures directed at the unemployed, especially the youngest age group (Scottish Government 2010a).

In summary, although during the last decade the policy has included social and personal development as part of its objectives, stress on human capital development and utilization continues to dominate policy. In addition, there has been an increased focus on younger learners, especially those from disadvantaged backgrounds. This is explored further in the findings reported after the methodology section.

METHODOLOGY: INTERVIEWS WITH MANAGERS OF LLL

Managers from six institutions and organizations participated in the interviews. In addition, one government official from Learning Connections and one senior official from the Scottish Funding Council took part (Table 4.2).

The interviews took place during late spring and summer 2009, at a time when the recession was beginning to have an impact but before the austerity cuts of 2010. Individual interviews were carried out with all of

Table 4.2 Overview of institutions and organizations and participants

Type of institution	No. of institutions	Total no. of interviews	No. of interviews
Colleges	2	6	College A: Vice-principal (1); Executive directors (1); Lecturer (1) College B: Principal (1); Department Head (1); Lecturer (1)
University: ancient	1	5	Registry/admissions/ widening participation (5)
Voluntary organization	1	2	Senior manager: 1; Work-based learning tutor organiser (1).
Local Authority Community and Learning Development (CLD)	2	3	CLD 1 semi-rural: Manager: 1 CLD 2 urban: Senior manager: 1; Manager of adult learning: 1
Government official; non-governmental public body (NDPB) official	–	2	Senior manager, Learning Connections (LC) (1) Senior manager, Scottish Funding Council (SFC) (1)
Total	6	18	

these participants, except the interview with the two urban CLD managers who were interviewed together. In each case, the interview lasted from 45 minutes to 1.5 hours.

LLL POLICY AND PRACTICE

This section draws on interviews with senior policy-makers of LLL in Scotland, one from Learning Connections (LC) and the other representing the Scottish Funding Council. LC is situated in the Directorate of Lifelong Learning within the Department of Education and Lifelong Learning. LC has two strands of work organized into two teams: Adult Literacies and Community Learning and Development (CLD). The latter includes both learning and social development for individuals and groups within their own communities. The Scottish Funding Council (SFC) is a non-departmental public body (NDPB) responsible for allocating government funding to higher and further education. In relation to definitions used with LLL2010 ('Towards a Lifelong Learning Society in Europe: The Contribution of the Education System'; see Chapter 1 in this volume), the Funding Council is responsible for funding formal education; LC supports non-formal community education but does not administer funding. A range of topics was covered in the interviews. In this section we focus on orientation of the new LLL strategy, target groups, transition and funding issues.

Views of the Skills Strategy

According to the Funding Council interview, the main differences between the earlier LLL strategy and the later skills strategy was that the latter had a clearer purpose, avoided overlaps and ensured that everyone involved were 'pulling in the same sort of direction'. The main emphasis of the new skills strategy was on the development and utilization of human capital:

> Interviewer: 'Would you say that it had a distinct focus on human capital?'
> Respondent: 'I hadn't thought of it in those terms actually . . . I'm not quite sure how I can answer that because the other bit of it which is new is the skills utilization bit. So it's not just the building of the human capital. It's the use of the human capital. But it is . . . I mean that's what it, that's the two bits of it really I think.'

The government official from LC was critical as he felt this focus failed to acknowledge learning in the wider sense: 'However, it [the skills strategy] doesn't for me acknowledge learning in life outside a learning institution and I think that is a massive gap . . . skills equals the chance to be employed' (Learning Connections interviewee).

These positions suggest tensions between different government departments in relation to the development of LLL provision. In terms of these two individuals, one sees human capital development as the most important aspect of LLL, whereas the other emphasizes a much wider definition of LLL encompassing all aspects of learning, a view more prevalent in the first LLL strategy. However, with the Funding Council having a budget of £1.7 billion for colleges and universities, the Council's interpretation of the skills strategy is likely to be highly influential. LC has no responsibility to fund learning provision in the two areas it is responsible for, community learning and development together with adult literacy and numeracy, as these are funded by local authorities. However, some of the adult literacy and numeracy programmes are provided by colleges and, in these cases, may be funded by the Funding Council.

Target Groups for Lifelong Learning Initiatives

In terms of target groups, the Funding Council manager was in no doubt that the focus had to be on young people:

> I don't think you can escape the school leaver, no the pre school leaver . . . You have got the dreadful [term], you used to call them the NEET [not in education, employment or training] group, you know, the MC[2], but all of them, and so many of them and some of them care-leavers of course, are a particularly vulnerable sub set.[1](Scottish Funding Council interviewee)

As can be seen from the speech made by the then Education Secretary Fiona Hyslop, this view clearly reflected government thinking: 'As we enter recession, young people are at disproportionate risk of becoming disengaged from education or training. Indeed, previous economic downturns, such as the 1980s and early 1990s, created a lost generation of young people who were not able to reach their full potential' (Fiona Hyslop, News release, 26 March 2009).

The Funding Council interviewee also noted that funding for older people was problematic for two reasons. Firstly, because of the potentially limited economic return on investment; and secondly, because training opportunities related to work were funded by the UK government:

> even at that stage, you are almost in sticking plaster . . . that sounds a terribly cynical thing [to say] but all the experience suggests that it requires a huge amount of effort to help people into a genuinely sustainable future, where they have an economic contribution to make and that requires enormous political will to make an investment that is probably disproportionate to the actual economic return. But saying that, it is right for society to do that and actually economically in the end it's right because if you look at the whole cost it's probably less than what you are actually paying out. The trouble is the whole cost is often done in Westminster with the payment of benefits, or it's the prison service to be blunt or whatever. (Scottish Funding Council interviewee)

The changing composition of the FE college population demonstrates the impact of funding regimes. The governmental policy to retain the EMA for younger people has encouraged many to remain in education. Support for older students is available through widening access initiatives, providing opportunities for access to higher education, though mainly via the college setting. In the view of the Funding Council manager, colleges were highly successful in providing for non-traditional students. The manager also felt that college followed by transition to university provided a good route for these students:

> Widening access in the college sector, if you look at their intake from the most deprived areas, it is proportionally high in comparison with the population of those areas. So on the whole, two stars to the college sector, not translating into higher education, and there are weaknesses in that articulation from college to university . . . it can sound patronising, but I think it's a really good route into universities for [non-traditional students]. (Scottish Funding Council interviewee)

However, the route for these students often involved less prestigious universities. In the view of the Funding Council manager, widening participation to the whole higher education sector had not been particularly successful:

> The Funding Council is charged with widening participation, and we have our 'Learning for All' initiative and are supportive of the widening access forums and the articulation hubs and all this sort of thing. So actually it falls on us significantly and our new corporate plan, like our previous one, has a focus on attempts at widening participation. But if one is brutally honest we haven't done very well so far, in times of rising student numbers, we got rising numbers from non-traditional backgrounds, but not rising at a faster rate than the whole shebang . . . and I suspect that we will really struggle this time round. We haven't cracked it, they haven't cracked it in England; it's really difficult. (Scottish Funding Council interviewee)

Access for mature students to elite higher education is thus limited and the Funding Council did not see ensuring a fairer admission regime as its responsibility.

Debates on the Funding of Higher Education

Universities and colleges in Scotland are currently under great financial pressures. As of January 2011, the government was considering graduate contributions or levy of student fees as means for creating a sustainable future for higher education in Scotland (http://www.scotland.gov.uk/Publications/2010/12/15125728/11). It is evident that the government wants to retain the state funding of higher education, in contrast to the English changes towards reductions in state funding and increased reliance on student fees and private investment. However, the government publication makes clear that, as in England, students will be expected to a pay for a large proportion of higher education through graduate contributions. The paper stresses that those who are able to benefit from higher education should not be barred from it due to lack of money. The paper notes the lack of success in the area of widening mature students' access to higher education (HE) and argues for the need to concentrate more on school pupils, in order to raise the aspirations of those young people who would not necessarily consider higher education as an option. Thus it seems that provision for less advantaged students within the formal education sector is focusing primarily on young people and access to higher education for mature students from low socio-economic backgrounds is at greater risk. By January 2013 Scottish students still do not have to pay fees; however, students from elsewhere in the United Kingdom are required to pay fees. These fees are set by each individual HE institution up to a maximum of £9000.

In summary, current policy measures strongly emphasize the importance of developing and utilizing human capital. Arguably, recent policies are moving away from LLL as a means of achieving personal development and social inclusion, and are focusing on young people as more salvageable. The human capital orientation is clearly reflected in the views of the Funding Council manager who also expressed concerns about the future of social inclusion measures. Colleges are seen as the key to widening participation, and new universities as providing a route to degree qualifications for non-traditional students. In the section that follows, the institutional context of learning is examined through the lens of education managers.

Educational Managers

As shown above, current policy strongly emphasizes the skills agenda with a focus on human capital development. Recent measures within formal higher and further education include a considerable and possibly increasing stress on participation in education by young people. Ensuring effective education for younger people is clearly important, especially at times when youth unemployment is increasing. In 2011, 12.2 per cent of the 16–19-year-old population in Scotland was not in education, training or work. The figure has fluctuated over the years from 11.7 per cent in 2004 to 13.7 per cent in 2010 before going down in 2011 (Scottish Government 2012). The national indicator for measuring levels of severe literacy and numeracy among the working-age population shows that no progress has been made in reducing the numbers in this category, in spite of the aspiration of the LLL skills policy to '[promote] equality of opportunity . . . to recognize people's different needs, situations and goals and remove the barriers that limit what people can do and can be' (Scottish Government 2007a: Statement of Equality).

This section examines interview data from senior managers in educational institutions and organizations, focusing on perceived impacts on funding of LLL, target groups of LLL initiatives, views on the skills strategy and transitions between non-formal and formal education.

Funding of LLL Initiatives

As mentioned above, the recession is affecting funding for all aspects of LLL and formal education in universities and colleges is going to see less generous funding settlements. However, learning provided in the non-formal sector through Community Learning and Development (CLD) and voluntary organizations is arguably more precarious. In 2008, local authorities agreed to freeze the council tax[2] in return for a slightly larger block grant and the removal of ring-fencing of funds, meaning that services considered less important, especially during a recession, are likely to lose funding. According to one of the CLD managers, adult education was particularly vulnerable:

> we are particularly concerned that in the current climate it [adult learning] is quite vulnerable. So the climate we are working in is difficult. And I'm trying to get a sense of what's happening across the other authorities . . . I'm in the process of contacting other authorities to find out what they are doing. The picture isn't consistent across the country but it's not, it's not looking [good], I've just had somebody from Moray contact me and they said that they don't have an adult education team any more. (CLD 2 senior manager)

Another difficulty faced by providers of adult education is that competition for funding might affect some of them more than others. According to the same manager, work that they would normally do in the community was now being channelled through further education (FE) colleges:

> I just heard that . . . the FE colleges have actually been given [funding] . . . to take a role in communities . . . apparently they have been given a huge injection of money in order to address . . . the gap with the numbers of growing unemployed etc. So they've just been given a lot of money to try and address the extra demand for, and . . . you'd think too in a period like this [the recession], the demand for social services in education would actually be, well will be greater and therefore . . . services like ours should be at least maintained if not topped up. But what's happening is the opposite. (CLD 2 senior manager)

The funding cuts also had a seriously detrimental effect on the voluntary organization. Competing for limited funds from alternative sources was time-consuming and detracted from the organization's aim of providing high-quality learning. In the view of the senior manager, her organization met many of the government objectives in learning provision but also faced considerable difficulties:

> You would think with the current credit crunch our role should be expanded. Because we're working in the workplace, we're working with unemployed, with

> disadvantaged groups. You would think that our aims meet so closely with government objectives that we should be getting poured in with money. But the reverse is true in that the ring fencing single outcome agreement has hurt us. And the lottery is just not forthcoming with large grants. I mean we've applied for two big grants recently and not got them. (Voluntary organization, senior manager)

It is worth noting that the policy-maker from the Funding Council claimed that sustainable funding for the third sector was seriously problematic, 'an absolute nightmare'. The funding issue had been around for a long time and nobody had managed to come up with a model providing sustainable and long-term funding. He also noted 'that significant numbers of organizations are plainly constrained by the lack of coherent funding'. Clearly, issues around funding are problematic for all institutions and organizations but particularly difficult for those engaging with learners who are the hardest to reach.

Target Groups for Different Institutions and Organizations

The university in our study had a range of initiatives focusing on widening access to non-traditional students. However, its main objectives were to produce high-quality research and to attract high-achieving students. Initiatives to attract students from low socio-economic backgrounds had not been particularly successful. The benchmarks set by the UK government on widening participation showed that the university had only attracted 17 per cent of students from lower social classes, falling short of its benchmark of 21 per cent. In relation to intake of those from low-participation neighbourhoods, the benchmark was 11 per cent, with the institution only recruiting 8 per cent in 2007–08. Despite these benchmarks there seemed to be little will from the UK and Scottish governments to enforce attainment of benchmarks by adjusting funding mechanisms. The university was clearly an elite institution focusing on research and those of high ability, mostly from advantaged backgrounds. Colleges, in contrast, were relatively successful in including learners from less advantaged backgrounds and the Funding Council used financial levers to ensure that this practice continued. However, as can be seen in Figure 4.3, the increase in younger learners and a decrease in the number of those aged 25–49 studying at colleges suggest that the impact of measures intended to capture younger learners potentially comes at the expense of older learners.

In CLD, adult education was under threat as greater emphasis was put on the work with young people and early intervention. In the words of the manager: 'it's quite clear now that the agenda for us within this government is early intervention, it's work with young people, it's positive distances for young people and family learning' (CLD 2 senior manager).

Although working with communities and adults was the core to CLD work, it was less likely to be a key priority. The manager noted that there was still a commitment at the higher level to make a more inclusive Scotland; a commitment that did not translate into action on the ground: '[There are] national objectives . . . in terms of helping make a more inclusive Scotland and the council has got high level objectives which support that but there does not seem be anywhere underneath for that to happen' (CLD 2 senior manager).

Views on the Skills Strategy

The shift in the skills strategy had been noted by all educational managers in colleges as well as in non-formal education. As voiced by one of the college lecturers:

> There is a bigger emphasis coming through now for skills, the government appears to be aligning itself with the skills issues. I think gone are the days where you bring people in and just put them on a course for the sake of it. Now it is, do they have the skills to get work and is the education and training good enough to get a job and prosper. (Lecturer, College A)

A similar shift was also noted in the voluntary sector. The manager explained that course provision had changed in order to take available funding into account. Learner numbers had remained the same, but the courses taken and the location had changed:

> the actual numbers of students over five years is about stationary . . . And that's because funding for community learning has declined . . . whilst project funding in the workplace has increased . . . so there's been a decline in community learning and a growth in workplace education. (Voluntary organization manager)

The increased emphasis on skills may provide fewer opportunities, particularly for older learners with low qualifications, to re-engage with learning in a non-threatening setting. A survey carried out among adult returners (Weedon and Riddell 2011) shows that learners with no previous qualifications are more likely than others to cite personal reasons for learning and to value the social aspect of learning. They are also less likely to be in employment, but particularly positive about their learning experiences when they participated in a non-formal setting, as opposed to a college setting. For this group of learners, the shift towards skills and workplace learning may lead to fewer opportunities.

Transitions between Non-Formal and Formal Education

Non-formal education can offer a first stepping stone towards a more formal educational setting and, as can be seen from the brief account above, this setting has been much appreciated by those with low levels of qualifications. However, the links between the non-formal and formal settings were not considered to be working well by the community learning managers because of the lack of effective support:

> [one of the area offices] did some work with [the local college] on links with the community and work supporting people and then they followed it on to doing courses. And that was excellent but I'm not sure if it's still going or what. And so I think probably we need a more, some kind of more structured pathway. (CLD 2 senior manager)

Differences in the ways the two settings engaged with the learners were also noted by the voluntary organization manager who stressed the learner-centred teaching methods used by her organization: 'We . . . say "what do you want to learn and how do you want to learn it" . . . [Formal institutions] say "here are the courses, do you want to sign up"' (Voluntary organization, manager).

Overall, the views of the education managers reflect the shifting emphasis of the new skills strategy. Funding mechanisms have led to an increased emphasis on the skills and employability agenda in colleges and the non-formal setting. The targeting of young people leaves fewer opportunities for adult learners and the increase in workplace learning potentially disadvantages older learners currently not in employment.

CONCLUSION

We raised two questions at the beginning of this chapter. The first one considered social justice principles in relation to target groups for LLL policy interventions. The two strategies on LLL and the 2010 update include commitments to ensure that all, including the most marginalized, are supported in accessing and benefiting from learning. Arguably, the wider vision of learning encompassing all aspects of LLL and learning for social and personal development in the first strategy has shifted to a much stronger emphasis on skills development and learning for work in the two later documents. All three documents include a commitment to provide learning for all, also recognized by those interviewed. However, educational managers felt that practice was driven by funding mechanisms that favoured younger learners. Measures such as widening access to higher education for adult learners from disadvantaged socio-economic backgrounds were not having a strong impact, especially in relation to accessing the most prestigious universities.

A further difference between the first and the latter two policy documents is the manner in which these were monitored. The first strategy was evaluated according to six indicators. Two of these focused on 16–19-year-olds: the first aiming to reduce the numbers of those not in employment, education or training; the second focused on increasing support for families to allow this group of pupils to stay in education.

The remaining four focused on those already in the workforce. The first of these aimed to increase the proportion of graduates in the workforce; the second to reduce the number of those with no or only lower secondary qualifications in the workforce; the third aimed at reducing the number of 18–29-year-olds with qualifications of lower secondary level or below; and the final indicator aimed to increase the proportion of adults in employment undertaking training.

The later strategies are evaluated using the National Indicators, which are part of Scotland Performs (http://www.scotland.gov.uk/About/scot Performs/performance). Only three of these indicators relate to learning: one refers to positive outcomes for school leavers, a second to positive outcomes for graduates, and the third to a reduction in the number of working-age people with severe literacy and numeracy problems. Of these three, the only indicator that has seen an improvement is the one in relation to positive outcomes for school leavers. There has been no change in the other two indicators. Although the Scottish LLL policy reflects the aims and objectives of the EU policy, the indicators used by the Scottish government are not reflecting EU benchmarks (CEC 2011). The EU aim to reduce the number of early school leavers to 10 per cent shows some overlap with the Scottish indicator on positive outcomes for school leavers. However, there is limited overlap between the other two Scottish and EU benchmarks. There is no Scottish indicator for improvement of literacy among school pupils, for increasing the proportion of school leavers with upper secondary education or for increasing the number of graduates in mathematics, science and technology. It could therefore be argued that Scotland is focusing on Scottish issues, and foremost for this government is to create a sustainable and vibrant economy. Lifelong learning is viewed as essential to this aim in that it will contribute to a skilled workforce.

The previous discussion shows that young people are increasingly targeted in relation to LLL measures and that provision for adult learners, especially in the less formal setting, is most vulnerable to funding cuts. In addition, a growing emphasis on the workplace as a site of learning restricts this group's access to job training programmes. Although the

2007 skill strategy aims to provide for all, irrespective of background, the measures taken suggest that provision for older learners, who are generally more reluctant learners but who stand to gain if provided with learning in a nurturing environment, is most at risk. Thus, the social justice principle of 'provision for all, irrespective of background' is not being fully realised.

The second question aimed to examine the Scottish LLL policy discourse in relation to the ideal types of discourse developed by Levitas. The policy documents and the consultation paper on higher education show that the government wishes to retain a role in funding and managing learning. The government also notes the need to assist those who may be discouraged from learning because of economic or other circumstances. Such attitude provides evidence of the redistribution discourse, although the target groups for this redistribution are under consideration. The consultation paper on higher education suggests that widening access measures aimed at socio-economically disadvantaged adults have remained rather ineffective and that it may be more effective to focus redistribution measures on young people currently in school. The EMA, as already mentioned, is one such measure. In contrast to England, the EMA has been retained in Scotland. In addition, the view of the Funding Council official indicates that access to higher education may be focused on colleges and new universities rather than on elite higher education institutions for non-traditional students. RED is evident, but its main target is younger learners and there seems to be no evidence for MUD. In terms of the working-age adult population, it is SID that predominates. Scotland's people are described as its most valuable resource and it is the duty of all to participate in LLL across their lifespan in order to contribute to the economy. Participation in learning is assumed to lead to, or at least increase, an individual's potential to engage effectively in the labour market and to increase the wealth of Scotland. This particular discourse is criticized by Mills (2002), who argues that the focus on employability and learning for work limited the role of learning as a social activity. In highlighting the need to retain the social aspect of learning, Mills is reflecting the views of the learners in the survey carried out by Weedon and Riddell (2011). Although Levitas's three discourses were developed to examine social exclusion and inclusion, they provide a useful way of examining LLL policy as they highlight how LLL is increasingly seen as a way of promoting integration through skills development. Field (2006) argues that 'social inclusion and exclusion' has replaced the term 'poverty' and that LLL is now central to social inclusion and social exclusion:

> lifelong learning plays a central part in the processes of inclusion and exclusion . . . It is actively used by particular groups and individuals to advance their

> interests and underpin their claims, and it is becoming more significant as an external marker of whether or not an individual or community is likely to prove a worthwhile investment for the future. (Field 2006, p. 124)

However, one aspect not explored by Levitas's framework is the shift from government responsibility of dealing with poverty towards placing the emphasis on the individual's role. A strong element of that individual responsibility is that each individual is expected to ensure that they have sufficient skills to enter and remain in the labour market. This emphasis on agency and autonomous learners has been criticized by researchers such as Hake (1999), who argues that this might increase the division between those included and those excluded. Although it is too early to comment on the outcomes of the austerity measures, they point towards a more negative impact on adult provision in the informal sector, and on provision for older people compared to other learners. Clearly, in response to the question in the chapter title, 'Has lifelong learning policy and practice in Scotland promoted social inclusion?', it has to be said that some measures, such as retaining the EMA, promote social inclusion. However, the lack of funding for some areas of adult education and a reduction in funding for adult literacy and numeracy is not promoting social inclusion. The recession is leading to very difficult decisions for the government and all stakeholders. However, the increasingly ageing population evident in the 2011 Census (http://www.scotlandscensus.gov.uk/en/news/articles/census2011pop.html) suggests that investment in older learners may become more important, not least to maintain a skilled workforce. However, the broader benefits of learning should not be forgotten. This would suggest that policy measures for those most vulnerable should be protected and that funding should be made available to ensure access to quality learning for those that find it most difficult to engage with learning. This would help to prevent the divide increasing further between those with high levels of qualifications and access to further learning opportunities and those that have few or no qualifications and fewer opportunities for learning.

NOTES

1. MC^2 refers to the young people not in education, employment or training and comes from the policy document *More Choices More Chances* which aimed to get away from the term NEET.
2. Council tax is a local tax set by each authority to fund local services.

REFERENCES

Boshier, Roger (1998), 'Edgar Faure after 25 Years: Down but Not Out', in John Holford, Peter Jarvis and C. Griffin (eds), *International Perspectives on Lifelong Learning*, London: Kogan Page.

Bryce, Tom and Walter Humes (2008), 'An Introduction to Scottish Education, 3rd edn: Beyond Devolution', in Tom G.K. Bryce and Walter M. Hume (eds), *Scottish Education, Third Edition: Beyond Devolution*, Edinburgh: Edinburgh University Press.

Commission of the European Communities (CEC) (2011), *Progress towards the Common European Objectives in Education and Training: Indicators and Benchmarks 2010/2011*, Brussels: CEC.

Devine, Tom M. (1999), *The Scottish Nation: 1700–2000*, London: Allen Lane.

Eurostat (2010), *Europe in Figures: Eurostat Yearbook 2010*, Luxembourg: European Union.

Field, John (2006), *Lifelong Learning and the New Educational Order*, Stoke on Trent: Trentham Books.

Hake, Barry J. (1999), 'Lifelong Learning Policies in the European Union: Developments and Issues', *Compare*, **29** (1), 53–69.

HM Treasury (2006), *Prosperity for All in the Global Economy – World Class Skills (the Leitch Review)*, London: HM Treasury.

Holford, John, Sheila Riddell, Elisabet Weedon, Judith Litjens and Guy Hannan (2008), *Patterns of Lifelong Learning: Policy and Practice in an Expanding Europe*, Wien: Lit Verlag.

Hudson, John (2006), 'Inequality and the Knowledge Economy: Running to Stand Still?', *Social Policy and Society*, **5** (2), 207–222.

Levitas, Ruth (2005), *The Inclusive Society? Social Exclusion and New Labour*, 2nd edn, Basingstoke: Macmillan.

Mills, Vince (2002), 'Employability, Globalization and Lifelong Learning – a Scottish Perspective', *International Journal of Lifelong Education*, **21** (4), 347–356.

OECD (2007), *Quality and Equity of Schooling Scotland*, Paris: OECD.

Ormston, Rachel, Fiona Dobbie, Nicky Cleghorn with Anna Davidson (2007), *National Adult Learning Survey (NALS) Scotland Report*, Edinburgh: Scottish Executive.

Rogers, Alan (2006), 'Escaping the Slums or Changing the Slums? Lifelong Learning and Social Transformation', *International Journal of Lifelong Education*, **25** (2), 125–137.

Scott, Gill and Gerry Mooney (2005), 'Conclusion: Social Policy in Scotland: Imagining a Different Future?', in Gerry Mooney and Gill Scott (eds), *Exploring Social Policy in the 'New' Scotland*, Bristol: Policy Press.

Scottish Executive (2001), *Adult Literacy and Numeracy in Scotland*. Available at: http://www.scotland.gov.uk/Resource/Doc/158952/0043191.pdf.

Scottish Executive (2003), *Life through Learning: Learning Through Life*, Edinburgh: Scottish Executive.

Scottish Executive (2006), *More Choices, More Chances: A Strategy to Reduce the Proportion of Young People not in Education, Employment or Training*, Edinburgh: Scottish Executive.

Scottish Funding Council (2010), *Measures of Success*, Edinburgh, Scottish Funding Council.

Scottish Government (2007a), *Skills for Scotland: A Lifelong Skills Strategy*, Edinburgh: Scottish Government.
Scottish Government (2007b), *Scotland Performs*, Edinburgh: Scottish Government.
Scottish Government (2010a), *Skills for Scotland: Accelerating the Recovery and Increasing Sustainable Economic Growth*, Edinburgh: Scottish Government.
Scottish Government (2010b), *SQA Attainment and School Leaver Qualifications in Scotland, 2008–09*, Edinburgh: Scottish Government.
Scottish Government (2012), *Local Area Labour Markets in Scotland: Statistics from the Annual Population Survey 2011*, Edinburgh: Scottish Government.
Scottish Office (1998), *Opportunity Scotland: A Paper on Lifelong Learning*, Edinburgh: HMSO.
Weedon, Elisabet and Sheila Riddell (2011), 'Social Justice, Inclusion and Lifelong Learning in Scotland: The Experiences of Adult Learners', in Sue Jackson (ed.), *Lifelong Learning and Social Justice: Communities, Work and Identities in a Globalized World*, Leicester: NIACE.

5. 'Renaissance' without enlightenment: New Labour's 'Learning Age' 1997–2010

John Holford and Thushari Welikala

> Technical education, though it must be an integral part of our educational system, is not an alternative to non-vocational education. The latter is a universal need; but whether the former is necessary depends on the character of the employment. (Ministry of Reconstruction 1919, p. 174)

> There is perhaps no branch of our vast educational system which should more attract . . . the aid and encouragement of the State than adult education . . . This ranks in my opinion far above science and technical instruction (Winston Churchill 1953 [1954], p. 173)

> Education is the best economic policy we have. (Tony Blair 1998, quoted in DfEE 1998, p. 9)

In the British general elections of 1997 and 2001, the Labour Party under Tony Blair's leadership achieved its largest parliamentary majorities ever – greater even than in 1945, the year generally seen as Labour's highest tide. Labour's victory in 2005 was also substantial, providing a working majority for two prime ministers: first Blair and then, after his resignation in June 2007, Gordon Brown. As a result, Labour had its longest ever period in government (1997–2010).[1] The Labour government of 1945–1950 was responsible for the bulk of Britain's welfare state. For many of its supporters, 1997 was also a moment of soaring hope, bringing an end to 18 years of increasingly neoliberal Conservative rule. Hopes were certainly high among those committed to adult education. In the event, vaulting ambitions went unrealized; achievements in lifelong learning were modest. In respect of adult and lifelong education, the government abandoned values which had previously been central to Labour thinking, and accepted policies and practices which were little different from those espoused by the previous Conservative administration. This chapter summarizes what the Labour government achieved, and explains how – at a very early stage – the ambitions of those who sought to ensure that citizenship, democracy and liberal education were key themes of a learning society were defeated.[2]

In Opposition, Labour had developed expansive rhetoric on the value of education: Blair famously announced in 1996 that his three top priorities for government would be 'education, education and education'. David Blunkett, Labour's education spokesman from 1994 and Secretary of State for Education and Employment throughout Blair's first government (1997–2001), had personal experience of adult education, having studied part-time to qualify for university. Prior to becoming a member of parliament, he had for 13 years been a further education lecturer. He had also been a notably radical leader of Sheffield's City Council, and was closely associated with a number of thoughtful and educationally influential Labour intellectuals such as Michael Barratt Brown, the founding principal of Northern College, Bob Fryer his successor, and Bernard Crick, Professor of Politics at Sheffield University (Taylor 2004; Fryer 2010). Fryer comments that, as the principal of a college established for working-class adult education, the new government – and Blunkett's appointment in particular – brought 'much relief and high expectations' (Fryer 2004, p. 69).

LABOUR'S RECORD

From a similar perspective, however, the actual record of the Blair governments on lifelong learning has been described as 'pretty dismal': 'As so often in the history of the British Labour Party . . . optimism, ambition and high hopes were all but dashed in the unfolding period of government' (Taylor 2009, p. 75). 'Overall', Taylor concluded, the Labour government's 'essential ideological drive, and the consequent practice' in lifelong learning policy was:

> geared to human capital perspectives, within a particular version of meritocratic expansion and marketised welfarism. Far from being a transformative agenda for social democratic change, [the government's] lifelong learning policy thus aims for the incorporation of an increasing number of learners into the existing free-market culture; thereby, it is argued, producing beneficial, wider social effects – reducing alienation, improving social cohesion and so on. (Taylor 2009, p. 75)

Taylor based his view on a consideration of three important policy areas: skills, widening participation, and civic or social purpose education. On the first, skills, he suggested that the Labour record was 'long on rhetoric and vision but rather short on delivery or even viable structures for delivery'. Citing 2004 research, he thought learning opportunities for employees had increased, but the actual increases in participation in training, whether on or off the job, had been 'slight' (Taylor 2009, p. 75).

If anything, the position deteriorated, despite frenetic policy development and rhetoric associated with the Leitch review (Leitch 2006; see below): participation in job-related education and training remained pretty constant (between 28.2 per cent and 28.7 per cent) between 2001 and 2006, but then declined quite sharply (to 27.2 per cent in 2007 and 25.6 per cent by 2010) (Aldridge and Tuckett 2011, p. 13). (It is, of course, probably fair to ascribe some of the post-2006 deterioration to recession, rather than to educational or 'skills' policies – though on the same argument, the business cycle should take some of the credit for earlier levels of participation.)

On the second policy area, widening participation in adult learning, Taylor's verdict was: 'the same mixture of rhetorical advocacy, some achievement but essentially modest progress'. In relation to higher education, the numbers participating had increased rapidly, but 'very largely through greater participation from the higher socio-economic groups' (Taylor 2009, p. 74). This verdict seems fair. By and large, different researchers have reached similar conclusions, using various data sources and methodologies (Bolton 2010; Stevenson and Lang 2010). The National Audit Office, drawing on a range of data, concluded:

> Participation in higher education in England . . . of young people (17–30 year olds) has fluctuated from 39.2 per cent in 1999–2000 to a peak of 42.5 per cent in 2005–06. It currently stands at 39.8 per cent in 2006–07 . . . Not all relevant groups in society are represented . . . in proportion to their representation in the population as a whole . . . Women are better represented than men and those from non-white ethnic groups are better represented than white people. Social class remains a strong determinant of higher education participation with the proportion from lower socio-economic backgrounds having remained largely static over the past five years. White people from lower socio-economic backgrounds, both men and women, are the most under-represented group. (National Audit Office 2008, p. 11)

There are, however, some indications that, so far as the social class mix of higher education is concerned, the situation began to improve in the government's later years: for instance, a 2009 study of 'Full-Time Young Participation by Socio-Economic Class' (in higher education) concluded:

> over the period 2002/03 to 2007/08, full-time young participation for the top three socio-economic classes fell from 45.2% to 41.2%, while for the bottom four socio-economic classes this has increased from 18.1% to 21.0%. The socio-economic class gap between these two participation rates has consequently narrowed by 7.0 percentage points. (DBIS 2009, p. 1)[3]

Higher education, though a dominating element of public expenditure on education for adults, is not typically regarded as lifelong learning or adult education. Taylor found Labour's record on adult participation in learning even more disappointing, and it is hard to disagree. According to the National Institute of Adult Continuing Education (NIACE), the proportion of adults 'currently' participating in learning in 2002 (23 per cent) was the same as it had been in 1996 (i.e., in the last year of the previous Conservative government), though there had been a slight increase (from 17 to 19 per cent) in the proportion who reported they had participated over the 'last three years'. By the end of the Labour government in 2010, the situation remained mixed: current participation had actually fallen back to 21 per cent (two percentage points below the figure for the year before Labour came to power), although 22 per cent now reported participation during the 'last three years' (Aldridge and Tuckett 2011, p. 11).

Disaggregating overall participation in adult learning, some more positive trends emerge. Between 1996 and 2010, the gender gap not only narrowed but reversed: participation (current and during the 'last three years') among men fell from 43 per cent to 41 per cent while among women it rose from 38 per cent to 44 per cent (Aldridge and Tuckett 2011, p. 14). In terms of social class, drawing on the 2004 NIACE report, Taylor commented that between 1996 and 2004, the learning divide had actually widened, with participation rates falling for all except the higher socio-economic groups. By 2010 the record was better; there had been a significant increase in participation among the lower socio-economic classes (although to levels still well below those among the more affluent groups: see Table 5.1).

Three other features of Labour policy on widening participation in lifelong learning emerge from Taylor's review. The 'overwhelming concentration' was on younger learners, particularly those aged 18–21 (and, in higher education, on full-time students living away from home); the 'large majority of widening participation learners in higher education' studied at 'lower-status' universities and colleges; and the government's 'overriding

Table 5.1 Current and recent participation in adult learning 1996–2010 by social class

	1996	1999	2002	2005	2008	2010
Total sample	40	40	42	42	38	43
Social Class AB	53	58	60	56	51	56
Social Class C1	52	51	54	51	46	51
Social Class C2	33	36	37	40	33	37
Social Class DE	26	24	25	26	26	30

Note: The figures relate to the UK as a whole.

Source: Aldridge and Tuckett (2011, p. 17).

purpose in widening participation policy' was 'to enhance the skills levels in the workforce through vocational training'. He comments, in relation to the last point, that: 'This perspective omits any recognition that there is a need to enable more and different learners to have access to a liberal and critical education; nor does it allow any collective or community notion of education – it assumes an entirely individualistic (and "marketised") frame of reference' (Taylor 2009, p. 75).

This limitation also applied to Taylor's third policy area, civic or social purpose education. This has 'a long history' in British (and perhaps particularly English) adult education, 'from the "Mansbridgean" [see below] ethos of education for personal enlightenment and development, to socialist and other radical – often community orientated – provision'. Labour gave 'rhetorical recognition in at least some government papers and policy statements' to 'the importance of "liberal adult education" and associated themes', thought Taylor, and 'a few' programmes (such as the Neighbourhood Renewal Initiative) had 'a real base in community development perspectives' (Taylor 2009, p. 75). Unfortunately, these were 'very much the exceptions. Exhortations to even modest and moderate liberal perspectives are rare, *sotto voce*, and very largely rhetorical: . . . through the period [1997–2010] this element has been consistently sidelined' (Taylor 2009, p. 75).

In sum, the Labour governments of 1997–2010 brought rhetoric aplenty, especially on the need for lifelong learning; and a good deal of new policy too. They also brought many new mechanisms and structures for delivery: funding agencies and systems, targets and the like. The cult of institutional 'modernization' sometimes seemed tantamount to a 'permanent revolution' of institutions. There were also broader policy priorities which had a significant impact on the policy and practice environment, and on the language of debate, in lifelong learning. For example, a Social Exclusion Unit, established in 1997 (and lasting until 2006), promoted social inclusion across policy areas; and 'citizenship' – often 'active citizenship' – became an important priority in certain areas (Millner 2008). These made discussion more civilized. But if one turns from rhetoric, language and policy debate to delivery and impact, the record disappoints; and in particular it disappoints from perspectives informed by traditions of social democracy and liberal adult education.

ENGLISH ADULT EDUCATION: ENLIGHTENED TRADITIONS

How were the high hopes dashed? Explanations can be found at a number of levels. It is true, of course, as Rizvi and Lingard argue, that a 'particular social imaginary of globalization, namely neoliberalism, has underpinned educational policy shifts around the world over the last two decades' (Rizvi and Lingard 2010, p. 184). Even while hopes remained high, Boshier saw the entire policy notion of lifelong learning, which emerged in the mid-1990s, as 'human resource development in drag' (Boshier 1998, p. 4) – in contrast to the broader, more humane, concept of 'lifelong education' found in the Faure Report (Faure et al. 1972). Field (2006) presents a more nuanced account of the emergence and growth of lifelong learning as a concept; but intensifying globalization and the need to respond to rapid economic change sit at its heart. Different kinds of explanation are to be found in political sociology. Michels (1916) would hardly have been surprised that Labour leaders supported the *status quo*. From similar positions, Miliband (1973), Coates (1975, 2000, 2003) and Panitch (1976) developed a socialist critique of the British Labour Party as never more than 'a party of modest social reform in a capitalist system within whose confines it is ever more firmly and by now irrevocably rooted' (Miliband 1973, p. 376). On this basis, as capitalism evolves the Labour Party adapts, but always in a 'functional' and supportive way.

The specific form this took in the mid-1990s was rebranding as 'New Labour' after Tony Blair became party leader in 1994. Initially for electoral reasons (Labour had lost four successive general elections, and won no convincing majority since 1966), 'New' Labour firmly distanced itself from 'old' Labour. But as Blair put it in his May 1997 victory speech, this was not merely an electoral strategy: 'we ran for office as New Labour, we will govern as New Labour'. This 'New Labour':

> emphatically rejected the idea that the state should use old-style statist social democratic methods to regulate the market. Instead economic policy had to empower and liberalise the market, not restrict or limit it; the free market, now more than ever, was the means to secure Labour's reformist ends. . . . New Labour's economic policy fell within the shadow cast by Thatcherism, [which had] . . . prioritised . . . the market in the governance of the economy; privatised and commercialised much of the state sector; marketised a great deal of state-centred activity; boosted financial capital over manufacturing; built a flexible labour market . . . asserted legislative control over trade unions; [and] . . . thereby helped further root pro-market, anti-corporatist, anti- (political) trade unionist, anti-public enterprise attitudes into British political life. (Heffernan 2011, p. 165)

From such perspectives, we need hardly be surprised by the docile and market-oriented character of the Labour government's *policies* on lifelong learning; by its acceptance of the general international trend, rather than the development of any 'democratic socialist' alternatives – though disappointment that the policies were so ineffective, even in their own terms, must remain. Yet though we may not be surprised by the Labour government's record on lifelong learning, it remains a dismal one; and we should perhaps reflect briefly on the *distance* that Labour thinking on lifelong learning had travelled. Policy development for a learning society in England could have drawn on rich traditions in further and higher education, and perhaps especially in adult education. During the twentieth century, these traditions had been particularly strongly entwined with the politics, ideology and thinking of the labour movement, though they had also been widely endorsed on the political right.

The relationship between Britain's labour movement and education was close, arguably symbiotic, especially through the first half of the twentieth century. The Workers' Educational Association (WEA) – formed in 1903, just three years after the Labour Party – thought of itself as 'a partnership of labour and learning' (Cole 1953; Jackson n.d.). Many of the most influential twentieth-century Labour politicians studied or taught in WEA classes. When the 1945–1951 Labour government enacted much of Britain's 'welfare state', one cabinet member was WEA vice-president, and 14 other ministers (including the Chancellor of the Exchequer), were WEA tutors, former tutors or executive committee members. Fifty-six members of parliament were active WEA tutors or students (Stocks 1953, p. 143). This proved the WEA's highest tide; but it was by no means the end of its influence. Two of the Labour Party's commanding post-war figures (Hugh Gaitskell, leader 1957–1962, and Neil Kinnock, leader 1983–1992) had taught extensively for the WEA before entering parliament. Of Tony Blair's first cabinet, Robin Cook (Foreign Secretary) and Ron Davies (Secretary of State for Wales) had each been full-time WEA tutors for four years (Cook 2007; Davies 2011), while Gordon Brown's Labour Party website stated that his 'first job after graduating [from university] was as a lecturer for the Workers [*sic*] Educational Association' (identical text was used on his personal website in 2012) (Brown n.d., 2012, 2013).

The WEA's origins were as an association of students in university 'tutorial classes' for adults, acting as a pressure group on universities and government to devote resources to the education of working class adults and children. What its founder – Albert Mansbridge – and early members valued above all was liberal education. This was 'true education': it 'directly induces thought, which permeates the whole of society'. In contrast, most education provided to the working classes promoted only 'unthinking absorption of facts', putting people 'at the mercy of the opinion of the hour, however irresponsible', and leaving them susceptible to 'flights of mere rhetoric' (Mansbridge 1944, p. 1) Liberal education for adults was thus vital, not only for the individual but also for the common good – for democracy and, in today's terminology, social cohesion.

Partly because of the WEA's close association with the labour movement, the necessity of liberal adult education became an accepted tenet of policy in England from the First World War to the 1980s. In 1918 'adult education' was defined in legislation as 'subjects of general as distinct from vocational education' (SR&O 1919, p. 31), and over the years the term developed connotations of 'specifically liberal education' (Jarvis 2004, p. 44). Churchill's assertion of the importance of liberal adult education, quoted in part at the start of this chapter, shows that it was valued on the Right as well as the Left for its political role – sustaining national identity and values – as well as for what it offered to individuals. Liberal adult education had a strong ethos of service; its leading intellectuals had been strongly influenced by the Oxford idealism of T.H. Green and Benjamin Jowett, which 'elevate[d] public service, whether to government, empire, church or community, as the highest ethical and professional imperative' (Goldman 2000, p. 299; see also Steele 1994). Churchill's paean continued:

> I have no doubt myself that a man or woman earnestly seeking in grown-up life to be guided to wide and suggestive knowledge in its largest and most uplifted sphere will make the best of all the pupils in this age of clatter and buzz, of gape and gloat. The appetite of adults to be shown the foundations and processes of thought will never be denied by a British Administration cherishing the continuity of our Island life. (Churchill 1953 [1954], p. 173)

Until the late 1980s all governments endorsed and funded liberal adult education. The rationale is to be found in a paragraph from the classic report of the Ministry of Reconstruction's Adult Education Committee – a paragraph quoted as 'even more relevant today' by the Russell Committee (Department of Education and Science 1973, p. 4):

> We do not wish to underrate the value of increased technical efficiency or the desirability of increasing productivity; but we believe that a short-sighted insistence upon these things will defeat its object. We wish to emphasise the necessity for a great development of non-technical studies, partly because we think that it would assist the growth of a truer conception of technical education, but more especially because it seems to us vital to provide the fullest opportunities for personal development and for the realisation of a higher standard of citizenship. Too great an emphasis has been laid on material considerations and too little regard paid to other aspects of life. (Ministry of Reconstruction 1919, p. 153; Department of Education and Science 1973, p. 4)

Later government reports endorsed the importance of liberal adult education. 'The whole range of evidence' considered by the Ashby Committee (which included Prime Minister Winston Churchill's comments, quoted above), was 'unanimous' that liberal adult education was 'still essential'

(Ministry of Education 1954, p. 33): 'adult education students represent in relation to the community at large a social and intellectual asset the loss of which would be deplorable; and we put on record our hope that their genuine educational needs will never go unfulfilled through lack of funds' (Ministry of Education 1954, p. 34).

The character of liberal adult education, and the depth of its connections with Labour thinking, can be seen in two rather different post-war contributions. The first is from the Marxist literary and cultural critic, Raymond Williams. After 15 years teaching WEA classes, he wrote an *Open Letter to WEA Tutors* in the early 1960s (Williams, n.d.). The Association, he wrote, 'has always stood for the principle that ordinary people should be highly educated, as an end justifying itself and not simply as a means to power'. Many people at that time thought that as secondary schools expanded, the need for adult education would decline: 'the exceptional mind in the poor family' would be 'spotted young, and . . . given a real chance'. But, wrote Williams:

> this was never at the heart of the W.E.A.'s purpose. Of course the exceptional minds must get their chance, but what about everyone else? Are they simply to be treated as rejects? The W.E.A. stands for an educated democracy, not for a newly mobile and more varied elite. (Williams n.d.)

The second contribution is from the Russell Report (DES 1973). Despite a background of expanding opportunities both at school and in higher education, which led them to expect demand for adult education to increase, they foresaw 'large areas of unmet need, especially among those little touched by the present provision of adult education'. The 'urgency of these unmet needs' was likely to 'sharpen'. In addition: 'The attainment of an acceptable quality of life for all and the development of a free, democratic society require that these demands and needs be met' (DES 1973, p. 3).

The quarter century between the Russell Report and the election of the first Blair government was, of course, largely filled by 18 years of (increasingly neoliberal) Conservative government (and Labour defeat). Liberal adult education, not to mention Russell's conception of 'unmet needs' and the social priorities they implied, came under considerable criticism. The chief agents of the assault lay, of course, on the political Right – notably Keith Joseph, Secretary of State for Education 1981–1986, often seen as one of the most powerful ideologues of neoliberal thinking in Britain, who saw 'education as central to Britain's economic plight', was strongly critical of what he called Britain's 'anti-enterprise culture', and 'relished the idea of challenging it at its heart' (Harrison 2004 [2011]). But there were also critics on the Labour side: liberal adult education was by no means the main target of (Labour Prime Minister) James Callaghan's Ruskin College speech (1976 [2001]), for instance; but he may well have regarded some collateral damage to it as acceptable.

THE 'LEARNING REVOLUTION' BETRAYED

The early months of the new Labour government saw a flexing of adult education's intellectual and political muscles. Within three weeks of taking office as the new Secretary of State for Education and Employment in May 1997, David Blunkett announced he was forming 'a new Advisory Group on Adult and Continuing Education', to be chaired by Professor Bob Fryer.[4] Fryer had long experience of and commitment to liberal adult education. The committee was to 'give us [i.e., ministers] advice as we prepare a White Paper later in the year' (DfEE 1997a). Two months later its membership and terms of reference were announced. Members included two WEA officials, representatives of the BBC and the Trades Union Congress, six distinguished academics with deep knowledge of liberal or social purpose adult education, as well as representatives of further education, local education authorities and business.[5] The group would 'have a crucial role in advising the Government as we prepare to publish our Lifelong Learning White Paper in the Autumn [of 1997]' (DfEE 1997b). Its terms of reference were:

> To advise the Secretary of State on matters concerning adult learning as required, and with particular reference to extending the inclusion in lifelong and work-based learning to those groups and individuals whose increased participation will contribute to improvements in employability, regeneration, capacity building, economic efficiency, social cohesion, independent living and citizenship generally; and to make proposals in respect of:
>
> - the preparation of a Government White Paper on Lifelong Learning;
> - the strengthening of family and community learning;
> - the contribution of further and higher education to adult learning, having regard to relevant recommendations of the Kennedy Committee on widening participation in further education and the national Committee of Inquiry into the future of higher education [two other government committees which had recently reported];
> - initiatives for development in the context of the University for Industry; and
> - the development of learning towns and cities. (NAGCELL 1997, p. 92)

The Advisory Group issued its first report in November 1997, recommending 'a culture of lifelong learning for all', and specifically:

- a 'strategic framework for the promotion of lifelong learning', to replace existing fragmented and incomplete arrangements;
- a 'fundamental change in attitude', based on a national publicity campaign;
- 'widening and deepening participation and achievement in learning', involving modified funding arrangements and 'systematic outreach and development work';
- 'increased emphasis' on 'the home, community and workplace as key places of learning': this would make use of 'individual learning accounts' and the University for Industry;
- simplification throughout the system, making it easier for learners to take up and continue lifelong learning;
- better 'partnership and greater collaboration' at regional and local levels;
- improved information and advice, incorporating a 'national learning helpline';
- better information to enable target-setting for specific economic sectors;
- effective harnessing of 'new technologies of communication and information', including broadcasting;
- over the following four years or so, 'step-by-step to increase the total volume of funding deployed to support lifelong learning by Government, other public authorities, employers, charitable bodies and individuals themselves' (NAGCELL 1997, pp. 3–10).

This was a substantial agenda for change (though by no means beyond criticism: see for example Jarvis et al. 1998, for a critique by other adult educators); and a short summary does not do justice to its creativity and imagination. Quite quickly, however, significant opposition mobilized within government. The white paper was delayed. Then, the *Times Educational Supplement* (*TES*) reported (6 February 1998):

> The delayed White Paper on lifelong learning has been finally torn up, leaving Government plans to support education from cradle to grave in tatters. David Blunkett . . . still backs the lifelong learning proposals. However, the Treasury wants no more open-ended cash commitments before its comprehensive spending review. Mr Blunkett promised the White Paper last May, as the centre-piece of the new Government's commitment to lifelong learning. But publication was postponed at least nine times as civil servants and task groups struggled to make coherent a wide range of commitments to education and industry . . .
>
> A range of promises which would have meant extra cash for further and adult education have now been pushed down the political agenda. The White Paper – which was to have been published next Tuesday – will be replaced by a series of

> consultation documents, concentrating on the Government's flagship proposals affecting industry. (Nash 1998a)

The same article claimed that the white paper had been 'at the printers . . . when the plug was pulled' – though the following week a junior minister denied this (Howells 1998). The same issue alleged the 'torn up' white paper would have included 'a series of initiatives including a special fund to support adult education and a commitment to expand further and higher education by 500 000 places by the year 2002' (Nash 1998b).

The following week, the *TES* returned to the topic, reporting:

> Tony Blair and Gordon Brown jointly decided to scrap the lifelong learning White Paper and go back to the drawing board, senior Government sources confirmed this week. [Blair and Brown] . . . were appalled by a lack of coherence, the lack of rigour when dealing with standards to be set and the open-ended costs of further education expansion.
>
> One senior official told *The TES*: 'The decision was taken by No 10 and No 11 [Downing Street: the official residences of the Prime Minister and Chancellor of the Exchequer respectively]. They wanted a paper of some coherence and were not getting it. Also, 500 000 more further education students would add hundreds of millions of pounds to costs next year.'
>
> [T]he work done on the paper was completely out of line with Mr Blair's own views, another senior source on a Government taskforce said. 'He (Mr Blair) said there was too much about trying to change the culture of training in Britain and not enough about standards and exams.' (Nash and Crequer 1998)[6]

Two weeks later, the government published a green – or 'white-turned-green' (Thomson and Tysome 1998) – paper, entitled *The Learning Age* (Cm 3790 1998). According to the *TES*, this was the same title as the white paper would have carried. (But the subtitles differed. The white paper, it was reported, would have been subtitled 'Towards a Learning Revolution for the 21st Century' (Nash 1998b); the green paper's subtitle was 'A Renaissance for a New Britain'.) Bob Fryer, chairman of NAGCELL, later commented that although *The Learning Age* had been:

> launched only after some internal Government wrangling . . . [it] contained what became a deservedly celebrated foreword by Blunkett. The foreword constituted a lyrical and visionary case for the vital contribution of lifelong learning to employment skills, personal and spiritual development, national prosperity, aesthetic life and creativity, civilised values and a sense of community. (Fryer 2004, p. 96)

But in Britain a 'white paper' is a statement of government policy, typically leading directly to new legislation. A 'green paper', on the other hand, is a consultation document – an opportunity for the government to make proposals, and receive feedback, but involving few if any commitments. One newspaper reported 'critics' as saying that the consultation exercise 'could mean that it takes the government another year to produce any real and significant policy creating a learning society' (Thomson and Tysome 1998). This prediction proved optimistic: the white paper eventually appeared in June 1999, 16 months after the first paper had been shelved – and under the title *Learning to Succeed: A New Framework for Post-16 Learning* (DfEE 1999).

'RENAISSANCE' STILLBORN

Though its contents may not have matched its 'lyrical and visionary' foreword, or the high hopes invested in the NAGCELL exercise, *The Learning Age* green paper did contain positive ideas, a good deal of rhetoric, and some proposals. Its aim was to develop 'a culture of learning' which would bring benefits for individuals, businesses, communities and the nation. Government would 'help create a framework of opportunities for people to learn' but not to 'force anyone to learn – individuals must take that responsibility themselves'. 'Together we can create a culture of self-improvement and a love of learning.' The chief specific commitments were to establish a 'University for Industry' (UfI) to 'connect those who want to learn with ways of doing so . . . as the hub of a brand new learning network', and to encourage 'individuals, employers and the state' to share the costs of learning. (The state would aim, through its funding, 'to widen participation and increase attainment at all levels where this will benefit society most'; the main specific mechanism was to be 'Individual Learning Accounts'[7] linked 'in the medium term' to tax incentives or other public funds.) There were also a number of less costly proposals. 'Learning Direct – a new national telephone helpline' would offer advice on 'how to get started and on courses to suit individual needs'. Partnership arrangements and other mechanisms would encourage learning 'at home and in the community', and 'open up access' to further and higher education. Use of 'new broadcasting and other technologies' would be strengthened. Various 'internal quality assurance systems, combined with regular independent inspections against a consistent framework of standards' would raise quality and achievement and reduce student drop-out rates. And there would be a qualifications and credit framework targeted at adults.

Yet it is clear in retrospect that *The Learning Age* represented a defeat for the innovative educational thinking of Fryer's National Advisory Group for Continuing Education and Lifelong Learning (NAGCELL). Its specific commitments were precisely, and only, those already announced by Blunkett in his speech *appointing* NAGCELL:

> [W]e will shortly be launching a National Learning Line. This will provide an early impetus towards our aim of a learning society. [T]he University for Industry, will engage a range of public and private partners to harness the contribution of modern technology . . . to open up opportunities to help adults realise their potential . . . [W]e must help people invest in their own skills . . . Individual Learning Accounts . . . will offer a million people the opportunity . . . to experience learning, in some cases for the first time since they left school. We will contribute £150 to each account to support those who make a small contribution themselves. We will also encourage employers to contribute to their employees' accounts. (DfEE 1997a)

Indeed, Blunkett and his adult educational band had been forced to retreat to commitments already made before the general election. Labour's 1997 manifesto, *New Labour: Because Britain Deserves Better*, had endorsed lifelong learning, though in a strongly vocational vein, with none of Blunkett's more 'lyrical and visionary' elements: 'We must learn throughout life, to retain employment through new and improved skills. We will promote adult learning both at work and in the critical sector of further education' (Labour Party 1997). Its only specific commitments were to individual learning accounts and the University for Industry:

> Employers have the primary responsibility for training their workforces in job-related skills. But individuals should be given the power to invest in training. We will invest public money for training in Individual Learning Accounts which individuals – for example women returning to the labour force – can then use to gain the skills they want. We will kickstart the programme for up to a million people, using £150 million . . . which could be better used [i.e. reallocating existing funding] and which would provide a contribution of £150, alongside individuals making small investments of their own. Employers will be encouraged to make voluntary contributions to these funds. . . .
>
> Our new University for Industry . . . will bring government, industry and education together to create a new resource whose remit will be to use new technology to enhance skills and education. The University for Industry will be a public/private partnership, commissioning software and developing the links to extend lifelong learning. (Labour Party 1997)

In short, *The Learning Age* represented a defeat for the creative policy thinking developed by the NAGCELL, and a retreat to the agenda developed by Labour in Opposition.

FROM 'INTIMACY OF CONNECTION' TO 'STRENGTHENING EMPLOYER VOICE'

The principal specific proposals in *The Learning Age* can, therefore, be traced back to the Labour Party's election manifesto, rather than to the more expansive thinking of the NAGCELL group. The traditions of community and citizenship learning, of collective learning, and of liberal adult education, had been substantially abandoned. NIACE's commentary reflected this disappointment:

> Whilst the [*Learning Age*] paper explores welcome practical steps to be taken to raise standards of achievement, and to revitalise Britain's skills, it has little to say in detail about how learning that fosters citizenship, or respects and celebrates cultural diversity can be developed . . . [In particular, it had] almost nothing to say on the different challenges facing the country in meeting the learning aspirations of people living in its inner cities, or its rural communities, although these will significantly affect the delivery of UfI; it has little to say about the contribution to be made to the achievement of the vision by Britain's black communities; or about the challenges facing people with learning difficulties in securing an adult curriculum that will support them in exercising their rights and duties as citizens in an informed way. It does not say enough about the learning needs of older people. (NIACE 1998)

David Blunkett's foreword to *The Learning Age* had captured the 'intimacy of the connection between creativity, learning, social movements and economic regeneration in his celebration of Victorian working people's ingenuity in using learning to create new social forms', but no policy proposals had been developed which would allow 'that intimacy to be renewed' (NIACE 1998). In particular, 'much more' was needed 'to foster active citizenship': 'The Green Paper concentrates on individual aspiration at the expense of what we learn together. It gives too little priority to the important role voluntary organisations can play in the evolution of a learning society' (NIACE 1998).

By its nature, NIACE works with government. It prefers making things just a little better (or just a little less bad) to complete exclusion from policy circles. Its reservations were, therefore, less than strident, and hedged with positives. But regrettably, *The Learning Age* was as good as it ever got for non-vocational adult learning.[8] The white paper, *Learning to Succeed* (DfEE 1999), NIACE thought 'understated' the challenge:

> Successive governments' understandable concern with measures relating to the skills needs of the economy has weakened a range of other dimensions of lifelong learning of the sort highlighted in the Secretary of State's introduction to *The Learning Age*. For more than a decade central Government has encouraged

> Local Education Authorities to . . . reallocate money to schools . . . [and] cut back on investment in community based adult learning . . . The result has been that for many pensioners, and others whose learning aspirations relate to personal development and cultural enrichment there has been a marked diminution in curriculum offer . . . . (NIACE 1999)

As the Labour government matured, so its vision for adult learning became further fixated by the 'imaginary' of global competitiveness. Adult learning policy – indeed, arguably all education policy – was dominated by the Leitch Review of Skills, appointed in 2004 and issuing its final report *Prosperity for All in the Global Economy – World Class Skills* (Leitch Review of Skills 2006) two years later. Lord Leitch, formerly Chief Executive of Zurich Financial Services, recommended 'the UK commit to becoming a world leader in skills by 2020, benchmarked against the upper quartile of the OECD [Organisation for Economic Co-operation and Development]'. This implied a 'focus on economically valuable skills' to 'provide real returns . . . in the labour market for individuals and employers', and 'strengthening the voice of employers' (Leitch 2006, pp. 3–4, 138). As NIACE pointed out, this might help individuals whose career aspirations 'are aligned totally with . . . their employer . . .. For those who have bigger or broader ambitions, things may be harder' (NIACE 2006).

A different kind of critique – perhaps politically more barbed – might have pointed to parallels between *The Learning Age* and two documents issued in the sunset days of the previous Conservative government. *Lifetime Learning – A Consultation Document* was issued in December 1995 (DfEE 1995); *A Framework for a Learning Society* (DfEE 1996) six months later. Their content shows some uncanny resemblances to *The Learning Age*. There were proposals to strengthen coordination in 'investing in the training and development of employees'. Proposals for 'gaining the commitment of individuals to return to and continue learning' included enlisting the support of broadcasters, working with banks to encourage 'career development loans', keeping tax relief and benefit rules 'under review' in order to encourage learning, and 'individual training (or learning) accounts' – though it found 'little support from the financial institutions' for ILAs and it preferred schemes 'run by employers for their own employees'. 'Developing an effective and high-quality infrastructure of information, advice and guidance' would include 'examining the scope for introducing a helpline service'. 'Improving access to learning' should involve encouragement to colleges to deliver courses 'where people live or work' and in 'partnerships with community and voluntary organisations and with employers'. Proposals to give 'people of all ages the opportunity to acquire the basic skills on which to build further learning' focussed on literacy and numeracy in schools, 'family literacy' and 'basic skills training for unemployed adults'. There would be measures to develop 'effective partnerships nationally and locally' – between government, educational providers, employers, trade unions, voluntary organizations and others. These, the document concluded, would contribute to 'establishing a society in which learning throughout life becomes a way of life. The Government has taken many initiatives . . . [b]ut *responsibility is shared* . . . [with] employers, individuals, providers and many others' (DfEE 1996 [1998]; emphasis in original).

In most respects, therefore, the Conservative vision of lifelong learning, at least as configured in the mid-1990s, shared the same features as Labour's post-1997 vision. There would be a national culture of lifelong learning, with responsibility (and costs) shared between individuals, employers and government. There would be measures to encourage individuals to commit themselves to continuing to learn – including financial and tax incentives. Better information and guidance, improved access, better basic skills provision, local partnerships, all formed part of both Labour and Conservative policy lexicons.

We suggested above – from the perspective of social and political theory – that we should not be surprised at the Labour government's acceptance of general international trends on lifelong learning, or at its failure to develop 'democratic socialist' alternatives. In fact, as we have seen, adult educators did attempt to develop and deploy an alternative perspective – hardly in the language of democratic socialism, but at the same time clearly distanced from neoliberalism. Those who worked on this were deeply rooted in the politics, ideology and thinking of the labour movement, and drew on rich national traditions of democratic citizenship in adult and lifelong education – yet also innovative thinkers, engaged with contemporary theoretical and policy debates. The evidence shows, however, that this alternative was decisively marginalized in the government's first two years, supplanted by a set of policies which was, in its fundamentals, uncontroversial across the political spectrum.

CONCLUSION

At first sight this story appears to contradict the view that 'national context: institutional, political, social, ideological' shapes how international (and specifically European Union) policies are configured in particular countries (Holford et al. 2008, p. 132). The family – genealogical – resemblances are very apparent between, for instance, the European Commission's white papers *Competitiveness, Employment, Growth* (CEC 1994) and *Teaching and Learning: Towards the Learning Society* (CEC 1995), the British

Conservative government's white paper *Competitiveness: Forging Ahead* (DTI 1995) and its *Lifetime Learning – A Consultation Document* (DfEE 1995), and the Labour government's white paper *Learning to Succeed* (DfEE 1999). All reflect the 'imaginary' (Rizvi and Lingard 2010) of neo-liberal globalization, and the role of competitiveness, flexibility and skills in an effective response.

Yet 'national context: institutional, political, social, ideological' is about much more than educational institutions, politics and ideology. Over its period in government, Taylor argues, 'New' Labour 'embraced enthusiastically the capitalist culture, the drive to individualism and the supposed need to indulge gross inequality' (Taylor 2009, p. 77). Under Blair, Labour's traditional language of 'class and social change' was supplanted by inclusion and exclusion, the individual rather than the collective, and the permanence of markets. For example, 'widening' and 'increasing' participation in higher education and lifelong learning were 'deliberately elided' (Taylor 2009, p. 77).

From this perspective, the 'national context' which international policy thinking on lifelong learning encountered in England was shaped principally by core agendas of the economy and electoral politics; the scope for sector-specific (or perhaps, given adult education's marginality, we should say subsector-specific) actors was highly circumscribed. Perhaps they had not realized how much the policy game had changed. Ball and Exley (2010) argue that a 'redistribution of policy influence within education policy-making towards informal policy networks' and a 'concomitant marginalisation of traditional "partners" – local authorities, teaching unions and the civil service, and academia – began during the 1980s' with connections between 'right-wing think tanks . . . such as the Institute for Economic Affairs (IEA), the Hillgate Group and the Centre for Policy Studies (CPS)' and the Thatcher government. Under New Labour – in many respects a highly centralized regime – 'the role and significance of Prime Ministerial advisers' led to a 'proliferation of think tank policy networks' (p. 152). 'In some respects,' they suggest, 'think tanks fill a vacuum of ideas created by the depletion or displacement of older policy orthodoxies – both neoliberal and welfarist' (p. 166).

Four months after its election victory, Tony Blair began his speech to the Labour Party's annual conference in light-hearted mood:

> As for Government, well, it beats the hell out of Opposition. They really do say 'Yes, Prime Minister.'[9] You have to learn a whole new language. They're not in the habit of calling anything a good idea, which given the last 18 years [of Conservative governments] is hardly surprising. When they describe a proposal as 'ambitious,' or, even worse, 'interesting,' what they really mean is they think it was a stupid idea, dreamed up at the last minute for the manifesto. When

> they describe it as 'challenging,' they mean there's not a hope in hell of making it work. And when they say of a policy 'that it really is quite a brave proposal Prime Minister,' it means they've got the doctor outside waiting to sign the certificates and they've just applied for a transfer to a senior job administering one of our few remaining dependent territories. (Blair 1997)

The irony is that, even as he spoke, a group of adult educators were working on ambitious ideas for building a learning society. Perhaps their proposals were too 'ambitious' and 'brave'; certainly they would have been 'challenging'. Unfortunately, they never got to first base: Blair himself, and his inner circle, had already appropriated the civil service lexicon. When adult educators played the policy game – attempting to colour an emerging discourse of lifelong learning with some democratic citizenship and liberal education gloss – they proved enthusiastic amateurs pitched against professionals: the civil servants fresh from 18 years of Thatcherism, fresh-faced prime-ministerial advisors, think-tankies and policy-networkers, all playing by new rules and destined for New Labour's premier league.

NOTES

1. Properly speaking, there were four Labour governments during this period: under Tony Blair (1997–2001, 2001–2005 and 2005–2007), and under Gordon Brown (2007–2010). In this chapter, however, unless otherwise specified, the term 'Labour government' refers collectively to all four.
2. This chapter focuses on England. Relationships between the countries of the United Kingdom are complex, and changed over this period. England is very much the largest country: a population of 52.2m in 2010 (84 per cent of the UK total of 62.3m); Scotland's was 5.2m, Wales's 3.0m, and Northern Ireland's 1.8m (ONS 2011). Until 1999 education in Scotland, Northern Ireland and Wales fell under the Scottish, Northern Ireland and Welsh Offices of the UK government, which were responsible to the UK parliament. In 1999 new legislatures and administrations were created in Scotland, Northern Ireland and Wales, to which responsibility for education was devolved. The UK parliament did not devolve its powers over education in England, which were the responsibility of the Department for Education and Employment (DfEE: this was renamed the Department for Education and Skills, DfES, in 2001). On taking office in 2007, Gordon Brown divided education in England between two government departments, broadly speaking responsible for children and adults, respectively: the Department for Children, Schools and Families (DCSF) and the Department of Innovation, Universities and Skills (DIUS). In 2009 the latter was amalgamated with the Department for Business, Enterprise and Regulatory Reform to form a new Department for Business, Innovation and Skills (BIS or DBIS).
3. There are frequent references to the weakness of data on social class and participation. This particular report, for instance, comments that as its 'measure draws from a number of data sources and therefore contains a number of weaknesses, it should be interpreted carefully' (DBIS 2009, p. 1).
4. The group, sometimes referred to as the Fryer Committee, was also known by its initials, NAGCELL (National Advisory Group on Continuing Education and Lifelong Learning).

5. For NAGCELL membership, which changed a little, see DfEE (1997b), NAGCELL (1997, 1999).
6. Elsewhere, the same issue of the *TES* reported that David Blunkett 'is understood to have fought to save the proposals' (Nash et al. 1998).
7. On Individual Learning Accounts, see Smith and Spurling (1995) and Schuetze (2007). The House of Commons Committee of Public Accounts (2003, p. 5) reported: 'The Government introduced Individual Learning Accounts in England in September 2000, to widen participation in learning and to help overcome financial barriers faced by individuals. Accounts were to be available to everyone, including the self-employed, and were to be used to help pay for learning of the learner's choice . . . [T]he Government was keen to target people with particular learning or skill needs . . . The scheme was successful in attracting over one million people back into learning. However, in November 2001, a fortnight after announcing the planned suspension of the scheme with effect from December, the Government withdrew it following allegations of fraud and abuse. Total expenditure is likely to exceed £290 million against a budget of £199 million. The scale of fraud and abuse could amount to £97 million, including £67 million fraud.'
8. A consultation paper, and then a white paper, on 'informal adult learning' were issued under Gordon Brown's administration. Their language was similar to *The Learning Age* a decade earlier. 'Our country enjoys a rich and diverse history of adult education . . . This consultation . . . will lead to a new vision for informal adult learning for the 21st century' (DIUS 2008, pp. 2–3). The resulting white paper, *The Learning Revolution* (the discarded subtitle of *The Learning Age*), asserted learning was important 'for its own intrinsic value'; it called for 'a culture which values informal adult learning in all its forms, with a wide range of organisations promoting it' (DIUS 2009, pp. 4–5). Unfortunately this statement appeared too late to have a significant effect. The government's emphasis on adult vocational education had 'led some to suggest' that it did not value informal adult education. 'Nothing could be further from the truth' (DIUS 2008, p. 2). However, within a 'spending on adult learning' (including vocational) of £4.8bn (DIUS 2008, p. 2), it had 'ring-fenced £210m for informal adult learning' (DIUS 2009, p. 10).
9. This is an allusion to the popular BBC television comedy series, *Yes, Minister* (broadcast 1980–84) and *Yes, Prime Minister* (1986–87). 'A benchmark for quietly civilised yet scalpel-sharp political satire', these were 'based on a very simple observation: that for all its claims towards democracy, the British political system is largely run by unelected civil servants who run Machiavellian rings around their supposedly superior masters' (Brooke n.d.). See also http://www.bbc.co.uk/comedy/yesminister/ and http://www.bbc.co.uk/comedy/yesprimeminister/.

REFERENCES

Aldridge, Fiona and Alan Tuckett (2011), *Tough Times for Adult Learners: The NIACE Survey on Adult Participation in Learning 2011*, Leicester: NIACE.

Ball, Stephen J. and Sonia Exley (2010), 'Making Policy with "Good Ideas": Policy Networks and the "Intellectuals" of New Labour', *Journal of Education Policy*, **25** (2), 151–169.

Blair, Tony (1997), 'Leader's Speech to Labour Party Conference, Brighton, 30 September'. Available at: http://www.britishpoliticalspeech.org/speech-archive.htm?q=&speaker=2&party=&searchRangeFrom=1997&searchRangeTo=1997 (accessed 17 January 2013).

Bolton, Paul (2010), 'Higher Education and Social Class', London: House of Commons Library Standard Note SN/SG/620. Available at: http://www.parliament.uk/briefing-papers/SN00620 (accessed 9 April 2012).

Boshier, Roger (1998), 'Edgar Faure after 25 Years: Down but Not Out', in John Holford, Peter Jarvis and Colin Griffin (eds), *International Perspectives on Lifelong Learning*, London: Kogan Page, pp. 1–20.

Brooke, Michael (n.d.), *Yes Minister* (1980–84), BFI Screenonline. Available at: http://www.screenonline.org.uk/tv/id/509969/ (accessed 22 April 2012).

Brown, Gordon (n.d), 'Archive: Gordon Brown, Prime Minister, The Leader of the Labour Party'. Available at: http://www2.labour.org.uk/biography (accessed 17 January 2013).

Brown, Gordon (2012), 'Biography'. Available at: http://gordonandsarahbrown.com/gordon-brown/the-biography/life-on-campus; http://www2.labour.org.uk/biography (accessed 12 April 2012).

Brown, Gordon (2013), 'Gordon Brown MP Kirkcaldy & Cowdenbeath Biography'. Available at http://gordonbrownmp.org/biography/ (accessed 17 January 2013).

Callaghan, James (1976 [2001]), 'Towards a National Debate', speech at Ruskin College, Oxford, 18 October. Full text reprinted in the *Guardian*, 15 October 2001. Available at: http://education.guardian.co.uk/thegreatdebate/story/0,9860,574645,00.html (accessed 9 April 2012).

Churchill, Winston S. (1953 [1954]), 'Letter to Sir Vincent Tewson', in *Report of Proceedings at the 85th Annual Trades Union Congress*, London: TUC, pp. 173–174. Reprinted in Ministry of Education (1954), *The Organisation and Finance of Adult Education in England and Wales*, Report of the Committee appointed by the Minister of Education in June 1953, London: HMSO, pp. 66–67.

Coates, David (1975), *The Labour Party and the Struggle for Socialism*, Cambridge: Cambridge University Press.

Coates, David (2000), 'The Character of New Labour', in David Coates and Peter Lawler (eds), *New Labour in Power*, Manchester: Manchester University Press, pp. 1–16.

Coates, David (ed.) (2003), *Paving the Third Way: The Critique of Parliamentary Socialism*, London: Merlin Press.

Cole, G.D.H. (1953), 'Adult Education and Workers' Education. Some Notes for the Attention of the Consultative Meeting of Experts at La Brévière . . .', Mimeo, Paris: UNESCO. Available at: http://unesdoc.unesco.org/images/0017/001791/179195eb.pdf (accessed 11 April 2012).

Commission of the European Communities (CEC) (1994), *Competitiveness, Employment, Growth*, Luxembourg: Office of Official Publications of the European Communities.

Commission of the European Communities (CEC) (1995), *Teaching and Learning: Towards the Learning Society*, Luxembourg: Office of Official Publications of the European Communities.

Cook, Robin (2007), 'Cook, Rt Hon. Robert Finlayson (Rt Hon. Robin)', in *Who Was Who, A and C Black, 1920–2008*, online edn, Oxford: Oxford University Press, December. Available at: http://www.ukwhoswho.com/view/article/oupww/whowaswho/U11722 (accessed 12 April 2012).

Davies, Ron (2011), 'Davies, Rt Hon. Ronald', in *Who's Who 2012*, London: A & C Black, 2012, online edn, Oxford: Oxford University Press, November. Available at: http://www.ukwhoswho.com/view/article/oupww/whoswho/U13122 (accessed 12 April 2012).

Department for Business Innovation and Skills (DBIS) (2009), 'Full-time Young Participation by Socio-Economic Class (FYPSEC) 2009 Update', London: Department for Business, Innovation and Skills. Available at: http://www.bis.

gov.uk/assets/biscore/corporate/migratedd/publications/f/fypsec-paper-2009.pdf (accessed 9 April 2012).

Department for Education and Employment (DfEE) (1995), *Lifetime Learning – A Consultation Document*.

Department for Education and Employment (DfEE) (1996 [1998]), 'James Paice Publishes a *Framework for a Learning Society*', DfEE Press Release 203/96. 24 June. *Framework for a Learning Society* is substantially reprinted in Stewart Ranson (ed.) (1998), *Inside the Learning Society*, London: Cassell, pp. 143–155.

Department for Education and Employment (DfEE) (1997a), 'Blunkett Boards the Lifelong Learning Bus', DfEE Press Release 105/97, 19 May.

Department for Education and Employment (DfEE) (1997b), 'Blackstone Announces Details of Continuing Education and Lifelong Learning Advisory Group', DfEE Press Release 183/97, 4 July.

Department for Education and Employment (DfEE) (1998), *The Learning Age: A Renaissance for a New Britain* (Cm 3790), London: Stationery Office.

Department for Education and Employment (DfEE) (1999), *Learning to Succeed: A New Framework for Post-16 Learning* (Cm 4392), London: Stationery Office.

Department for Innovation, Universities and Skills (DIUS) (2008), 'Informal Adult Learning – Shaping the Way Ahead', London: DIUS. Available at: http://www.bis.gov.uk/assets/biscore/innovation/docs/s/urn-ial2008-shaping-the-way-ahead (accessed 14 April 2012).

Department for Innovation, Universities and Skills (DIUS) (2009), 'The Learning Revolution', Cm 7555, London: Stationery Office. Available at: http://www.bis.gov.uk/assets/biscore/corporate/migratedd/publications/l/learning_revolution.pdf (accessed 15 April 2012).

Department of Education and Science (DES) (1973), *Adult Education: A Plan for Development. Report of a Committee of Inquiry . . . under the Chairmanship of Sir Lionel Russell*, London: HMSO.

Department of Trade and Industry (DTI) (1995), *Competitiveness: Forging Ahead*, London: HMSO.

Faure, Edgar, Felipe Herrera, Abdul-Razzak Kaddoura, Henri Lopes, Arthur V. Petrovsky, Majid Rahnema and Frederick Champion Ward (1972), *Learning To Be. The World of Education Today and Tomorrow*, Paris: UNESCO.

Field, John (2006), *Lifelong Learning and the New Educational Order*, 2nd edition, Stoke on Trent: Trentham Books.

Fryer, Bob (2004), 'The Northern College from Thatcherism to "New Labour": A Personal Reminiscence', in Malcolm Ball and William Hampton (eds), *The Northern College: Twenty-five Years of Adult Learning*, Leicester: NIACE, pp. 69–100.

Fryer, Robert (2010), *Promises of Freedom: Citizenship, Belonging and Lifelong Learning*, Leicester: NIACE.

Goldman, Lawrence (2000), 'Intellectuals and the English Working Class 1870–1945: The Case of Adult Education', *History of Education*, **29** (4), 281–300.

Harrison, Brian (2004 [2011]), 'Joseph, Keith Sinjohn, Baron Joseph (1918–1994)', *Oxford Dictionary of National Biography*, Oxford: Oxford University Press; online edn May 2011, http://www.oxforddnb.com/view/article/55063 (accessed 18 January 2013).

Heffernan, Richard (2011), 'Labour's New Labour Legacy: Politics after Blair and Brown', *Political Studies Review*, **9** (2), 163–177.

Holford, John, Sheila Riddell, Elisabet Weedon, Judith Litjens and Guy Hannan

(2008), *Lifelong Learning: Policy and Practice in an Expanding Europe*, Vienna: Lit Verlag.
House of Commons, Committee of Public Accounts (2003), 'Individual Learning Accounts', HC544. London: Stationery Office. Available at: http://www.publications.parliament.uk/pa/cm200203/cmselect/cmpubacc/544/54402.htm (accessed 14 April 2012).
Howells, Kim (1998), 'Lifelong Learning not Dead' (Letter to the Editor), *Times Educational Supplement*, 13 February.
Jackson, Trudy (n.d.), 'A Brief History of the Early Years of the WEA: The Partnership between Labour and Learning', London: WEA. Available at: http://www.online.wea.org.uk/mod/resource/view.php?id=1121 (accessed 12 April 2012).
Jarvis, Peter (2004), *Adult Education and Lifelong Learning: Theory and Practice. 3rd edition*, London: RoutledgeFalmer.
Jarvis, Peter, Colin Griffin, John Holford, Linda Merricks and Paul Tosey (1998), 'Why Lifelong Learning Is Not a Policy', *Times Higher Education Supplement*, 16 January.
Labour Party (1997), *New Labour: Because Britain Deserves Better*, London: Labour Party.
Leitch, Alexander (2006), *Prosperity for All in the Global Economy – World Class Skills. Final Report*, London: Stationery Office (with the permission of HM Treasury on behalf of the Controller of HMSO). Available at: http://webarchive.nationalarchives.gov.uk/+/http:/www.hm-treasury.gov.uk/leitch_review_index.htm (accessed 14 April 2012).
Mansbridge, Albert (1944), *The Kingdom of the Mind: Essays and Addresses 1903–37*, London: J.M. Dent & Sons.
Michels, Robert (1916), *Political Parties; a Sociological Study of the Oligarchical Tendencies of Modern Democracy*, London: Jarrold & Sons.
Miliband, Ralph (1973), *Parliamentary Socialism: A Study in the Politics of Labour*, London: Merlin Press.
Millner, Sophie (2008), 'A Review of the Civil Renewal and Active Citizenship Debate', London: National Council for Voluntary Organisations. Available at: http://www.ncvo-vol.org.uk/sites/default/files/UploadedFiles/NCVO/Publications/Publications_Catalogue/Sector_Research/Civil_renewal_active_citizenship_debate.pdf (accessed 12 April 2012).
Ministry of Education (1954), *The Organisation and Finance of Adult Education in England and Wales*, Report of the Committee appointed by the Minister of Education in June 1953, London: HMSO.
Ministry of Reconstruction (1919), *Adult Education Committee: Final Report*, Cmd. 321, London: HMSO.
Nash, I. (1998a), 'Plans for Lifelong Learning Torn Up', *Times Educational Supplement*, 6 February.
Nash, I. (1998b), Lifelong Learning Paper Is Scrapped', *Times Educational Supplement*, 6 February.
Nash, Ian and Ngaio Crequer (1998), 'Red Faces after White Paper is Torn Up', *Times Educational Supplement*, 13 February.
Nash, Ian, Ngaio Crequer and Ben Russell (1998), 'Blair Bins White Paper', *Times Educational Supplement*, 13 February.
National Advisory Group for Continuing Education and Lifelong Learning (NAGCELL) (1997), *Learning for the Twenty-First Century: First Report of*

the National Advisory Group for Continuing Education and Lifelong Learning, NAGCELL.

National Advisory Group for Continuing Education and Lifelong Learning (NAGCELL) (1999), *Creating Learning Cultures: Next Steps in Achieving the Learning Age. Second Report of the National Advisory Group on Continuing Education and Lifelong Learning*, NAGCELL.

National Audit Office (2008), *Widening Participation in Higher Education*, London: Stationery Office.

National Institute of Adult Continuing Education (England and Wales) (NIACE) (1998), 'Realising The Learning Age', A NIACE Response to the Government Green Paper. Available at: http://archive.niace.org.uk/Organisation/advocacy/Archive/Learningage.htm (accessed 10 April 2012).

National Institute of Adult Continuing Education (England and Wales) (NIACE) (1999), 'NIACE Response to the White Paper "Learning to Succeed"'. Available at: http://archive.niace.org.uk/Organisation/advocacy/White_paper/Response.htm (accessed 14 April 2012).

National Institute of Adult Continuing Education (England and Wales) NIACE (2006), 'Prosperity for All in the Global Economy: World Class Skills', A NIACE response to the Leitch Review of Skills. Available at: http://archive.niace.org.uk/Organisation/advocacy/Leitch/default.htm (accessed 14 April 2012).

Office for National Statistics (ONS) (2011), 'Population Estimates for UK, England and Wales, Scotland and Northern Ireland, Population Estimates: Timeseries 1971 to Current Year'. Available at: http://www.ons.gov.uk/ons/rel/pop-estimate/population-estimates-for-uk--england-and-wales--scotland-and-northern-ireland/population-estimates-timeseries-1971-to-current-year/index.html (accessed 20 April 2012).

Panitch, Leo (1976), *Social Democracy and Industrial Militancy. The Labour Party, the Trade Unions and Incomes Policy 1945–1974*, Cambridge: Cambridge University Press.

Rizvi, Fazal and Bob Lingard (2010), *Globalizing Education Policy*, London: Routledge.

Schuetze, Hans G. (2007), 'Individual Learning Accounts and Other Models of Financing Lifelong Learning', *International Journal of Lifelong Education*, **26** (1), 5–23.

Smith, Jim and Andrea Spurling (1995), *Individual Lifelong Learning Accounts: Towards a Learning Revolution*, Leicester: NIACE.

Statutory Rules and Orders (SR&O) (1919), *Regulations for Technical Schools. &c.*, dated August 24, 1918, made by the Board of Education, for Technical Schools, Schools of Art, and other forms of Provision of Further Education in England and Wales (SR&O 1919, No. 2231), London: HMSO.

Steele, Tom (1994), 'The Colonial Metaphor and the Mission of Englishness: Adult Education and the Origins of English Studies', in Stuart Marriott and Barry Hake (eds), *Cultural and Intercultural Experiences in European Adult Education: Essays on Popular and Higher Education since 1890*, Leeds: University of Leeds Department of Adult and Continuing Education, pp. 70–91.

Stevenson, Jacqueline and Mel Lang (2010), 'Social Class and Higher Education: A Synthesis of Research', York: Higher Education Academy. Available at: http://search.heacademy.ac.uk/kb5/hea/evidencenet/resource.page?record=vBfcqjLkNbk (accessed 9 April 2012).

Stocks, Mary (1953), *The Workers' Educational Association: The First Fifty Years*, London: WEA.

Taylor, Richard (2004), 'Creating Northern College', in Malcolm Ball and William Hampton (eds), *The Northern College: Twenty-five Years of Adult Learning*, Leicester: NIACE, pp. 36–50.

Taylor, Richard (2009), 'Lifelong Learning under New Labour: An Orwellian Dystopia?' *Power and Education*, **1** (1), 71–82.

Thomson, Alan and Tony Tysome (1998), 'Blunkett's Dream Awaits Cash', *Times Higher Education Supplement*, 27 February.

Williams, Raymond (n.d.), *An Open Letter to WEA Tutors*, London: Workers' Educational Association.

6. Rising to the challenge of realizing lifelong learning for one and all: the role of community adult education in widening participation for traditionally marginalized groups in Irish society and beyond

Catherine Maunsell and Paul Downes

Adult learning and education play a critical role in responding to contemporary cultural, economic, political and social challenges. (UNESCO 2010, p. 43)

INTRODUCTION

The impact of education on an individual's options in life is unequivocal (European Commission 2011a). Lifelong and 'life-wide' learning has a fundamental part to play in addressing social exclusion and the intergenerational cycles of educational disadvantage and poverty. Educational policies and practices aimed at widening participation in educational activities for marginalized groups are a prerequisite to successfully meeting the challenges of promoting social inclusion and reducing poverty (Cedefop 2009; European Commission 2010).

A recent European Union (EU) Commission examination of the impact of ongoing educational policy reform on the adult learning sector affirms these principles: 'in a very real way, adult learning can help to overcome the main challenges related to demographic change, poverty, social exclusion, early school leaving and low literacy and thus provide opportunities for all individuals, notably the most disadvantaged groups' (European Commission DG EAC 2010).

Furthermore, in its 2011 review of the impact of its 2007–2010 *Action Plan for Adult Learning* (European Commission 2007), the European Commission (European Commission 2011b) highlighted the multiplicity of challenges that must be addressed to ensure that the most disadvantaged groups, particularly early school-leavers and low-skilled adults, have access to lifelong learning (LLL) opportunities. Some of the challenges highlighted in the Action Plan include *inter alia*: 'the need for political will to develop and implement relevant policies . . . the lack of data on the competences of low-skilled individuals in Europe . . . the multiple barriers to participation including pressures on funding due to the economic crisis' (European Commission 2011b, p. 30).

Over the recent decades, the EU agenda on LLL has been central to member state policy developments in the field of adult education, including community-based adult education. Downes (forthcoming), in a systems-level focus on access to education for traditionally marginalized groups in Europe, cites a range of examples of community-based education found across countries including Belgium, Bulgaria, Estonia, Hungary, Scotland and Ireland. Indeed, social forces, alongside the economic forces at play, have always been viewed as key drivers of the Irish LLL agenda (Maunsell et al. 2008; Downes et al. 2006; Holford et al. 2009).

The important role of social factors may be traced to the historical strengths of the community-based adult education sector in Ireland, characterized by a predominance of women's community groups and high levels of volunteerism (Bane 2007; Kavanagh 2007; Fleming 2004; Connolly 2005; Aontas 2001, 2003, 2004, 2010; Owens 2000). The principle of LLL itself, underpinned by the six priority areas of consciousness raising, citizenship, cohesion, competitiveness, cultural development and community building, has become central to the rhetoric of the Irish state's educational policies since the publication of its White Paper on Adult Education entitled *Learning for Life* in 2000 (Maunsell et al. 2008). In particular, the White Paper stresses the importance of: 'equality of access, participation and outcome for participants in adult education, with proactive strategies to counter barriers arising from differences of socio-economic status, gender, ethnicity and disability. A key priority in promoting an inclusive society is to target investment towards those most at risk' (Department of Education and Science 2000, p. 13).

Drawing on a range of research, scholarship and practice as the basis for ongoing policy reform in adult education, in this chapter we outline the potential of community-based non-formal education as the route to engaging marginalized groups in formal education, including higher education. We will approach community LLL centres as the key to meeting the educational needs of those most marginalized within their own local communities. Such a model of community-based adult education has the potential for wider application across European countries. Building stronger alliances between the non-formal and formal education sectors is fundamental for rising to the challenge of realizing LLL for everyone.

PARTICIPATION IN ADULT EDUCATION

There have been significant changes in Ireland's economic profile across the timeframe of LLL2010. In 2005, when the research commenced, Ireland's 'Celtic Tiger' was regarded as a model economy, particularly for other like-sized EU member states. Since 2008, however, the Irish economy and labour market have been significantly and adversely affected by the recent global economic downturn and national banking crisis. Average unemployment rates have more than trebled since 2007, rising from 4.6 per cent at its lowest in 2007 to 14.7 per cent in 2011 (CSO 2011). Younger people and the lesser-skilled are at greatest risk of unemployment – with the unemployment rates of those aged under 25 reported to have been twice as high as the unemployment level of those aged 25–54 (Forfas 2010).

Comprehensive data on adult participation in LLL is sparse at the national level. According to the 2009 Labour Force Survey, Ireland reported a participation rate of 6.3 per cent, compared to the EU average of 9.3 per cent (Eurostat 2010). Recent data available from the Quarterly National Household Survey on Lifelong Learning published in 2010 indicates that 5 per cent of adults aged 25 and over in Ireland were engaged in formal education. Just under 20 per cent of adults reported being engaged in non-formal education (CSO 2010a).

Such patterns of participation are of particular significance, given the objectives as set out in *Tomorrow's Skills: Towards a National Skills Strategy*, which documents the strategic mission of the government-established Expert Group on Future Skills Needs (EGFSN). The key objective of the strategy, in direct relation to the Lisbon agenda, is cited as being 'to identify the skills required for Ireland to make the transition to a competitive, innovation-driven, knowledge-based, participative and inclusive economy by 2020' (Department of Enterprise, Trade and Employment 2007, p. 5). The National Skills Strategy sets out a range of targets to be achieved, but acknowledges that the requirement to enhance the skill level of the Irish population will present a major challenge. Compared to other EU member states, Ireland's participation rates in continuous learning (non-formal learning) are relatively poor. Only 14 per cent of those aged 25–64 were engaged in non-formal learning in Ireland in 2002, compared to 34.5 per cent in the UK (Department of Enterprise, Trade and Employment 2007). The 2007 report also notes Ireland's poor ranking in terms of adult literacy, citing data from the International Adult Literacy

Survey (IALS) undertaken in Ireland in 1995 and reported in 1997. The IALS results revealed that a quarter of Irish adults aged between 16 and 65 achieved level 1 on the IALS scale for document literacy (Department of Education and Science 1997). A 2009 report on research undertaken by the National Adult Literacy Agency (NALA) found that Irish people with literacy and numeracy difficulties are less likely to participate in LLL opportunities, providing further evidence for the 'Matthew effect'. According to the latter, those who need educational support the most are the least likely to make use of opportunities provided, thereby compounding existing inequalities (NALA 2009).

Further examples of these patterns of inequality can be found in a recent study on the experience and views of a non-random sample of 1000 adult learners who had returned to education after two years or more (Maunsell et al. 2009; Maunsell et al., forthcoming). Data from respondents who had initially left education prior to upper secondary level (International Standard Classification of Education – ISCED – levels 1 and 2) was compared with data from those who had initially left education at or after their Leaving Certificate qualification (equivalent to ISCED levels 3–6). Two-fifths, or 39.6 per cent, of all respondents indicated that they had initially left education before upper secondary level, with 60.4 per cent of respondents having left at later levels. The majority of participants who had reported leaving the education system early, that is, before upper level secondary education, were currently studying at ISCED levels 1–3. Less than one in ten respondents were identified as early school leavers engaged in higher education. In contrast, the majority of participants who had left education at or after upper secondary level were engaged in post-secondary, non-tertiary education or tertiary education at ISCED levels 4–6 (Table 6.1).

A third of the respondents listed work as the reason for leaving education before upper level secondary, whereas only 16.9 per cent among those who

Table 6.1 Percentage breakdown of current stage of education by ISCED level

Current stage of education	Left school before upper secondary (%)	Left school after upper secondary (%)
ISCED 1+2 Primary and lower secondary	40.3	3.8
ISCED 3 Upper secondary	34.7	9.9
ISCED 4 Post secondary non-tertiary	16.5	26.9
ISCED 5+6 Tertiary	8.5	59.4

Source: Maunsell et al. (2009).

Table 6.2 Percentage breakdown of parental highest level of education by ISCED level

Parental highest education level	Left school before upper secondary (%)	Left school after upper secondary (%)
Mother's highest education level		
ISCED 1+2 Primary and lower secondary	85.4	51.0
ISCED 3 Upper secondary	9.6	20.1
ISCED 4 Post-secondary non-tertiary	4.0	12.1
ISCED 5+6 Tertiary	1.0	16.9
Father's highest education level		
ISCED 1+2 Primary and lower secondary	83.0	51.2
ISCED 3 Upper secondary	8.9	19.9
ISCED 4 Post-secondary non-tertiary	4.3	11.2
ISCED 5+6 Tertiary	3.9	17.7

Source: Maunsell et al. (2009).

had left education at higher stages had done so because of occupational obligations. In contrast, the most common reason cited by over half of the respondents for leaving education at a later stage was the obtaining of the necessary qualification. Less than 5 per cent of early school leavers stated that they had obtained the necessary qualification at the time they had left school. One in ten among early school leavers listed either lack of interest in the study programme or personal and emotional problems as secondary factors in their decision to leave school. Among later school leavers, 5.5 per cent and 2 per cent chose these respective categories. Thus, based on these findings, financial reasons were central to respondents leaving school early without feeling they had obtained the necessary qualification. For a significant minority, participation in education was adversely impacted by motivational and intrapersonal factors.

Table 6.2 highlights the impact of intergenerational influences on early school leaving. The overall majority of participants who initially left education before upper level secondary reported that their mothers had also left before this stage, compared to just half of those who had left education at later levels. For those who had left early, only 1 per cent of their mothers went on to tertiary education, compared to 16.9 per cent for those who left later. As presented in Table 6.2, the highest level of education respondents' fathers also showed a similar pattern across the two groups.

While a stated priority of the Irish (and EU) educational policy is addressing early school leaving, almost 12 per cent of all persons aged

18–24 had left school early according to the Central Statistics Office (CSO) 2006 national census figures (CSO 2006). The most up-to-date data, based on a Special Module on Educational Attainment (December 2010), similarly shows that 11 per cent, or one in nine, of the population aged 18–24 may be defined as early school leavers. The latter are defined as persons aged 18–24 who have completed their education and whose highest level of education attained is lower secondary or below ISCED levels 1 and 2 (CSO 2010b).

Unequivocal evidence shows that patterns of early school leaving only serve to reinforce existing social and economic inequalities. The personal and societal 'price' of missing out on learning is, clearly, significant. Smyth and McCoy (2009) and Byrne and Smyth (2010) include difficulties in accessing further education, training and employment among the consequences of early school leaving. Other researchers have found strong correlations between early school leaving and drug misuse (Department of Community, Rural and Gaeltacht Affairs 2009; Downes et al. 2006; Downes and Maunsell 2007), engagement in criminal activity and imprisonment (O'Mahony 1997; Morgan and Kett 2003). Smyth and McCoy (2009) reported in their longitudinal study of early school leaving on the significant disparity between the imprisonment rates among early school leavers, estimated at 46.6 per 1000, compared with those who had completed their Leaving Certificates, estimated at 1.6 per 1000. Prisoners and ex-prisoners comprise a significant, educationally marginalized group and are at a high risk of social exclusion.

Such rates and patterns of participation in education among those most marginalized give a stark picture of the educational situation in Ireland. In the current context of economic recession, the persistent challenges presented by social and economic exclusion, experienced by the most marginalized, will require targeted and proven approaches. Otherwise, the benchmark of 15 per cent of adults participating in LLL by 2020, as set out in the Strategic Framework for European Cooperation in the area of Education and Training (ET2020), is unlikely to be met.

CURRENT ECONOMIC CONTEXT

In terms of infrastructure, human resources and range and diversity of provision, the field of community education in Ireland has developed significantly since the publication of the White Paper on Adult Education in 2000. While progress has been made, 'the main competing perspective in Ireland is not so much ideological as simply giving financial priority to adult education over other areas' (Maunsell et al. 2008, p. 5). Spending for adult education in 2009 was €420 497 000, representing 0.27 per cent of gross national product (GNP). In 2008, funding of circa €9.3 billion was available to the education sector, with approximately €182 million designated for adult and further education, equating to less than 2 per cent of the overall education allocation (European Commission 2011b, p. 10). Given the recessionary economic conditions experienced in the Republic of Ireland since 2008, the level of future fiscal investments by the state in adult education remains uncertain. Indeed, in the recent past significant cutbacks in funding have been experienced by the adult education sector as a whole and, in particular, by community-based initiatives. Few of the localized community adult education initiatives have been mainstreamed and their funding sources have remained fragmented and unpredictable (Dooley et al. 2010). One of the community education providers interviewed as part of that research study noted that:

> in the last financial year we would have been funded by eleven State funding lines. It's important to be aware of that, because that is one of the . . . [unusual] things about the way the sector is funded . . . funding for the organization is from year to year . . . predominantly year to year unfortunately. (Dooley et al. 2010)

In many cases, financial support has been dramatically reduced since the economic downturn, particularly in relation to community adult education initiatives. Thus, already limited resources are being further stretched, with those most marginalized becoming even less likely or able to access adult educational opportunities.

One community education provider interviewed by Dooley et al. (2010) indicated their deep concerns about the effects of such significant cuts on the community education sector, stating that:

> If you start cutting back classes and things like that, you're really cutting back not just classes but hope . . . people need to have hope, hope that their situation or their lives will improve, and we're not even talking financially, we're talking about that their lives are improved . . . so if they're cut back . . . you're limiting the amount of learning that people can do. (Dooley et al. 2010)

She went on to explain the wider value of the support that community education offers to participants, 'by coming to classes, sitting down with other people, sharing their worries and their cares, the classes provide that, not just as in an academic way but the support, otherwise you have communities falling apart'.

Given our current context, Lyn Tett (2006) cogently articulates many of the prevailing tensions arising for community adult educators. High levels of expectation position community adult education at the forefront of such key policy areas as LLL, while the capacity for teaching is constrained by lack of investment and withdrawal of funding:

> a key challenge will be to ensure that investment is made by the state in prioritising spending in preference of those most disadvantaged and to ensure that opportunities for equal access, participation and outcome at every level of the system are available to disadvantaged groups and those most vulnerable. Further challenges are ensuring accessibility to all learners; the removal of barriers to access; provision of a continuum of education and transfer, progression and accreditation for all learners. (Pobal 2009, p. 4)

THE POTENTIAL OF NON-FORMAL, COMMUNITY-BASED EDUCATION

The Irish Government's White Paper on Adult Education (2000) identifies the community as the key learning site for adults. The White Paper envisages a central role for the community education sector as a 'key agent in successfully meeting the needs of communities and groups who are most marginalized' (Department of Education and Science 2000, p. 118). While the White Paper recognizes the valuable contribution of community education in Ireland, it also acknowledges that the constraints inherent in the sector include, *inter alia*, inadequate resourcing, isolation from other educational sectors and lack of research support. These constraints still apply equally, more than a decade later (Aontas 2010; Maunsell 2010).

The White Paper on Adult Education explicitly acknowledged the contribution of community adult education providers in formulating innovative and effective bottom-up educational strategies. The White Paper saw these strategies as having the potential to engage 'highly marginalized people' (Department of Education and Science 2000, p. 71) and 'pioneering new approaches to teaching and learning in non-hierarchical, community-based settings' (2000, p. 110). In this respect, the Irish model of adult education can trace its influences on the international stage to the writings of Freire (1970 [1972]) and Mezirow (1981, 1991, 1997) among others. In both the Republic of Ireland and Northern Ireland, the work of educationalists such as O'Sullivan (1993, 2005) and Lovett (1971, 1980) on the links between education, community development, and political and social change are notable.

Thus, non-formal, community-based education is a fundamental strategic 'opportunity' for EU policy and practice, adding an important dimension to those strategies already proposed by the EU Action Plan for Adult Learning for widening participation in LLL activities, particularly for those who have been traditionally marginalized. 'Lifelong learning in a non-formal context provides a forum for the development and practice of citizenship competencies in all forms of interaction: multicultural, demographic, intergenerational, environmental, spiritual etc.' (European Commission 2011a, p. 67).

Research has indicated that in a range of ways, non-formal learning can play a key role in widening access to education for traditionally under-represented groups through, *inter alia*, helping to overcome fear of failure or fear of success, and alleviating potential alienation from friends, family and community (Ivers 2008).

Moving beyond a 'deficit' model for adults experiencing social exclusion and educational disadvantage, the non-formal education sector recognizes that a person's life experience also carries significance for learning (Pobal 2006). According to Boldt (1997), a personal development dimension, enhancing of self-esteem and having the opportunity to engage in a wide range of learning opportunities aimed at learners' expressed needs are cornerstones of non-formal educational provision in the community.

The European Commission explicitly recognized the community as the setting for LLL, particularly for traditionally marginalized groups: 'Community and voluntary groups have unique opportunities to deliver targeted learning, to promote learning amongst (potential) learners and to articulate their needs and interests' (European Commission 2001).

The significance of non-formal community-based education is that by its presence in the local community it is located 'where it is needed', taking the form of outreach for those who have had to leave school early and who have been marginalized by the mainstream education system (Dooley et al. 2010). The director of the school-based community education project Kileely Community Project, interviewed as part of the Dooley et al. (2010) report, explained that in Ireland 'the community education sector is very accessible, you're just welcome'. The director believes that education should be available locally: 'I believe that if we want to reach the adults who most deserve a second chance [in education], we have to provide them with it, within their community. It is their right; they must know that and in time maybe come to demand it' (cited in Boldt 1997).

In regard to the transformative potential of community-based education, she went on to stress that community education 'has the opportunity for local empowerment, local leadership, social capital, educational capital, reinventing the community, enormous power and potential in it'. Such an approach, based on identified local needs and adopting a 'bottom-up' strategy of stakeholder engagement, emerges as a more effective model in relation to educational leadership and programmes aimed at addressing school exclusion. When establishing community education in an area for the first time, the director recommends that it is important to:

> listen to people in the community, they're the experts, they will identify what their needs are if they're given a safe place to do it, they will identify their strengths if given a safe place to do it, you can grow goodwill given a safe place to do it . . . In order to address school exclusion, those who are excluded should be included in the process, decision-making and overall delivery of educational provision. You have to be very conscious of power, of attitudes, not making decisions over people's heads. (Dooley et al. 2010)

The Director highlights the particular part that community education plays in addressing educational disadvantages when explaining why institutions, particularly formal educational institutions, have difficulty attracting certain groups: 'I think sometimes institutions and the formal educational sector, we are too quick to judge why people aren't participating, we need to ask them . . . what is it that will make it more accessible for them'. The way in which the Kileely Community Project reaches out and engages with the local community is a model of good practice in respect of outreach to traditionally marginalized groups, relying on the relational dimension of person-to-person communication and networking:

> We encourage them and it's word of mouth, and a little bit of push here and a knock at the door there and say come out . . . even if you don't want to do it, come up and have a cup of tea when we're all sitting down and a chat . . . so it's basically word of mouth as well, if somebody comes and they enjoy it, they will say to someone else oh, there's a great class going on in the school . . . in terms of outreach, in terms of . . . I think word of mouth is really important . . . you cannot beat the personal touch, if I want to increase the number of people . . . stand in the corridor and actually talk to people. (Dooley et al. 2010)

Such relational outreach strategies have tremendous potential for use in other education sectors and, indeed, also outside the Irish context (Downes forthcoming).

At the national level, Pobal as part of its commitment to delivering LLL in disadvantaged communities has similarly recognized that:

> Community based educational access is a dynamic process that involves the localised delivery of a range of educational supports by community education practitioners aimed at enhancing access to educational opportunities . . . at all levels by building the capacity of individuals, families, communities and the education sector to identify the barriers to education and to develop the strategies necessary for addressing them. (Pobal 2006, p. 13)

Pobal identifies a range of strengths of community-based approaches to education which place the sector at the vanguard for LLL:

1. commitment to meeting the needs of adult learners;
2. commitment to social inclusion and addressing educational disadvantage;

3. commitment and capacity to reach hard to reach groups;
4. shared sentiments with new social movements;
5. flexible and responsive to people's needs;
6. focus on fostering self reliance and empowerment;
7. builds community capital. (Pobal 2009, p. 35)

The concept of 'community capital' is explicated by Connolly and defined as 'a combination of cultural and social capital, the intellectual, educational, social relationships – the collective resources for the entire community' (Connolly 2009, p. 10). Thus, community-based education, with its commitment to widening access to education for traditionally marginalized groups, potentially 'builds up communities in sustainable ways by linking education theory with practice, local issues with the global issues and the personal with social advocacy' (Dooley et al. 2010, p. 49).

THE POTENTIAL OF COMMUNITY LLL CENTRES

Predicated on being embedded in wider regional and national strategies for LLL and access to education, Community Lifelong Learning Centres offer a key pathway and bridge in reaching out to marginalized communities and fostering the connection over time between the non-formal and formal systems. The key objective of community LLL centres is to develop a new alliance between the formal and non-formal education sectors. Such alliance would work towards achieving parity of esteem across both sectors and serve to strengthen and expand the role of education in the lives of the marginalized.

The following section presents an overview of a model community-based LLL centre, included in Dooley et al.'s (2010) report on access to education for adults experiencing educational disadvantage in Ireland. This community LLL centre engages with the vision of learning as being lifelong and 'life-wide', in line with the national and EU Commission definitions. The LLL centre also provides a community-based range of pathways for the individual to progress from non-formal to formal education, including higher education.

EXEMPLAR OF A COMMUNITY-BASED LLL CENTRE: AN COSÁN ('THE PATH')

An Cosán is one of the largest independent community-based education centres in Ireland. An Cosán developed from the Shanty Educational Project Ltd, established in 1986. The Shanty aimed at providing 'second-chance' community-based education opportunities to meet the needs of people living in the Tallaght West community, with the primary focus on women's education. In 1999, the organization relocated to a multipurpose community facility and was renamed An Cosán, meaning 'the path'. The organization offers community-based education, childcare and enterprise through its three main endeavours:

- The Shanty, which provides adult community education.
- Rainbow House, an early childhood education centre.
- Fledglings Training and Fledglings Childcare.

An Cosán demonstrates lifelong and 'life-wide' learning in action, as it engages with whole communities of non-traditional learners. The centre provides community-based educational opportunities across generations from early childhood education to adult basic, further and higher education. As reported by its chief executive officer (CEO), An Cosán is 'of intergenerational education, where adults and young children are given parallel opportunities to learn' (Dooley et al. 2010, p. 71).

Adult learners who avail of An Cosán educational programmes and services include those most at risk of social exclusion: early school leavers, ethnic minorities, long-term unemployed and underrepresented social groups. The Shanty Education Programme, 'responsible for the adult education dimension, has had particular success in attracting and retaining participants who otherwise would be unlikely to engage in lifelong learning' (Waters 2007, p. 160). The programme offers participants the opportunity to take the first step back into education in a supportive environment. The programme is based on the belief that adult community education is transformative both for the individual as well as for the community and that social exclusion and poverty can be challenged and transformed through education.

The CEO of An Cosán went on to explain that:

> As early school leavers there's a whole gap in your development . . . it's the move from the verbal and experiential into the written and it is very challenging and we have had to build a whole lot of supports in place . . . each of our classes includes an element of critical social analysis . . . people need to know and to look at why they're facing the challenges of doing basic literacy when they are 35, 45 . . . the basic classes are where our social analysis must be deeply rooted and begin. (Dooley et al. 2010, p. 77)

In An Cosán, learners have the option to progress through advancing levels of educational programmes, from non-formal to formal education, including higher education. The typical starting point for adult learners is through non-formal education: courses such as personal development, communication skills, and basic literacy and numeracy. Another series of courses reflect the needs of the local community for training in leadership. These courses have been developed at the behest of local community groups and include training for community drug workers and community development workers. Courses that facilitate progression into formal education include those run under the Young Women's Programmes. Some past students have gone on to third-level colleges and universities, gaining certificates, diplomas and degrees. The CEO explained:

> We would always encourage students . . . to consider where they might go next, either within the organization or beyond. There is a variety of progression routes . . . up to the degree, and a lot of supports . . . put in place to support students make that progress. (Dooley et al. 2010, p. 78)

A significant development by An Cosán, realizing the vision of the continuum of LLL inherent in both national and EU definitions, is the provision of a BA degree programme on Leadership in Community Development. The CEO noted that: '[We] always have had programmes that would be focused on developing community leadership and that has developed right up to now'. The CEO went on to highlight the significance of this degree programme as An Cosán: 'Having what I think is a first for a community development organization . . . we developed a degree entirely ourselves . . . that's quite unique and I think it's the first undergraduate degree with the word leadership in its title' (Dooley et al. 2010, p. 83).

The CEO explained that An Cosán contributes to community development through a focus on local educational issues. 'What is needed locally and how can we support that . . . a lot of our courses have been developed really in partnership with groups in the community'. These courses include, for example, the community drugs programme, community development courses and childcare courses.

The CEO set out several areas that are important in developing a strategy for the non-formal sector, including:

> To develop tools to evaluate the impact of our work, to be able to present the State with cost benefit analysis . . . the community education sector . . . ensure that we do not simply become service providers, providing services that the State has failed to provide, but that we ensure that . . . that service provision is one where there's also advocacy, voice given . . . social analysis . . . and real key commitment to social change . . . there's a huge danger that we might just become service providers. (Dooley et al. 2010, p. 84)

POTENTIAL TO BUILD RELATIONSHIPS BETWEEN THE NON-FORMAL AND FORMAL EDUCATION SECTORS

The role of community-based LLL centres as a path to accessing and participating in formal education opportunities is not without challenges, wrought not least by historical fragmentation of the community education sector. Nonetheless, non-formal community-based adult education, linked with formal education providers and provided through local community LLL centres, can play an important role in delivering education and training for members of their communities if adequately resourced.

As part of a national lifelong learning strategy, there is a need to support authentic partnerships between the non-formal, community-based education sector and other formal education sectors and, indeed, with other sites of non-formal and formal education, such as prison education. In examining the perils of confusing lifelong learning with lifelong education, Billett cautions against 'ignoring the importance and ubiquity of learning experiences' outside of the formal education sector (Billett 2010, p. 401). Billet further calls for a reinterpretation of LLL in its broadest sense, inclusive of both socio-personal and institutional processes. He contends that what is advanced is 'a narrow conception of how learning might best be promoted and supported' (ibid.).

Furthermore, from a life course perspective, building links between community-based adult education and earlier primary and secondary stages in the continuum of LLL can have the effect of strengthening 'first-chance' education for individuals, which ultimately supports their accessing further and higher education. Operationalizing a clear 'lifelong learning' strategy tailored to meet the individual's needs within their communities carries the potential to lead to what the White Paper on Adult Education envisaged as 'a new synergy between the sectors thereby . . . providing the greatest return from the community sector's capacity to innovate and engage with the most marginalized in society' (Department of Education and Science 2000, p. 117).

SCHOOL AS A SITE FOR COMMUNITY EDUCATION

The use of local schools as community LLL centres would clearly increase connections between the formal education system and community education. The model of practice for Kileely Community Project also included in Dooley et al.'s 2010 report illustrates the potential of a dynamic relationship between the school and the local community where the school has become a learning centre for that community.

It is important, however, to also consider that many adults may not wish to learn in school environments because of negative childhood experiences of mistreatment and failure by the education system. Therefore other arrangements and learner sites, such as those offered in a community LLL centre, will also need to be available in the local community (Maunsell et al. 2008); a position endorsed in the Pobal report, which notes that 'Learning centres that offer an alternative to the traditional "schools" model and make-up should be established to reflect the "whole" community to enhance integration of all learning models' (Pobal 2009, p. 15).

COMMUNITY EDUCATION LINKS TO HIGHER EDUCATION

A particular challenge highlighted by Dooley et al. (2010) is the identification and recognition of non-formal community-based adult education within higher education structures and/or systems. The CEO of An Cosán in particular spoke about difficulties with creating more links with third-level institutions both locally and further afield, explaining that 'It is hard to get third level engagement', and drawing on her personal experience of working with the formal education sector:

> I've been very involved in this with three different formal educational institutes. The commitment to working with disadvantage is limited in the formal education sector. The commitment to working with our sector, I don't see that formalized, I don't see that supported in order to get colleges to work with us. You have to show them very clearly what's in it for them. (Dooley et al. 2010, p. 205)

Clearly, the formal links between higher education institutions and community education providers representing traditionally marginalized groups need to be strengthened.

As the Senior Access Official of one Higher Education Institution, interviewed as part of the Dooley et al. (2010) study, explained, fostering such engagement between higher education institutions and local community education has led to: 'The community feel at home, being able to access the university. Through the outreach programmes . . . that has helped to consolidate that and encourage people into. . . [the University] as well' (Dooley et al. 2010, p. 27).

LINKS TO OTHER EDUCATIONAL SECTORS

The promotion of LLL opportunities for those most marginalized carries significant potential for building links between prison education and post-release educational provision in community-based settings. Prisoners and ex-prisoners are particular groups of socially excluded, young male, early school leavers, long-term unemployed. Within the Irish Prison Service, LLL is a key feature of the strategic plan as set out in Part 12 of the 'Prison Rules, 2007'. The latter sets out that:

> In so far as is practicable, a broad and flexible programme of education shall be provided in each prison to meet the needs of prisoners, through helping them cope with their imprisonment, achieve personal development, prepare for life after their release from prison, and establish the appetite and capacity for lifelong learning. (Department of Justice, Equality and Law Reform 2007, p. 72)

Despite the importance of the national report in addressing social exclusion and participation for a key sector, the authors of Sub project 5 Irish National Report highlight that:

> Provision of education in Irish prisons is restricted by a lack of political support for prison education, which is connected to negative public attitudes to prisoners enforced by the media in Ireland. There is an over emphasis on security above all else in Irish prisons, which results in restrictions or barriers to the education of prisoners as the priorities within these institutions are system security and containment. (Dooley et al. 2010, p. 223)

When questioned about the adequacy of educational provision, a prison senior manager responded in an interview: 'To ask is the education system in place here adequate to deal with the needs of the prison population that are in . . . [the prison] at any given time, my answer is they are not, they are totally inadequate for the real volume' (Dooley et al. 2010, p. 89).

A range of institutional obstacles prevents prisoners from accessing education provision within the prison context. The annual Inspector of Prisons report claims that prisons are chronically overcrowded, education is not being prioritized and prisoners are prevented access to education centres in prisons and/or significantly delayed in attending classes. Such barriers, contravening the European Prison Rules,[1] need to be addressed as a matter of educational priority (Maunsell et al. 2008, p. 29).

RISING TO THE CHALLENGE

The Country Report on the Action Plan on Adult Learning: Ireland (2011) refers explicitly to the Education Equality Initiative (EEI)[2] in terms of rising to the challenge of widening participation for those traditionally marginalized groups in Irish society and providing a continuum of education. The Initiative, which operated in 2000–2006, supported 'a range of action research projects to generate policy and practice lessons to address educational disadvantage among adults, including participation challenges' (European Commission 2011b, p. 12). The Initiative summarized that the major policy 'lesson' from this initiative was 'that an integrated national and local approach is the only effective way to address educational disadvantage' (ibid.).

Clearly, on the national level, education as a whole needs 'joined-up thinking' and active partnership across government departments. As the recent Economic and Social Research Institute (ESRI) report *Investing in Education: Combating Educational Disadvantage* highlights:

> The necessity of joined-up planning and provision between education, health and welfare services to meet the needs of those experiencing social exclusion in society. It stresses that with the current recession it is important that the long-term importance of investment in education, particularly for those experiencing marginalization is not forgotten. (Smyth and McCoy 2009, p. 58)

Greater links between the community education, primary, secondary, further education and higher education sectors are clearly warranted to enable individuals who have experienced educational disadvantage to continue their education. Specifically referring to access to higher education, the *National Action Plan 2005–2007: Achieving Equity of Access to Higher Education in Ireland* highlighted that strengthening effective connections and partnerships between all elements of the Irish education system from primary, secondary-level, further, community and higher education, should be a key aspect in promoting equity of access to higher education for groups experiencing educational disadvantage (Higher Education Authority 2004).

The current *National Plan for Equity of Access to Higher Education, 2008–2013* indicates that: 'Ireland now needs to look towards the development of . . . greater connectivity across the different sectors/agencies. A more integrated approach at national and local level will better allow Ireland to more effectively meet the challenges of achieving wider societal goals and the delivery to the citizen of more coherent and integrated services' (Higher Education Authority 2008, p. 69).

Indeed, the Higher Education Authority of Ireland refers to 'the near theoretical consensus that integrated strategies have the greatest potential to address the multi-dimensional causes and consequences of educational disadvantage and social exclusion' (Higher Education Authority 2008, p. 35).

CONCLUSIONS

Clearly, community-based and community-led adult education as a primary means of widening access for those traditionally marginalized in our society needs to be further strengthened and supported. Such an approach can contribute to a process of change not only on the part of the individual, but more broadly in terms of cultural change within educational institutions, communities and society at large. Such transformation can have the effect of normalizing expectations that each and every individual, 'one and all', can participate successfully in learning opportunities across their life course. As Pobal (2009, pp. 7–8) claims, 'increasing equality of access to education and educational attainment for learners is of key importance in making lifelong learning a reality for all citizens'.

Realizing the intrapersonal, interpersonal, institutional, societal and cultural transformation envisaged requires ongoing and authentic engagement of and dialogue with adults experiencing educational disadvantage (Brookfield and Holst 2010; Preskill and Brookfield 2008). Thus, widening participation in LLL for traditionally marginalized groups through community-based adult education 'continues to create new opportunities for active inclusion and enhanced social participation' (Mark 2010, p. 9) and can be transformative for both the individual and the wider society.

To conclude, the potential of the model of non-formal, community-based adult education offered through community LLL centres, as a key route to engaging traditionally under-represented groups in formal education, including higher education, has been the central tenet proposed in this chapter. Such a model is central to an integrated, holistic response to increasing participation in LLL of adults experiencing social and educational disadvantage and has much potential for wider application both within and beyond the European Union.

NOTES

1. The European Prison Rules (Council of Europe, Committee of Ministers 2006) state that prisons shall seek to provide all prisoners with access to as comprehensive education as possible, while meeting individual needs and taking into account future aspirations.

2. Funded by the Department of Education and Science (now Skills) through the National Development Plan (NDP) (2000–2006) with support from the European Social Fund.

REFERENCES

Aontas (2001), *At the Forefront: The Role of Women's Community Education in Combating Poverty and Disadvantage in the Republic of Ireland*, Dublin: Aontas.

Aontas (2003), *Gender and Learning*, Dublin: Aontas.

Aontas (2004), *Community Education*, Dublin: Aontas.

Aontas (2010), *Community Education: More than Just a Course. Exploring the Outcomes and Impact of Department of Education and Skills Funded Community Education*, Dublin: Aontas.

Bane, Liam (2007), 'A Seagull's Eye View: Adult and Community Education', in Paul Downes and Ann Louise Gilligan (eds), *Beyond Educational Disadvantage*, Dublin: IPA.

Billett, Stephen (2010), 'The Perils of Confusing Lifelong Learning with Lifelong Education', *International Journal of Lifelong Education*, **29** (4), 401–413.

Boldt, Scott (1997), *The Kileely Community Project: A Case Study*, Lyon: Institut National de Recherche Pédagogique.

Brookfield, Stephen and John Holst (2010), *Radicalizing Learning: Adult Education for a Just World*, San Francisco, CA: Jossey Bass.

Byrne, Delma and Emer Smyth (2010), *No Way Back: The Dynamics of Early School Leaving*, Dublin: ESRI and National Council for Curriculum and Assessment (NCCA).

Cedefop (2009), *Continuity, Consolidation and Change; Towards a European Era of Vocational Education and Training*, *Cedefop Reference Series 73*, Luxembourg: Publications Office.

Central Statistics Office (CSO) (2006), *Principal Statistics 2006*.

Central Statistics Office (CSO) (2010a), *Quarterly National Household Survey: Educational Attainment*.

Central Statistics Office (CSO) (2010b), *Quarterly National Household Survey: Lifelong Learning*, Quarter 3, 2008.

Central Statistics Office (CSO) (2011), *Live Register*, March.

Communication from the Commission (2010), *Europ. 2020: A European Strategy for Smart, Sustainable and Inclusive Growth*, Brussels: European Commission.

Connolly, Bríd (2005), 'Learning from the Women's Community Education Movement in Ireland', in Jim Crowther, Vernon Galloway and Ian Martin (eds), *Engaging the Academy*, Leicester: NIACE.

Connolly, Bríd (2009), 'The Role of Community-based Access in Delivering Lifelong Learning', presentation at Pobal seminar on Community Based Access as a Route to Further and Higher Education, Cork, September.

Council of Europe, Committee of Ministers (2006), 'Recommendation (2006)2 on the European Prison Rules', Brussels: Council of Europe

Department of Community, Rural and Gaeltacht Affairs (2009), *National Drugs Strategy Interim 2009–2016*, Dublin: Government Publications.

Department of Education and Science (1997), *International Adult Literacy Survey IALS: Results for Ireland*, Dublin: Government Publications.

Department of Education and Science (2000), *Learning for Life: White Paper on Adult Education*, Dublin: Government Publications.
Department of Enterprise, Trade and Employment (2007), *Tomorrow's Skills: Towards a National Skills Strategy*, Dublin: Government Publications.
Department of Justice, Equality and Law Reform (2007), *Prison Rules*, Dublin: Government Publications.
Dooley, Catherine, Paul Downes, Catherine Maunsell and Valerie McLoughlin (2010), *Lifelong Learning 2010: Sub Project 5 Irish Country Report: Access to Adult Education, LL2010: SP5*, Dublin: Educational Disadvantage Centre, St Patrick's College.
Downes, Paul (forthcoming), *A Comparative Analysis of Policy and practice in Relation to Access across Europe, LLL2010: SP5 Comparative Report*, Dublin: Educational Disadvantage Centre, St. Patrick's College.
Downes, Paul and Catherine Maunsell (2007), *Count Us In: Tackling Early School Leaving in South West Inner City Dublin: An Integrated Response*, Dublin: SICCDA and EDC.
Downes, Paul, Catherine Maunsell and Jo-Hanna Ivers (2006), *A Holistic Approach to Early School Leaving and School Retention in Blanchardstown*, Dublin: Blanchardstown Area Partnership.
Downes, Paul, Catherine Maunsell, Valerie McLoughlin and Meilutė Taljūnaitė (2006), 'Lifelong Learning in Ireland and Lithuania: Some Examples of Irish Policy and Practice for Lithuania to Consider?' *Filosofija Sociologija (ed Lithuanian Academy of Sciences)*, **4**, 29–36.
European Commission (2001), *Making a European Area of Lifelong Learning a Reality*, Brussels.
European Commission (2007), *Action Plan on Adult Learning: It is Always a Good Time To Learn (2007–2010)*, Brussels.
European Commission (2011a), *Final Conference on the Action Plan on Adult Learning Background Document*, Budapest, March.
European Commission (2011b), *Country Report on the Action Plan on Adult Learning: Ireland*, Brussels: Research voor Beleid.
European Commission DG EAC (2010), *Impact of Ongoing Reform in Education and Training on the Adult Learning Sector, Final report, p. XI–XII*, Brussels: Research voor Beleid.
Eurostat (2010), *Labour Force Survey 2009*.
Fleming, Ted (2004), 'The State of Adult Education', *Adult Learner: The Journal of Adult and Community Education in Ireland*, **21**, 9–17.
Forfas (2010), *National Skills Bulletin*, Dublin: Expert Group on Future Skills Needs.
Freire, Paulo (1970 [1972]), *Pedagogy of the Oppressed*, Harmondsworth: Penguin.
Higher Education Authority (2004), *National Action Plan 2005–2007: Achieving Equity of Access to Higher Education in Ireland*, Dublin: HEA.
Higher Education Authority (2008), *National Plan for Equity of Access to Higher Education, 2008–2013*, Dublin: HEA.
Holford, John, Sheila Riddell, Elisabet Weedon, Judith Litjens and Guy Hannan (2009), *Patterns of Lifelong Learning: Policy and Practice in an Expanding Europe*, Vienna: Lit Verlag.
Ivers, Jo-Hanna (2008), 'A Phenomenological Re-Interpretation of Horner's Fear of Success in Terms of Social Class', unpublished thesis (MA) Dublin City University /St Patrick's College, Drumcondra.

Kavanagh, Maureen (2007), *Women, Learning and the Labour Market in Ireland. Irish Country Report: EAEA Study on Gender Aspects in Lifelong Learning*, Dublin: Aontas.

Lovett, Tom (1971), 'Community Adult Education', *Studies in Adult Education*, **3**, 2–14.

Lovett, Tom (1980), 'Adult Education and Community Action: The Northern Ireland Experience', in Colin Fletcher and Neil Thompson (eds), *Issues in Community Education*, London: Falmer Press.

Mark, Rob (2010), 'Editorial Comment', *Adult Learner: Irish Journal of Adult and Community Education*, **26**, 7–10.

Maunsell, Catherine (2010), 'Tracing Our Roots, Imagining Our Future: A Life History of Adult Education in the Republic of Ireland', presentation at Standing Conference on University Teaching and Research in the Education of Adults (SCUTREA), University of Warwick, July 2010.

Maunsell, Catherine, Jane Carrigan, Paul Downes, Valerie McLoughlin and Imelda Byrne (2009), *National Report of a Survey of 1000 Adult Learners' Experiences of Returning to Education*, LLL2010: Sub-project 3, 1st edn, Dublin: Educational Disadvantage Centre, St Patrick's College.

Maunsell, Catherine, Jane Carrigan, Paul Downes, Valerie McLoughlin and Imelda Byrne (forthcoming), *Realising Lifelong Learning: Findings from the National Report of a Survey of 1000 Adult Learners' Experiences of Returning to Education*, LLL2010: Sub-project 3, 2nd edn, Dublin: Educational Disadvantage Centre, St Patrick's College.

Maunsell, Catherine, Paul Downes and Valerie McLoughlin (2008), *National Report on Lifelong Learning in Ireland*, LLL2010, Sub-project 1.

Mezirow, John (1981), 'A Critical Theory of Adult Learning and Education', *Adult Education Quarterly*, **32** (1), 3–24.

Mezirow, John (1991), *Transformative Dimensions of Adult Learning*, San Francisco, CA: Jossey-Bass.

Mezirow, John (1997), 'Transformative Learning: Theory to Practice', *New Directions for Adult and Continuing Education*, **74**, 5–12.

Morgan, Mark and Mary Kett (2003), *The Prison Adult Literacy Survey Results and Implications*, Dublin: Irish Prison Service.

National Adult Literacy Agency (NALA) (2009), *Seeking a Refreshed Adult Literacy and Numeracy Strategy*, Dublin: NALA.

O'Mahony, Paul (1997), *Mountjoy Prisoners: A Sociological and Criminological Profile*, Dublin: Department of Justice, Equality and Law Reform.

O'Sullivan, Denis (1993), *Commitment, Educative Action and Adults*, Aldershot: Avebury.

O'Sullivan, Denis (2005), *Cultural Politics and Irish Education since the 1950s: Policy Paradigms and Power*, Dublin: IPA.

Owens, Toni (2000), *Men on the Move: A Study of Barriers to Male Participation in Education and Training Initiatives*, Dublin: Aontas.

Pobal (2006), *Community-Based Access to Further and Higher Education: A Model Drawing on the Experience of Partnerships and the Local Development Social Inclusion Programme 2000–2006*, Dublin: Pobal.

Pobal (2009), *Delivering Lifelong Learning in Disadvantaged Communities within the EU Programme 'Raising Awareness of Life Long Learning Strategies – Education and Training 2010'*, Community-Based Access as a Route to Further and Higher Education Seminar Report, October.

Preskill, Stephen and Stephen Brookfield (2008), *Learning as a Way of Leading: Lessons from the Struggle for Social Justice*, San Francisco, CA: Jossey Bass.
Smyth, Emer and Selina McCoy (2009), *Investing in Education: Combating Educational Disadvantage*, Dublin: ESRI and Barnardos.
Tett, Lyn (2006), *Community Education, Lifelong Learning and Social Inclusion*, Edinburgh: Dunedin Academic.
UNESCO Institute for Lifelong Learning (2010), *(CONFINTEA VI): Final Report: Living and Learning for a Viable Future: The Power of Adult Learning*, Hamburg: UNESCO Institute for Education.
Waters, Liz (2007), 'Community Education: A View from the Margins', in Paul Downes and Ann Louise Gilligan (eds), *Beyond Educational Disadvantage*, Dublin: IPA.

7. Flemish formal adult education: (g)rowing against the stream?

Ellen Boeren and Ides Nicaise

INTRODUCTION

Flanders is an outlier in terms of the share of formal adult education in its overall provision of adult education. Recent legislation has indeed aimed to streamline and strengthen formal adult education, contrary to the trends in neighbour countries (the Netherlands in particular) where governments have deregulated the sector and dismantled large public institutions (Doets et al. 2008). The Flemish approach also seems to ignore Gibbons's (1994) statement about the growing importance of contextualized, non-formal and informal learning in the knowledge-based society.

It is worth examining the rationale underpinning this atypical policy. Should it be attributed to old-fashioned views of the role of the state in the education sector? Or is this a voluntary strategy with the aim of boosting participation, especially among socially disadvantaged groups?

Our hypothesis is threefold. Firstly, not all forms of formal adult education can be substituted with non-formal learning – as the second-chance and social upgrading functions in particular involve long pathways along a ladder structure. Secondly, the Department of Education sees catering for 'life-wide' learning (languages, arts, hobbies, etc.), as opposed to lifelong learning for employability, as one of its missions. Thirdly, formal education, which is the main policy instrument of the government, aims to redistribute opportunities to lower-educated groups.

In this chapter, we start with the some theoretical discussions describing the (non-)formality of learning in order to better understand the relationships between formal and non-formal education. Next, we show an overview of European participation rates in adult education based on the recent Eurostat Adult Education Survey and highlight the unique position of Flanders vis-à-vis the ratio between formal and non-formal participation. Further, we describe the Flemish adult education policy of the last decade and the availability of education offers, both formal and non-formal. Before showing empirical results – based on the Flemish part of the Eurostat Adult Education Survey – we describe some technical aspects of this survey. In the results section, we analyse the individual profiles of adult learners and explore their motives for participation. Special attention is paid to the diversification between formal and non-formal education, the main focus of this chapter. The chapter ends with a discussion of our hypotheses and findings.

(NON-)FORMALITY OF LEARNING

Before discussing Flemish policy and showing empirical results, we want to provide some details on the theoretical discussions about the (non-)formality of learning. Simkins (1977) describes the main differences between formal and non-formal education by their purposes, the timing of learning activities, the learning content, the delivery methods and the level of control (Table 7.1). Formal education takes places in a strongly institutionalized context outside the social environment and consists of long-term programmes. After a successful completion of the course, the adult gets an officially recognized credit. The programmes are organized or subsidized by the government and the curricula are generally standard-

Table 7.1 (Non-)formality of learning

	FORMAL	NON-FORMAL
Purpose	Long-term, general	Short-term, specific
	Credential-based	Not credential-based
Timing	Long cycle	Short cycle
	Preparatory	Recurrent
	Full-time	Part-time
Content	Input focused	Output focused
	Standardised	Recurrent
	Clientele determined by entry requirements	Entry requirements determined by clientele
Delivery	Institution-based	Environment-related
	Teacher-centred	Learner-centred
	Isolated from social environment	Community-based and action-oriented
	Rigid structures	Flexible structures
	Resource-intensive	Resource-saving
Control	External	Self-governing
	Hierarchical	Democratic

Source: Simkins (1977) in Colley et al. (2003, p. 12).

ized. Non-formal education is more tailored towards a specific context and is action-oriented. Programmes are shorter in time and no credits are awarded. Non-formal education can be subsidized by the government or provided exclusively on a commercial basis.

Although Simkins's distinction is certainly useful to clarify some basic differences between the two types of adult education, some aspects of the picture are probably overemphasized and may no longer apply in the present context. As Colardyn and Bjornavold (2004) have emphasized, both types tend to converge and new types of blended learning (careers) are multiplying. Formal education today has evolved into a much more flexible system. In Flanders, for example, periods of workplace learning are integrated into education curricula, accreditation of competences acquired through work or non-formal learning is being introduced and the Decree on Adult Education forces all centres to offer modular courses instead of classical linear-year programmes.

Colley et al. (2003) state that the process of learning differs in formal and non-formal learning activities. In formal activities, teaching and instruction take place within specialist education institutions while non-formal activities take place – at least partly – outside these officially recognized and credential-based institutions. Knowledge and skills learned in the formal education system can be applied to a wide range of contexts, while non-formal learning provides very context-specific knowledge and skills. A major criticism of the formal education system is that it is strongly dominated by the values of the social elites, and therefore it is less accessible and leads to fewer success experiences for people from lower socio-economic backgrounds (Bourdieu and Passeron 1990). This certainly applies to the Flemish context, which, according to Programme for International Student Assessment (PISA) findings, is highly segregated and has a strong tendency to reproduce social inequalities (Hirtt et al. 2007). Comparative research on the impact of system characteristics on participation in adult education indeed suggests that the disappointing participation rates in Flanders may be due to the discouraging effect of the stratified initial education system on low achievers (Nicaise et al. 2007). Disadvantaged groups have more negative experiences in highly stratified education systems, such as grade repetition, demotion, school failure and dropout rates, and supposedly tend to develop more negative attitudes to learning in adulthood. Therefore, disadvantaged adults would supposedly benefit more from less 'schoolish', non-formal adult education systems. In practice, however, we notice that most non-formal adult education offers are organized in the private sector and focus specifically on job skills or in-company training (Vermeersch and Vandenbroucke 2010). As a result, disadvantaged groups are excluded, either because employers tend

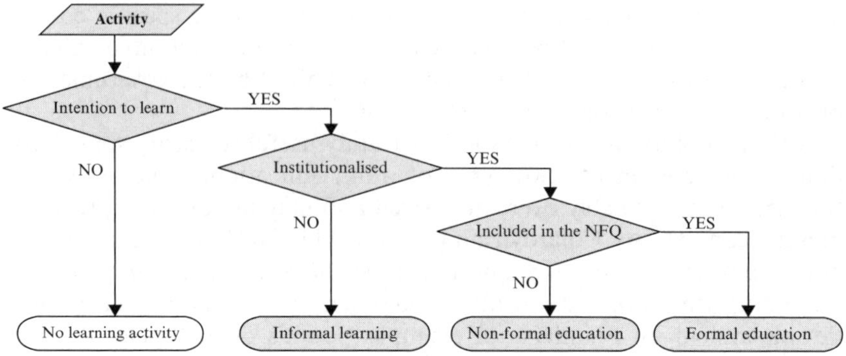

Source: Eurostat (2007, p. 23).

Figure 7.1 Schematic definition of (non-)formality of learning

to privilege investment in their most competitive employees, or indeed because they are unemployed and cannot rely on employers. In Flanders, adult basic education as well as second-chance education – within the formal adult education system – aim to reactivate a positive learning experience in the school system and prepare adults for future participation in the formal education system by strengthening their basic knowledge and skills. Adult basic education develops basic skills in writing, reading, arithmetic, information and communication technology (ICT), and so on, while second-chance education prepares adults to obtain the official final diploma of Flemish secondary education. Empirical data on the transition from adult basic education to other forms of adult education are lacking and information on the effectiveness of this policy is thus not transparent.

In this chapter we make use of the Eurostat Adult Education Survey (AES), within which the definitions of formal, non-formal and informal learning deviate slightly from standard definitions (Figure 7.1). In their communication about participation in learning activities, they use non-formal and formal education only. The AES starts from the assumption that learning is always intentional, although this is highly controversial in the international literature. Mainstream definitions of informal learning use terms such as incidental learning and random learning. In the AES, informal learning refers to self-study outside the educational context, but includes, for example, borrowing learning materials from a library. Non-formal and formal education take place in an institutionalized context, although the main difference is that non-formal learning is not credential-based and that these courses are not included in the National Qualification

Frameworks. At an overall level, the definition is based on two main dimensions: institutionalization and the orientation towards qualification.

Note that the most widely accepted definition of formal learning includes the 'ladder' criterion, that is, qualifications acquired through formal learning are ranked by level and build on each other, as is the case in initial education. This is not the case with the AES definition, in which formal learning leads to any kind of certified qualification. In practice, this means that certified training courses provided by a public employment agency, or indeed by private accredited training institutions, are seen as formal learning activities, even if they do not give access to further training at a higher level.

PARTICIPATION RATES

According to the results of the Eurostat Adult Education Survey, more than a third of European adults between 25 and 64 years old participate in formal or non-formal learning activities on a yearly basis (Boateng 2009). There are significant differences between countries. Figure 7.2 ranks countries in order of increasing (overall) participation rates, but also distinguishes between formal and non-formal participation. Adults in

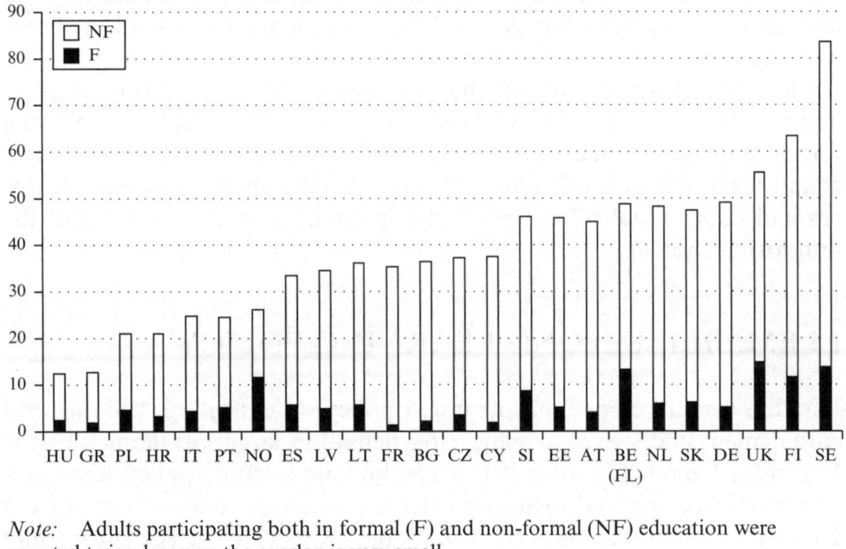

Note: Adults participating both in formal (F) and non-formal (NF) education were counted twice, however the overlap is very small.

Source: Eurostat Adult Education Survey.

Figure 7.2 Participation rates: formal versus non-formal

Scandinavian countries (except Norway) and the United Kingdom participate most. Countries with the lowest rates are mainly located in Southern and Eastern Europe, although exceptions exist (e.g. Slovakia, Slovenia, Estonia). Note that some adults participate both in formal and non-formal education: countries are ranked based on the overall participation rates (including overlap).

Although Flanders does not belong to the leading group in terms of overall participation, its rate of participation in formal adult education rises above the level of other countries with comparable overall rates (i.e. between 40 and 50 per cent), and reaches the level of Scandinavia and the United Kingdom (the only regions where participation in formal adult education exceeds 10 per cent). In all comparable countries, participation in non-formal adult learning activities is higher, but the distribution between formal and non-formal varies. Although participation in Sweden is very high, the proportion of formal education is rather low.

At an overall level, it is agreed that participation rates in adult education reflect more or less the different stages in the modernization process (Rubenson and Desjardins 2009). The large variation in participation rates suggests major differences in public policies, adult education structures, learning cultures and learning opportunities at work. Nevertheless, this type of comparative research often does not distinguish between formal and non-formal adult education and uses participation as a single dichotomous variable.

Flemish research on system characteristics influencing participation in adult education in the EU-15 used a participation indicator combining formal and non-formal learning (Desmedt et al. 2006). The aim of this chapter is to examine differences in policy actions, profiles of adult learners and educational offers specifically pertaining to the formal and the non-formal system.

FLEMISH LIFELONG LEARNING POLICY

Flanders has developed an integrated policy on education, training and employment and strives to achieve participation targets as defined by the European Union (Eurydice 2011). The lifelong learning policy stimulates 'life-wide' learning and focuses on the socio-cultural development of the Flemish population, along with other objectives such as a smoother functioning of the labour market. The policy aims to equip all adults with the necessary competencies (knowledge, skills and attitudes) to participate in society at the level of personal and professional development, and to obtain recognized credits, diplomas or degrees of study.

During the past decade, various policy documents were produced to set out these policy lines. In 2000, the year of the Lisbon Treaty, the Flemish government launched a scheme called On the Right Track for Lifelong Learning (*Een Leven Lang Leren in Goede Banen*) (Vlaamse Regering 2000). The plan outlined objectives to boost labour market participation and economic growth, but also to promote social cohesion and active citizenship. Personal development is a central concern, which means that learning is presented as an individual's right that has to be ensured by the government in cooperation with social partners and other stakeholders. The Vilvoorde Treaty (*Pact van Vilvoorde*) (Vlaamse Regering 2001) put forward 21 social and economic objectives to be achieved by 2010. With regard to education, the main priorities included a decrease in unqualified school leaving, a reduction in the number of adults with low literacy or ICT skills and an increase in the participation rates for lifelong learning activities.

In 2009, one year before the 'Vilvoorde targets' had to be achieved, the participation rate in lifelong learning was still far below 12.5 per cent on a four-weeks basis (Vlaamse Regering). Therefore, the Flemish Government developed a new scheme called 'Pact 2020 – Flanders in Action (*Pact 2020 Vlaanderen in Actie*) (Vlaamse Regering 2009), which includes the achievement of a Flemish learning society by 2020 as one of the key priorities. A few years earlier, in 2005, the Flemish government had launched the Flemish Strategic Plan for Literacy (*Strategisch Plan Geletterdheid*), as results of the International Adult Literacy Survey had indicated that 15 to 18 per cent of the Flemish adult population did not have the literacy level required to function properly in society (Van Damme et al. 1997). In addition to the screening of adults with literacy problems, the government also stresses the importance of identifying the specific learning needs and difficulties of this target group as well as creating appropriate learning opportunities for them. The Centres for Basic Education (*Centra voor Basiseducatie*) also played an important role in this debate.

Flemish formal adult education is coordinated mainly by the Department of Education and the Department of Work (Boeren 2008). Courses supported by both departments grant credits or certificates, but the courses of the Department of Education have a stronger civic value, whereas credits granted by the Department of Work are seen as vocational qualifications, which are not classified within the educational ladder. Formal adult education has been reformed in recent years and is regulated by the Act of 15th June 2007. The Department of Education is responsible for:

1. Adult basic education, providing courses to adults who lack the basic reading, writing, arithmetic, ICT, etcetera, skills necessary to function

properly in society. In addition, Dutch as a second language for immigrants is another major type of course. Adult basic education is organized in 13 Centres for Basic Education, each with its own regional catchment area.

2. Centres for Adult Education offer a wide range of courses in many fields (cooking, languages, carpentry, ICT, economics, etc.). Every adult should be able to find a course within their field of interest in one of the 113 Centres for Adult Education. Furthermore, they offer second-chance education for low-skilled adults who want to obtain a final secondary school qualification. The Centres for Basic Education (*Centra voor Basiseducatie*) and the Centres for Adult Education (*Centra voor Volwassenenonderwijs*) are organized according to a separate Decree on Adult Education (*Decreet Volwassenenonderwijs*) (Boeren 2008). They are supported by the Flemish Resource Centre for Adult Education (*Vlaams Ondersteuningscentrum voor Volwassenenonderwijs*, VOCVO).
3. Arts education provides part-time artistic education for children, teenagers and adults. Specific adult tracks are organized for anyone aged 15 and over. Course offers are divided between performing arts (music, dance, drama) and visual arts (painting, sculpture, etc.). Arts education is organized according to the Decree on Art Education signed on 31 July 1990.
4. Higher education includes non-university colleges and universities. At around the age of 18, secondary school graduates can start a Bachelor course at college or university. Most of these programmes take place in full-time daytime education and can also be followed by older adults. Some universities and colleges organize specific programmes – for example evening classes or distance education – for adults who want to combine higher education with other life spheres such as work or family. Nevertheless, research has demonstrated that specific offers for adult learners in higher education (such as evening or weekend classes) are mainly situated in the human sciences (sociology, education, philosophy) and nursing.

In addition, the Department of Work offers specific labour market courses:

1. VDAB training. VDAB is the Flemish Employment, Training and Counselling Agency which offers mediation, guidance and work-related training, mainly to unemployed adults. These courses are offered in almost all vocational fields. For unemployed adults, courses at VDAB are free of charge. E-learning courses are also available.

2. SYNTRA offers entrepreneurship training for adults who want to start a career in self-employment and focuses on small and medium-sized enterprises. The programme includes training on specific legislation and management. In addition, SYNTRA offers training to dropouts from full-time compulsory education (aged 15 and above) who want to combine education with work. Syntra has five regional centres.

As regards non-formal education, the AES defines the concept by listing the following forms: private lessons or courses, distance education, seminars or workshops and supervised on-the-job training (Eurostat 2007). On the one hand, we can distinguish providers receiving state funding to organize courses such as social-cultural organizations. For example, folk high schools (*Vorming Plus*) offer many short courses, seminars and workshops without granting certificates. Socio-cultural work is organized by the Decree on Socio-Cultural Adult Work signed on 4 April 2003. The Department of Culture is responsible for policy preparation, follow-up and evaluation in this field. There are no specific requirements to enroll for a course in socio-cultural adult work as the aim is to serve a wide audience regardless of formal qualifications or socio-economic background.

Arts education is seen as non-formal adult education in the AES, although it is officially organized by the Department of Education and follows the traditional ladder structure in which learners can move on to the next grade if they have passed the previous grade. We assume that it is placed under non-formal adult education because of its leisure-oriented content (for most participants), however, many courses in the Centres for Adult Education are also followed as leisure courses (e.g. cooking, language courses).

In addition to the above, there are many private providers of adult education, for example in companies or firms, although it is hard to identify them all as detailed data are lacking. All forms of workplace learning (on-the-job training offered by the employers for their employees) are considered non-formal learning. Overall, we can conclude that there is a wide variety of educational programmes, offered by a large number of different education providers (see Hefler 2010, p. 57).

RESULTS

In this section, we are mainly interested in the participation differences between formal and non-formal adult education. We look at the personal profile characteristics of participants, but also at their main motives for participation. At some points, we make a comparison with other countries

Table 7.2 Main motive for participation in adult education (%)

Motive	Formal	Non-formal
Job	50	69
Personal	50	31
Total	100	100

Source: Adult Education Survey 2009.

that reach high participation rates in formal adult education (Sweden, Finland, Norway and the United Kingdom).

As previously shown in Figure 7.2, 43.2 per cent of all Flemish adults between 25 and 64 years old participated in at least one course in the 12 months preceding the interview. Participation in non-formal education is higher than in formal education (35.4 per cent versus 13.3 per cent). A small proportion (5.5 per cent) participates in both forms.

Although formal as well as non-formal education in Flanders has a broad scope – personal development as well as securing labour market positions – we notice that the purpose of participation differs markedly between participants in formal and non-formal adult education (see Table 7.2). Nearly 70 per cent of all learners in non-formal education participate in the first place for job-related reasons, while 30 per cent report personal reasons as the main motive for participation. In formal education, this distribution is 50:50. This result indicates that – despite the success of regulated socio-cultural work – non-formal education is dominated by vocational education and training, often organized in a private context and sponsored by an employer. Lifelong learning has been criticized for being 'human resource development in drag' and as being 'lifelong earning' (Field 2000). This is especially the case for non-formal learning.

Trends in motives enable us to gain a deeper insight into the specificity of the adult education offers – as experienced by the adult learners themselves (Figure 7.3). In this regard, it is clear that Flanders is also rather unique in the number of adults reporting personal development as the main motive for participation. In other countries with more than 10 per cent participation in formal adult education, these percentages are lower. In the United Kingdom, no more than 8 per cent of all adults enrolled in formal education said they participated mainly for personal reasons. In Sweden, 41 per cent of the adults reported personal reasons, but this is still nearly 10 per cent below the Flemish results. Overall, this confirms the hypothesis that, in addition to economic targets, Flemish formal adult education policy aims to cater for 'life-wide' learning.

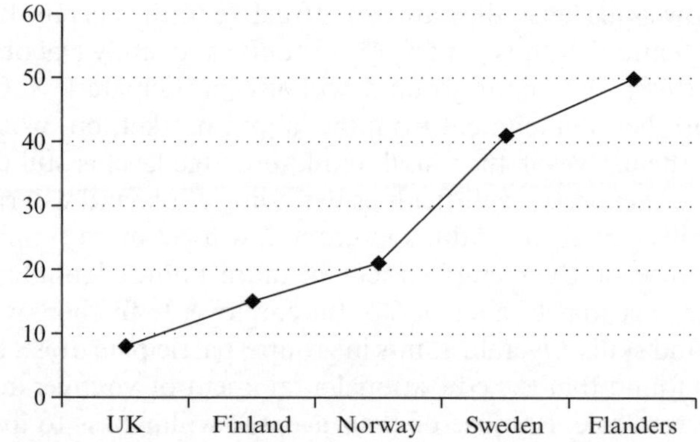

Source: Adult Education Survey 2009.

Figure 7.3 Percentage of participants in formal adult education reporting personal motivations, in Flanders and selected other Western European countries

Apart from motives, we look at the profile of adult learners. Desjardins et al. (2006) analysed the individual profiles of adult learners based on the International Adult Literacy Survey 1994–1998, the Adult Literacy and Lifeskills Survey 2003 and the EU Barometer 2003, surveys conducted in various countries in the developed world (in Europe, the USA and Canada). Desjardins et al. identified six distinct profiles on the basis of the three main determinants of participation: age, educational attainment and activity status:

- group 1: mid- to late-career workers (aged 45–65) who are less educated, less skilled and employed in low-skill blue-collar jobs;
- group 2: mid- to late-career workers (aged 45–65) who are highly educated, highly skilled and employed in high-skill white-collar jobs;
- group 3: employed early- to mid-career adults (aged 26–45);
- group 4: unemployed or out-of-the-labour-market mid- to late-career adults (aged 45–65) who are less educated and less skilled;
- group 5: unemployed or out-of-the-labour-market mid- to late-career adults (aged 45–65) who are highly educated and highly skilled;
- group 6: unemployed or out-of-the-labour-market early- to mid-career adults (26–45).

Adults in groups 1 and 4 have a very low probability of being an adult learner. They are in the final stage of their labour market career or do not have a job (any more) and are low skilled. Because of their age (Doets et al.

2001) and low skills level, they are not attractive to the current knowledge-based society and will thus get few opportunities to study (Jacobs and Van der Kamp 1998). Adults in group 5 will also participate less, because of their age and their detachment from the labour market, but would be able to relaunch themselves if their skill and knowledge level is still up-to-date. If not, they will experience difficulties in finding a job, and will run the risk that their skills depreciate. Adults in group 2 will get more training opportunities because of their employment in more knowledge-intensive jobs, although their age may be a barrier for the employer to further invest in their knowledge and skills. Overall, adults in group 3 participate most. Desjardins et al. (2006) found that the educational attainment of younger adults plays a less important role. Because of their age, the willingness to invest in the future is present, both at the level of the individual and at the level of the employer. Adults in group 6 do not have a job, but because of their younger age, it remains worthwhile to invest in their knowledge and skills and thus improve their chances of actively participating in the labour market.

Although Desjardins et al. (2006) did not find large differences in participation between men and women, gender roles might influence participation behaviour (Jackson 2004). On the one hand, men earn more than women (Ngo et al. 2003). Together with their responsibilities at home, due to motherhood, women have more discontinuous jobs and get less training opportunities in the workplace (Summers 2003; Light 2007). On the other hand, women increasingly outperform men within initial education, and tend to participate more in adult learning for non-work-related reasons. Work and education are thus not gender-neutral domains (Blackmore 2006). Unlike Desjardins et al. (2006), we will look at the differences between formal and non-formal education and analyse whether discrepancies exist.

Another potentially relevant socio-demographic determinant is nationality. Apart from their low socio-economic status, many foreign-born adults have poorer skills when it comes to reading, writing and speaking the national language. This double disadvantage leads to employment in less-knowledge-intensive jobs and thus affects the opportunities to participate in training. Many governments are aware of the unequal training opportunities for immigrants and try to compensate for this by offering language and other basic courses for these groups (Desjardins et al. 2006). In Flanders, too, we expect to find more non-Belgian adult learners in the formal education system.

Figure 7.4 reflects the participation rates in Flemish adult education, by each of our five key variables, separately for formal and non-formal adult education. As expected, men participate more in non-formal adult education, and women more in formal adult education. Because of the strong work-related nature of non-formal education, we can conclude that

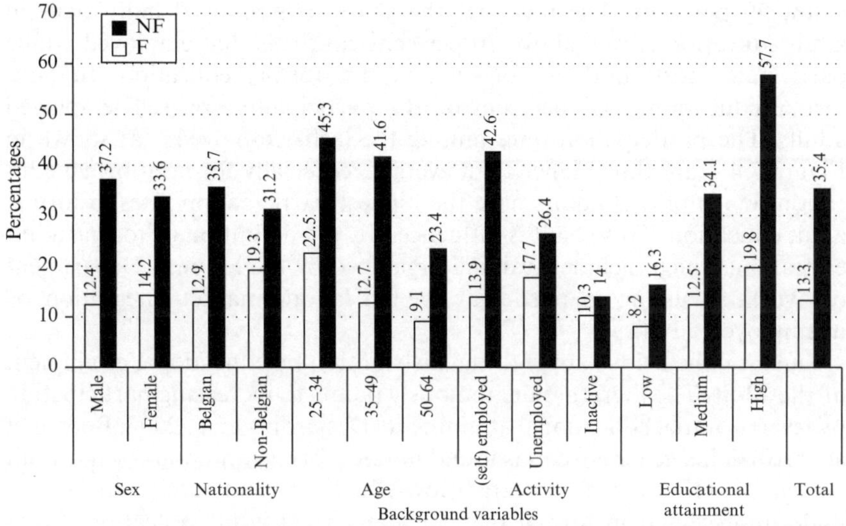

Source: Adult Education Survey 2009.

Figure 7.4 Participation rates of adult learners in formal versus non-formal adult education

traditional gender roles still persist to some extent in Flanders (Koelet 2005). Further investigation of barriers preventing participation (available in the AES) showed that, while all adults suffer from time squeeze, men suffer mainly from time pressure related to job responsibilities and women mainly from time pressure related to family responsibilities (Boeren et al. 2010).

Looking at nationality, we notice that participation in formal education is higher among non-Belgians than among Belgians. As mentioned earlier, Centres for Adult Basic Education and the Centres for Adult Education have special programmes for immigrants, such as Dutch as a second language, second-chance education and citizenship courses. Because of the under-representation of immigrants in knowledge-intensive jobs, we would expect lower participation in non-formal learning.

As regards the age distribution, it is well known that adults in the oldest age group participate less – as expected. Participation decreases by age, for formal as well as non-formal education. Nevertheless, the participation gap between the youngest group and the population average is larger in formal education (69 per cent) than in non-formal education (28 per cent).

During the AES data collection, the employment rate in Flanders was below 70 per cent. The fact that the share of employed individuals in adult education is well above 70 per cent confirms that employed adults participate most, both in formal and non-formal education. In non-formal education, 87.5 per cent of the participants are (self-)employed adults. The participation rates among the (self-)employed – as shown in Figure 7.4 – are thus higher than average, especially for non-formal education. Unemployed adults have the highest participation rates in formal adult education. This result is influenced by the definition of formal adult education, which includes training organized by the Flemish Department of Work, focussing in particular on the labour market integration of unemployed adults.

Similar conclusions apply to the distribution by educational attainment of the adult. The literature unanimously points to increasing participation by level of initial educational attainment (Desjardins et al. 2006; Boeren et al. 2010). This general trend is found in both formal and non-formal adult education. However, as expected, low-educated adults are relatively less under-represented in formal than in non-formal adult education. More specifically, they participate in Centres for Adult Basic Education and in the Second Chance programme of the Centres for Adult Education. Highly educated adults participate relatively more in non-formal education, probably because their jobs require continuous updating of knowledge and skills and because training opportunities are more available to them.

One of our hypotheses was that the Flemish formal education policy aims to redistribute education towards low-educated groups. In this regard, it is interesting to compare the shares of low-educated adults in the population of learners in the formal adult education system in different countries. Whereas low-educated adults in Flanders are under-represented in formal adult education (8.2 per cent compared with the population average of 13.3 per cent), this participation gap is smaller than in other countries: for example the United Kingdom (7.8 per cent versus 15.1 per cent), Finland (3.7 versus 10.2 per cent), Slovenia (2.1 versus 8.7 per cent), Spain (1.7 per cent versus 5.9 per cent).

Summing up, our results are in line with the findings of Desjardins et al. (2006). Participation is stronger among high-educated adults who have a job and are below the age of 50. These trends apply for both formal and non-formal education, although there are systematic differences between the two types of adult education: traditional inequalities in participation by gender, age, citizenship, labour market status and level of education are stronger in non-formal education.

CONCLUSIONS

In this chapter, we started from the observation that the focus on formal adult education in Flanders is considerably stronger than in other European countries. Our hypothesis was threefold:

- firstly, not all forms of formal adult education can be substituted with non-formal learning – as the second-chance and social upgrading functions in particular involve long pathways along a ladder structure;
- secondly, the Department of Education sees catering for 'life-wide' learning (languages, arts, hobbies, etc.) as opposed to lifelong learning for employability as one of its missions; and
- thirdly, formal education, which is the main policy instrument of the government, aims to redistribute opportunities to lower-educated groups.

In our description of Flemish adult education policy, we explained that the aims and objectives of the adult education system are very broad. Whereas national and EU policies in this field are often criticized for being too narrowly focused on vocational and economic objectives (Holford et al. 2008), the Flemish formal system seems to foster the 'life-wide' approach to learning. Looking at motivations to participate in formal learning, the personal 'life-wide' perspective of Flemish learners clearly deviates from patterns in other European countries. We can thus state that the second hypothesis is confirmed.

In addition, the personal values of learning, the new Decree on Adult Education also focuses on the need to boost the proportion of adults with a qualification (Boeren 2008). Despite the general recognition of the additional value of a qualification for the labour market, the possibility of obtaining a formal qualification (usually referring to a final secondary school qualification) is also a strong aim in itself. As many adults lack skills and knowledge, they have to (re)start their educational careers at the very lowest level in Centres for Basic Education, or they have to enroll for second-chance education. Although many policy-makers see the non-credential-based specificity of non-formal education as a positive point to attract more disadvantaged groups – as it gives adults the opportunity to enroll without previous qualification requirements – non-formal adult education is in practice less accessible for low-educated groups (and weaker groups in general). As the non-formal system is so dominated by vocational aspects, the same 'Matthew effect' applies: the strongest groups and those with the highest qualifications are employed in the best jobs, which provide more training opportunities (Boeren et al. 2010). This Flemish philosophy confirms the first hypothesis, that the ladder structure is seen as important in order to decrease the social, cultural and economic gaps in society. Furthermore, with the introduction of European and National Qualification Frameworks, we notice a tendency to formalize non-formal learning (Coles 2007). Qualification Frameworks strive towards recognition of skills and knowledge ranging from levels 1 to 8. In the end, learning outcomes and the related competencies are important, regardless of whether they were gained by formal or non-formal learning activities.

The third hypothesis was confirmed by showing that adults from vulnerable groups participate relatively more in formal adult education than within non-formal adult education. We would call this phenomenon the 'formal–non-formal accessibility paradox'. Nevertheless, the paradox itself is relative, in view of the general trend that stronger groups of adults participate more in adult education 'at large', and also in formal learning. In other words, the 'Matthew effect' in adult education applies to formal as well as non-formal education, but relatively less to formal education. Perhaps this can be seen as a step in the desired direction.

REFERENCES

Blackmore, Jill (2006), 'Unprotected Participation in Lifelong Learning and the Politics of Hope: A Feminist Reality Check of Discourses around Flexibility, Seamlessness and Learners Earners', in Carole Leathwood and Becky Francis (eds), *Gender and Lifelong Learning: Critical Feminist Engagements*, London: Routledge, pp. 9–26.

Boateng, Sadiq Kwesi (2009), *Significant Country Differences in Adult Learning*, Luxembourg: Eurostat.

Boeren, Ellen (2008), 'Een nieuw decreet volwassenenonderwijs' (A New Decree for Adult Education), *School en samenleving*, **19**, 65–80.

Boeren, Ellen, Ides Nicaise and Herman Baert (2010), 'Intentions and Constraints of Non-Participants in Adult Education', presentation at ESREA Conference Linkoping, Sweden.

Bourdieu, Pierre and Jean-Claude Passeron (1990), *Reproduction in Education, Society and Culture*, London: Sage.

Colardyn, Danielle and Jens Bjornavold (2004), 'Validation of Formal, Non-Formal and Informal Learning: Policy and Practice in EU Member States', *European Journal of Education*, **39** (1), 69–89.

Coles, Mike (2007), 'Qualifications Frameworks in Europe: Platforms for Collaboration, Integration and Reform: Presidency Conference "Realizing the European Learning Area"', Munich.

Colley, Helen, Phil Hodkinson and Janice Malcolm (2003), *Informality and Formality in Learning: a Report for the Learning and Skills Research Centre*, London: Learning and Skills Research Centre.

Desjardins, Richard, Kjell Rubenson and Marcella Milana (2006), *Unequal Chances to Participate in Adult Learning: International Perspectives*, Paris: UNESCO.

Desmedt, Ella, Steven Groenez and Gert Van den Broeck (2006), *Onderzoek naar de Systeemkenmerken die de Participatie aan Levenslang Leren in de EU-15 Beïnvloeden* (Research into System Characteristics influencing Participation in Lifelong Learning in the EU-15), Leuven: HIVA.

Doets, Cees, Wil van Esch and Anneke Westerhuis (2008), *Een Brede Verkenning van een Leven Lang Leren* (A Broad Exploration of Lifelong Learning), Hertogenbosch: CINOP.

Doets, Cees, Barry Hake and Anneke Westerhuis (2001), *Lifelong Learning in The Netherlands. The State of the Art in 2000's*, Hertogenbosch: Cinop.

Eurostat (2007), *Task Force Report on Adult Education Survey*, Luxembourg: Eurostat.

Eurydice (2011), *Educational Structures and Education Systems for Vocational Training and Adult Education in Europe. Belgium – Flemish Community – 2009*, Brussels: Flemish Government.

Field, John (2000), *Lifelong Learning and the New Educational Order*, Stoke on Trent: Trentham Books.

Gibbons, Michael (1994), *The New Production of Knowledge: the Dynamics of Science and Research in Contemporary Society*, London: Sage.

Hefler, Gunther (2010), *The Qualification Supporting Company – the Significance of Formal Adult Education in Small and Medium Organisations. Comparative Report, Subproject 4 – LLL2010*, Krems: Danube University.

Hirtt, Nico, Ides Nicaise and Dirk De Zutter (2007), *De School van de Ongelijkheid* (The School of Inequality), Berchem: EPO.

Jackson, Sue (2004), *Differently Academic? Developing Lifelong Learning for Women in Higher Education*, Dordrecht: Kluwer Academic Publishers.

Jacobs, Ineke and Max van der Kamp (1998), 'Deelname en Behoeften in de Volwasseneneducatie' (Participation and Needs in Adult Education), *Stoho*, **18**, 1–25.

Koelet, Suzana (2005), *Standvastige Verschillen. Een Analyse van Theoretische Benaderingen over de Verdeling van het Huishoudelijk Werk tussen Vrouwen en Mannen op Basis van Tijdsbudgetonderzoek* (Persistent Differences. An Analysis of Theoretical Approaches to the Distribution of Domestic Tasks between Women and Men based on Time Budget Research), Brussels: Vrije Universiteit Brussel.

Light, Ivan (2007), 'Women's Economic Niches and Earning Inferiority: The View from the Ethnic Economy', *Journal of Ethnic and Migration Studies*, **33** (4), 541–557.

Nicaise, Ides, Steven Groenez and Ella Desmedt (2007), 'How do System Characteristics Affect Participation in Lifelong Learning? The Experience of the EU15', presentation at European Conference for Education Research, Gent, 19–21 September.

Ngo, Huang-yue, Sharon Foley, Angela Wong and Raymond Loi (2003), 'Who Gets More of the Pie? Predictors of Perceived Gender Inequity at Work', *Journal of Business Ethics*, **45**, 227–241.

Rubenson, Kjell and Richard Desjardins (2009), 'The Impact of Welfare State Regimes on Constraints to Participation in Adult Education. A Bounded Agency Model', *Adult Education Quarterly*, **59** (3), 187–207.

Simkins, Tim (1977), *Non-Formal Education and Development*, Manchester: Department of Higher and Adult Education.
Summers, Anne (2003), *The End of Equality: Work, Babies and Women's Choices in 21st Century Australia*, Sydney: Random House.
Van Damme, Dirk, Luc Van de Poele and Els Verhasselt (1997), *Hoe Geletterd/Gecijferd is Vlaanderen. Functionele Taal- en Rekenvaardigheden van Vlamingen in Internationaal Perspectief* (How Literate/Numerate is Flanders. Functional Language and Arithmetic Skills of Flemings in an International Perspective), Leuven/Amersfoort: Garant.
Vermeersch, Lode and Anneloes Vandenbroucke (2010), *Het Leren Zoals het Is . . . bij Volwassenen met een Geletterdheidsrisico* (Learning as it is . . . among Adults with a Literacy Risk), Leuven: HIVA Institute for Labour and Society.
Vlaamse Regering (2000), *Actieplan 'Een Leven Lang Leren in Goede Banen'* (Action Plan 'On the Right Track for Lifelong Learning'), Brussels: Vlaamse Regering.
Vlaamse Regering (2001), *Het Pact van Vilvoorde* (The Vilvorde Treaty), Brussels: Vlaamse Regering.
Vlaamse Regering (2005), *Strategisch Plan Geletterdheid* (Strategic Plan for Literacy), Brussels: Vlaamse Regering.
Vlaamse Regering (2009), *Pact 2020. Vlaanderen in Actie (ViA)* (Pact 2020 – Flanders in Action), Brussels: Vlaamse Regering.

APPENDIX: ADULT EDUCATION SURVEY

In this chapter, we use data from the Flemish Eurostat Adult Education Survey (AES) gathered in 2007. The preparation of the AES started in June 2004 with the creation of an Adult Education Questionnaire Development Group. The aim of the AES was to collect data on adult education and learning as a response to an increasing demand for information about this sector, which has to continuously anticipate the development of a knowledge-based society.

In addition to data on adult education participation, the AES database contains information on socio-demographic and socio-economic background variables, on language and ICT skills and on participation in various social and cultural activities (Eurostat 2007). Furthermore, barriers preventing participation and general attitudes towards learning and education were surveyed.

The survey was carried out in most EU-27 countries in the period 2005–2008. All participating countries were provided with a common codebook – constructed by the Questionnaire Development Group – which had to be adapted into a country-specific questionnaire.

The Flemish sample was stratified by gender and age (Vermeersch and Vandenbroucke 2010). In total, 8677 adults aged 25 to 64 were invited to participate and received a web link to where they could complete the questionnaire. Non-respondents were contacted again by telephone or visited by interviewers who offered support in filling out the questionnaires. This resulted in 3104 respondents, which is a response rate of nearly 36 per cent. A weighting procedure was applied to obtain a representative sample by gender, age, occupational status, educational attainment, nationality and family size. The main variables in this survey, those relating to participation in adult education – both formal and non-formal – were measured using a reference period of 12 months preceding the interview. Adults who did not participate at the moment of the interview but during the preceding 12 months also had to answer these questions.

8. In search of building blocks for lifelong learning: motivation and institutional support in Norwegian education and training

Odd Bjørn Ure and Bjørg Eva Aaslid

INTRODUCTION

Lifelong Learning as a Field of Educational Practices

Contemporary EU policy-making for lifelong learning (LLL) tries to 'build effective adult learning systems' (European Commission 2009, p. 27) and to 'modernise education and training systems' (European Council 2010, p. 3). The Norwegian government equally announces in its annual education budget its intention to 'further develop a national system for lifelong learning'. If these ambitions are to become reality, various education and training practices need to support the aims of LLL.

Research on possible transformations of national education and training systems into a state of lifelong learning should look into the policy interventions behind the efforts to put the systems on an LLL track. It is equally pertinent to scrutinize agency mechanisms, for example how various actors, such as interest groups, promote or resist such transformations, which can lead to educational practices gradually forming patterns pointing towards the existence of building blocks of a lifelong learning system.

In this chapter, we will concentrate on tracing motivational and institutional aspects that affect such LLL patterns. As we will detail below, it is assumed that LLL can be understood as an 'organizational field', composed of actors with their identities and roles. Our aim is to contribute to conceptual frameworks for analysing the institutional preconditions for learners' life and learning trajectories and, in the last instance, to inform policy-makers in matters of lifelong learning. The main traits of our theoretical framework are illustrated in Figure 8.1.

LLL as an organizational field

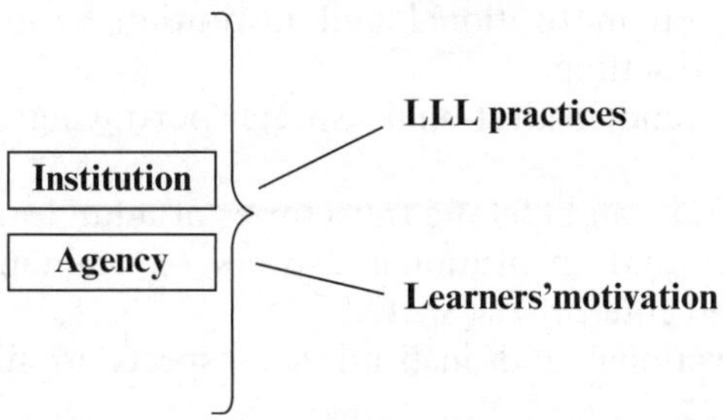

Figure 8.1 LLL as an organizational field

LLL Practices Sustained by the Institutional Capacity and Learners' Motivation

Against the background of the educational landscape and theoretical framework depicted above, this chapter has a twofold aim: we will look at LLL practices in adult education institutions as well as the motivation of adult learners. If the education system is to realize the goal of providing lifelong learning, it has to stimulate the number of participants in adult education while reducing inequalities in access to participation. More precisely, we will scrutinize whether there is a change of practices supporting the emergence of LLL at macro, meso and micro levels. Within this perspective, we will operationalize LLL as follows:

1. individual aspects of LLL (in practice, the motivation of adult learners to attend further and continuing training);
2. institutional (and structural) aspects of LLL (in practice the existence of LLL practices in education institutions and firms).

This discussion will be related to the judicial path of Norwegian formal education in terms of numerous statutory rights for individuals. For this purpose, a range of policy documents were analysed. On two occasions, semi-structured interviews were conducted in adult education institutions and combined with a survey of 750 learners. The methods used have varied between the five sub-projects underpinning this chapter, thus allowing for analyses of micro, meso and macro relations of lifelong learning.

Outline of the Chapter

The chapter is structured in the following way:

1. The framework and operationalization of LLL in Norway.
2. Perspectives on motivational and institutional aspects of LLL in organizational settings.
3. Motivational and institutional aspects: portraying adults in formal education.
4. Instant portraits and lifelong trajectories of adult learners.
5. Motivational and institutional aspects of training in small and medium-sized enterprises (SMEs).
6. From motivational and institutional aspects to life and learning trajectories.
7. LLL within labour market and economic structures: Norway in country typologies.

The concluding section will contextualize the motivational and institutional aspects affecting Norwegian LLL patterns. This will be done by positioning Norway within typologies that notably capture countries' labour market as well as education and training structures.

THE FRAMEWORK AND OPERATIONALIZATION OF LLL IN NORWAY

The Framework: Lifelong Learning in the Educational Landscape

Whereas the concept of LLL has probably had a stronger impact on decision-makers than on the Norwegian research community, researchers have to a large extent approached LLL via older notions such as further and continuing training. This discrepancy reflects a reticence towards new and possibly rhetorical concepts (Ure 2007). The high ambitions behind LLL targeting everyone sometimes add a political flavour to the slogan; but this also pinpoints a need to address simultaneously many learning contexts (school, home, workplace, community). Some dimensions of lifelong learning seem to have transformed the traditional education and training system. In a vague sense of the word, a kind of LLL system can be traced in Norway, meaning that education and training practices show signs of systemic change.

Given that LLL is basically a policy concept, it is pertinent to refer back to the European Union (EU) *Memorandum on Lifelong Learning* (European Commission 2000), which contains a widely used definition embracing all levels of learning activities, from early childhood education and care to adult learning, and addressing all forms of learning, independent of the learning context in which it takes place (formal, non-formal or informal).

A recent study on *Lifelong Learning Strategies* conducted on behalf of the European Commission (GHK 2010) sheds more light on mechanisms for change at a system level. Here, the point of departure was to analyse how policy can improve lifelong learning as a continuum (in terms of its quantity, quality, effectiveness and efficiency). The study notably looked at mechanisms and practices that:

1. entail changes in terms of facilitating transition and progression across education and training sub-systems or different forms of learning;
2. address more than one education and training subsystem (e.g. policies that combine adult learning with pre-school learning);
3. ensure learners develop the right competence sets and attitudes to engage in learning throughout their life.

We will enlarge on such change mechanisms in a specific section devoted to perspectives on lifelong learning.

Operationalization of LLL in a Norwegian Context

A historic overview of the Norwegian education and training system with regard to the LLL discourse allows us to outline what makes lifelong learning operational for the average learner. This discourse is primarily promoted by public actors (Ure 2007). For a more complete picture it is therefore urgent to link national LLL frameworks with learning conditions for individuals. We assume that the concept boils down to three characteristics:

1. Better learning opportunities for the individual leads to improved access ('LLL for all').
2. More tailor-made training during the initial education period as well as later leads to improved offer, which is a challenge for public and private providers of further and continuing training.
3. More opportunities for validation and recognition of non-formal and informal learning create a need to mobilize more learning spaces during a person's life span.

Coupled to these characteristics several statutory rights have been introduced leading to LLL practices that can be related to the same characteristics. Our attempt to make the concept of LLL more operational is accordingly illustrated in Figure 8.2.

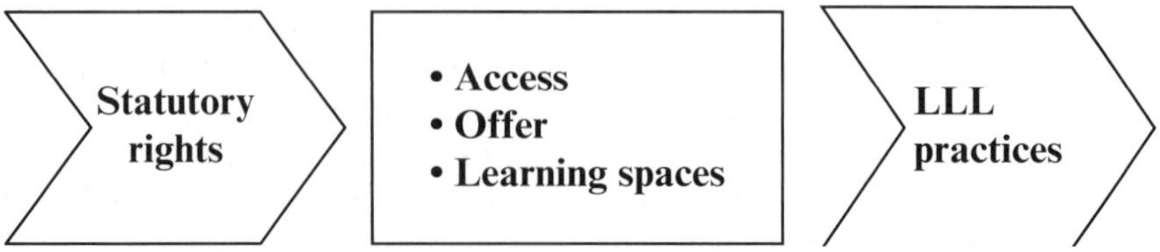

Figure 8.2 Main characteristics of lifelong learning in a Norwegian context

Short Retrospective

An ambitious LLL reform, coined the Competence Reform, tried to reshape the educational and labour market landscape during the period 1999–2006. 'Second-chance' learners were offered improved access to formal education by allowing them to complete their education at the level of primary or upper secondary education. In addition, the reform enshrined a right to training leave for employees and equal treatment of adolescent and adult learners by the State Educational Loan Fund. A third statutory right guarantees adapted education according to learners' individual needs. This right applies to everybody and is undoubtedly a very ambitious goal, depending on how it is being implemented at local level. These statutory rights have definitely put LLL in Norway on a judicial path, guaranteed by the state.

Following local and sector experiments launched in the late 1990s, the validation of non-formal and informal competencies aims to evaluate and compare learning experiences from the labour market, civil society and the education system. In light of experiences gained so far, the ambition to develop a unitary validation system at national level has been scaled down to the benefit of one framework document for the labour market and another for civil society. The dissemination of the validation framework for the civil society has been quite slow in spite of good involvement of Norwegian study associations during the pilot phase. Likewise we do not experience any convergence of assessment tools in the labour market. Hence, the average learner is not yet offered substantial tools for translating learning experiences gained in these two settings. Comparisons of such experiences to the education system are not widespread either, although several pilot projects have been launched at a county level in Norway and within European projects aiming to spur partnerships that could facilitate appreciation of prior learning experiences (GHK 2011).

PERSPECTIVES ON MOTIVATIONAL AND INSTITUTIONAL ASPECTS OF LLL IN ORGANIZATIONAL SETTINGS

The wide scope of LLL policy invites researchers to look at the field from numerous theoretical perspectives, ranging from (socio-)psychological perspectives to institutional theory of political sciences. Within learning theory inspired from pedagogy, attitudes of adult learners are explained by distinguishing individual motivation for attending a limited number of training lessons from motivation for entering a long-lasting learning trajectory. There is equally a scientific discourse on how personal motivation and institutional factors can be related to individual life and learning trajectories (see Mayer 2009 for an overview of research on life course).

When looking deeper into motivation, various subtypes can be distinguished, such as intrinsic and extrinsic motives, thus featuring the goals and means related to attending some kind of education or training course (cf. Dæhlen and Ure 2009). Knud Illeris argues for example that low-skilled adults understand very well the importance of formal education or training, but they strongly wish that attending it were not necessary (Illeris 2003, 2006). Many such learners had bad experiences in school, where success was a rare phenomenon. Nonetheless, they recognize that formal education may be the only way out of a vulnerable situation. In other words, education is necessary but not desired. Consequently, low-skilled adults could be motivated mainly by job-related factors. This does, however, not rule out that other people, in addition to low-skilled adults, can also consider further and continuing education more as a compulsion than an opportunity (Tight 1998).

The theoretical perspective guiding this chapter searches for the organizational preconditions and sources for the motivation of individual learners. The weight of institutions within the (emerging) LLL system then comes to the fore, but not as a stereotyped opposition between individual agency and institutional structures. We suggest instead combining these two with the main characteristics of LLL in Norway, including the LLL practices that we identified as well as the learners' motivation. This framework is illustrated in Figure 8.3.

Before enlarging upon this, a short retrospective on institutional theory is needed. In their chapter on 'Perspective of Governance', two rather 'early institutionalists' explain their perspective in the following way:

> In the institutional theory, people act, think, feel and organize themselves on the basis of exemplary or authoritative (and sometimes competing or conflicting) rules derived from socially constructed identities and roles. Along the way,

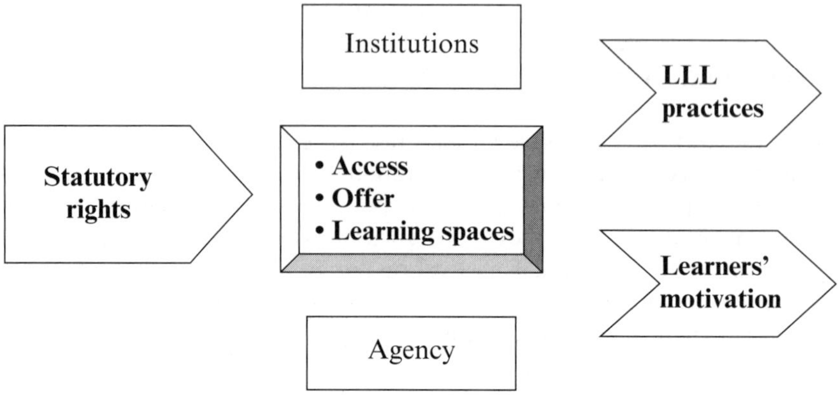

Figure 8.3 Organizational setting for motivational and institutional LLL factors

> political institutions create rules regulating the possession and use of political rights and resources. Even the conception of an autonomous agent, with a particularistic way of self-understanding . . . is a conception of an acquired identity, a socialized understanding of self and others. (March and Olsen 1995, p. 30)

Less concerned with political institutions, Richard Scott has further developed the Bourdieu-inspired concept of 'field', which is seen together with individuals and organizations:

> organizations provide institutional contexts within which particular actors are located and take action. Generalized models – beliefs, norms, menus and scripts – flow 'down' through the various levels, carried by socialisation, social construction and sanctioning powers. These models are carried and reproduced, but also modified and reconstructed, by the interpretations and inventions of subordinate actors: individuals, organizations and fields. (Scott 1995, p. 141)

Departing from the assumption that LLL can be understood as an 'organizational field', composed of actors with their identities and roles, this chapter discusses the role that institutions exercise within this field. How they influence the LLL agenda can be elucidated by looking at the institutional freedom or leeway to define and put in place their own strategies, compared with implementing policies defined from above, regardless of whether the command chain is of a public or private nature. The interaction between adult learners and institutions within the LLL field will also be discussed. Such institutions, possibly forming part of a nascent LLL system, do not only implement public policy or policies defined by other stakeholders. They also have institutional capacity to meet the needs of adult learners materialized in pedagogical practices adapted to the specific conditions pertaining to (groups of) individual learners. The capacity to meet these needs points to a discussion of the possibility of changing the formal education system in order to put it on a distinct LLL track.

A key concept in this regard is 'institutional package', implying that individual educational opportunities are shaped by reciprocal actions between, notably, the education system and the labour market (cf. Ure and Saar 2008). The concept complies with the theoretical approach derived from attempts to discern varieties of welfare capitalism. It seeks out 'institutional complementarities' far beyond the education system and the labour market by also accounting for different production regimes, industrial relations and social protection systems (cf. Hall and Soskice 2001; Streeck 1989). Rather than grouping countries under a single regime, the concept of 'institutional package' allows for multidimensional models of institutional structures, which are country-specific. In the present chapter we therefore identify specific building blocks for LLL, before situating Norway among other European countries.

MOTIVATIONAL AND INSTITUTIONAL ASPECTS: PORTRAYING ADULTS IN FORMAL EDUCATION

Motivational and institutional aspects come to the forefront in discussions on how LLL practices can be sustained. The broadly defined motivational and institutional aspects were particularly scrutinized in a Norwegian survey of 750 adult learners, concluding that characteristics such as gender, age, employment and citizenship affect adults' motivations to attend further and continuing education. Previous research suggests that adults' motivations for education are multifaceted. Although many learners state that they enrol in education programmes because they want to learn something new, they often attend training because they are (or feel) obliged to do so (Illeris 2003). This perspective is particularly pronounced in scholarly works harvesting from Foucault's notion of 'governmentality', implying that the necessity and value of learning form part of the governing of the population (for an overview, see Fejes and Nicoll 2008).

In the Norwegian study six reasons for participation were grouped into three clusters: social aspects (to meet new people; to contribute to the community), personal aspects (desire to learn more) and job-related and financial aspects (to claim benefits; to find a job). The list then reads as shown in Box 8.1.

The survey data showed that high-skilled learners less frequently state getting a job as a reason for starting a course, compared with low-skilled

BOX 8.1 MOTIVATIONAL ASPECTS REVEALED IN A SURVEY OF NORWEGIAN ADULT LEARNERS

Reasons for tending adult education:

- Learn more about a subject that interests me.
- Contribute more to my community.
- Somebody advised me to do it.
- I was obliged to do it.
- Get a new job.
- Meet new people.

Source: Daehlen and Ure (2009).

learners. In an article detailing these findings, Dæhlen and Ure (2009) demonstrate that low-skilled adults more often say they were obliged to participate in the courses. Hence, the importance of social motivation for participating in a course (e.g. to meet new people) remained unequal across educational levels. The authors maintained that learners at the primary and secondary level put significantly greater emphasis on social aspects than those at the upper secondary and master's level.

Moreover, qualitative interviews in 50 adult education institutions were conducted and this information was coupled with data arising from a survey to which 750 adult learners responded. One conclusion was that adult education institutions at all levels put emphasis on non-traditional access routes through assessment of prior learning experiences gained outside the classroom. At lower education levels, many institutions are offering administrative and pedagogical support to adult learners. In this regard, institutions at the lowest educational levels seemed somewhat more flexible than institutions at higher levels. One implication is that universities and university colleges often take for granted that the Norwegian State Educational Loan Fund provides sufficient economic support to adult learners by covering their living expenses and teaching material.

Still, the survey of 750 adult learners referred to above revealed that this difference between education levels does not seem to impact on adult learners' confidence in completing their studies, nor in their satisfaction with the training actually offered. Overall, the high level of confidence in completing training courses, and the low level of satisfaction with the training offered to adult learners at all education levels, did not support the assumption that institutions play a significant role in increasing adults' participation in formal education and in reducing inequalities in participation (Dæhlen and Ure 2009). Flaws in our data may however explain or at least modify this observation. A further attempt to link data from the surveyed 750 adult learners with qualitative interviews in 50 adult education institutions was to produce five 'images' or portraits that describe typical elements or characteristics of the adult learners enrolled in courses at different educational levels. These images are not meant to describe one particular person or institution, nor the average learner. We use them as 'idealizations of real cases' (Ragin 1994, p. 70). Inspired from the Weberian *Idealtypen*, the images should illuminate the relationship between the formal education system and adult learners. They are presented below.

The Image of a Student on an Introductory Programme (ISCED[1] 1 + 2 Level of Education)

Samira (32) is married and has three small children. She is a refugee from Somalia and has been living in Norway for the last three years. She has education only at a primary level from Somalia and her skills in Norwegian are relatively poor. In order to apply for permanent settlement and Norwegian citizenship, Samira was obliged to start her educational programme. Samira is relatively negative towards the course she is attending and also towards adult education in general. She has few positive experiences with education. In general, she thinks that money spent on adult education is not well spent.

The course Samira is attending is free of charge and includes 250 hours' Norwegian language training and 50 hours' introduction to social conditions (the introductory programme). Although Samira was obliged to enrol in the programme, she thinks this is an important step in getting a job.

The introductory course is developed in cooperation between the municipality and the Norwegian Labour and Welfare Organization (NAV). It is provided by a competence centre that specializes in education for refugees. As a participant at this centre, Samira is offered education on one of three tracks of the introductory programme. These tracks are adjusted to the educational background of the participants, ranging from elementary to more independent and advanced levels. As Samira has very limited prior education, enrolment at track 1 was most suitable for her. On this track, her native language is used and progression is rather slow. Reading and writing skills are emphasized. The class consists of people facing a similar situation, most of them of her age or even younger, with a small majority of women. The teacher speaks both Somalian and English, which makes it easier to follow the classes.

After finishing the introductory programme she has been thinking about progressing to education at ISCED 1+2 level, which is offered by a competence centre in the municipality where she lives. As she was registered on a National Introductory Register (NIR), she received a letter with information regarding such offers. The fact that there are neither formal admission requirements at this level nor any enrolment fees is an incentive for Samira to participate in primary education. To a certain degree, the easy access to training neutralizes her low level of motivation.

The Image of a Student at ISCED 3 Level; Private School

Line (24) is unmarried and has no children. After finishing upper secondary school she studied social sciences at university. Over the last three years she has been working and also travelling around in Asia. She has now decided to become a doctor and is spending this year improving her marks in order to commence university studies in medicine. Since Line has already finished her upper secondary education, she is not covered by the statutory right of free upper secondary education. She decided nevertheless to apply to a private school that adapts its training courses to individual learning needs. There are no formal admission requirements but she has to attend an interview where her documented prior education is assessed. Line receives grant aid and a limited loan from the Norwegian State Educational Loan Fund. The school she attends is relatively expensive. She has to cover a study fee of €5000 in addition to the expenses of study material and she is facing financial problems. She manages, however, due to savings and help from her parents.

The school has a policy for providing exams to adults. The average pupil has either missed out one or more subjects, or wants to improve their previous results (as in the case of Line) in order to enter a particular field of study. Line had the offer to take the courses as electronic distance learning, but since she lives in a larger city with offers from private schools, she decided to attend classroom education. The students work in smaller groups from time to time. In her class there are about 30 pupils, many sharing the same educational goal.

Line found out about the school after noticing a commercial campaign on the metro addressing students who wanted to upgrade their skills, and thereafter through checking the school's website. The educational institution does not receive any public subsidies and regards itself more of a course supplier than a school. Its management does not perceive the institution as a competitor with the state school but as a course supplier targeting a different group: namely those who already have benefitted from their statutory rights in the public education system and now want to improve their marks, while being offered flexible learning solutions.

The Image of a Student at ISCED 3 Level; Vocational Education Provided by a State School

Lars is 55 years old. After finishing compulsory education he had various short-term contracts in the labour market. At that time the unemployment rate in Norway was low and Lars found it relatively easy to get a job. At the age of 23 Lars got a permanent job as a warehouse worker. However, in 2002 his company was closed down and Lars became unemployed. During his unemployment period Lars was encouraged to join a course under the auspices of NAV. This course offered six weeks of work placement in a company that produces steel structures. After the work placement period Lars was offered a job. Lars was, however, obliged to enrol on a course in welding and to pass the exams before getting a permanent position.

He applied to an upper secondary school offering vocational education in the county where he lives. The school offers altogether five different educational paths or programmes in general and vocational education, in addition to adjusted part-time training and some compressed offers. The school has a separate (but integrated) resource centre that specializes in further and continuing education for adults within specific fields.

The school has flexible admission requirements. Lars submitted documentation of his compulsory education and attended an interview, mostly in order to map his competencies and needs in relation to the course he is attending. During the interview he found out that there are long waiting lists for attending vocational upper secondary courses and he feels lucky to have the opportunity. The school administration also informed him that there are possibilities of attending preparatory programmes and extra courses, for example a so-called 'reading and writing workshop' for those in need of increasing their basic skills.

There are 11 other pupils attending the welding course, which runs on a part-time basis to make it possible to combine study with work commitments. It lasts for 20 hours, distributed over four evenings of five hours teaching and practical activities. The total course costs around €300, but this includes teaching material and necessary equipment. This fee is covered by his employer. Lars is satisfied with the teachers who have an offer of in-service training from their employer where education adapted to individual needs is one of the central topics.

The Image of a student at ISCED 4 Level of Education

Kristian was born in 1978. He is married and has no children. In 2000 he got a certificate as a carpenter. After advice from his employer he started in 2006 at a state vocational school in order to obtain a master craftsman certificate. The programme that Kristian is attending is one year's full-time study. The course is mainly based on Internet studies with only four gatherings (normally comprising of 15 people) over three days during a year. Traditional class instruction and working in smaller groups is the regular teaching mode. Since Kristian has problems with dyslexia, he attends some additional remedial classes.

The school has a policy of recruiting adult learners at a local and regional level and it collaborates with local industry, especially the private business sector. The education is free of charge and Kristian maintains his salary even if his work hours are somewhat reduced.

The vocational tertiary education institution cooperates with an upper secondary school, but consists of a separate department offering three different educational paths. It is possible to take smaller units of courses, but no final diploma is issued before completing the entire educational path. This diploma qualifies for education at university and university college level. For the time being, Kristian does not intend to take this step.

The Image of a Student at ISCED 5 + 6 Level of Education

Anne is 43 years old. She is married and has two children, aged 16 and 20. After finishing lower secondary school Anne continued into upper secondary education. She left it after nearly two years without getting a certificate or degree. After that, she had various jobs until she became a mother. Anne returned to work as a part-time worker at a local nursing home when her youngest child started school. Although Anne lacks formal credentials she was accepted at a public university college to the Bachelor programme in nursing in 2006 on the basis of her 'real competencies'. For admission she had to send in documentation of her prior education and working experience. After advice from a colleague who had attended continuing education at another university college, she decided to apply for a shortening of the study period on the basis of prior working experience and some in-service courses, but this was not accepted by the admission office.

At the university college where Anne is a student, the importance of adult education is part of the institutions' strategy document. However, this issue has lately to some extent been ignored at the expense of issues such as internationalization and multicultural issues. Since the university college is in the process of applying for university status, a lot of the administration's strategic and economic efforts are now put into this process.

Anne thinks it is a great advantage having a university college in her own municipality. This is crucial when trying to take care of her family and home besides her studies. The university college charges Anne only a very small enrolment fee (less than €100 per semester). Anne also receives loans and grants from the Norwegian State Educational Loan Fund. She was positively surprised by the small study fee, while her sister who lives in the north of Norway was charged larger fees for distance learning through a local study association.

Anne has a positive attitude towards adult education and she thinks that money spent on adult education is money well spent. Her main reason for returning to school was that she wanted to learn more on a subject that interests her.

In Anne's class there are six other adult learners. Classroom teaching and working in smaller groups are the most common educational practice, but they are also followed up individually by their teachers. Most of her fellow students are Norwegian women with children of school age or older. In addition, she has one classmate who has migrated from Pakistan. He has lived in Norway for some years and has been working as an auxiliary nurse for four years. Getting a permanent job is his main reason for attending the course.

INSTANT PORTRAITS AND LIFELONG TRAJECTORIES OF ADULT LEARNERS

The aforementioned portraits emerged when data from interviews with educational staff were pooled with data from a survey of adult learners. The portraits mirror variations in individual motivation and institutional contexts along education levels (from ISCED 1 to 6) and according to a public–private divide. The life and learning history of the adults partly come to the surface but not yet systematically. Nevertheless, the portraits depict one approach for how institutional and motivational aspects can nurture analyses of trajectories of adults' learning biographies over a longer time span. The portraits may therefore point to a future research agenda.

MOTIVATIONAL AND INSTITUTIONAL ASPECTS OF TRAINING IN SMEs

A critical analysis of these LLL aspects needs to challenge conventional ideas; for instance that small and medium-sized enterprises (SME) with unsystematic learning strategies give low priority to formal training of their employees. This hypothesis was investigated by conducting case studies, charting formal training, in six Norwegian SMEs as part of their overall strategy for training and human resources development.

The case studies revealed that formal training is intertwined with various forms of informal and non-formal training. The conclusion therefore stressed that formal education in an informal Norwegian training culture is not a contradiction in terms. It coincides with the nature of the enterprises under scrutiny; that is, SMEs of a size allowing for smooth and informal work procedures, including training practices. Also, the informality cohabits with deliberate strategies for empowering employees in a labour market context by means of formal education leading to recognized exams (Ure 2010).

Personal Motivation among Learners in Small and Medium-Sized Enterprises

Our interviews in SMEs also revealed that employers pay most of the training costs for employees enrolled in formal education. The other part of the deal is that the learners have to invest their spare time in studying. This requires a quite high motivation among the learners, who state that they depend on patience from their families. This coincides with data from the Norwegian Learning Conditions Monitor (Dæhlen and Nyen 2009):

1. Twenty-five per cent of those enrolled in formal further education studied during their work hours, with no wage reduction.
2. Two per cent of those in formal further education were on study leave with no wage reduction.
3. Most job-related training takes place during work hours. More than three out of four received pay during such training, which mostly was non-formal.
4. Employees spend an average of 20 hours at courses, seminars and in other job-related non-formal training.

Self-Selection to Further and Continuing Training

The act of sacrificing their spare time implies that those employees who are most committed to enrol in education courses tend to be selected. This mechanism can ensure that, from the viewpoint of the management, the training investments are channelled to the employees who most likely will succeed. It might however reduce the number of employees willing to enrol in formal education.

There is, furthermore, a tendency that younger workers are those contacting the human resources development (HRD) department to discuss their plans for formal education. Such self-selection of young and often already qualified staff to undertake training is a very common phenomenon and does not stem from any deliberate discrimination from the side of the enterprise. Instead, our interviewees suggested the following explanations:

1. Young workers are more in need of upskilling than their experienced colleagues.
2. Experienced workers have climbed the hierarchy and have less time to leave their commanding and coordinating positions to start up training.
3. Workers aged around 55 tend to ponder more on their pension and retirement than on further upskilling.

This selection makes it more likely that the management invests in training for those who are motivated enough to complete a demanding educational trajectory. The other side of the coin is that self-selection is probably not to the advantage of an enterprise in a long-time perspective.

Attention should be given to the fact that the management is often willing to pay for training of relevance for the enterprise without looking too much into budgets. Such rough accounting procedures for training expenses will probably become more formalized when the (in many cases) nascent HRD strategies become full-fledged. They reflect however a more or less conscious strategy of seizing opportunities to fill skill gaps when learners are willing to start up training and when company profits allow for unforeseen training expenditures.

This observation has however to be attenuated by the fact that our interviews were conducted at the height of a business bonanza with severe skills shortages in certain sectors of the economy. The annual Learning Conditions Monitor shows that 52 per cent of the employees participating in formal further education were subsidized by their employers (Dæhlen and Nyen 2009).

Our results from the study of learning conditions in SMEs, and the comparison with surveys of training in the entire Norwegian labour market, have certain implications for the Norwegian LLL agenda. For researchers to understand learners' motivation and for policy-makers to design measures and instruments, note should be taken of the fact that a (long) training course intervenes in a person's life trajectory, whose learning trajectory is constructed by negotiations with family and friends as well as colleagues and managers.

On the one hand, this can question the financial support received by employees attending formal training. On this point, our interviews in SMEs revealed a positive attitude to formal education, which often was financed by employers who did not neatly assess whether the courses strictly fell in line with company needs. Hence, the somewhat nebulous borderline of training for the company versus training for personal upskilling, which the basic agreements between social partners reside on, seemed be crossed without much ado.

On the other hand, the intertwinement of a person's life and learning trajectory puts pressure on the Norwegian LLL agenda in terms of developing guidance and counselling services, and likewise for the EU.[2] Our observations point to a need for specialized services reflecting the various phases in a person's life, while respecting specific learning environments for each education level. We will enlarge on the different conditions for effective LLL strategies across education levels in the section below.

FROM MOTIVATIONAL AND INSTITUTIONAL ASPECTS TO LIFE AND LEARNING TRAJECTORIES

The link between (personal) motivation and institutions' capacity to meet the needs of adult learners was investigated by interviewing 14 staff members in adult education institutions at all educational levels (Stensen and Ure 2010). The underlying idea was to identify institutional practices that underpin this capacity. Our train of thought is as follows: from the outset, an educational course can be adapted to certain learners with a view to recruit them to adult education. Equally, adaptation services are set up to retain certain target groups. Finally, institutional practices are put in place in order to assist adult learners so that they can complete their courses.

Theoretically, the terms 'recruitment', 'retention' and 'completion' can be grouped into educational pathways (or trajectories) of which there are at least four oppositions (cf. Doray et al. 2009). These can be understood as tensions between, respectively:

1. the individual and the institution;
2. an individual's subjective and objective situation;

3. school-based learning and extra-curricular experiences;
4. an individual's past experiences and achievements, and future expectations.

The second and fourth points both address motivation to learn; the third point captures learning and life trajectories of high relevance for the appreciation of learning experiences; and the first point features the structural constraints for learners' access to educational institutions.

For Norwegian lifelong learners, a statutory right to adapted education according to individual needs can partly pave educational pathways (cf. Law on Education, §4A-1 from 1998). This right implies that different scholastic demands are catered for during compulsory schooling and also at upper secondary level. The statutory right leads to multiple pedagogical and administrative support initiatives, for example preparatory programmes, supplementary workshops and remedial classes. These initiatives contribute to motivating non-traditional groups of learners. Tertiary education institutions are not affected by the statutory right to adapted education but they are obliged to put in place some procedures destined for adult learners, such as assessment of prior learning. Our interviews with 14 staff members in adult education institutions confirmed that counselling and career advice are services of particular value for learners at all educational levels who come from backgrounds of social marginalization.

With inspiration from the theoretical framework proposed by Doray et al., the main results of our interviews are illustrated in Figure 8.4. The institutional and pedagogical practices are structured with regard to recruitment, retention and completion.

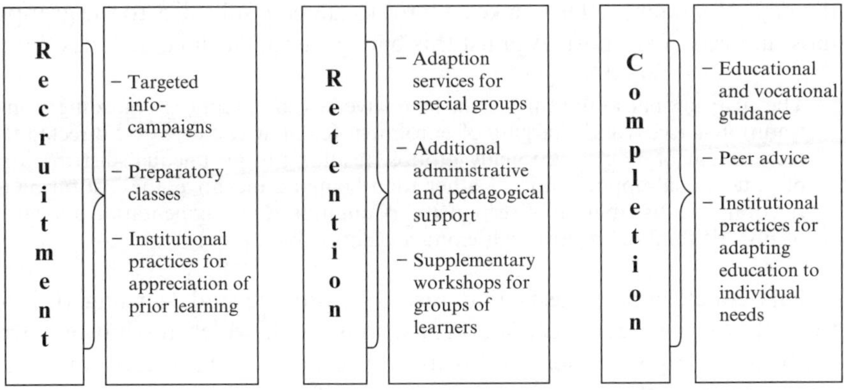

Figure 8.4 Institutional and pedagogical practices structured with regard to recruitment, retention and completion

When looking jointly at institutional and motivational aspects, it appears that they can be scrutinized from a perspective of learning and life trajectories. This joint perspective can build on insights from disciplines such as political science, sociology, psychology and pedagogy (cf. West et al. 2007; Merrill 2009). The three categories of recruitment, retention and completion are useful for linking institutional practices to life and learning trajectories. The aim of this categorization is however not to arrive at a mutually exclusive classification of institutional practices, because some of the practices observed cannot easily be listed as recruitment, retention or completion. It is particularly cumbersome to subsume the individual right to adapted education under one of the three categories. As was revealed in the text above, the adaptation to individual needs, which is a statutory right in Norway, affects recruitment, retention and completion. This means that, from the outset, a course can be adapted to certain learners with a view to recruiting them to adult education. Equally, adaptation services are set up to retain certain target groups. Finally, institutional practices are put in place in order to assist adult learners so that they can complete their courses.

When combining a survey of 750 learners with qualitative interviews in 50 adult education institutions, we *inter alia* built on the theoretical framework of Hans G. Schuetze. For higher education, Schuetze distinguishes between policy and institutional factors influencing the access of non-traditional learners (cf. Schuetze 2000). Correspondingly, higher education institutions within our sample of 50 institutions were subject to a separate analysis (Aaslid 2008). While summarizing observations on institutional freedom, the author maintains that this freedom is in practice 'combined with an outcome-based funding formula that necessitates an effective run-through of students'. This makes it hard to allocate subsidies to the groups most in need of support. Against this background, Aaslid concludes that:

> The institutional autonomy leads to a diversity of practices regarding non-traditional access and charging of enrolment fees, few resources are directed to recruitment of non-traditionally groups, resulting in an unequal distribution of educational opportunities. Rather than being an incentive, the institutional freedom and distribution of responsibility might lead to fragmentation and lack of holistic thinking regarding lifelong learning. (ibid., p. 69)

This conclusion suggests that research into life and learning trajectories have to reflect the policy constraints with which institutions are confronted. Higher education institutions exercise certain freedom when implementing strategies ranging from scientific excellence to social inclusion. In their efforts to recruit and retain learners from backgrounds of social marginalization, adult education institutions at higher educational level can normally mobilize more institutional resources than schools at lower levels of the education system. Independent of whatever institution is under scrutiny, an issue cutting across education levels is that social inclusion does not need to be restricted to implementation of minimum standards defined at a central level. Institutions succeeding in recruiting and retaining groups exposed to social exclusion tend to define their own institutional objectives, earmark their own money and get additional funding from public (or private) programmes or initiatives. Such deliberate institutional strategies can also embrace the design of courses that support certain groups of non-traditional adult learners (Stensen and Ure 2010).

LLL WITHIN LABOUR MARKET AND ECONOMIC STRUCTURES: NORWAY IN COUNTRY TYPOLOGIES

In Norway, the above-mentioned institutional LLL strategies unfold within constraints notably posed by public policy. This has to do with the strong position of the state and its bifurcations when the Norwegian education and training policy is ironed out (cf. Ure 2007).

As illustrated in the introductory chapter to this book, LLL strategies are rooted in deeper labour market and economic structures that have been subject to analysis of country typologies. Figure 8.3 in this chapter depicts the organizational setting for motivational and institutional factors structuring the LLL field. In order to position Norway within country typologies reflecting labour market and economic structures, in this section we will revisit such typologies, particularly those pertaining to socio-economic and social models in addition to education and training systems. They are both accounted for below.

Socio-Economic and Social Models

The so-called Nordic model has caught the attention of scholars analysing national variations of capitalism. While drawing heavily on Gøsta Esping-Anderson, the country typology suggested by Aiginger and Guger (2007) emphasizes the importance of education and lifelong learning but strongly reflects traditional economic indicators such as annual growth, gross domestic product (GDP) per capita and employment rates. The Nordic countries stand out in their extensive redistribution mechanisms and social benefits financed by high taxation. The model also features active labour market policies and high employment rates (cf. Ure and Saar 2008).

The economic structure of the Norwegian labour market is said to favour a high skills equilibrium (Schøne 2001). Norwegian skill formation has consequently been explained by a compressed wage structure, with small median differences in remuneration between low-paid and high-paid employees (cf. Schøne and Torp 2005). This makes high-skill labour relatively cheap and leads Norwegian industries into highly priced market niches, where quality – combined with decent safety standards – may count more than the price ticket. What is often added to this picture are comprehensive industrial relations played out at national, sector and local levels (Moene 2009). All this points to a highly regulated labour market, albeit recently attenuated by labour immigration into less transparent sectors of the labour market (Alsos and Eldring 2008); in other words a coordinated market economy opposed to liberal and mixed-market economies (cf. Hall and Thelen 2008; Hall and Gingerich 2004).

A theoretical approach permitting analysis of barriers to participation in adult education within the frame of Nordic welfare state regimes is offered by Kjell Rubenson and Richard Desjardins (2009). They explain that:

> broad structural conditions and targeted policy measures are seen to directly affect the extent and impact of institutional and situational (job and family related) barriers. Structural conditions play a substantial role in forming the circumstances faced by individuals and limit the feasible alternatives to choose from, and therefore they can bound individual agency.

The two authors conclude that the understanding of barriers to adult education depends on analysing the interaction between structural factors and individuals' dispositions, thus addressing the agency–structure dimension referred in the theoretical section above. On this point, Rubenson and Desjardin qualify that: 'welfare state regimes can affect a person's capability to participate through the way they construct cultural conditions and helps individuals overcome both structurally and individually based barriers.'

By this means, the authors are able to pin down the structural conditions, mirrored in education reforms as part of welfare state arrangements, to conditions facing individual learners. There is a tradition of literature on welfare aspects of Scandinavian education, such as access and the comprehensiveness of education; notably embodied in the 'unitary school' with its low level of streaming, alongside other measures to prevent social exclusion (cf. Arnesen and Lundahl 2006; Estevez-Abe et al. 2001). Some even refer to a deliberate use of 'educational policies as a strategy for creating social justice' (Tjeldvoll 1998); but often without addressing individual agency within the welfare state arrangements.

Education and Training Systems

As pointed out in the introductory chapter of this book, Andy Green situated in his early work on typologies (Green 1999), the modes of articulation between central governments, education systems, labour markets and firms. Below, we sum up how the Norwegian education and training system is situated in this regard.

A stocktaking of LLL in Norway (Ure 2007) maintained that the main constituent elements of the education and training system are the labour market, the civil society and the state. The winding-up of a trade union-instigated LLL reform (1999–2006) confirmed that the state is one prime driver in Norwegian education and training. The reform put Norwegian LLL on a judicial path, guaranteed by the state, but did not entail new structures of social partner regulation. In the long run and if stakeholders in the labour market continue relying on the state as the main vehicle in pursuing further and continuing education and training, the social partner cooperation for lifelong learning might therefore lose strength. Under such a scenario, it would be hard to count social partner arrangements for collective action in training among the pillars in what is often called a Nordic model of cooperation (Ure 2007).

Prior to the above-mentioned LLL reform, the Norwegian education and training system had gone through changes supporting an LLL vision. In general, there is a low level of stratification. One example is the smooth transition between education levels for the age group 6–16 on their passage from primary to lower secondary level. A vocationally specific model of upper secondary education can imply apprenticeship training in firms. It is however easy to switch between vocational and general education programmes in upper secondary education. Continuous attempts to equalize the status of these programmes add to the picture of a low-stratified education system, which is close to the LLL policy objective of having permeable borders between educational pathways.

CONCLUSION

A low level of stratification of students, and a low degree of compartmentalization between education trajectories, bear proof of attempts to instal practices that fall under an LLL paradigm. While LLL hinges not only on educational practices but also on changes in the civil society and the labour market, we have looked into an ambitious LLL reform, the Competence Reform. It was planned as an answer to challenges in the labour market and was stamped with an employability perspective that was not really challenged. To the contrary, the reform was defended by most stakeholders. The few grievances centred on terminating the various actions of which it was composed. The LLL reform has therefore been characterized as 'episodic' (cf. Grepperud et al. 2010, p. 133) and 'with limited diffusion throughout working life' (Payne 2005). Although there are reasons for questioning its long-term effects, the employability stamp on the reform coincides with a European pattern, sometimes called a 'narrow labour market focus' in lifelong policies (Holford et al. 2008, p. 112).

Different from assessing lifelong learning in Norway as the fulfilment of one single reform – that is, the above-mentioned Competence Reform – the present chapter has set out to identify LLL practices over a longer time span. LLL as a field in an institutionalist Bourdieu-like sense puts the education system, labour market and civil society under scrutiny. Consequently this opens up possibilities for cross-country typologies embracing several societal spheres: mainly the labour market, civil society and the state.

A condensed description of the Norwegian landscape reveals LLL practices that partly fall into patterns pointing to systemic elements, embracing institutional and motivational aspects, mediated through institutional strategies that are moulded into a relatively centralized system. The institutions exercise a certain freedom in defining their own LLL strategies, for example in terms of recruiting students from backgrounds of social exclusion. This leeway does not seem to be more frequently used in higher education institutions, which are more independent from the local or central government, than in institutions at upper secondary level. It therefore turns out that institutional strategies, being more ambitious than mirroring minimum requirements and mainstream public policy, do matter.

All in all, LLL in Norway seen as a field creates the framework around which individual agency and structural constraints play out. As disclosed in policy documents, these practices can easily be considered building blocks for lifelong learning, not least because the broad definition of LLL allows few systemic improvements to escape from its scope.

When studying adult learners' motivation to enrol in training courses, numerous analyses of LLL barriers suggest that not only the learning trajectory in a strict sense, but also the way in which training intervenes in a learner's life trajectory should be increasingly theorized and lead to policy recommendations. If these recommendations are transformed into practices affecting several forms of learning (i.e formal and informal), some elements sustaining a LLL system could emerge; thus replacing ad hoc solutions such as the tacit compromise implying that employers may pay for formal education, provided the employees agree to devote quite a lot of their spare time to education and training.

NOTES

1. International Standard Classification of Education.
2. cf. http://eur-lex.europa.eu/LexUriServ/LexUriServ.do?uri=OJ:C:2008:319:0004:0007:EN:PDF

REFERENCES

Aaslid, Bjørg Eva (2008), *Lifelong Participation and Equalisation: Barriers and Incentives at Higher Education Level in Norway?* Master's thesis delivered at NTNU (Norges teknisk-naturvitenskapelige universitet), Trondheim.

Aiginger, Karl and Alois Guger (2007), 'The European Socioeconomic Model', in Anthony Giddens (ed.), *Global Europe, Social Europe*, Cambridge: Polity Press, pp. 124–150.

Alsos, Kristin and Line Eldring (2008), 'Labour Mobility and Wage Dumping: The Case of Norway', *European Journal of Industrial Relations*, **14** (4), 441–459.

Arnesen, Anne-Lise and Lisbeth Lundahl (2006), 'Still Social and Democratic? Inclusive Education Policies in the Nordic Welfare States', *Scandinavian Journal of Educational Research*, **50** (3), 285–300.

European Commission (2000), *A Memorandum on Lifelong Learning*, Commission Staff Working Document, SEC (2000) 1832 Brussels 2000.

European Commission (2009), *Key Competences for a Changing World. Progress Towards the Lisbon Objectives in Education and Training. Analysis of Implementation at the European and National Levels*, COM(2009) 640, Brussels.

Dæhlen, Marianne and Torgeir Nyen (2009), *Livslang læring i norsk arbeidsliv. Resultater fra Lærevilkårsmonitoren 2009*, Fafo-paper 2009: 22, Oslo: Institute for Labour and Social Research.

Dæhlen, Marianne and Odd Bjørn Ure (2009), 'Low-Skilled Adults in Formal Continuing Education: Does Their Motivation Differ from other Learners?' *International Journal of Lifelong Education*, **28** (5), 661–674.

Doray, Pierre, France Picard, Claude Trottier and Amélie Groleau (2009), 'Educational Pathways: Some Key Concepts', Canada Millennium Scholarship Foundation, Millennium Research Series no. 44, June.

Estevez-Abe, Margarita, Torben Iversen and David Soskice (2001), 'Social Protection and the Formation of Skills: A Reinterpretation of the Welfare State', in Peter A. Hall and David Soskice (eds), *Varieties of Capitalism. The Institutional Foundations of Comparative Advantage*, Oxford: Oxford University Press, pp. 145–183.

European Council (2010), *Council Conclusions on 'New Skills for New Jobs: The Way forward'. Brussels*, 7 June, Brussels. Available at: http://www.consilium.europa.eu/uedocs/cms_data/docs/pressdata/en/lsa/114962.pdf (accessed 24 May 2011).

Fejes, Andreas and Katherine Nicoll (eds) (2008), *Foucault and Lifelong Learning: Governing the Subject*, London: Routledge.

GHK (2010), 'Lifelong Learning Strategies: Critical Aspects and Good Practice in Implementation', Final report submitted by GHK Consulting to DG Education and Culture of the European Commission. December (report to be published by the European Commission).

GHK (2011), 'Norwegian Country Report', for DG Education of the European Commission for the 2010 Update of the European Inventory on Validation of Non-Formal and Informal Learning. Available at http://libserver.cedefop.europa.eu/vetelib/2011/77643.pdf (accessed 21 November 2011).
Green, Andy (1999), 'Education and Globalization in Europe and East Asia: Convergent and Divergent Trends', *Journal of Education Policy*, **14** (1), 55–71.
Grepperud, Gunnar, Berith Bergersen, Odd Einar Johansen and Geir Sæhle (2010), *Kunnskapssamfunnet – hva vil vi med voksnes kvalifisering?* Oslo: Gyldendal Forlag.
Hall, Peter A. and Daniel W. Gingerich (2004), 'Varieties of Capitalism and Institutional Complementarities in the Macroeconomy', Max-Planck-Institut für Gesellschaftsforschung Discussion Paper 04/5.
Hall, Peter A. and David Soskice (2001), 'An Introduction to Varieties of Capitalism', in Peter A. Hall and David Soskice (eds), *Varieties of Capitalism: The Institutional Foundations of Comparative Advantage*, Oxford: Oxford University Press, pp. 1–69.
Hall, Peter A. and Kathleen Thelen (2008), 'Institutional Change in Varieties of Capitalism', *Socio-Economic Review*, **7** (1), 7–34.
Holford, John, Sheila Riddel, Elisabet Weedon, Judith Litjens and Guy Hannan (2008), *Patterns of Lifelong Learning: Policy and Practice in an Expanding Europe*, Vienna: Lit Verlag.
Illeris, Knud (2003), 'Adult Education as Experienced by the Learners', *Journal of Lifelong Education*, **22** (1), 13–23.
Illeris, Knud I. (2006), 'Lifelong Learning and the Low-Skilled', *International Journal of Lifelong Education*, **25** (1), 15–28.
March, James G. and Johan P. Olsen (1995), *Democratic Governance*, New York: Free Press.
Merrill, Barbara (ed.) (2009), *Learning to Change? The Role of Identity and Learning Careers in Adult Education*, Frankfurt am Main: Peter Lang.
Moene, Kalle (2009), *Den skandinaviske modellen og økonomisk ulikhet*, NOU 2009:10: Fordelingsutvalget. Vedlegg til utredning fra et utvalg oppnevnt av Finansdepartementet. Available at http://www.regjeringen.no/nb/dep/fin/dok/nouer/2009/nou-2009-10.html?id=558836 (accessed 24 May 2011).
Payne, Jonathan (2005), *What Progress is Norway Making with Lifelong Learning? A Study of the Norwegian Competence Reform*, Research paper 55, Oxford and Warwick: SKOPE Publications, Oxford and Warwick Universities.
Ragin, Charles (1994), *Constructing Social Research*, Thousand Oaks, CA, USA; London, UK; and New Delhi, India: Pine Forge Press.
Rubenson, Kjell and Richard Desjardins (2009), 'The Impact of Welfare State Regimes on Barriers to Participation in Adult Education: A Bounded Agency Model', *Adult Education Quarterly*, **59** (3), 187–207.
Scott, Richard W. (1995), *Institutions and Organizations*, Thousand Oaks/London/New Delhi: SAGE Publications.
Schøne, Pål (2001), 'Analysing the Effect of Training on Wages – Using Combined Survey Register Data', *International Journal of Manpower*, **22**, 138–158.
Schøne, Pål and Hege Torp (2005), 'Opplæring i arbeidslivet', in Bente Rasmussen (ed.), *Et bærekraftig nytt arbeidsliv. Kunnskapsstatus og problemstillinger*, Oslo: Norges forskningsråd.
Schuetze, Hans G. (2000), *Tumbling Walls, Changing Landscapes – 'Non-Traditional*

Students' and Lifelong Learners in Higher Education, Vancouver: University of British Columbia.

Stensen, Ole-Anders and Odd Bjørn Ure (2010), 'Social Inclusion in Adult Education is More Than Implementing Mainstream Public Policy: A Compilation of Interviews in Norwegian Adult Education Institutions', Fafo-paper 2010:16, Oslo: Institute for Labour and Social Research.

Streeck, Wolfgang (1989), 'The Social Dimension of the European Economy', a paper prepared for the 1989 Meeting of the Andrew Shonfield Association, Florence, 14–15 September.

Tight, Malcolm (1998), 'Education, Education, Education! The Vision of Lifelong Learning in the Kennedy, Dearing and Fryer reports', *Oxford Review of Education*, **24** (4), 473–485.

Tjeldvoll, Arild (1998), *Education and the Scandinavian Welfare State in the Year 2000*, New York: Garland.

Ure, Odd Bjørn (2007), 'Lifelong Learning in Norway. A Deflating Policy Balloon or an Act of Piecemeal Implementation?' Fafo-report 2007: 30, Oslo: Institute for Labour and Social Research.

Ure, Odd Bjørn (2010), 'Formal Education in an Informal Norwegian Culture of Enterprise Training: Six Cases Collected from Maritime and Offshore Environments', Fafo-paper 2010:21, Oslo: Institute for Labour and Social Research.

Ure, Odd Bjørn and Ellu Saar (2008), 'Some Micro – Meso – Macro Relations in Lifelong Learning. Conceptual Framework paper for LLL2010', Working Paper No. 17, Oslo and Tallinn. Available at: http://lll2010.tlu.ee/publications/working-papers/lll2010-working-papers-on-overall-theoretical-framework/d13-2-lll2010-working-paper-17_ad-hoc.pdf/view (accessed 24 May 2010).

West, Linden, Peter Alheit, Anders Siig Andersen, and Barbara Merrill (eds) (2007), *Using Biographical and Life History Approaches in the Study of Adult and Lifelong Learning*, European Perspectives, Frankfurt am Main: Peter Lang.

9. Nobody's darling: dynamics and inertia of formal adult education in Austria

Jörg Markowitsch, Günter Hefler, Stephanie Rammel and Paul Ringler

INTRODUCTION

Adult education (*Erwachsenenbildung*) in Austria is generally perceived as the opposite of formal education. Rooted in the history of liberal adult education, with its early and strong movements of *Volkshochschulen* (folk high schools), the core notion of adult education does not include training or adult learning in schools and higher education institutions. Thus, 'formal adult education' – although increasingly gaining ground – was and still is an exotic and foreign matter in adult education. Only very recently, the concept of adult education has broadened and is increasingly used synonymously with *Weiterbildung* (continuing education and training) (for example, Gruber 2011; Lenz 2005, p. 21; Schlögl and Schneeberger 2003, p. 7).

Formal adult education was historically treated as 'second-chance education' to prepare for access to university studies. It was rarely conceived as part of adult education, but instead as a marginal element of the public education system. More recent national policy initiatives have focused on widening access routes to higher education and improving qualifications for school drop-outs. While continuing higher education also attracts some attention, Austria's lifelong learning policy overlooks almost all other fields of formal adult education.

There is neither a comprehensive view of formal adult education in Austria, nor a perceived need for systematic analysis beyond statistical compilations such as mapping Austria's education provisions for global education databases. The European-wide 'formal–non-formal' distinction is still translated into, on the one hand, 'the public education system' with its schools, colleges and universities (formal), and on the other hand, 'adult education' with its traditionally large number of private providers (non-formal).

We will argue that examining various elements of formal adult education in Austria and fitting them together results in a new way of conceiving adult education and a key to understanding and revitalising Austria's lifelong learning policy. Firstly, we will show the deficits in the current structure of adult education, explore the distinction in formal and non-formal education and reveal the problems resulting from the previously mentioned simple, but incorrect, translation. By using an organizational-field approach that borrows from organizational institutionalism (Greenwood et al. 2008), we will propose a new way of looking at formal adult education. We then apply to the Austrian situation a typology presented in Chapter 3 in this volume.[1] We will not present an overall picture for Austria, rather, we concentrate on recent developments in four of the seven organizational fields of formal adult education. This allows us to better understand and describe the dynamics of adult education in Austria, and to come up with lessons to be learned for Austria's future lifelong learning policy.

ELEMENTS OF FORMAL ADULT EDUCATION IN AUSTRIA: AN ORGANIZATIONAL FIELD APPROACH

The most recent major surveys of adult education in Austria have been produced for the United Nations Educational, Scientific and Cultural Organization (UNESCO) (Schneeberger et al. 2008), the Organisation for Economic Co-operation and Development (OECD) (Schlögl and Schneeberger 2003), the European Centre for the Development of Vocational Training (Cedefop) (Schneeberger and Petanovitsch 2004), and the German Institute for Adult Education (Lenz 2005). These reports categorize adult education mainly into: firm-based training, labour-market programmes for the unemployed, upgrade-training for employed workers, liberal and civic education, and second-chance education. Interestingly, higher education, although addressed in all reports elsewhere, is not explicitly on this list and formal adult education – as mentioned above – is only covered by second-chance education. Most of these reports deliberately provide common ways of further structuring adult learning by distinguishing competences (national, provinces, public employment service, companies, trade unions, etc.), providers (schools, universities, private training organizations, etc.), financing sources (private, public, etc.) and others.

However, although the studies sometimes compare and use cross-tabulations (e.g., type of providers cross-tabulated by financing sources), they do not provide a comprehensive picture, apart from listing individual measures or provisions. The reader has a sort of 'product information sheet' that provides all sorts of technical details but does not offer a mental image leading to an understanding of the social phenomenon. Despite the authors' uncontested expertise, they do not comprehensively represent social reality by effectively using the social categories and statistics. We do not claim to be able to do this for adult learning in general, but at least we offer an approach to doing a part of it, namely for formal adult education. Before analysing the social statistics, we briefly explore the distinction between formal and non-formal education and give some accounts of their quantitative relation in Austria.

The largely accepted, European Union-wide distinction of formal, non-formal and informal learning is translated in Austria into the national education system (formal) as represented in diagrams of the ministry of education; private provider training courses[2] (non-formal); and everyday learning (informal) in companies or at home. This understanding is evident in the public and semi-public discourse among politicians, non-professionals and researchers; it is visible in the governance and administration structures of education, in teacher and trainer education, in research structures and academic communities; and it can be found in various policy documents.

For example, Austria is currently developing a national qualifications framework (Luomi-Messerer et al. 2009, 2007). The key document has undergone an extensive countrywide consultation resulting in dozens of responses from stakeholders. It suggests developing the qualifications framework in three distinct, but combined, 'corridors': 'Corridor 1 encompasses qualifications within the formal education system, Corridor 2 involves non-formally acquired qualifications (above all from adult-education providers), and Corridor 3 intends to develop approaches that include qualifications awarded on the basis of informal learning' (BMUKK and BMWF 2008, p. 6, translated by the authors). In practice, this was intended less to clearly distinguish between formal and non-formal education, and more to make the whole process manageable by grouping together actors, such as providers and governing bodies, with similar interests.

Another example can be found within the ministry for education. The department for adult education only deals with non-public, adult-education providers. However, formal offers for adults, such as evening schools for employed people, belong to another department responsible for initial education. This increases the difficulties of learning from each other and implementing reforms.

A third example is the academic research that not only reflects these borders, but also uses its well-established authority to strongly defend the borders. There is a small, distinct circle of adult-education scholars in

Austria, all rooted in andragogy, who pursue a tradition of liberal adult education, which has eroded in many aspects. However, this liberal adult education also gained new ground in related areas (such as vocational training or higher education), although this has not, or only with great delay, resulted in research topics, dedications of academic chairs or study programmes. As is well known, crossing borders and joining efforts is a bigger challenge for scholars than for practitioners, who must often transcend divisions because of simple economic pressure. Thus, it is not surprising that no coherent view has been developed that touches upon research areas usually perceived as distinct from adult education.

The continual underestimation in Austria of the importance of formal adult education provides a further reason – apart from its heterogeneity – why formal adult education has not been considered a distinct social phenomenon (Markowitsch et al. 2008; Rammel and Markowitsch 2009). Indicators based on the Labour Force Survey are somewhat misleading: in 2003, only 3 per cent of 25–65-year-olds in Austria participated in formal education, whereas 25 per cent participated in non-formal education within a 12-month period (Statistik Austria 2004; Hefler et al. 2011). This proportion changes dramatically if one looks at the overall instruction hours in adult learning: one-third can be found in formal settings. After correcting for all the inconsistencies caused by different definitions and survey concepts, we can estimate that between 75 000 and 135 000 adults are enrolled in programmes leading to a nationally recognized certificate (Ringler 2010; Markowitsch et al. 2008). Austria does not have data on lifetime participation in formal adult education.[3] Based on estimates, however, we could expect that from 20 to 40 per cent of all adults participate in formal adult education sometime between the ages of 25 and 64 (Ringler 2010). Apart from the underestimated quantitative role of formal adult education, its qualitative role is generally unrecognized and undercut by lifelong learning policy rhetoric that continually insists on the equal importance of all forms of learning. Yet, formal (adult) education provides potential access to particular social positions in a different way from other forms of learning. Although evident in the daily lives of education practitioners and policy-makers, the effects of the 'social charter' of formal adult education (Hefler and Markowitsch 2012; see also Chapter 3 in this volume) is clearly misjudged in research and official policy discourses.

Formal adult education is a disparate and highly diverse part of the overall skill formation system. It can hardly be looked at in the same way as the relatively more homogenous systems of schools or higher education institutions or firm-based training, from all of which it 'borrows' elements or in which parts of it may be rooted. In Chapter 3 in this volume, we presented a new approach to structuring this diverse field by distinguishing seven different types of formal adult education. Table 9.1 shows the seven types for Austria, provides a brief characterization and examples for each one, and lists main actors and financing sources. Due to lack of space, we cannot discuss all of the seven types here. We will focus on four types – basic-skills programmes, second-chance education, higher education and continuing higher education – to give insights into a changing landscape of formal adult education in Austria. This selection is somewhat arbitrary, because the fields that are not discussed are equally interesting. Within the field of retraining programmes, we could have shown the rise of active labour market policy and the public employment service as a new key player. It would have been worth analysing the renewed interest in the certification of companies in the field of customized vocational programmes (Markowitsch and Jonach 2006). And finally, the field of continuing professional education would have been a perfect example to illustrate ongoing tendencies to formalize and make more academic that are part of professionalization (Eraut 1994). The four selected fields are innately closer to the initial education system, which makes them potentially more interesting for the national qualifications framework we will discuss.

INERTIA AND DYNAMICS: EXAMPLES FOR A CHANGING LANDSCAPE

When looking from the outside at adult education in Austria, one can get the impression that things do not change. There is still no law regulating adult education, the large adult education institutions still dominate the landscape, and the universities have not yet realized their involvement in adult education. The participation rate in lifelong learning (participation within the past four weeks) oscillates around the European Union (EU) target of 15 per cent. A political strategy for lifelong learning has been in constant development since the European Year of Lifelong Learning 1996 – culminating in a new strategy paper in 2011 (Republik Österreich 2011).

However, if we shift our focus to formal adult education and if we try to look at it from the inside and examine each part separately, we recognize highly dynamic changes and growth happening in the past 15 years (approximately 1995–2010), particularly during the 'Towards a Lifelong Learning Society in Europe: The Contribution of the Education System' (LLL2010) project's lifetime (2005–2011). This ambivalent picture of inertia and dynamics also arises because the widely unconnected developments in the various fields are driven by various other policy fields and by

Table 9.1 Overview of formal adult education in Austria

	Characterization	Main Providers	Financing	Population	Examples
I Basic skills programmes	Compared to international standards, an underdeveloped field dominated by non-formal provision, with only one programme classified as formal	Non-profit adult education providers, in particular *Volkshochschulen*; specialised non-profit providers	Ministry of Education, Public Employment Service	1000+	Only one formal programme: preparation course for general secondary school (*Hauptschule*) qualification
II Second-chance education	A well-established sector with programmes preparing for entrance permission to higher education and lower and higher secondary vocational education programmes, leading to defined broad vocational qualifications	Schools, non-profit adult education providers	Ministry of Education, *Länder*; private households	35 000+	Academic upper-secondary schools or colleges of engineering for employed; preparation courses for the university entrance examination or *Berufsreifeprüfung*
III Higher education programmes	Part-time study programmes grew over the last 15 years, but most 'non-traditional' students still enrol in traditional full-time programmes	*Fachhochschulen*, public universities	Ministry of Science, local public bodies; private households	40 000+	Part-time *Fachhochschule* degree programmes, university programmes
IV (Re)training	Within the highly expanded area of active labour market (a quarter of all funding for lifelong learning in Austria, see: Markowitsch and Hefler 2006) the field of formal retraining forms a very small part	Adult-education providers, non-profit and for profit providers	Public Employment Service, municipalities	No figures available; less than 5 per cent of participants in formal adult education	Specific temporary programmes: e.g. college of engineering (for unemployed women); placement programmes for care workers

Table 9.1 (continued)

	Characterization	Main Providers	Financing	Population	Examples
V Customized vocational programmes	Niche-products in the training market for enterprises, allowing for 'formalization' of in-house training or customization of formal programmes for employees of a single enterprise paying for the programme	Schools, public and private universities, *Fachhochschulen*; for-profit training providers (in cooperation with organizations of formal education)	Companies, Ministry of Education; Ministry of Science; provinces	No figures available; less than 5 per cent of participants in formal adult education	Customized programmes in 'mechatronics' by higher secondary technical schools; university training course 'Professional Workforce Management' for *Trenkwalder* (a major temporary work agency)
VI Continuing higher education	New, but fast-growing field of post-secondary and post-tertiary programmes for further specialization, typically provided at full cost plus profit with weak social charter in a supply-driven market	Public universities, *Fachhochschulen*; non-profit and for-profit providers in adult education	Ministry of Science; private households; employers	20000+	University and *Fachhochschulen* training courses, MBAs, MAS
VII Continuing professional education	A field with many highly autonomous sub-fields encompassing preparation courses for various examinations/accreditations for professions, typically legally regulated	Professional Associations, Chambers of Commerce, employer organizations; Universities, *Fachhochschulen*	Ministry of Science; private households; employers	No overall figures available	Formal: Master craftsperson courses (participants: 3800 in 2007); not yet recognized as formal: 'psychotherapy' (4700 participants)

the market; they do not come from a central 'coherent strategy for lifelong learning' (DUK 2007; BMUKK 2008; Republik Österreich 2011).

We identify and discuss four main forces for change: the overall expansion of formal education and increasing competition between providers; the emergence of active labour-market policy as the new key player for financing lifelong learning; the increasing importance of local bodies for supporting lifelong learning by administrating European funds; and a renewed interest in certified programmes by employer organizations.

Basic Skills Programmes: A Marginalized Education Field (I)

While other countries, such as England, Scotland and Norway, provide a wide selection of basic skill programmes in formal adult education, Austria has only one type of formal programme, which has approximately 1000 participants in preparatory courses for the *Hauptschulabschluss*. The *Hauptschulabschluss* is an important marker, signifying successful completion of the last year of lower secondary education. However, it is not formally required to advance to vocational education at International Standard Classification of Education (ISCED) level 3 and has little value as a 'signal' within the labour market. Programmes preparing for the *Hauptschulabschluss* are 'formal' due to the 'goal' and the public funding, yet they frequently pursue a wide range of therapeutic goals (Steiner et al. 2006).

The *Volksbildung* movement and adult education centres began as efforts to use education to reduce social disadvantages due to poverty, low income or class and to facilitate access to cultural events previously restricted to the middle and upper classes. With the enormous expansion of education in the twentieth century, the 'disadvantaged' were increasingly marginalized. Illiteracy became one of the great taboos in Austria's society in the second half of the century. Only in the last two decades has the perception in Austria seem to have changed – partly due to the international awareness-raising campaigns of UNESCO and the OECD, as well as by Austria's large neighbour, Germany (Rath 2007; Wieser and Dér 2011).

However, teaching basic skills remains a marginalized, under-resourced field in Austria and outside the official vision of 'formal education' except for the above-mentioned example. Data on overall formal and non-formal activities are missing; reported activities represent only a tiny fraction of course participation in lifelong learning. Along with a long-established reluctance to admit to the problem of low literacy, several mainly institutional reasons for the weak position of basic education in Austria include the following:

1. A deeply rooted approach of 'educational selectivity' contradicts individualized support to adults for improving elementary skills to enable participation in existing second-chance programmes or other programmes; anyone not able to follow a defined pace of learning is expected to leave programmes. Therefore, institutions do not have publicly funded tutoring opportunities to build bridges for adults who simply cannot participate in the most frequent education opportunities.
2. For young people (15–24 years old) who need basic skills, the public employment service has become the major provider of further education: basic skills are taught within a dense net of labour market programmes that particularly include vocational training programmes for school drop-outs and long-term unemployed young workers. However, the mandatory character and the stigmatized nature of the programmes do not fit with the principles developed by adult basic education. In any case, voluntary adult basic education (for the employed) is rarely financed by the system of active labour market policy in Austria.
3. The mandatory German language courses for migrants from non-EU-member states (implemented in 2003, latest amendment 2011) has only a comparatively low level of public co-funding for the required course work. Learning German is understood as an individual obligation, not as an individual right guaranteed by the state: consequently, German courses are not understood as part of 'formal' adult education – as they are for example in Norway or Sweden and as recommended by statistical manuals (UNESCO et al. 2010).
4. The weak funding for basic education has not allowed the development of specialized adult educators. Courses and certification for educators were established only recently.

The Austrian qualifications framework currently under development will need to deal with the lack of formal programmes below the *Hauptschulabschluss*. On the one hand, Austria decided to implement the eight-level structure of the European Qualifications Framework (EQF); on the other hand, the *Hauptschulabschluss*, the 'absolute skills minimum' (Steiner et al. 2006, p. 17), cannot be lower than level 2, because the next-higher certificate, the 'apprenticeship leave certificate' is currently discussed as being at level 3 or 4 (BMUKK and BMWF 2008; Markowitsch 2009). This will give plenty of room for new basic skills qualifications at level 1. Interestingly, countries such as Scotland and Ireland, which developed their qualifications framework prior to the EQF, have introduced more than eight levels in order to better distinguish between skills qualifications at the lower levels (Markowitsch 2009). This coincides with a distinctive provision of formal basic skills programmes in these countries, and underlines the potential to integrate basic skills programmes into the upcoming Austrian qualifications framework and to speed up ongoing institutionalization. Potential for such an action is high, but chances are low because that field depends heavily on public spending (both by public employment service and ministry of education), and comes partly from other policy areas, for example the obligatory German language courses for immigrants. Thus, although a distinct field, basic skills programmes do not have a clear advocate in Austria.

Second-Chance Education: An Unexpected Revitalization (II)

Second-chance education represents a highly differentiated, long-established, well-developed field within formal education in Austria with approximately 40 000 adult participants (2008). In the mid-1990s, this field began to change dramatically, as we will describe in this section.

In Austria, as in many other countries, the opportunity to have a second chance to acquire a school-leaving certificate at a higher secondary level goes back to the 1920s. The former *Arbeitermittelschulen* (evening secondary schools) (Engelbrecht 1988, pp. 213ff.) were transformed into today's 'evening gymnasiums', which expanded dramatically in the 1960s during the first wave of post-war education expansion (ibid., pp. 446ff.). To correctly evaluate second-chance education in Austria, one has to consider two particularities of the Austrian education system. Firstly, access to higher education has long been limited to pupils who pass the *Reifeprüfung*[4] (upper secondary school leaving exam allowing enrolment in higher education) at the end of higher secondary education. Most young adults were excluded from higher education because of early segregation at the age of ten into academic and non-academic streams, and then at the age of 14, another separation into higher secondary education preparing for *Reifeprüfung* or the 'dual apprenticeship system', which does not provide access to university. In 2005, only 40 per cent of a cohort were permitted to enter university. Beyond access to higher education, the *Reifeprüfung* has been the entrance requirement for any upper-level careers in public administration (including the military) and many private bureaucratic organizations (for example, in banking and insurance). Consequently, second-chance education had and still has many potential participants seeking the qualifications to begin higher education or making progress in their careers.

Because the *Reifeprüfung* has long dominated the system of educational stratification, alternative routes for access to higher education were forcefully opposed by conservative political parties and by the proponents of higher secondary education and universities. Alternatives to evening schools preparing for *Reifeprüfung*, such as the constantly reformed and renamed *Studienberechtigungsprüfung* (university entrance qualification examination) available since 1945 (ibid., p. 531f.) remain fairly unattractive with restrictive access requirements. The primacy of *Reifeprüfung* weakened only after the introduction of the *Berufsreifeprüfung*[5] (examination providing general access to higher education for skilled workers and graduates of three- to four-year full-time vocational schools) in 1997 (see below).

Similarly to initial education, part-time secondary technical and vocational colleges for the employed were introduced alongside the general and academic track. They are mainly attended by young adults (20–25-year-olds) and the high level of isomorphism with the initial education system is not only due to the offered qualifications (equal to the initial education in all aspects), but it is also manifest in curricula, teaching and learning modes, teacher education and administration. Instruction takes place by classes, by the same teachers and in the same premises for those who are between 15 and 19 years old. Until recently, curricula were congruent with full-time schools, and apart from the older target group and the fact that instruction takes place in the evening, it would be difficult to distinguish evening schools from their full-time equivalents. Evening schools remained pretty much unchanged until very recently, when they came under increasing pressure from the introduction of the *Berufsreifeprüfung* (see Figure 9.1). As a result, the number of participants in second-chance programmes in Austria has doubled and the programmes have undergone two important developments. Firstly, the (private) adult education associations gained the right to offer at least sections[6] of the examination leading to a nationally recognized (formal) certificate, and therefore partially dissolving the long-standing equation of 'adult education equals non-formal learning' as noted in the introduction. Secondly, by introducing their tradition of teaching, adult education providers broke with the image of second-chance education as school education for adults. In contrast to learning in schools, learning at adult education organizations means learning within a modularized course system with individual learning time and no compulsory attendance. Elements of these classical adult education approaches are now also infiltrating the evening schools; for example, all programmes have introduced modularizations.

However, the *Berufsreifeprüfung* affected not only the evening schools, but also the university entrance qualification examination, which was the traditional way to have access to university courses without a school leaving certificate. Whereas the *Berufsreifeprüfung* in principle offers access to all university courses, the university entrance qualification examination

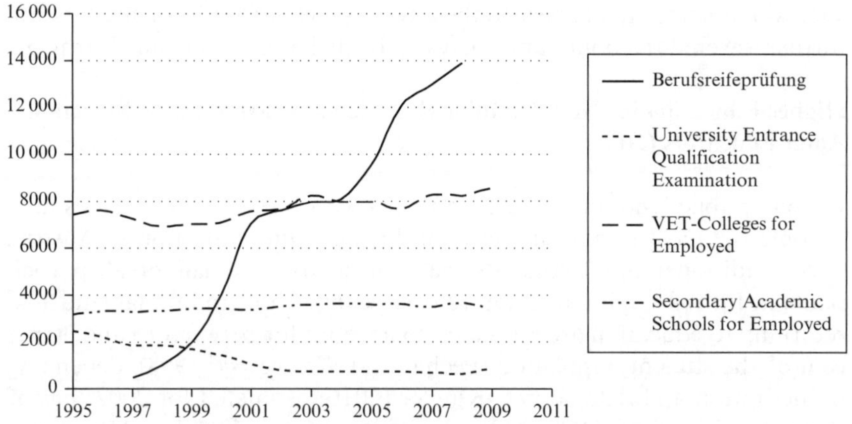

Sources: Statistics Austria; Austrian Federal Ministry for Education, Arts and Culture; Klimmer et al. (2006); Markowitsch et al. (2008); Lachmayr (2011); authors' own calculations.

Figure 9.1 Development of student population for selected offers of second-chance programmes in Austria, 1995–2010

offers only restricted access to universities, and therefore it lost influence over time (see also Figure 9.1; Markowitsch et al. 2008; Birke et al. 2001). Finally, in 2010, the university entrance qualification examination Act was abolished, leaving it entirely to the universities to organize this particular method of access. It will be interesting to see if this leads to a decrease in preparatory courses of the adult-education providers, or if this will result in new forms of cooperation between them and the universities.

The vocational courses of evening schools were less affected by the *Berufsreifeprüfung*. A highly prestigious system of higher-secondary vocational education exists in Austria, which also offers *Reifeprüfung* and therefore entrance to higher education, while also preparing for a direct transition to occupational career pathways in various economic sectors. This system came under pressure from the expansion of higher education, notably by introducing universities of applied sciences (see below). Thus, second-chance education streams included pathways dedicated solely to preparing for entrance to higher education or terminal vocational degrees. Consequently, the field consists of two relatively independent segments.

To conclude, since the mid-1990s, we can see a considerable expansion of second-chance education in Austria that can mainly be attributed to introducing a new qualification, the *Berufsreifeprüfung*, which further strengthened the role of adult education providers in this field. Its organization and success has somewhat tarnished the attractiveness of traditional offers and further lowered the boundaries between formal and non-formal learning.

Higher Education for Non-Traditional Students: Universities as Reluctant Adult Educators (III)

Despite public ignorance and even their own resistance, universities have become the most important actors in formal adult education in Austria. 'Non-traditional' adult students make up at roughly half of all participants in formal adult education (25–64 years). Non-traditional students[7] returning to education are estimated to account for between 15 and 30 per cent of the student population (Pechar and Wroblewski 1998), depending on definition and data source. Ringler (2010) estimated for 2002 that of the approximately 175 000 students with Austrian citizenship, 16 per cent worked before beginning their studies. Unger et al. (2010) found that in 2009 around 42 per cent of all students above the age of 25 worked before beginning their studies. Therefore, while Austria has fewer adult non-traditional students than, for example, England or the United States, the numbers are far from negligible. However, only in the mid-1990s did policy initiatives start to openly support adult participation in higher education.

Austria has experienced delayed progress from 'elite' to 'mass' higher education. Education reforms began in the early 1960s (for example, abolishing entrance examinations and tuition fees for higher secondary education, and the foundation of three new local universities) and new subsidies for pupils and their families were introduced in the late 1960s. These changes helped, by the early 1970s, to overcome the cutbacks in education participation caused by Austro-Fascist (1934–1938) and National Socialist regimes (1938–1945). In 1970, only 8 per cent of a cohort (11 per cent of men and 5 per cent of women) took up university-level studies. After 1985, Austria finally entered 'mass' higher education (Trow 1973, 2006) with more than 15 per cent of a cohort in higher education. Even today, after 25 years of further expansion and creation and inclusion of new types of higher education institutions, graduation rates for 25–34-year-olds (19 per cent) at the typical age are clearly below the EU average (33 per cent) (Statistik Austria 2011). Graduates still make up only 18 per cent (2008) of the working-age population (compared to 24 per cent for the EU-25).[8] To reach the recently proposed EU 2020 target of higher education graduates making up 40 per cent of the working-age population, Austria would have to double the existing rate.

Paradoxically, while Austria supports the EU 2020 targets and programme, strong forces resist any further expansion of the higher education sector. Condemnation of the 'massification' of higher education has become a constant trope of Austrian education policy since the late 1970s. As an example, the Minister of Science, appointed in 2011, publicly questioned the need for more graduates.[9] In any case, we will discuss some of the simultaneous opening and closure tendencies particularly important for adult non-traditional students. Universities in Austria receive a lump-sum budget, not connected to the number of student places they provide. Much of the expansion of the student population has been accomplished without expanding university budgets, resulting in extraordinarily bad ratios of teaching staff to students in many programmes and universities. Universities have no interest in attracting and retaining additional student populations: the 'old' universities do not attempt to attract adult students into regular programmes. In 2006, entrance examinations were introduced in some disciplines (for example, medicine and psychology).[10] This was partly in response to high inflows of German students after a European court decision that overturned Austria's restrictions on foreign students from EU member states. Qualification for university studies is no longer enough to choose freely between study programmes.

Non-traditional students have always entered Austrian universities in high – although unreported – numbers. The highly liberal organization of programmes – for example obligatory attendance for most lectures was abolished in 1966 and reintroduced only partly in the past decade – has allowed a combination of study and work even with no institutional support, mainly by individuals increasing the number of years of study. However, reorganization of university studies through the Bologna reforms have started to considerably reduce individual flexibility, restricting options for working while studying. Partly as a response to these reduced opportunities, in the mid-1990s, major reforms began to explicitly support employed adults. They included introducing study courses for the employed at *Fachhochschulen* (universities of applied sciences) and developing financial support schemes for employed adults. Moreover, the ministry encouraged universities to consider their employed students' needs, for example, with regard to opening hours and lecture schedules.

Thus, in the mid-1990s, the sector divided into old and new higher education sectors. Among the new actors the most important are the *Fachhochschulen*. This new sector was continuously developed to fulfil tasks that had seemed unachievable by universities: for example, providing shorter, more practice-oriented studies, particularly in regions with no university. These programmes are open to students with work experience but without *Reifeprüfung*; they have an external quality assurance system; and their financing is based on predefined study places. Shortly after introducing *Fachhochschulen* (1993), the first courses for the employed (1995) started and were gradually expanded. In addition, due to political

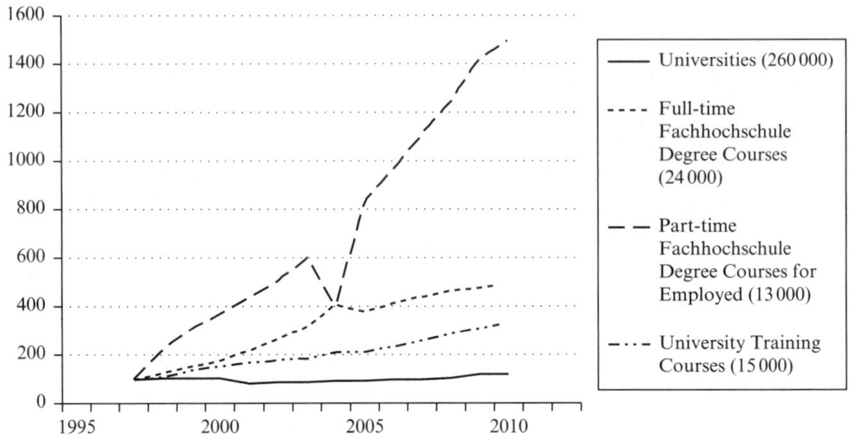

Note: numbers in brackets show absolute figures for 2010.

Source: Statistics Austria, Uni-data, FH Council.

Figure 9.2 Overview of trends in student population (growth rates) of selected streams in the Austrian tertiary sector

focus and funding, study courses for the employed at *Fachhochschulen* have experienced higher growth rates than other types of formal adult education in the last 15 years (see Figure 9.2), so that meanwhile around 40 per cent of all students in this study sector are enrolled in part-time programmes. This chance was also seized by the large adult education providers; for example, the Vocational Training Institutes of the Chamber of Labour (*Arbeiterkammer*) and the Training Institutes of the Chambers of Commerce started *Fachhochschule* courses and form part of the diverse provider landscape.

While competitive entrance examinations are generally foreseen for all programmes, many *Fachhochschule* programmes – in particular, in technical areas – openly compete for applicants, because there might be more places available than suitable candidates. Reaching out for an adult clientele is therefore an important strategy for securing maximum public funding. Moreover, retention of non-traditional students becomes important because – contrary to the universities – funding for study places stops when students drop out. Because of this, 'old' universities take an interest in 'adult' employed students only for their high-priced continuing higher education programmes (see the next subsection), and *Fachhochschulen* have become more engaged in offering openly formal adult education. Thus, they partly close the gap in the provision of higher education that results from universities' reluctance to open their programmes to the employed.

To sum up, the higher education sector is a highly dynamic field in formal adult education, with a constant tension between waves of expanding and restricting developments. However, the field is not regarded as part of 'adult education', nor as an important part of policies fostering lifelong learning. Given the extraordinary difficulties and tensions within the Austrian higher education sector, after decades of underfinancing and continual reform, the various actors place a low priority on non-traditional adult students.

We find an equally surprising inertia regarding offers for non-traditional students among the 'old' universities. These universities in Austria constantly underplay the role they have or could have regarding lifelong learning. Either they take the position that they are too busy with other issues (see above), or they maintain the more arrogant position that their courses are free to any student, traditional or non-traditional. The ministry has so far failed to negotiate target agreements obliging universities to offer part-time programmes. By contrast, Germany, which faces a similar situation, recently initiated a multi-million euro measure to 'open' universities.[11] Most European countries have already developed their part-time university course offers. A further expansion of formal adult education in Austria depends on the willingness of universities to open their regular studies and to actively adapt them for non-traditional students, that is, to become lifelong learning organizations. A neighbouring country provides an example of what happens when 'the giant awakes': in the Czech Republic, the number of students accepted into tertiary studies went up from 50000 in the year 2000 to 126000 in 2009. This increase mainly resulted from study programmes designed for those who work (Kuchar and Dobes 2010). Paul Downes used interviews to reveal the distance of Austrian universities from 'opening access' (while pretending to have, and being proud of, open access):

> A common thread emerges from the above example of this Austrian university: There is an absence of strategic policy level commitment at institutional level to access and social inclusion . . . Against this backdrop, it is unsurprising that there are no institutional supports at the university to facilitate access and social inclusion. This is not a case of lip-service being paid to access issues, there is not even lip-service being paid. (Downes 2011, p. 146f.)

Continuing Higher Education: Austria's 'Academic Capitalism' (VI)

Continuing higher education is a strongly expanding field, driven by market forces: universities – and other eligible organizations – seek to attract paying students for degree programmes that are not accepted as 'normal' studies but only as continuous education. The high tuition fees must fully cover additional costs, but also result in a steady stream of additional income. Because normal study programmes have no or moderate tuition fees, continuing higher education forms a market of particular economic interest: adults are very welcome as paying customers.

Before 2002, university studies used to be regulated in detail by law in Austria. However, universities and other approved organizations have now been allowed to issue degrees at both post-secondary and post-tertiary levels. The programmes offered should react flexibly to social and market needs for highly specialized competences in any possible field of expertise. Universities should guarantee the professional and research-based quality of programmes. At the level of education policy, new organizations such as the Interuniversitäres Forschungsinstitut für Fernstudien (IFF) (1979, reformed 1992) have been, and are, founded with the goal of developing new innovative programmes, answering societal demands for further education based on interdisciplinary research. Even more important, the Danube University Krems was founded in 1995 as a public university engaged only in the for-pay provision of continuing higher education. Today it delivers an extraordinarily wide range of degree programmes in medicine, natural sciences, technical sciences, law, social sciences and humanities. Student numbers increased from 100 in the first year (1995) to 5000 in 2010. Various 'old' universities have founded their own for-profit centres for providing continuing higher education, among them the Austrian Business School (University of Linz), the WU Executive Academy (Vienna University of Economics and Business) and the Postgraduate Centre (University of Vienna). Meanwhile, more or less all universities, and all universities of applied sciences, are active in the continuing higher education market. Together, they cater to more than 12 000 participants (Statistik Austria 2010, p. 282). Various other non-higher education providers have also been accepted to provide degree programmes within continuous higher education, among them both traditional adult education organizations and long-term established providers for particular professions. In 2008, 50 providers offered so-called *Lehrgänge universitären Charakters* (university-level courses) for around 4000 students. Together, approximately 20 000 participants (or their employers) spend an estimated €50 million to €100 million a year on tuition fees – a considerable share of Austria's education market.

The emerging organizational field of continuing higher education awaits a critical institutional analysis. It certainly delivers highly specialized formal adult education, although the 'social charters' of these programmes are often unclear and acceptance in the labour market is, at best, selective. While there are examples of well-arranged links between programmes and occupational or professional fields, participants risk suffering from a new version of the 'great training robbery' (Berg and Govelick 1970). The formal status of programmes seems to be secured mainly by ritual compliance with institutional rules and not by a firm institutionalization of its acceptance: participants may actually 'buy' a title, while they could have received similar education services at lower rates within the normal higher education system. Universities play a double role: while they 'cold-shoulder' adult students who, as students, pay no or low fees, the universities embrace paying students in continuing higher education and introduce them to the world of 'academic capitalism'. The expansion of continuing higher education is driven by various factors that include status competition among these new 'education enterprises'. However, this expansion hardly results from a deliberate, lifelong learning policy (although public co-funding opportunities for tuition fees help the market to develop), nor from universities expressing an active interest in lifelong learning.

CONCLUSIONS AND OUTLOOK: FORMAL ADULT EDUCATION IN THE GROWING SHADOW OF THE NATIONAL QUALIFICATIONS FRAMEWORK

We have seen that while Austria has little societal space available for formal adult education in the field of basic education, policy interventions and adults' choices have enabled strong expansion and structural change since 1997 in the field of second-chance education. We have seen the stalemate in higher education for non-traditional students, where any progress, such as introducing specialized programmes for employed students at universities of applied sciences, could be nullified by the inertia of 'old' universities, which prefer to 'divert' potential students away from their doors instead of attracting them. Finally, we have seen the development of a market-driven field of continuing higher education, where the money of adult students is welcome, yet which can provide few institutional guarantees for the quality and the 'social charter' of their educational 'products'.

By looking closer into the selected fields of formal adult education, we observed both highly dynamic and stagnant aspects coexisting within each field. If we now try to summarize the most important trends across the analysed fields, we can assert the following.

In three out of the four fields described, we observed a strong increase in provisions for and participation of adult learners in formal education, which exceeds the ongoing general educational expansion, best shown by second-chance programmes and programmes for non-traditional students at universities of applied sciences. We also saw how adult education providers and private education organizations, previously restricted to non-formal offers, are increasingly entering new fields and appear as new actors within formal education, in particular in offering preparation courses for formal qualifications, but also as providers of part-time study courses and university-level courses. The expansion of the continuing professional education field has not been discussed here due to lack of space. We have also left out the highly complex field of retraining with its comparatively restricted access to formal education. We can further expect that introducing the Austrian Qualifications Framework will promote the rise of new formal programmes (or the acceptance of existing non-formal programmes as formal) in all seven fields of formal adult education. However, this will not reach the speed of countries that have introduced systems of recognition for non-formal and informal learning. Thus, we can see an overall expansion of formal adult education along three lines: new programmes, increasing numbers of students, and transformation of existing programmes.

Apart from these tendencies, two even more important issues became evident. Firstly, although traditional adult education became an active player in formal adult education, the provision of formal education to adults – with the exception of second-chance programmes – remains outside the scope of the adult education community. Areas where adult education providers still play a minor role (for example, part-time *Fachhochschule* degree courses or university training courses) are not perceived as adult education by relevant administrators, policy-makers, the participants and the wider public. A complete picture of adult education in Austria is only possible if one crosses traditional demarcation lines and considers various branches of formal adult education, firm-based training, liberal and civic adult education, and so on.

A comprehensive and accurate view is consequently the precondition for any attempts at making serious, coherent lifelong learning policy. This insight does not touch upon the problems and difficulties inherent in coordinating a coherent lifelong learning strategy against the background of these diverse fields, logics and traditions. In fact, we have sketched an overview that makes clear the tensions. Any lifelong learning policy must seek to mediate these problems, although with no guarantee that there actually is a way to build bridges between the divergent interests, logics and cognitive frames of the organizational fields.

Assumed success stories disabuse us of a seductive faith in a 'perfect' policy. Ivančič and Radovan (2011; also see their Chapter 10 in this volume) show that Slovenia's remarkable expansion of lifelong learning, which exceeds even many of the old EU member states, cannot be attributed to adult education policy.

The ongoing failure of lifelong learning policy in Austria as well as in many other countries is thus not surprising. It is more convenient to blame ineffective policy on lack of resources and competences than to admit that it might be hopeless to attempt to develop 'perfect' policy, as any policy is held hostage by the institutional contradictions of organizational fields, which are rarely made explicit. People have excessive expectations for most action plans for lifelong learning (e.g., European Commission 2011) and the related short-term solutions. Experience shows that any serious lifelong learning policy must cover at least 10 or 15 years.

Leaving these fundamental problems aside, we will finally concentrate on the positive and prospective outcomes of our analysis. We used the typology presented in Chapter 3 of this volume to highlight some recent dynamics in formal adult education in Austria. An institutional analysis would allow the identification of blind spots and neglected fields of lifelong learning policy. Focusing on formal education that leads to a qualification would provide a tool for investigating the existing types of learning that would be mapped by the upcoming qualifications framework. Consequently, this focus provides the insight required for the political process of creating the national qualifications framework (NQF), which is likely to intervene in the existing fields of formal provision. By applying our sevenfold typology, we can spot areas for development within the qualifications framework (e.g., the basic skills programmes). Furthermore, we are able to provide a tool for understanding institutional logics and ongoing processes in developing a qualifications framework. With this tool, we can examine how education programmes classified by the framework actually arrange for the social acceptance – the social charter – of their education programmes and their issued qualifications. This goes beyond a traditional, but simple, grouping of actors by institutional similarities, or grouping of qualifications by programme type. As we were able to show, neither the type of organization nor the type of programme provides a sufficient criterion to mark the blurred borders between fields. Thus, the typology also offers a new way of thinking about how to develop the Austrian qualifications framework.

The same applies to future research on organizational fields, rather than traditional research on particular actors or programmes. The analysis further reveals that international comparisons are doomed to failure if they rely upon ISCED levels or, worse, on only aggregated data instead of considering an organizational-field approach. Formal adult education, as we were able to show, is particularly interesting because of its hybrid position between further training and initial education. In addition to further investigations of particular fields across countries, for example comparing evening schools or basic skills programmes, it would be promising to expand this approach to study the remaining organizational fields in adult education beyond formal provision. Using this process, we could better see how formal and non-formal provision interact in society.

Regarding formal adult education, lifelong learning policy faces both dilemmas and opportunities. On the one hand, any coherent policy is limited by the persistence of both segregation in initial education that 'charters' many youth to educational failure and precarious employment opportunities, and also the heavily under-resourced universities, which deny their role as the key players in formal adult education. On the other hand, the ongoing growth of formal adult education in the fields mentioned needs coordination and further development. The national qualifications framework (NQF) is a promising new starting point for a more coherent approach towards formal adult education. At the same time, the crucial role unfolding for formal adult education in lifelong learning provides a new impetus for the NQF.

Finally, our framework of seven organizational fields of formal adult education only provides a proper starting point for an in-depth analysis and for further research. Beyond incidental comments, we have scarcely pointed out the competing roles of various organizational actors – the providers, the professions, the business-interest organizations, the trade unions, various social movement organizations, the political parties – strategically seeking institutional advantages from any changes in education policy. We have not presented a systematic account of social mechanisms – structural and institutional – responsible for institutional stability and the gradual drift or disruptive change as outlined by recent contributions within historical (Streeck and Thelen 2005; Mahoney and Thelen 2010) and organizational institutionalism (Scott 2008; Beckert 2010). We have not interpreted how in the same time frame (1995 – 2010) lifelong learning was affected by Austria's accession to the European Union against the background of transnational – truly global and world-culture related – institutional developments (Baker and LeTendre 2005; Meyer 2010) which might exert their influence beneath the surface of local policies and politics and all-powerful 'folkways' of educational ideology (Turner 1960; Meyer 2011). To conclude, we understand our contribution as an early step towards a view on lifelong learning in Austria that could incorporate structural, human-capital, conflict and institutional perspectives (Rubinson and Browne 1994).

NOTES

1. We characterize 'formal adult education' by its ability – its 'social charter' (Meyer 1970) – to provide eligibility for further steps on the education or occupation ladder. We dem-

onstrate that formal adult education is provided in seven organizational fields, enjoying considerable autonomy and characterized by their particular institutional processes and logics. Although our arguments in this article could be followed without it, we strongly recommend looking at Chapter 3 in this volume, as we cannot repeat many of the theoretical foundations and general statements here.

2. Predominantly adult education centres and the vocational training institutes of the Chamber of Labour and the Chambers of Commerce.
3. For Germany see Hillmert and Jacob (2003) and Hillmert and Mayer (2004). For the USA see Elman and O'Rand (2007).
4. The everyday term used in Austria is *Matura*; *Abitur* in Germany. There is a difference between the academic and the vocational track insofar as the latter in addition to the *Reifeprüfung* also provides a labour market qualification (*Diplomprüfung*) in a specific vocational field.
5. After an experimentation phase in the past decade, mainly driven by business interest organizations facing declining attractiveness of the dual apprenticeship, a large-scale programme (2008–2012) was set up to promote the combination of dual apprenticeship and *Berufsreifeprüfung* for 15–19-year-olds (http://www.bmukk.gv.at/medienpool/16691/berufsmatura_richtlinien.pdf).
6. Three out of four exams – German, a foreign language, mathematics and a vocational topic – can be taken at an adult education organization; at least one has to be taken at a school. This perfectly reflects the negotiations and trust between the different systems, and partly explains why it has been criticized as a 'low-cost' school leaving certificate by representatives of schools.
7. Students returning to education, working while studying, or studying without the university entrance examination.
8. Low participation rates in higher education also reflect the particularities of Austria's 'German-like' skill formation system with occupational space clearly dominating (Hefler and Markowitsch 2012). By the mid-1980s, the state was regarded as the single most important employer for university graduates beyond the traditional 'liberal professions'. Incremental innovation, coming from polyvalent vocationally trained worker elites, 'craft master', 'engineers' and 'traders' educated at higher secondary level, have been long regarded as the backbone of Austrian manufacturing and trading.
9. *Kurier*, 21 May 2011.
10. In 1999, the *Privatuniversitätengesetz* allowed the foundation of private universities. In 2008, 12 private universities catered for approximately 5000 students in niche markets (Statistik Austria 2010, p. 243). These universities provide study places in disciplines with limited study-places and competitive entrance examinations such as in medicine, psychology, and also in the performing arts. Moreover, private universities are engaged in management studies. Together, private universities play – as in Germany (Fernández Darraz et al. 2010) – a subordinated role in higher education, although they are of more importance within continuing professional education.
11. http://www.wettbewerb-offene-hochschulen-bmbf.de/

REFERENCES

Baker, David Jan and Gerald K. LeTendre (2005), *National Differences, Global Similarities: World Culture and the Future of Schooling*, Stanford, CA: Stanford Social Sciences.

Beckert, Jens (2010), 'How Do Fields Change? The Interrelations of Institutions, Networks, and Cognition in the Dynamics of Markets', *Organization Studies*, **31**, 605–627.

Berg, Ivar and Sherry Govelick (1970), *Education for Jobs. The Great Training Robbery*, New York: Praeger Publishers.
Birke, Barbara, Helmut Hafner, Susanna-Maria Henkel and Johanna Wagner (2001), *Die künftige Entwicklung der Studienberechtigungsprüfung*, Wien: Industriewissenschaftliches Institut.
Bundesministerium für Unterricht, Kunst und Kultur (BMUKK) (2008), 'Wissen – Chancen – Kompetenzen: Strategie zur Umsetzung des Lebenslangen Lernens in Österreich', Konsultationspapier.
Bundesministerium für Unterricht, Kunst und Kultur (BMUKK) and Bundesministerium für Wissenschaft und Forschung (BMWF) (2008), 'Konsultationspapier: Nationaler Qualifikationsrahmen für Österreich', Wien.
Downes, Paul (2011), 'A Systems Level Focus on Access to Education for Traditionally Marginalized Groups in Europe: Comparing Strategies, Policy and Practice in Twelve European Countries', Comparative Report: Subproject 5, LLL2010, Dublin: Educational Disadvantage Centre, St Patrick's College.
Donau-Universität Krems (DUK) (ed.) (2007), 'Leitlinien einer kohärenten LLL-Strategie für Österreich bis 2010: In einer ersten Konsultation abgestimmte Vorschläge einer facheinschlägigen ExpertInnengruppe', Final Version, 20 January.
Elman, Cheryl and Angela M. O'Rand (2007), 'The Effects of Social Origins, Life Events, and Institutional Sorting on Adults' School Transitions', *Social Science Research*, **36**, 1276–1299.
Engelbrecht, Helmut (1988), *Geschichte des österreichischen Bildungswesens: Von 1918 bis zur Gegenwart*, Vol. 5, Vienna: Österreichischer Bundesverlag.
Eraut, Michael (1994), *Developing Professional Knowledge and Competence*, London: Falmer.
European Commission (2011), 'Action Plan on Adult Learning: Achievements and results 2008–2010', Commission Staff Working Paper, SEC (2011) 271-final, Brussels.
Fernández Darraz, Enrique, Gero Lenhardt, Robert D. Reisz and Manfred Stock (2010), *Hochschulprivatisierung und akademische Freiheit: jenseits von Markt und Staat: Hochschulen in der Weltgesellschaft*, Bielefeld: Transcript Verlag.
Greenwood, Royston, Christine Oliver, Kerstine Sahlin and Roy Suddaby (eds) (2008), *The SAGE Handbook of Organizational Institutionalism*, Los Angeles, CA: Sage Publisher.
Gruber, Elke (2011), 'Anbieterstruktur der Erwachsenenbildung/Weiterbildung: Befunde aus dem Forschungs- und Entwicklungsprojekt PERLS', in Jörg Markowitsch, Elke Gruber, Lorenz Lassnigg and Daniela Moser (eds), *Turbulenzen auf Arbeitsmärkten und in Bildungssystemen: Beiträge zur Berufsbildungsforschung*, Innsbruck: StudienVerlag, pp. 293–307.
Hefler, Günter and Jörg Markowitsch (2012), 'Bridging Institutional Divides: Linking Education, Careers and Work in "Organizational Space" and "Skill Space" Dominated Employment Systems', in Rachel Brooks, Alison Fuller, Johanna Waters (eds), *Changing Spaces of Education: New Perspectives on the Nature of Learning*, London: Routledge, pp. 160–180.
Hefler, Günter, Paul Ringler, Stephanie Rammel and Jörg Markowitsch (2011), *Formal Adult Education in Context: The View of European Statistics*, Synthesis Report of SP2 – LLL2010, Krems: Danube University Krems.
Hillmert, Steffen and Marita Jacob (2003), 'Bildungsprozesse zwischen

Diskontinuität und Karriere: Das Phänomen der Mehrfachausbildungen', *Zeitschrift für Soziologie*, **32**, 325–345.

Hillmert, Steffen and Karl Ulrich Mayer (eds) (2004), *Geboren 1964 und 1971 – Neuere Untersuchungen zu Ausbildungs- und Berufschancen in Westdeutschland*, Wiesbaden: VS-Verlag.

Ivančič, Angela and Marko Radovan (2011), 'Inequality of Access of Underrepresented Groups in Formal and Non-Formal Education in Slovenia: The Role of National Adult Education Policy', unpublished manuscript.

Klimmer, Susanne, Peter Schlögl and Barbara Neubauer (2006), *Die Berufsreifeprüfung – Höherqualifizierung für den beruflichen Aufstieg oder für den Umstieg? Eine Status-quo-Erhebung*, Materialien zur Erwachsenenbildung Nr. 3/2006, Vienna: Bundesministerium für Bildung, Wissenschaft und Kultur.

Kuchar, Pavel and Martin Dobes (2010), 'SP2 National Report: Czech Republic', National Training Fund.

Lachmayr, Norbert (2011), 'Berufsreifeprüfung – eine österreichische Erfolgsgeschichte', *WISO – Wirtschafts- und Sozialpolitische Zeitschrift*, **2**, 153–163.

Lenz, Werner (2005), *Porträt Weiterbildung Österreich*, Bielefeld: W. Bertelsmann Verlag.

Luomi-Messerer, Karin, Sonja Lengauer and Jörg Markowitsch (2009), 'Die Entwicklung eines Nationalen Qualifikationsrahmens in Österreich im Kontext internationaler Beispiele und Erfahrungen', in Jörg Markowitsch (ed.), *Der nationale Qualifikationsrahmen in Österreich: Beiträge zur Entwicklung*, Vienna: Lit-Verlag, pp. 29–48.

Luomi-Messerer, Karin, Jörg Markowitsch and Sonja Lengauer (2007), 'Nationaler Qualifikationsrahmen: Aktuelle Ansätze in Österreich im Vergleich mit anderen Ländern', *Berufs- und Wirtschaftspädagogik online – Bwp@ Spezial*, **3**. Available at: http://www.bwpat.de/ATspezial/luomi-messerer_etal_atspezial.shtml.

Mahoney, James and Kathleen Thelen (2010), 'A Theory of Gradual Institutional Change', in James Mahoney and Kathleen Thelen (eds), *Explaining Institutional Change: Ambiguity, Agency, and Power in Historical Institutionalism*, New York: Cambridge University Press, pp. 1–37.

Markowitsch, Jörg (ed.) (2009), *Der nationale Qualifikationsrahmen in Österreich: Beiträge zur Entwicklung*, Vienna: Lit-Verlag.

Markowitsch, Jörg, Silvia Benda-Kahri and Günter Hefler (2008), 'The Underestimated Role of Formal Adult Learning in Austria's Lifelong Learning Policy', *Berufs- und Wirtschaftspädagogik online – Bwp@ Spezial*, **3**. Available at: http://www.bwpat.de/ATspezial/markowitsch_etal_atspezial.shtml.

Markowitsch, Jörg, Silvia Benda-Kahri, Monika Prokopp, Stephanie Rammel and Günter Hefler (2008), *Neuausrichtung der berufsbildenden Schulen für Berufstätige. Eine Studie im Auftrag des BMUKK*, Studies in Lifelong Learning, Vol. 7, Krems: Donau-Universität Krems.

Markowitsch, Jörg and Günter Hefler (2006), '(K)ein Markt, viele Märkte? Zur Marktsituation und Professionalisierung der Weiterbildung in Österreich', in Brigitte Mosberger and René Sturm (eds), *Zwischen Lifelong Learning, Qualitätsdebatte und Werkvertrag* – Beiträge im Anschluß an die Fachtagung 'Kompetenzen, Berufsfelder und Arbeitsbedingungen von TrainerInnen' vom 5. Oktober 2005 in Wien, Vienna: Hofstätter, pp. 9–27.

Markowitsch, Jörg and Michaela Jonach (2006), *Anerkennung und Zertifizierung betrieblicher Aus- und Weiterbildungsleistungen im Kontext nationaler*

und internationaler Entwicklungen. Eine Überblicksexpertise, Vienna: Bundesministerium für Wirtschaft und Arbeit.
Meyer, Heinz-Dieter (2011), 'Path Dependence in German and American Public Education: The Persistence of Institutional Difference in a Globalizing World', in Douglas Mitchell, Robert Crowson and Dorothy Shipps (eds), *Shaping Education Policy – Power and Process*, London: Routledge, pp. 189–211.
Meyer, John W. (1970), 'The Charter: Conditions of Diffuse Socialization in Schools', in Richard W. Scott (ed.), *Social Processes and Social Structures: An Introduction to Sociology*, New York, USA and London, UK: Holt, Rinehart & Winston, pp. 564–578.
Meyer, John W. (2010), 'World Society, Institutional Theories, and the Actor', *Annual Review of Sociology*, **36**, 1–20.
Pechar, Hans and Angela Wroblewski (1998), *Non-traditional-Students in Österreich: Studienbedingungen bei Nebenerwerbstätigkeit, verspätetem Übertritt und alternativem Hochschulzugang*, Vienna: Institut für interdisziplinäre Forschung und Fortbildung.
Rammel, Stephanie and Jörg Markowitsch (2009), 'Formale Erwachsenenbildung in Österreich: Stellenwert und Reformpotential', in Lorenz Lassnigg, Helene Babel, Elke Gruber and Jörg Markowitsch (eds), *Öffnung von Arbeitsmärkten und Bildungssystemen: Beiträge zur Berufsbildungsforschung*, Innsbruck: StudienVerlag, pp. 394–411.
Rath, Otto (2007), 'Netzwerk Basisbildung und Alphabetisierung in Österreich: Hintergründe, Bestandsaufnahme, Perspektiven', *MAGAZIN erwachsenenbildung.at*, **1**. Available at: http://erwachsenenbildung.at/magazin/07-1/meb07-1_02_rath.pdf.
Republik Österreich (2011), *Strategie zum lebensbegleitenden Lernen in Österreich LLL: 2020*, Vienna. Available at: http://www.bmukk.gv.at/medienpool/20916/lllarbeitspapier_ebook_gross.pdf.
Ringler, Paul (2010), *Limits and Possibilities of quantitative Data on Participation in Formal Adult Education in Austria*, Austrian National Report of SP2 – LLL2010, Krems: Danube University Krems.
Rubinson, Richard and Irene Browne (1994), 'Education and the Economy', in Neil J. Smelser and Richard Swedberg (eds), *The Handbook of Economic Sociology*, Princeton, NJ: Princeton University Press, pp. 581–599.
Schlögl, Peter and Arthur Schneeberger (2003), *Adult Learning in Austria: Country Background Report of the OECD Thematic Review on Adult Learning*, Paris: OECD.
Schneeberger, Arthur and Alexander Petanovitsch (2004), *Continuing Vocational Education and Training*, Report of the Austrian ReferNet for CEDEFOP, Vienna: ABF-Austria.
Schneeberger, Arthur, Alexander Petanovitsch and Peter Schlögl (2008), *Entwicklung und Stand der Erwachsenenbildung in Österreich: Länderbericht für die UNESCO 6th International Conference on Adult Education (CONFINTEA VI)*, Materialien zur Erwachsenenbildung Nr. 1/2008, Vienna: Bundesministerium für Bildung, Wissenschaft und Kultur.
Scott, W. Richard (2008), *Institutions and Organizations: Ideas and Interests*, London: SAGE.
Statistik Austria (2004), *Lebenslanges Lernen – Ergebnisse des Mikrozensus 2003*, Vienna.
Statistik Austria (2010), *Bildung in Zahlen – Tabellenband*, Vienna.

Statistik Austria (2011), *Bildung in Zahlen*, Vienna.
Steiner, Mario, Elfriede Wagner and Gabriele Pessl (2006), *Evaluation der Kurse zur Vorbereitung auf den Hauptschulabschluss – Studie im Auftrag des Bundesministerium für Bildung, Wissenschaft und Kultur*, Materialien zur Erwachsenenbildung 1/2006, Vienna: Bundesministerium für Bildung, Wissenschaft und Kultur.
Streeck, Wolfgang and Kathleen Thelen (2005), 'Introduction: Institutional Change in Advanced Political Economies', in Wolfgang Streeck and Kathleen Thelen (eds), *Beyond Continuity: Institutional Change in Advanced Political Economies*, Oxford: Oxford University Press, pp. 1–39.
Trow, Martin (1973), *Problems in the Transition from Elite to Mass Higher Education*, Berkeley, CA: Carnegie Commission on Higher Education.
Trow, Martin (2006), 'Reflections on the Transition from Elite to Mass to Universal Access: Forms and Phases of Higher Education in Modern Societies since WWII', in James J.F. Forest and Philip G. Altbach (eds), *International Handbook of Higher Education*, Amsterdam: Kluwer, pp. 243–280.
Turner, Ralph H. (1960), 'Sponsored and Contest Mobility and the School System', *American Sociological Review*, **25**, 855–867.
UNESCO, OECD and EUROSTAT (2010), *UOE Data Collection on Education Systems: Volume 1, Manual Concepts, Definitions and Classifications*, Montreal, Canada; Paris, France and Luxembourg.
Unger, Martin, Sarah Zaussinger, Stefan Angel, Lukas Dünser, Angelika Grabher, Jakob Hartl, Gerhard Paulinger, Johanna Brandl, Petra Wejwar and Regina Gottwald (2010), *Studierenden-Sozialerhebung 2009, Studie im Auftrag des Bundesministeriums für Wissenschaft und Forschung*, Institut für Höhere Studien: Wien.
Wieser, Regine and Krisztina Dér (2011), 'Basisbildung in Österreich und ein weiter Blick über die Grenzen', in Peter Schlögl, Regine Wieser and Krisztina Dér (eds), *Kalypso und der Schlosser Basisbildung als Abenteuer im Land des Wissens und Könnens*, Austria: Forschung und Wissenschaft – Erziehungswissenschaft, 9, Vienna: LIT-Verlag, pp. 17–30.

10. Implementation of lifelong learning in Slovenia: institutional factors and equality of access of adults to formal and non-formal education

Angela Ivančič and Marko Radovan

INTRODUCTION

Rubenson (2006) points out that there are numerous factors of inequality in adult education. They extend from individual characteristics of learners to characteristics related to institutions and a particular cultural context. Similar to a great majority of other countries the available evidence for Slovenia indicates that inequalities characteristic of youth education are also reproduced in the education of adults. People with better educational achievements profit most from education later in their lives. In this chapter we argue that the institutional environment is an important factor in the development of participation patterns of adult education in Slovenia. We especially wish to highlight the degree of openness (or lack) of the national education system with respect to the inclusion of adults who are traditionally underrepresented in formal and non-formal education. We focus on adults with less than upper secondary education, and on older age groups (older than 49 years). Access of adults to formal education is considered in particular.

The chapter is primarily based on results of analyses performed in five sub-projects of the project Lifelong Learning 2010 (LLL2010). These are: a review of literature and policy documents (Mirčeva et al. 2007); analysis of participants and non-participants in formal learning based on data from the Eurostat-driven Adult Education Survey (AES) and the ad hoc module on lifelong learning within the European Labour Force Survey (LFS) (Ivančič and Radovan 2010); a survey of adult learners in formal education (ALiFE) (Mohorčič Špolar et al. 2008); case studies on formal learning practices in small and medium-sized enterprises (SMEs) (Mirčeva et al. 2008); and interviews with other stakeholders in adult education (Ivančič et al. 2009).

The chapter begins with a brief survey of adult participation in lifelong learning in Slovenia, and a review of how European lifelong education theorists have explained the role of institutions in participation. It then examines the main institutional features of the Slovenian educational system, and its relationship to the labour market as the main context within which opportunities for access to the education of adults are generated and maintained and also differentiated. Finally, the chapter explores the impact of national policy initiatives, and the impact of Slovenia's joining the European Union (EU) in 2004. We suggest that Slovenia has not yet been able to turn its legal opportunities and formal policy on the education of adults based on lifelong learning principles into concrete operational schemes, measures and mechanisms, which in reality would visibly target the groups defined as priority groups in national policy documents. While the better-educated segments of the population appear to recognize the importance of upgrading their educational attainment, and invest in their own education and training, this is not the case for those with low educational attainment.

Participation and Equity

Following the most recent available comparative data on participation in education of adults, with 41 per cent of adults of age 25–64, Slovenia belongs to the group of EU countries in the middle of the participation scale (Eurostat 2007). This evidence shows that a greater percentage (37.6 per cent) of Slovenian adults participate in non-formal education. The share of the adult population improving their educational attainment within formal programmes of education amounts to about 8.7 per cent. Mohorčič Špolar et al. (2008) point out that longitudinal statistical data for more recent years indicate a constant decline of numbers of adult participants in programmes of formal education leading to primary (International Standard Classification of Education – ISCED – 2) and secondary (ISCED 3) education. On the other hand the number of participants in higher education, university education and postgraduate studies has been constantly increasing over the last decade. The decline of participation in primary and secondary education cannot be explained just by the improved education structure of the adult population. The data show that there is still a considerable share of adults in older age groups without any post-primary education but who have completed secondary vocational training. Looking at the results of analyses of the data collected by two national surveys – the national survey, conducted in 2004 by the Slovenian

Institute for Adult Education, and the Adult Education Survey (AES) in 2007 by the National Statistical Office (SORS) it is not likely that any improvements have occurred in recent years. In 2004 the participation rate of the population of age 25–64 years in formal education amounted to 9.4 per cent and in 2007 to 8.7 per cent. The rate of participation of the same population in non-formal education amounted in 2004 to 43.1 per cent and in 2007 to 37.6 per cent. The differences in participation of adults in formal education are not statistically significant, while those calculated for non-formal education are statistically significant. However we are primarily interested in changes in opportunities of traditionally underrepresented groups of adults in education and training. Therefore we particularly investigate the chances of participation by less-educated adults and the oldest age group in formal and non-formal education.

While analysing effects of the attained level of education and age on the participation rate the results show that these individual characteristics remain the most significant predictors of the likelihood of participation in education after completion of initial education, and thus comply with those obtained in previous research (Mohorčič Špolar, Radovan and Ivančič 2011). The higher the attained level of education, the more likely a person is to participate in formal and non-formal education later in their life. On the other hand age categories 25–34 years and 35–49 years do not significantly differ in their likelihood of participation, whereas the chances of participation within the age category 50–64 years are significantly reduced (ibid.). The opportunities of all educational levels to participate in adult education decreased in 2007 with the chances of the middle-aged categories decreasing more strongly compared to the youngest age group. Participation by adults in formal education shows a slightly different picture. It appears that the chances of the secondary vocational education have significantly worsened compared to those of tertiary education. On the other hand the chances of all age categories decreased equally in 2007. Somewhat different evidence was found in relation to participation of adults in non-formal education: the chances of the intermediate education groups worsened more compared to the chances of the most educated adults. Also in this case it appears that no significant differences exist in the deterioration of participation chances of different age categories.

Looking at the comparative data, Slovenia is among the EU countries with the largest differences in shares of participants in education of adults from the lowest and the highest educational category (SORS 2010). The data on barriers to participation in the education of adults confirm that time and money are the most important barriers (Mohorčič Špolar et al. 2005; SORS 2010), which allows the assumption that low levels of education significantly affect access to education of adults who are in a weak economic position.

Institutions and Participation

Most recently researchers in Western Europe have been concentrating on analysing the significance of institutional factors for educational achievements and for broader social achievements of individuals (cf. Müller and Gangl 2003; Shavit and Müller 2000). The structure of a particular education system determines how individuals acquire education, how education is distributed across the population, and how credentials are valued in the labour market.

Schuetze and Slowey (2002, p. 318) argue that the following institutional and policy factors are likely to affect not just participation in initial education but also participation, of non-traditional students, in higher education:

1. Institutional differentiation in the adult education system: for example horizontal and vertical differentiation, articulation and transfer routes, student choice and information, no dead-end routes, equivalence of general and vocational routes, coordination between different sectors and programmes.
2. Institutional governance: for example institutional autonomy and flexibility.
3. Access: for example specific policy and outreach strategy for lifelong learners, open or flexible access, recognition of work and life experience, special entry routes, involvement in regional development and service for the community.
4. Mode of study: for example modular courses and credit transfer, part-time mode, distance learning, independent study.
5. Financial and other support.
6. Adult education opportunities: for example provision of relevant courses, appropriate scheduling, affordable fee levels.

More comprehensive approaches view the institutional environment as multidimensional and highly interactive (cf. Blossfeld 2003; Hall and Soskice 2001). They consider the education system as part of a country-specific institutional package. Accordingly, educational opportunities are formed involving different institutions and actors.

Recent explanations of participation in non-formal education take into account the rather complex character of the link between the education system and participation in non-formal education. Among the theoretical frameworks that inform such explanations are those of labour market segmentation and internal labour markets (Maurice et al. 1986), and welfare production regimes, as well as social, economic and supportive political institutions (Estevez-Abe et al. 2001).

Some authors argue that to implement the philosophy of lifelong learning it is necessary to adjust the education systems to the needs of people of all ages and to characteristics of different life periods. Lifelong learning does not require more of what is already available in individual education sectors but a type of systemic change that enables the development and articulation of the vision of lifelong learning (Papadopoulos 2000).

Following these theoretical considerations we now turn to the main characteristics of the Slovenian education system (and its interrelation with the employment system) which might explain the persistence of inequalities related to age in the formal education of adults, and the role of education and age inequalities in participation in non-formal education.

THE SLOVENIAN EDUCATION SYSTEM AND ADULT EDUCATION

Before the independence of Slovenia a unified education system of young and adults – so-called 'career-directed education', was in force (within the Yugoslav Federation) involving a traditional concept of formal education carried out in traditional educational settings (Act on Career-Directed Education 1980). After independence (in the early 1990s) the educational system experienced important changes as well. National education reform enacted in 1996 again established education of adults as an independent education subsystem, which complemented the education of young people. The lifelong learning concept was introduced in Slovenia following the Rome conference organized by the European Lifelong Learning Initiative (1994).

More thorough analysis of the national strategic and political documents suggests that similar to many other European countries the term 'lifelong learning' is used as a synonym for adult education, particularly the part covering non-formal and informal learning. No serious changes have been made so far to create conditions for the implementation of the concept and philosophy of lifelong learning (Holford et al. 2007). A national strategy on lifelong learning (MoES 2007), which delineates a more comprehensive concept of lifelong learning in Slovenia, has not been followed by an adequate national implementation action plan.

Currently the national education system encompasses initial and continuing and further education and training programmes that provide nationally recognized level of formal education as defined by the school laws, and publicly recognized certificates of non-formal education. Despite this, education of adults is not treated equally to education of children or the young and is often taken as an appendage of the national education system. At the level of formal education there are distinctions made between regular and irregular education. Irregular education is intended for adult learners while regular education can be taken as a synonym for youth education (Vocational Education and Training Act 2006; Higher Education Act 2004), which contradicts the lifelong learning concept and strategy promoting transitions between education and work throughout the lifetime of an individual (Memorandum on Lifelong Learning 2000).

Commonalities of Formal Education of Youth and Adults

While primary education in Slovenia is comprehensive and lasts nine years (until the age of 15), secondary education is clearly differentiated on vocational and general tracks. The vocational track is primarily directed towards the labour market while the general track enables access to the most advanced levels of education at tertiary level. It should be stressed that in Slovenia the level of educational attainment is the most important indicator of of an individual's social status. By being selected for the vocational track an individual is automatically directed towards positions in the labour market, which are linked with lower social status. Therefore strong competition exists for places in secondary general schools (gymnasia), while the interest for vocational education training (VET) is in constant decline. About 40 per cent of the generation gets enrolled in general secondary education.

The basic entry requirement to all initial secondary education programmes is the certificate of successfully completed primary education. However for young people intending to enrol in upper secondary education their achievements in primary education are extremely important. The best performers go to general schools; second-best performers go to the vocational track that enables double exit – to employment and to certain tertiary studies; while the rest can enrol in the vocational track leading to employment.

Contrary to the regular education it is not usual that meritocratic criteria would apply so strictly at sorting people into programmes of formal education of adults. This also enables weaker performers at matriculation examinations to get enrolled (as mature students). As already mentioned, the number of adult students in tertiary programmes is constantly increasing. While speaking of irregular students at the tertiary level one has to point to the fact that the majority of irregular students are young people who cannot enrol as regular students because they did not attain the required scores in the matriculation examination or do not fulfil additional requirements. However, adults without proper educational credentials are not allowed to enrol. Within the Slovenian education system it is not foreseen that work experience or validation and recognition of non-formal education and learning may count towards fulfilling entry requirements. The formal education system strongly opposes the idea of also enabling access to adults without the required certificates who may produce evidence that they can be successful in the programme. This may be an important obstacle to adults who, for different reasons, were not able to continue their education to enrol in tertiary education as they needed first to obtain the missing credentials. These are usually people with a weaker socio-economic background who are neither financially able nor motivated to pass the required previous stage of formal education. Certificates and diplomas obtained in formal regular and irregular education programmes are nationally recognized.

Differentiation of the education system between vocational and general tracks is supposed to provide opportunities for all to choose education according to their abilities and interests and develop their potential. However it is more likely that, in the first place, it corresponds with the hierarchy in which work is organized in the labour market. The fact that curricula in 2–3-year VET do not stress the development of general and key skills and competences that enable lifelong learning, coupled with adverse selection, finally results in low motivation and abilities of this educational category of adults to return to education and learning after completing their initial education. The results of the international adult literacy survey conducted in 1998 showed rather low levels of literacy achievements of the population with completed secondary vocational training (Mohorčič Špolar et al. 2001).

Adjustment of Formal Education to the Needs and Possibilities of Adults

A unified system of formal education for young people and adults (*White Paper* 1996) may be an advantage since it enables equivalency of certificates obtained in regular and irregular education and thus their equal treatment in the education system and the labour market. However this may also be an obstacle to the enrolment of adults since the programmes leading to individual levels of education are of long duration and quite rigid in their method of execution. At the same time all available data from national surveys show that time and money are the most important barriers preventing adults enrolling in education (e.g. Mohorčič Špolar et al. 2008). The Slovenian education system has tried to capture this through legally defined possibilities of using different paths to obtain standards of knowledge and skills defining individual levels of formal qualifications (*White Paper* 1996; Primary Education Act 1996; Vocational Education and Training Act 1996, 2006; Gymnasium Act 1996).

Adjustment of Curricula to the Needs of Adults

At the level of secondary education irregular students may enrol either in educational programmes specially prepared for adults or in educational programmes for youth which are adjusted to the needs and peculiarities of adults. The adjustment concerns the duration of education and training, organizational forms of delivering curricula, recognition of prior education and learning, teaching and learning methods and techniques, and learning material. In practice adjustments most often include the duration of individual programmes, the method of organization and timing of delivery. Unfortunately, these most often depend on the financial possibilities of providers and do not comply with real needs of adult learners. To be more specific, the number of hours of organized work with adult learners is reduced to the legally allowed minimum irrespective of individual characteristics of the participants. The modular approach has not yet gained ground in Slovenia and the entire programme has to be finished to obtain a recognized formal qualification. Modularization seems to be more common in higher education. Though providers of adult education are quite slow in adopting modularization, they are offering a variety of other possibilities, for example e-learning, online study, autonomous learning, seminar work and so on.

The Slovenian formal education system is quite rigid in terms of shifts from vocational secondary education to general and technical secondary education, as well as between programmes in different education fields within the same track. It largely rests with individual schools to decide how permeable are the training programmes that they carry out. According to some case studies not knowledge and skills attained but similarity or dissimilarity in structure of the programme is observed, mostly in terms of similarity of subject content and the hours assigned to an individual subject (Drofenik et al. 2001; Klemenčič et al. 2006). This was also confirmed by some interviews with participants in secondary technical education (Mirčeva et al. 2008).

Recognition of Prior Learning

Recognition of prior learning in formal education is the most important base for the adjustment of execution of a particular curriculum to individual needs and possibilities of adults. The Slovenian formal education system has only most recently begun to open up to accommodate this issue. Previous legislation limited recognition of prior learning to that which was proved by adequate evidence (see Ivančič and Svetina 2008). Recognition of non-formal and informal learning not proved by publicly validated evidence was legalized by laws passed after 2004 (Vocational Education and Training Act 2006; Higher Education Act 2004). However the legal basis is the first step only. Findings based on interviews carried out with representatives of providers of the education of adults and policy-makers (Ivančič et al. 2009, pp. 106–107) show that regardless of the level or mode of education (formal, non-formal) it still holds true that the recognition is first and foremost based on hard data – something that can be 'shown on paper', and is verified by institution, for example other faculties, schools or other education institutions.

The responsibility for validation and recognition is decentralized to schools while national educational authorities provide some general guidelines. However schools and teachers are not ready to assume this responsibility. They expect national educational authorities to provide them with procedures and methodologies standardized at the national level. Drawing on the interviews referred to above, it seems that the main obstacle to recognize prior non-formal learning is transparency and standardization of acquired knowledge and skills as well as mutual trust between the main actors (ibid.).

Traditional higher education institutions seem to be the least in favour of the idea to recognize any knowledge and skills obtained outside the higher education space. More positive attitudes are evident in other higher non-university institutions, especially private ones established to carry out programmes for adults. They also raise the question of the availability of adequate assessment tools.

Surprisingly, findings from the survey on adult learning do not confirm that exemption from tuition based on assessment and recognition of prior learning would increase learners' satisfaction; rather the contrary (Mohorčič Špolar et al. 2008).

Tuition Fee

At the beginning of this chapter it was pointed out that cost of education is the second most often cited barrier by the Slovene participants in education of adults. This is also among the most important reasons for early school leaving of young people revealed by a survey on formal adult learning (Mohorčič Špolar et al. 2008), though there is no fee for regular education and diverse forms of grants supporting regular pupils and students are available. In the case of formal education of adults only primary education is free of charge for participants. Participation in secondary and tertiary education must be paid for by adult students. For the time being there is no unified approach to financial support provided to adults enrolled in formal education. Those below 27 years of age who are not employed or registered as unemployed have legally guaranteed access to the benefits connected to regular study (health insurance, student work, subsidized transportation and scholarship) (Adult Education Act 2006, art. 4). At the same time no accessible loans or special state or social partners' schemes or funds are available on a systemic basis to those who are older than 27 years. The state carries the costs when adults are entitled to subsidized participation in education within individual state-sponsored schemes and programmes. Ivančič et al. (2009) point out that in practice participants have to pay the fee themselves and get the money reimbursed after successfully completing their education, which excludes access by persons with a weak socio-economic background who are not able to pay for their study. We can conclude from the survey results that organizations providing formal education for adults try to motivate students to enrol and stay in the process by enabling them to pay tuition fees in instalments, or by postponing individual instalments and the like. However such measures are decided individually and are not specially directed to particular more disadvantaged groups. They also do not dispose of special funds to support enrolments of members of those groups. When it comes to publicly financed education the education authorities limit the fees (ibid.).

Providers of Formal Education of Adults

No particular network of providers of formal education of adults exists in Slovenia. Legally, formal education may be delivered by schools, colleges and adult education organizations that fulfil legally defined criteria for carrying out a particular programme. As demonstrated by the data collected in the survey on adult learning in formal education (Mohorčič Špolar et al. 2008), the largest share of secondary formal education of adults is provided by schools for young people and school centres. Slovenia has a strong network of people's universities; however, as the only public organizations for the education of adults, they are rather exceptional providers of formal adult education. Usually peoples' universities provide primary education for adults while at post-primary levels they most often cooperate with vocational schools and colleges and higher education institutions.

Some upper secondary schools have special units for the education of adults. These employ adequately trained staff (andragogues, organizers of adult education, counsellors in education of adults); others carry out courses for adults as an additional function with staff already engaged in the education of youth. Teaching staff often develop teaching competences in regular education.

A great number of private schools and colleges have emerged over the last two decades providing educational programmes for adults especially at the tertiary level. These schools and colleges are self-financing but some of them, for example vocational colleges, also carry out publicly financed programmes. Some provide programmes exclusively for adults at the whole educational vertical. They try to attract as many students as possible by also organizing and delivering programmes (as extensions) outside their premises in several major centres in Slovenia.

It is often argued that schools providing formal education for adults as an additional activity to the regular education, using staff who carry out the education process as additional (separately paid) work, do not have the competences needed to take into consideration the needs and particularities of adults. It is further argued that these schools do not invest in motivating adults to enrol in education and be successful in the process. Results show that the institutional influence on adult learners' general satisfaction seems to be great (Mohorčič Špolar et al. 2008). However it is not the type of institution itself but mainly the quality of teachers and, to a certain extent, other institutional support provided for adult learners that affect the satisfaction. According to the data, from 88.9 per cent (ISCED 4) to 98.1 per cent (ISCED 1–2) of providers of adult education pay in-service training of their teaching staff. Almost two-thirds of institutions conduct individual performance reviews of teachers either once a year (35 per cent) or more than once a year (30.9 per cent). More than half of them have an external quality control every five or more years.

The majority of students irrespective of the ISCED levels of their programmes perceive high levels of teacher support. This is maybe most obvious for attendees of programmes at ISCED levels 1 and 2 which are provided by people's universities. Learners who perceive a lack of teacher effort to help students succeed also have difficulties competing with younger students, experience lack of preparation for the study programme, have no time for studying, and think that studies are scheduled at an inconvenient time. Students with the same problems also feel that teachers do not respect them (Mohorčič Špolar et al. 2008, pp. 56–59). The data also show that a majority of providers of formal adult education provide some additional services to adult students, such as Internet access, libraries, information and counselling, and (in a more limited way) also social services.

There seems to be an important difference among various types of institutions delivering education to adults with regard to facilitating access of underrepresented groups of adults. Findings propose that providers of formal education pay a lot of attention to outreach strategies and LLL policies (ibid.). Of all interviewed providers, 44 per cent organize preparatory courses, 70 per cent organize refresher courses and 56 per cent organize workshops for special skills development. However, given individual data, only a small percentage of adult learners attended preparatory courses and, most surprisingly, of those enrolled in primary school programmes no one participated. Among the respondents 86 per cent of providers of formal adult education answer that they try to access vulnerable groups of adults. The providers try to access these vulnerable groups by contacting other institutions in local communities – mainly social services and employment services, but also other education institutions (ibid.). An additional analysis of institutional data indicates that secondary schools invest the least in outreach measures and programmes aiming to attract traditionally underrepresented groups while on the other hand peoples' universities seem to be most active developing measures for the recruitment of these groups. This may be connected to the highest satisfaction of participants in ISCED 1–2 programmes with the process and outcomes (Mohorčič Špolar et al. 2008). Tertiary education institutions, public as well as private, currently do not pay special attention to measures increasing enrolment of marginalized groups (Ivančič and Radovan 2010).

Links between the Education System and the Labour Market

It has to be accentuated that strong ties exist in Slovenia between the education system and the labour market. This was the case during the socialist era and has been even more strongly emphasized after transition to the market economy. Employers play an important part, directly or indirectly, in the design of education programmes and their outcomes as well as their execution (vocational training). Skilled occupational positions in the labour market are based on formal qualifications produced in the education system. We could speak of the operation of so-called qualification spaces or occupational markets (cf. Maurice et al. 1986; Marsden 1990). Particular level and type of educational qualification is directed to a corresponding occupational or qualification segment in the labour market. Shifts between individual qualification or occupation segments are possible only by having the required level and type of formal qualification attested by respective educational credentials. This holds equally true for new entrants to the labour market, recruitment from the external labour market, and internal shifts of employees. Moreover, the development of an individual occupational career is as a rule linked to an upgrading of individual educational attainment. Occupational labour market segmentation is especially evident in relation to secondary and post-secondary VET since these curricula are based on occupational standards prepared by the economy. Since recognition of non-formal learning has not yet taken place in the Slovenian education system, only one path is available to acquire the required level of formal education: to enrol in programmes of formal education delivered by respective educational institutions.

Educational expansion, which has extended from the secondary to the tertiary education sector, has decreased but also blurred the value of individual levels of education in recruitment processes. More than 90 per cent of the Slovenian population aged 18–24 years has finished upper secondary education (CEC 2009) and about 60 per cent of that age group is enrolled in tertiary education (Ministry of Higher Education, Science and Technology – MVŠZT 2008). Graduates from vocational colleges and secondary technical and vocational-technical education compete for the same occupational positions in the labour market. Upgrading one's formal education has thus become a 'defensive necessity' (Thurow 1975). Not just generations in initial education but also the employed and unemployed try to obtain ever higher levels of education or upgrade their educational attainment to keep up with younger generations coming from the education process. Given the great disproportions of enrolment in individual education fields ever greater qualification mismatches exist in the labour market (cf. Ivančič 2008). This represents one more factor pressuring the employed and unemployed to invest in additional qualifications either by upgrading the attained level of education or by broadening it with another qualification at the same level. However, as shown by quantitative data, such trends are above all characteristic of younger generations who managed to pass the matriculation examination. On the other hand those finishing two- and three-year VET more or less successfully struggle to fulfil criteria to access vocational maturity examinations. According to statistical data a great majority of young people finishing three-year VET continue in two-year vocational-technical programmes in order to attain the criteria to enrol in tertiary studies or at least improve their occupational position.

At the same time one may still observe rather high levels of legal employment protection compared to other transition countries (cf. Ivančič 2008). Permanent employment is still the main type of employment. This may additionally explain the low motivation of the employed with lower educational attainment for investment in upgrading their formal qualifications. On the other hand the available data confirm that employers also generally prefer to invest in job-specific skills, via supporting non-formal training, as they are not keen on investing in education of the least-educated workforce because there is a large availability of affordable and flexible well-educated labour (Radovan 2009).

National labour legislation stipulates the right and duty of the employed to participate in education and training required by the employer, but also for their career development. Types and extent of employers' support are specified in collective agreements. These agreements involve paid and unpaid days off to prepare and sit for exams as well as cases when employers bear the training expenses. However, at the end of the day employers choose the kind of education and training they support. The increasing deregulation of employment, enabled by the renewed Employment Relationship Act (2006), seems to have additionally decreased employers' willingness to invest in workers' education and shifted the responsibility for education and training to employees themselves. Consequently education and training opportunities for low-educated workers has further decreased. This is reflected by the fact that the right to training is increasingly losing its legal basis in collective agreements and is left to individual training contracts. A representative of one of the SMEs interviewed stated that: 'acquiring formal education is an individual matter that should be finished before the employment. If someone decides to study after he has been employed in order to realize individual needs and projects, it should be done in his/her spare time' (Mirčeva et al. 2008).

Reduction of employers' support to employees' education and training is evident also from the results of an analysis where data from the national Adult Education Survey conducted in 2007 (Eurostat 2007) were compared to data from the national survey conducted in 2004 (Mohorčič Špolar et al. 2005). Significant decreases of participation by all educational categories and all age categories of the employed in formal as well as non-formal education of adults were calculated (see Mohorcic Špolar et al. 2011). Interestingly enough while comparing effects of decreasing individual levels of education, the employees with two- and three-year vocational training proved to be the most disadvataged compared to those with higher and university education. Such trends clearly suggest that the state will also have to take the responsibility for the improvement of educational attainment of the employed with completed VET not leading to the matriculation examination.

NATIONAL POLICIES AND INEQUALITIES IN PARTICIPATION IN FORMAL EDUCATION OF ADULTS

McGivney (2001) underlines that patterns of participation in education of adults can be changed only with the support of a large array of political strategies at all levels, but only if they are also supported with ample financial resources. Referring to the Slovenian situation one may argue that, despite the acceptance of lifelong learning principles in national political and strategic documents, there are still rather persistent traditional perceptions that formal education is a preparation for working life occurring during childhood and youth within traditional educational settings. Lifelong learning is mostly understood as non-formal and informal education and training, taking place after the highest attained level of initial (regular) education, which is mainly intended for maintaining productivity and employability. Accordingly, employers, individuals and state agencies should share responsibility for it. Formal education of adults, on the other hand, is as a rule related to qualification needs of employers and individual career promotion with employers and individuals as main beneficiaries. Wider societal benefits are rarely taken into account. Considering this, individuals themselves and/or employers are expected to take financial and other responsibility for it (cf. Becker 1964 [1975]).

The attitude of the state towards investment in formal education of adults started to change with the transition to the market economy. Economic restructuring during the transition from the socialist to the market economy was accompanied by rapidly increasing unemployment, which proved to be structural in nature, encouraged the introduction of active labour market policy (ALMP). Expenditure on ALMP amounts to about 0.34 per cent of Slovenian gross domestic product (GDP) (Kajzer 2005). Education and training of the unemployed, and the employed threatened by unemployment, has become an important ALMP measure mainly in the form of short-term job-related training. However it became evident that in the long run low-educated unemployed and employed members of the population had to upgrade their level of attained education in order to maintain their employability and to be able to adjust to changes in the labour market and job structure. In 1997 the government introduced a special programme supporting formal education of the unemployed, which has turned into a permanent measure that has been, since 2004, financially supported by the European Social Fund. The priority is given to young unemployed adults and drop-outs from initial education. Only recently have some measures been introduced to subsidize formal education of the employed.

In 2004 Slovenia became a fully fledged member of the EU. Part of the accession process involved modernization of the education system in line with EU policy and strategies. National strategic and political documents defining national goals and priorities of economic and social development foresaw the development of lifelong learning as an important measure, supporting their realization. Education of adults as an important part of lifelong learning was the focus of a great deal of those activities. The key document in this respect, the Resolution on the National Programme of Adult Education until 2010 (NPAE), was adopted by the Parliament in 2004. This document has, for the first time, defined goals and priorities in the field of adult education and created foundations for greater equity and equality in access to education opportunities. An improvement in formal education of the population has been among priority goals resulting in a considerable increase in participation in non-formal general and vocational education. The NPAE states that four-year secondary education should become the national education standard. The three priority fields defined by the NPAE until 2010 – increasing participation in general education and learning of adults; raising the level of individual educational attainment; and increasing participation in education and training for the labour market – are defined so as to promise considerably improved access to groups of adults underrepresented in education and training in terms of greater equity and equality.

After Slovenia gained access to the European Social Fund, in 2004, a considerable amount of funding has supplemented national financial means earmarked for the education of adults. In order to make use of the European Social Fund the area of lifelong learning in the adopted Single Programming Document was set up as a priority with the following specific aims (SVRL 2007):

1. to improve knowledge and capacity of teachers and others involved in adult education;
2. to achieve greater flexibility of adult education and learning provision in accordance with the needs of the economy sector and labour market;
3. to ensure quality information, counselling and access to all through local and regional information centres and contact points of lifelong learning;
4. to stimulate the system of quality assurance by adopting the model of self-evaluation;
5. to decrease the educational gap of adults having only basic or lower vocational education, a low level of literacy and a low level of digital literacy;
6. to increase participation in learning of persons who have not completed their schooling or who have left school early.

Judging from the available data on developments in the system of the education of adults it may be argued that in the preparation period of Slovenia to become an EU member, EU policies in the field of lifelong learning and employment as well as good practices from some European countries contributed importantly to the development of a coherent system and new systemic solutions which should facilitate participation in formal and non-formal education of all adults. The most important achievement was the formulation of the adult education policy based on the lifelong learning concept that was defined in the above-mentioned NPAE adopted by the Parliament at the same time as Slovenia became an EU member. In the accession phase some innovative approaches were also developed and implemented, such as programmes for improving adult literacy skills, project learning for young adults, study circles, and centres for informing and counselling in adult education. Slovenia was among the first countries introducing Lifelong Learning Week in 1996 and even disseminated this event in some other EU countries. The work on the development of a system for assessment and recognition of qualifications based on all education and learning, regardless of the learning setting, also started in that period and gained its legal basis in the Act on National Occupational Qualifications passed in August 2000. However it appears that the concept of lifelong learning gained stronger ground in the Ministry of Labour and Social Affairs compared to respective education ministries, which may be explained by the great need for the improvement of education and skills of the labour force to successfully combat unemployment and the risk of social exclusion.

The period after becoming a member of the EU has been a period of designing concepts and policies and legal documents. To a lesser degree it has also been the period of their implementation. Slovenia has actively participated in all EU processes and activities concerning education and lifelong learning, but the guidelines have been mainly followed on the declarative level. The Slovenian Lifelong Learning Strategy was prepared in 2007 but it was not adopted by the government or Parliament and has remained a paper of the Ministry of Education and Sport. To date no efforts have been made for the systemic implementation of the Strategy, as similar to some other EU countries, Slovenia also applies a neoliberal approach to lifelong learning. The state takes great care of formal education of children and youth, with special emphasis on increased investments in higher education, while education of adults is more or less left to the market. As revealed in the analysis of interviews, authorized representatives of respective ministries specially underline the market nature of adult education (Ivančič et al. 2009). No stable and consistent operational programmes and measures exist to facilitate greater participation of underrepresented groups at the macro as well as the meso level. National policy defined in the NPAE was not followed up by adequate programmes and strategies for its implementation. Public finances earmarked for the implementation have been insufficient and the allocation instruments have not been properly used. Current debates mostly concern the availability of public finances and their allocation to providers of adult education. Public and private providers bid on an equal footing for publicly financed courses. Private provision of adult education heavily outnumbers public provision, which may increase inequality even further in access to education of adults. There is great imbalance in provision of training programmes directed towards occupational and labour market needs and general personal and community development-oriented programmes in favour of the first group. Issues such as intergenerational learning, migrant education and intercultural learning have not yet been properly tackled. There is no effective coordination among ministries and local authorities and non-governmental organizations (NGOs) are not involved in developing and implementing lifelong learning policies. Consequently there is no efficient and equitable use of available resources directed to this area.

CONCLUSIONS

Slovenia belongs to the group of the EU countries situated in the middle of the scale of participation in the education of adults (Eurostat 2007). Following the available empirical evidence a conclusion can be drawn that in general all inequalities in participation of adults in education stemming from low educational attainment still existed in 2007. It is characteristic that in 2007 training opportunities worsened equally for all adults regardless of their educational attainment. However there are differences when referring participation in formal and non-formal education. Age remains the main factor affecting access to formal education. At the same time unequal access to non-formal education is strongly connected with individual educational attainment while differences among age groups are less pronounced. Despite the significance of formal education in the Slovenian labour market and society in general the share of adult participants in formal education also shows a slight decline in 2007. According to the official data the number of adults in secondary education has been decreasing while the number of participants in tertiary education has been increasing constantly (Mohorčič Špolar et al. 2008). This confirms that adults who have already crossed the threshold between low and better educational attainment tend to improve their educational level, but adults who belong to deprived educational groups do not. It might be argued that formal education of adults in Slovenia is less likely to narrow the education gap by increasing the educational attainment of the least-educated population; it primarily contributes to the improvement of human capital to support individual career development and respond to changes in the occupational structure in the labour market.

Slovenia has adopted in its formal and strategic documents the concept of lifelong learning as defined by the EU structures but it has more or less remained at the declarative level. Similar to many other EU countries, in Slovenia lifelong learning is also understood narrowly as education of adults – predominantly the non-formal part. Typically education of adults is not treated as complementary to youth education with its own requirements. Results of the analysed data allow the conclusion that structures and institutions of the education system which are defined by Schuetze and Slowey (2002) as those affecting participation in adult education have not experienced changes which would ease access of adults to formal education. This lack of change is particularly true when speaking of access of the educationally most deprived groups. This involves adequate educational provisions (programmes, providers, links between formal and non-formal education, investment in adequately trained teaching staff) as well as the enrolment requirements to enter formal programmes. Moreover, there are no stable financial mechanisms in place which would enable access of adults with a weak socio-economic background. Slovenia has also undergone financial cuts for public services in common with other European countries. Consequently adult education has been experiencing big funding cuts while at the same time there is no political will to reconsider the current allocation of national funds earmarked for education from the point of view of the needs of individual life cycles. Following EU guidelines, higher education is defined as the great priority.

Taking all this into consideration it might be argued that not coherent national goals and strategies followed by adequate institutional changes in the education system, which would ease the access of underrepresented groups to formal education, but the developments in the education, training (expansion of private colleges and schools in tertiary education and private adult education providers) and labour markets mainly determine the developments in adult education participation in Slovenia.

In addition to the lack of appropriate systemic solutions to facilitate lifelong learning, there is also no political will to adequately implement the existing ones. In line with the neoliberal discourse prevalent in Europe the responsibility of education and learning is increasingly shifted to individuals, which is expected to additionally increase inequality in access. Better-educated populations recognize the importance of upgrading their educational attainment by investing in education and training on their own and simultaneously exploiting available state mechanisms supporting access. On the other hand, vulnerable groups, which are also educationally deprived, do not have the resources (financial and other) needed to take their learning into their own hands.

REFERENCES

Adult Education Act (2006) (amended), *Official Gazette of the Republic of Slovenia*, No. 69/2006.

Becker, Gary S. (1964 [1975]), *Human Capital*, New York: Columbia University Press.

Blossfeld, Hans-Peter (2003), 'Globalization, Social Inequality and the Role of Country-Specific Institutions: Open Research Questions in a Learning Society', in Pedro Conceicao, Manuel V. Heitor and Bengt-Ake Lundvall (eds), *Innovation, Competence Building and Social Cohesion in Europe*: *Towards a Learning Society*, Cheltenham, UK: Edward Elgar Publishing, pp. 303–324.

CEC (2009), *Progress towards the Lisbon Objectives in Education and Training. Indicators and Benchmarks – 2009*, Luxemburg: Publications Office of the European Union.

Drofenik, Olga, Vera Mlinar, Sonja Klemenčič, Livija Knaflič, Jasmina Mirčeva, Ester Možina, Tanja Možina, Zvonka Pangerc Pahernik, Marko Radovan, Metka Svetina, Tanja Vilič Klenovšek, Darka Kosec (2001), *Evalvacija srednješolskega formalnega izobraževanja brezposelnih – program 5000* (Evaluation of Secondary Formal Education of the Unemployed – Programme 5000), research report, Ljubljana: Slovenian Institute for Adult Education.

Employment Relationship Act (2006), *Official Gazette of the Republic Slovenia*, No. 79/06, issued 27 July.

Estevez-Abe, Margarita, Torben Iversen and David Soskice (2001), 'Social Protection and the Formation of Skills: A Reinterpretation of the Welfare State', in Peter A. Hall and David Soskice (eds), *Varieties of Capitalism: The Institutional Foundations of Comparative Advantage*, Oxford: Oxford University Press, pp. 145–183.

Eurostat (2007), *Adult Education Survey*.

Gymnasium Act (1996, 2007), *Official Gazette of the Republic of Slovenia*, No. 12/1996 & No. 1/2007.

Hall, Peter A. and David Soskice (eds) (2001), *Varieties of Capitalism: The Institutional Foundations of Comparative Advantage*, Oxford: Oxford University Press.

Higher Education Act (1993, 2004), *Official Gazette of the Republic of Slovenia*, No. 67/1993 & No.1000/2004.

Holford, John, Sheila Riddell, Elisabet Weedon, Judith Litjens and Guy Hannan (2007), *Patterns of Lifelong Learning, Policy and Practice in an Expanding Europe*, Studies in Lifelong Learning 2, Vienna, Austria and Berlin, Germany: Lit Verlag GmbH & Co. KG.

Ivančič, Angela (2008), 'Slovenia', in Irene Kogan, Michael Gebel and Clemens Noelke (eds), *Europe Enlarged: A Handbook of Education, Labor and Welfare Regimes in Central and Eastern Europe*, Bristol: Policy Press, pp. 353–369.

Ivančič, Angela and Marko Radovan (2010), *Inequality of Access of Underrepresented Groups in Formal and Non-Formal Education in Slovenia: The*

Role of National Adult Education Policy (SP2 National Report), Ljubljana: Slovenian Institute for Adult Education.
Ivančič, Angela, Vida A. Mohorčič Špolar and Marko Radovan (2009), *Opportunities of Vulnerable Target Groups in Formal and Non-Formal Education in Slovenia: National and Institutional Strategies and Polities (National Report on SP5), Lifelong Learning 2010*, Ljubljana: Slovenian Institute for Adult Education.
Kajzer, Alenka (2005), 'Spremembe na trgu dela v Sloveniji v obdobju 1995–2005' (Changes in the Slovenian Labour Market in the Period 1995–2005'), Working Paper No. 5/2006, Ljubljana: Institute for Macroeconomic Analyses and Development.
Klemenčič, Sonja, Tanja Možina, Metka Svetina, Vera Mlinar, Tanja Vilič Klenovšek, Marija Velikonja and Maja Zupančič (2006), *Oblikovanje izvedbenega kurikula v poklicnem in strokovnem izobraževanju odraslih* (Formation of executive curriculum in vocational and technical education), Ljubljana: ACS, RIC.
Marsden, David W. (1990), 'Institutions and Labour Mobility: Occupational and Internal Labour Markets in Britain, France, Italy and West Germany', in R. Brunetta and C. Dell'Aringa (eds), *Labour Relations and Economic Performance*, Houndmills: Macmillan, pp. 414–438.
Maurice, Mark, François Sellier and Jean-Jacques Silvestre (1986), *The Social Foundation of Industrial Power*, London: MIT Press.
McGivney, Veronica K. (2001), *Fixing or Changing the Pattern? Reflections on Widening Adult Participation in Learning*, Leicester: NIACE.
Mirčeva, Jasmina, Angela Ivančič and Vida A. Mohorčič Špolar (2008), *A Review on the Participation of Employees of SME in Formal Education – The Case of Slovenia. SP 4 – National Report, Lifelong Learning 2010*, Ljubljana: Slovenian Institute for Adult Education.
Mirčeva, Jasmina, Vida A. Mohorčič Špolar and Peter Beltram (2007), *LLL2010: Sub-project 1 (National Report)*, Ljubljana: Slovenian Institute for Adult Education.
Mohorčič Špolar, Vida A., Angela Ivančič, Jasmina Mirčeva, Ester Možina, Marko Radovan, Tanja Vilič Klenovšek, Zvonka Pangerc Pahernik, et al. (2001), *Udeležba prebivalcev Slovenije v izobraževanju odraslih*, Ljubljana: Andragoški Center Republike Slovenije.
Mohorčič Špolar, Vida A., Jasmina Mirčeva, Marko Radovan, Ester Možina and Angela Ivančič (2005), *Pismenost in ključne življenjske veščine v družbi znanja: družbeno skupinski vplivi udeležbe odraslih v izobraževanju kot dejavnik razvoja družbe znanja, zaključno poročilo* (Literacy and Key Life Skills in the Knowledge Society: Socio-Group Effects on Participation in Education), Research Report, Ljubljana: Slovenian Institute for Adult Education. Available at http://porocila.acs.si/datoteke/naslovnica.pdf (accessed 20 December 2010).
Mohorčič Špolar, Vida A., Marko Radovan and Angela Ivančič (2008), *Adults in Formal Education. Slovenia. National Report on SP 3 – Lifelong Learning 2010*, Ljubljana: Slovenian Institute for Adult Education.
Mohorčič Špolar, Vida A., Marko Radovan and Angela Ivančič (2011), *Vseživljenjsko učenje – tek čez ovire?: mednarodni vidiki politike vseživljenjskega učenja in udeležbe v izobraževanju odraslih*, Ljubljana: Slovenian Institute for Adult Education.
MoES (2007), *The Slovenian Lifelong Learning Strategy*, Ljubljana: Ministry of

Education and Sport. Available at http://www.mss.gov.si/fileadmin/mss.gov.si/pageuploads/podrocje/razvoj_solstva/IU2010/Strategija_VZU.pdf (accessed 1 July 2011).
Müller, Walter and Marcus Gangl (2003), 'The Transition from School to Work: A European Perspective', in W. Müller and M. Gangl (eds), *Transition from Education to Work in Europe: The Integration of Youth into EU Labour Markets*, Oxford: Oxford University Press, pp. 1–22.
MVŠZT (2007), *Resolucija o nacionalnem programu visokega šolstva 2006–2010* (Resolution on the National Programme of Higher Education 2006–2010). Available at: http://www.mvzt.gov.si/fileadmin/mvzt.gov.si/pageuploads/pdf/visoko_solstvo/RNPVS.pdf (assessed 30 March 2011).
National Occupational Qualifications Act (2000), *Official Gazette of the Republic of Slovenia* No. 81/2000.
Papadopoulos, Georgiou (2000), 'Lifelong Learning and the Changing Policy Environment', in David Istance, Hans G. Schuetze and Tom Schuller (eds), *International Perspectives on Lifelong Learning: From Recurent Education to the Knowledge Society*, Buckingham, UK and Philadelphia, PA, USA: SRHE and Open University Press, pp. 39–46.
Primary Education Act (1996), *Official Gazette of Republic Slovenia*, No. 12/96, 29 February.
Radovan, Marko (2009), 'Značilnosti zaposlitve ter udeležba v formalnem in neformalnem izobraževanju odraslih' (Characteristics of Employment and Participation of the Employed in Formal and Non Formal Education), *Organizacija*, **42** (3), 153–165.
Rubenson, Kjell (2006), 'The Nordic Model of Lifelong Learning', *Compare*, **36** (3), 327–341.
Schuetze, Hans Georg and Maria Slowey (2002), 'Participation and Exclusion: a Comparative Analysis of Non-Traditional Students and Lifelong Learners in Higher Education', *Higher Education*, **44** (3–4), 309–327.
Shavit, Yossi and Walter Müller (2000), 'Vocational Secondary Education: Where Diversion and Where Safety Net?' *European Societies*, **2** (1), 29–50.
SORS (2010), *Anketa o izobraževanju odraslih* (Adult Education Survey), Ljubljana: Statistical Office of the Republic of Slovenia.
SVRL (2007), *Enotni programski dokument 2007–2013* (Single Programming Document 2007–2013), Ljubljana: Služba Vlade Republike Slovenije za Lokalno Samoupravo in Regionalno Politiko.
Thurow, Lester (1975), *Generating Inequality*, New York: Basic Books.
Vocational Education and Training Act (1996, 2006), *Official Gazette of the Republic of Slovenia* No. 12/1996 and No. 79/2006.
White Paper on Education in the Republic of Slovenia (1996), Ljubljana: Ministry of Education, Science and Sport.

11. Why are the participation rates in lifelong learning so low in Hungary?

Péter Róbert, Saida Ayupova and Szilvia Altorjai[1]

INTRODUCTION

According to the rank order of nations in various comparative datasets (Adult Education Survey, Labour Force Survey ad hoc module on LLL – lifelong learning), Hungary is among the last in regard to participation rates in formal adult learning. Country typologies developed in the framework of the 'Towards a Lifelong Learning Society in Europe: The Contribution of the Education System' (LLL2010) project (Hefler et al. 2011) empirically confirm Hungary's poor placement in the league tables. In accordance to the main focal points of the project, five aspects expected to influence the practice of formal adult learning activities at the level of the individual will be investigated in this chapter. These aspects are:

1. The policy context of LLL in Hungary from the viewpoint of the declared aims as well as of the applied legislation. Legislation can be instrumental in creating either a helpful or an ineffective constrictive environment.
2. The institutional context of LLL in Hungary:
   a. Practices of employers in either helping or hindering possible adult learners in their decisions on returning to school. As the research in LLL2010 focused on small and medium-sized enterprises (SMEs), utility of LLL for the companies in contributing to the (further) human capital investments of their employees is one of the crucial points that will be discussed.
   b. Educational institutions offering courses and programmes for adults are regarded as providers. Most of the educational institutes, either public or private, look at adult education from a market perspective. Adult learners, if paying tuition fees, are a

financial resource to improve and extend the (narrow) institutional budget. Another viewpoint to elaborate is the content and nature of the programmes, as to how they reflect the needs of the labour market.
3. At the level of the individual, participants of LLL are approached from two perspectives:
   a. Learners and non-learners are compared in order to reveal the main sociological and demographic differences between the two groups and to track down the mechanisms that motivate some, and not others, to return to school.
   b. Individuals participating in an adult education programme at a certain level of schooling (primary, vocational, secondary, post-secondary, tertiary) are studied in the context of their personal motivations and goals for studying, as well as their satisfaction with their experiences in the Hungarian school system.

After the introduction, the chapter goes through these stages in this order, leading to a conclusion where policy-related, institutional and individual aspects of LLL in Hungary are summarized. In the conclusion, we also return to the starting point of the chapter, the low level of participation in a comparative sense, and reflect on the place of the country from a comparative perspective.

THE POLICY CONTEXT OF LLL IN HUNGARY[2]

The Hungarian system of education and skill formation went through a series of transformations during the last few decades. Firstly, following the collapse of Communism in 1990, Hungary reformed the inherited government-owned schooling system. This divergent process included curriculum destandardization, leading to a decrease in the 'signalling function'[3] of education, a decline of vocational specificity, growing marketization, and stratification when private and church-run institutions emerged (Bukodi and Róbert 2008). Secondly, the character of the national LLL policy has markedly changed. The earlier 'second-chance' policy, driven by a political equality principle to support those unable to study because of their poor social background (Kolosi and Róbert 1985), has gradually lost its former social and political role. Thirdly, the national LLL policies had to be harmonized with the Community's concepts upon Hungary's accession to the European Union. Moreover, most recently the system had to further readjust itself in order to fulfil the requirements of the Bologna practice, in accordance with the EU principles on higher education. These processes have had an impact on the various educational institutions, including those concerned with adult learning courses and programmes. During the four decades of Communism, formal adult education was chiefly responsible for increasing the level of schooling of the population. Furthermore, adult education gave an opportunity for those who had missed out on proper schooling to achieve a higher level of education. The collapse of the Communist regime brought about substantial changes, including the disruption of state monopoly over education, resulting in the rise of private institutions and market elements in adult education. There has also been a shift towards regarding adult education as a practical matter designed to serve the labour market needs beyond providing a 'second chance' for schooling, thus dramatically changing the role of LLL from the 1990s onwards.

At the same time, educational policies have to take into account the general situation in terms of the population in the country. Namely, the Hungarian population is ageing and the labour force has been shrinking over the last two decades, resulting in one of the lowest labour force participation rates in the European Union (EU). Furthermore, significant regional gaps exist in terms of levels of education and access to training or job opportunities: the Western parts of Hungary provide much better prospects than the Eastern parts. Finally, Hungary has a particular minority problem, that is, the Roma population, which has serious social deficits and is the target of substantial prejudice. The majority of the people in the Roma community are undereducated and underemployed, with the problem of early school drop-outs being the most critical matter for them. The Roma population represents a disproportional percentage of these drop-outs, emphasizing the need for an increased attention to their adult schooling. The latter could serve as a mechanism to reintegrating them into the educational process, the labour force and, as a complex socio-economic moderator, to the whole society (Kertesi 2010).

The facts and circumstances outlined above call for a policy discussion and development towards LLL in Hungary. Though several related actions and measures can be and will be mentioned, the most problematic point is that the responsibility for LLL policy development had been bounced back and forth between two governmental bodies in Hungary: the Ministry of Education and the Ministry of Labour. Although this circumstance may not be exceptional in Europe, the almost non-existing cooperation between these institutions during the previous years further demonstrates the troublesome nature of this sphere of education. As compared to other EU states, the situation is specifically worrying because of the particularly low level of fertility (1.4 children per woman) and the exceptionally low level of employment (about 61 per cent for males and 50 per cent for females aged 15–64). Upon the governmental reconfigurations after the elections in Hungary in 2010, the Ministry of Education ceased to exist. At the moment, the Ministry of National Resources is responsible for the whole education system from elementary level to higher education, including, in principle, the adult education. The Ministry of Social Affairs and Labour is also in charge of LLL, from the perspective of the labour market.

Despite the institutional conflicts mentioned above, a number of essential Acts and policy papers were adopted in order to strengthen the system of education with a special focus on LLL. The first important document was the *Act CI of 2001 on Adult Education*, which established the framework for certification of informal learning. The Act introduced three requirements regulating adult education: (1) compulsory registration of training providers; (2) institution accreditation; and (3) programme accreditation. Only those institutions which had received accreditation could apply for state support. Individuals wishing to take part in these programmes could apply for a tax reduction. Training providers, in turn, were required to enter into a written contract with the participants. The accreditation requirement for training providers was introduced as an attempt to improve the quality of education. However, at this point, reality failed to match expectations. The Act also contained a reference to the recognition of experience-based knowledge, obliging training provider institutes to take it into account when assessing the overall knowledge level of an individual. The system is not yet fully functional and remains at an experimental stage.

The next policy paper is considered to be one of the two documents establishing the basis for the Hungarian policy on LLL. The *National Lifelong Learning Strategy Paper* was prepared in collaboration between the Ministry of Social Affairs and Labour and the Ministry of Education in 2005. Among others, the paper paid special attention to such aspects of adult education as: (1) the development of institutional and methodological backgrounds; (2) readjustment of vocational education and training according to economic needs; (3) boosting the system of higher education to better fit the current economic demands; and (4) advancement of basic competences in the sector of public education.

Utilizing an educational approach in order to decrease unemployment remains the foundation of the document. The paper is in line with the European Union requirements on LLL as well as with the labour market perspective of the Hungarian adult learning system, focusing primarily on vocational adult education. The document makes an attempt to reconsider public education system in terms of quality and effectiveness, as well as access to education and training, and equal opportunities. Therefore, the document emphasizes the need for: development of basic skills and competencies in the sphere of compulsory education; an increase in the number of institutions providing vocational and higher education, including those for adult learners; the establishment of guidance services and follow-up of school leavers; recognition of non-formal and informal learning; assistance to disadvantaged social groups in terms of access to education; and the development of a new teaching and learning culture. The main flaw of the Strategy Paper is the absence of any social control built in the programme, which has already resulted in the inability to keep up with the schedule of policy implementations.

Accepted roughly at the same time (2004), the *National Action Plan on Social Cohesion 2004–2006* tries to address some of the problems identified earlier. In particular, the National Action Plan targets high rates of school drop-outs, low rates of participation in LLL and strong regional differences. The document set the target of reaching a 10 per cent participation rate in LLL by 2010 as well as reducing the number of young vocational school drop-outs by half, to 15 per cent. The Action Plan further emphasizes the need to create LLL opportunities for socially disadvantaged groups. A considerable part of the document discusses the strategies of achieving 'social cohesion' through social assistance, education enablement, facilitation of participation in employment through training and LLL etc. The document also underlines the need for special programmes for integrating the Roma minority into the socio-economic life of the country.

The most recent document from the 2006 II National Development Plan is the *Human Resources Development Operative Programme 2007–2013*. In addition to the goals set in the *National Lifelong Learning Strategy Paper*, the Programme elaborates on the need to pay special attention to social inclusion, proposing special programmes for disadvantaged groups to facilitate their integration into the labour market. Other elements of the policy document include development of skills, increasing motivation and further capability for learning.

All documents highlight the need for a number of policy changes in order to address some of the obstacles to LLL in Hungary, such as low participation rates of social partners and other stakeholders (e.g. civil organizations). Yet, other issues, including the limited scope of learning which neglects non-formal education, are not covered in a satisfactory manner. A range of institutions offering non-formal education exists in Hungary: cultural centres, libraries, telecottages, folk high schools and others. However, policy-makers continue to disproportionately favour institutionalized forms of education. As the first years of compulsory education are considered to be crucial for individual development, policy documents contain a massive gap between formal and informal channels of education, further restraining the incentives for individual learning activities.

Various policy and national strategy documents have so far led to only modest results. Participation rates in adult education remain far below the European average and are increasing at a slow pace. That being said, it is important to keep in mind that statistical information does not account for informal learning, which plays an important role in competence development. The slow rate at which social integration programmes develop points to the need for continuing efforts in coordination of different agents and promotion of adult education through financial assistance. In some cases, the adopted measures have led to opposite results from what was originally intended, benefiting the already advantaged portion of the population. For example, the tax allowance legislation adopted in 2002 offered the participants enrolled in LLL programmes a chance to receive a tax reduction in the amount of 30 per cent of the tuition fees spent in that year. The legislature was intended to increase participation rates by giving a financial stimulus, even if failing to take into account that most of those who would benefit from this measure would already have sufficient funds to cover their training costs. The most disadvantaged groups usually do not have enough financial resources to enrol in tuition-based programmes to start with, meaning they do not really benefit from the tax-reduction strategy.

Continued presence of obstacles could, in part, be explained by the fact that a number of key concepts in LLL policy have yet to solidify within the framework of Hungary. For example, the concept of the 'knowledge society', although used more frequently today than before, remains more of a slogan without much meaning behind it. While the *National Strategy Paper* of 2005 uses this concept in the introduction, the 'knowledge society' is not explained or elaborated upon in the document.

Another term that requires further exposition is the 'learning city'. There has been some progress on a local level, mainly initiated by local governments, to create 'smart cities' and 'smart regions'. The project entails the development of e-government through local electronic networks and interactive services accessible to local citizens as well as small enterprises. Among other aims, the project has attempted to launch small-scale e-learning programmes and other individual learning activities. However, such initiatives remain small in number and require constant support.

The concept of a 'learning city' brings us back to the regional needs in terms of policy formulation and implementation. A new regional development concept was approved in 1998, resulting in the creation of seven administrative regions. Each region has established its own councils in charge of the regional development plans and integration of various stakeholders into the process. 'Regional knowledge centres' and 'knowledge transfer agents', represented by the institutions of higher education, play an important role within this programme.

Overall, due to the above-mentioned transformations in policy development and implementation on the governmental and local levels, LLL remains an area with much room for improvement. The gaps in LLL policies can only be filled through intergovernmental cooperation, inclusion of social partners and closer attention to non-formal and informal channels of education. Needless to say, social inclusion and reintegration of the disadvantaged groups should be important criteria for any future legislature.

THE INSTITUTIONAL CONTEXT OF LLL IN HUNGARY[4]

The institutional context of LLL in Hungary represents a diverse range of practices which cannot be generalized as one model. However, exploring the strengths and weaknesses from various angles, including the institutional one, is crucial to promoting any serious modifications in the system and approaches to adult education. In this section we will take a closer look at two main branches of institutions: the workplace, the role of SMEs in particular; and educational institutions.

The Perspectives of Employers and Employees

The concept of a 'learning organization' is usually associated with the workplace, especially in the context of large international companies. Unfortunately, this concept is not yet fully integrated in the everyday practices of Hungarian enterprises, with a very limited number of companies offering such opportunities to their employees. Therefore, the analysis of practices, policies and attitudes remains at an early stage of investigation. It is important to bear in mind that the conclusions arrived at in this chapter are based on initial results derived from interviews with employees as well as managerial staff. Two clear frameworks can be identified based on this research: attitudes of the managerial staff towards LLL and the type of support they are willing to provide to employees who decide to participate in further education.

High variations make generalizing attitudes and practices towards LLL in SMEs risky. For example, some of the companies interviewed in Hungary had up to 90 per cent of their employees taking part in formal adult education, while others only had 4–5 per cent. Yet, some commonalities and differences can be identified.

The human resources (HR) departments of SMEs seem to favour

informal over formal adult education. None of the interviewed companies denied the importance of continued development of practical and general skills of their employees. However, due to the high competitiveness of the market, most of the enterprises perform very specific, technology-oriented lines of work. According to the managerial staff, education provided in certified established institutions is outdated as well as primarily focused on theoretical aspects of a relevant field. These programmes are not capable of keeping up with the rapid development of technology. Instead of supporting participation in formal adult learning, SMEs in Hungary find more benefit in organizing internal, informal training for their employees in order to maintain their skill and knowledge levels. For this purpose, SMEs sometimes try to build contact with certain educational institutions, although cooperation with other agencies such as cultural centres, libraries or telecottages is rarer.

At the same time, the high number of school drop-outs in Hungary and the overall low participation rates in LLL result in many low-skilled jobs being performed by undereducated people. Consequently, companies acknowledge the potential benefits of their employees taking part in continued formal education. The interviews revealed different perceived benefits, such as the development of communication skills, learning habits and commitment to the job. Employers believe that constant interaction with peers positively impacts their workers while providing an opportunity for personal development, which in turn increases the employees' level of satisfaction and happiness. Moreover, some HR development (HRD) departments of SMEs find theoretical knowledge received through formal channels of education rather useful, because it complements the practical knowledge already acquired in the workplace. Therefore, these employees can approach their tasks from different angles, possibly leading to increased productivity.

Since many of the companies offer very specific ranges of products and services, finding the right person for a leadership position from outside the company might be challenging. The employers prefer to fill such positions with their employees who already have the necessary practical skills. Often, promotions imply the need for improved educational levels of employees, resulting in the company's overall support for LLL. However, it is important to note that in most companies, participation in continued education and obtainment of a certificate does not guarantee increased pay or promotion upon graduation.

Hungarian SMEs can be further divided into two categories: those that put emphasis on certification and those that do not. The first category consists of companies whose clients require (or at least strongly prefer) the employees to have certification, seen as a proof of qualification.

Certification constitutes an integral part of the ability to compete in the market. Therefore, such companies strongly encourage, if not require, their workers to enrol in certain programmes. At the same time, most of these companies already employ people with high levels of education (International Standard Classification of Education – ISCED – level 4 and higher). The second category, on the other hand, consists of companies that employ people with low levels of education (ISCED 0–2). Consequently, the ability to perform a certain type of job is valued more than certification and, as a result, less attention tends to be paid to employees' participation in educational programmes.

Finally, companies have to consider the financial implications of participating in LLL. Very often, individuals are not capable of covering the costs of education on their own and they seek their companies' support. Although some HRD departments successfully manage to secure state funds, others either do not qualify for such subsidies or find the process too complicated and overly bureaucratic even to apply.

Most of the companies interviewed try to accommodate the needs of their employees to some extent. Providing financial assistance, which usually entails covering the costs of tuition fees and sometimes travelling costs, is more challenging for small and start-up companies. Those capable of providing such support usually condition it upon an employee's commitment to continue to work for the company for a specified amount of time after the training. In case of breaching this contract, the employees are obligated to repay the company the expenditures on their education. However, significant variations exist. While some HRD policies require a company and an employee to enter into a written agreement outlining rights and responsibilities, others have no such practice. Such variations result from the lack of institutionalization of adult education in workplace in Hungary.

Another type of support, more or less common for different types of companies, is time flexibility. Companies can permit a number of days off for taking examinations, granting a few hours a week to accommodate class schedules and/or a possibility to work from home during exam periods. Depending on the type of job performed by an employee, a company would be more or less lenient in this regard. Some of the interviewed SMEs simply cannot afford their employees being absent, resulting in reduced willingness to accommodate their school schedules. Others have the possibility to allow their workers to complete job-related tasks from home. Overall, even the most rigid companies make an attempt to allow for some sort of time flexibility.

The last aspect of LLL in workplace deals with companies' partnership with educational institutions. Some companies have established such patterns of cooperation, which often serve as the main recruitment tool for companies. After offering placements for vocational training to students and upon their successful completion of the programme, companies hire them as full-time employees. Yet, most of the interviewed companies have not yet established such cooperation; mainly because of a lack of belief in such institutions being able to provide employees with the required job-specific knowledge. Another important element that in some cases prevents companies from cooperating with educational institutions is the way the Hungarian higher educational system has adapted to the Bologna process. In many cases, this transformation has been quite formal. The two-level (BSc and MSc) curriculum was not restructured, with the previous curriculum only modified and shortened without substantial changes to its character. To a large extent, focus was maintained on theoretical elements, thus preventing students' participation in more practical training.

Clearly, there exists a gap between companies' attitudes towards institutional forms of education and institutions themselves. Considering the number of workers who could benefit from closer cooperation between companies and educational institutions, as well as the currently low rates of participation in LLL, a closer look at the training provider's perspective is required.

The Perspective of Training Providers

The distribution of educational opportunities continues to be very uneven in Hungary. Social background strongly affects school performance, while the selective nature of education creates further difficulties for those already disadvantaged (Bukodi and Róbert 2008). Similarly, post-secondary education tends to benefit those who already have relatively high educational qualifications. Following the Lisbon Treaty, Hungary has implemented a number of social policies aimed at reducing levels of inequality. Such actions are monitored by the European Commission.

One of the possible reasons for the continued unequal distribution of education among the Hungarian population could be the fact that state policies continuously favour institutionalized forms of education, excluding informal and non-formal types of LLL. Moreover, most efforts are directed towards the development of basic compulsory education, because, as is commonly believed, during these years individuals learn at the highest rate and develop most of their competencies and learning habits. To illustrate the differences in approaches towards compulsory versus higher, formal versus non-formal and other forms of education, what follows is a look at these various educational providers along with a number of examples for each of the categories of schools.

Primary and secondary school opportunities are available to all adult learners, including those in prison. Classes run on a different schedule, usually in the evenings. Upon successful graduation, students enjoy the same rights as those who completed education in a regular manner. The following example shows the difficulties many educational institutions with a focus on adult learners may face.

A school in Budapest, specializing in preparing adult learners for high school diplomas, provides a number of learning options to its participants, including distance and correspondence education. The school's funding comes from three different sources: state, local government and students. Since the students only pay a part of the tuition costs, a significant number of them are representatives of disadvantaged groups (for example, Roma students constitute more than 10 per cent of the student body). Although this model contains a number of strengths – for example high professionalism of the teaching staff, establishment of close relationships between teachers and students, and other benefits – the lack of funding remains the biggest challenge. As a result, the school is limited in its capabilities. For example, the institution cannot afford to offer its teachers sabbatical years for their further development or to enrol more students from disadvantaged groups.

A number of secondary schools in Hungary focus on disadvantaged adults in particular. In order to accommodate financial difficulties of the participants, such schools search for alternative ways of funding. For example, one such school receives funding from the city's secondary school, the university and the local innovation centre. Thus, the school is able to offer education free of charge or for a small fee. As a result, approximately 50 per cent of the student body comes from the disadvantaged Roma population. However, even schools that manage to find alternative sources of funding remain highly vulnerable in this aspect, once again highlighting the need for allocating more resources towards institutions focusing on providing educational opportunities for disadvantaged groups.

The government tried to address the problem of under-representation of the disadvantaged populations in education by implementing a number of programmes, such as tuition-based tax reductions and various civil scholarships. The Arany János programme enables gifted, underprivileged children to enrol in high school education. The 'Útravaló' programme assists the underprivileged to get into higher educational institutions.

Mindful of existing regional differences, the Hungarian government started paying more attention to vocational training. Upon the development of administrative regions, integrated vocational training centres have been created. Such centres have established patterns of cooperation with the regional employment centres with the goal of increasing the training opportunities for disadvantaged groups. The centres focus on school-age participants as well as on adult learners. Regional development plans envisage close collaboration between various stakeholders: employers, civil society organizations, 'regional knowledge centres' and 'knowledge transfer agents' (those providing higher educational opportunities).

Higher education runs on the basis of full-time, part-time and evening schedules in order to accommodate diverse groups of people. Distance learning is also an option. For example, one of the biggest universities in Budapest, Hungary, though offering primarily engineering programmes, also contains a Centre for Learning Innovation and Adult Learning. The centre offers a wide range of postgraduate specialization programmes as well as continued education programmes in engineering. Postgraduate programmes are combined with distance and correspondence education, incorporating e-learning and face-to-face consultations. In addition, the university offers vocation programmes providing the participants with supplementary education. Since the university is entirely dependent on students' funding, at least for the adult learning programmes, the majority of those enrolled in the latter should have full-time jobs to allow them to cover the costs of education. As a result, the unemployed and representatives of other disadvantaged groups do not constitute a substantial part of the student body. Moreover, the emphasis remains on postgraduate programmes, meaning that fewer resources are allocated towards the adult education sector. Under the Hungarian Universitas Program, the government is planning to establish more educational programmes working directly with adult learners.

Prison education mainly provides basic and secondary-level qualifications and is state-sponsored. Since most prisoners are either low-qualified or unqualified, prisons are obligated to provide elementary education. In many cases, the programme is outsourced to external educational institutions within the prison boundaries. Prior to taking classes, prisoners might be split into groups based on results of knowledge-assessment exams. The programmes require a commitment of approximately 20–22 hours per week. Upon graduation, the participants receive a certification no different from those provided by regular schools. Those wishing to enrol in secondary education must be given such an option, provided they have completed the elementary level of schooling. Considering the low number of prisoners expressing the wish to carry on with their education, prisons tend to cooperate amongst each other and organize common classes. Vocational training initiatives, however, are not numerous: partly because of financial limitations, partly because of the level of initial schooling of the prisoners. Thus, labour market vocational training, which could be considered extremely useful and relevant, is not capable of providing up-to-date equipment for professional practice, and the majority of the prisoners are unskilled.

Due to the limited statistical information on informal and non-formal learning, one runs the risk of underestimating the overall rates of learning activities. Non-formal education is mainly run by such institutions as cultural centres, libraries, telecottages, folk high schools, and so on. Often, these institutions provide mentoring programmes aimed at assisting disadvantaged groups in finding appropriate educational opportunities, vocational training programmes and/or jobs. Some of these institutions are located outside of Budapest, thus attempting to address regional issues. These institutions are in a constant search for funding, which usually comes from multiple sources; for example, from the Regional Public Employment Services and private businesses.

To summarize, the institutional context for LLL is full of challenges. Formal adult education remains unpopular among employers, mainly because of lack of funding, lack of trust in educational institutions or simply due to lack of motivation on behalf of employees as well as employers. The educational system itself needs to be reconsidered in terms of resource allocation, scrutiny of the non-formal sector and the role of adult education in social integration.

INDIVIDUAL FACTORS IMPACTING PARTICIPATION IN FORMAL ADULT LEARNING[5]

This section discusses individual factors which determine both the participation level in and the satisfaction with formal adult learning. Firstly, learners and non-learners are compared in order to reveal main sociological and demographic differences between the two groups for understanding the mechanisms behind the variations in people's decisions to return to school. The Hungarian data of the Adult Education Survey (AES) are used for this purpose. Secondly, the attitudes and personal motivations of LLL participants are investigated along with their satisfaction, enjoyment, confidence and wider opinion on the teaching and learning processes of their course. The Hungarian survey carried out in the framework of the LLL2010 project is used for this purpose.

Learners and Non-Learners

We claim that the reasons for and correlations of the particularly low level of attendance in formal adult education in Hungary are related to various forms of inequalities in access to adult education. Three types of explanatory variables shed light on the nature of these inequalities:

1. demographic variables (gender, age, place of residence, presence of small child in the family);
2. sociological variables (initial level of schooling, time elapsed since leaving school, labour market integration and type of occupation, e.g. manual versus non-manual);
3. attitudes towards learning (Róbert 2010).

Starting with the last explanation, subjective attitudes towards adult education contained elements such as: the importance of skill development in being successful at work; employers' responsibility in providing training; the attitude that learning is fun and gives self-confidence; the opinion that learners should share the financial burden of adult learning, and so on. The division of these attitudes is displayed in Table 11.1. Not surprisingly, when respondents are divided into two groups by participation, those taking part in formal adult learning are significantly more likely to possess

Table 11.1 Learners' and non-learners' attitudes towards adult learning (%)

Attitude items	Proportion of complete agreement by the respondents' participation	
	Participated in formal adult education	Did not participate in formal adult education
If you want to be successful at work you need to keep improving your knowledge and skills	**78**	51
Employers should be responsible for the training of their employees	**48**	39
The skills you need to do a job can't be learned in the classroom	**47**	39
Education and training can help you manage your daily life better	**61**	38
Learning new things is fun	**41**	22
Learning gives you more self-confidence	**68**	45
Individuals should be prepared to pay something for their adult learning	**30**	19

Note: Bold = significantly deviates from the total percentage (over-represented).

positive attitudes towards learning than those not studying. In addition, those participating in adult education tend to agree with the need to pay for their studies, unlike those not learning.

Multivariate analysis combines the demographic, sociological and attitude variables to estimate the probability of participation in adult learning. In Hungary, the demographic indicators could explain 16 per cent of the variance among adults returning to school. The sociological indicators in total account for 21 per cent of the variance in returning to school, with the attitude measures explaining only 5 per cent of the variance.

However, demographic, sociological and attitudinal characteristics are not independent from each other, having stronger or weaker correlations. The complete multivariate analysis of the three groups of predictors sheds light on these interdependencies. This complete model with all of the explanatory factors explains about 26 per cent of the variation in returning to formal adult education in Hungary. The most influential effects highlight the combination of those barriers which contribute to the low participation rates in formal adult education. In this context, neither gender nor region has direct impact in Hungary. However, having one or more children under three years of age remains a significant obstacle to studying. Furthermore, the role of the time elapsed since one has left school adversely predicts the odds of participation in formal adult education. The same holds true for the unemployed, the self-employed and manual workers. In contrast, those fully integrated in the labour market (working with a permanent contract in a full-time position) are less likely to participate in adult learning than their counterparts. Regarding attitudes towards learning, the belief that skills and knowledge improve success at work and help to manage daily life increases the odds of returning to formal education even when all socio-demographic features are taken into account.

Adult Learners' Experiences and Perspectives

After comparing learners and non-learners, the next step is to discuss the more detailed information on learners' attitudes and personal motivations for studying, along with their satisfaction, enjoyment, confidence and wider opinion on the teaching and learning processes of their course (Róbert et al. 2009).

For the purpose of in-depth analysis of participants in formal adult education, as a first step, two comprehensive indexes show 'attitudes towards learning' and the 'enjoyment of learning'. In Hungary, respondents generally enjoy learning, as well as having a very positive attitude towards learning (60 per cent and 72 per cent respectively). Also, the more time the

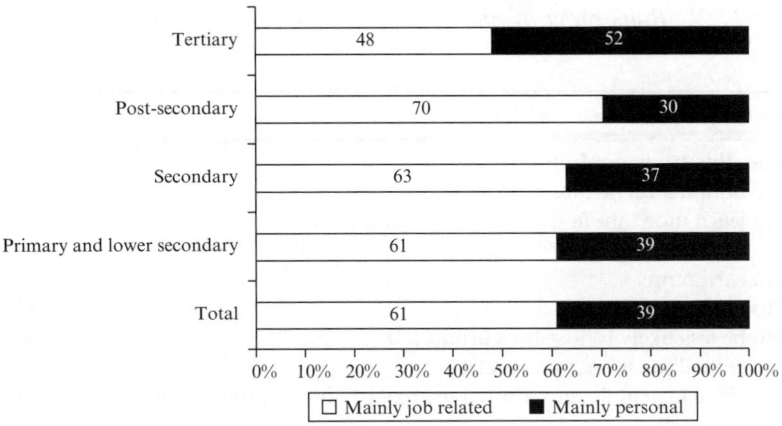

Figure 11.1 Job-related versus personal motivation of participation in formal adult education

individuals have spent in the education system (i.e. the more qualified), the more positive their experiences and attitudes towards learning.

Nevertheless, motivations for learning can be quite different. In Hungary, 60 per cent of all participants enrolled on their courses because of job-related reasons and 40 per cent out of personal interest. As Figure 11.1 shows, job-related motivations are more prevalent among post-secondary level students (70 per cent) and less important (less than 50 per cent) among tertiary level learners. This difference suggests that the general idea about the purpose of LLL might be different depending on the level of the initial qualification and the exact courses students have chosen. For example, the majority of the learners at post-secondary level have secondary school qualifications from grammar schools where the vocational character of their studies was low. Apparently, adult learners prefer to study something that improves their chances in the labour market.

A large number of motivators concerning social control, human capital, social capital and personal fulfilment were investigated in order to capture the more detailed aspects of the drive to gain new skills or qualifications. Although all of these reasons have their role in increasing adult learning, they can be divided into three groups according to the order of the items as displayed in Table 11.2. More than 70 per cent of the respondents provided reasons such as 'obtain a certificate', 'earn more' or 'doing the job better'. Reducing the risk of losing the current job is also quite a frequent motivator in Hungary. These responses echo the fundamental economic rationale of learning, namely that the new skills might help people in gaining a better position in the labour market. At the same time, reasons

Table 11.2 Rank order of motives to study in an adult learning programme (%)

Order of motives	%
I chose this study programme. . .	
. . . to obtain a certificate	86
. . . to learn more about a subject that interests me	83
. . . to learn knowledge/skills useful in my daily life	79
. . . to earn more	74
. . . to do my job better	73
. . . to be less likely to lose my current job	58
. . . to contribute more as a citizen	55
. . . because my employer required me to enrol in the programme	54
. . . to get a job	53
. . . to meet new people	52
. . . to contribute more to my community	46
. . . to gain awareness of myself and others	39
. . . to participate in group activities	37
. . . to get a break from the routine at home and work	36
. . . because someone advised me to do it	25
. . . because I was obliged to do it, e.g. to claim benefits, to avoid redundancy	23
. . . to start up my own business	20
. . . because I was bored	5

such as personal interests or usefulness in daily life score also high among Hungarian learners.

The motivators listed above can be grouped into controlled and autonomous categories. Controlled motivators are purely extrinsic, stemming from external pressure or from the learners themselves. Autonomous motivations are driven by the individual wanting to undertake a given course because of the joy of learning or because of the added value to one's own life. Two indexes were created accordingly: the 'controlled motivation index' and the 'autonomous motivation index'. The importance of controlled motivators is significantly greater among students attending primary and lower secondary level courses in Hungary, meaning that external factors are more important to these students than to those learning at higher levels. The autonomous motivators also play a relatively important role. Interestingly, the least educated group scores the highest in this measure. To those studying at post-secondary level, autonomous reasons were significantly less important when deciding whether or not to participate in adult education, confirming what has been said about these learners and their job-related attitudes towards adult education.

Another issue for adult learners is their confidence regarding their own success in formal adult education. Approximately 80 per cent of the respondents are confident of being able to complete their studies. The problems which potentially jeopardize the completion of their course include: too little time for studying, trouble arranging childcare, inconvenient schedule, financial problems, transportation problems, lack of preparation for the course, difficulties competing with younger students and family problems. In Hungary, only one-fifth of the respondents say that they do not face any obstacles in completing their study programmes. Around two-thirds of learners have 1–3 problems and another 17 per cent face 4–6 problems. Therefore, those participating in adult education invest considerable time and effort juggling with different duties and obstacles to be able to complete their studies.

The general assumption is that satisfaction is the main driver for persistence in participation in learning. When adult learners do not experience any satisfaction from their studies, they are likely to discontinue learning. The satisfaction of adult learners was investigated from five dimensions, as shown in Table 11.3. Although the vast majority of learners were satisfied with their course, those studying at tertiary level appeared to be less content. The lowest levels of satisfaction (less than 50 per cent) in the table appear among these learners and for those items that refer to the practical organization of the educational institution and to what the students can do after the completion of the course. Such a low level of satisfaction seems

Table 11.3 Learners' satisfaction with various aspects of the course (%)

Satisfied with. . .					
Type of course	General progress of study	Learning climate	Practical organization of educational institution	What you learned so far	What you can do after this course
Tertiary education	61	59	46	59	45
Post-secondary education	78	77	78	85	59
Secondary education	75	74	71	76	55
Primary and lower level of secondary education	77	81	78	81	59
Total	73	73	68	75	55

Table 11.4 Evaluation of teaching and learning processes (%)

Proportion of having a positive opinion on. . .				
Type of course	Strong affiliation between students	Very active involvement of students	High level of teacher support	High level of task orientation
Tertiary education	47	30	30	17
Post-secondary education	48	38	81	25
Secondary education	52	38	82	16
Primary and lower level of secondary education	52	46	85	31
Total	50	38	69	22

to confirm what has been said in the previous section on the low level of utility of the curriculum in the tertiary education institutions. However, Hungarian learners are less satisfied (less than 60 per cent) with what they can do after their studies, coinciding with employers' attitudes on the usefulness of what people can study on formal adult courses in Hungary.

The teaching and learning processes include affiliation between students, the level of teacher support, task orientation, personal goal attainment, organization and clarity and student involvement. As Table 11.4 shows, Hungarian learners are less satisfied with these aspects of their courses as compared to the percentages in the previous table. Only satisfaction with affiliation between students is close to 50 per cent. College and university level learners are even more critical about teaching and learning process. Satisfaction regarding the level of teacher support is about 80 per cent among other groups of adult learners and only 30 per cent in tertiary education. Similarly, satisfaction with the level of task orientation is very low among students at tertiary level.

CONCLUSION[6]

In this chapter we have attempted to search for an explanation for the low participation rates in formal adult learning activities in Hungary. At least three kinds of reasons can be taken into account: policy-level deficits, institutional-level deficits and individual-level deficits.

On the governmental level, the lack of cooperation between ministries is the most noticeable challenge. Until the enforcement of EU requirements, which introduced new interdepartmental cooperative processes, the cross-check of the policy documents remained a primary point of intersection. Further restructuring of governmental departments in regard to vocational education resulted in the establishment of subsectors, where each person would be responsible for a certain function. The downside of the system is the absence of an appointed person for a number of important tasks. Overall, very few actual changes have occurred in terms of interdepartmental cooperation. In addition, competition for limited financial resources takes place on the intra- as well as the interministerial levels, further diminishing the motivation to cooperate.

Another problem with the policy documents investigated and discussed in the chapter is the lack of attention to how the relevant policy issues are handled in these Acts and declarations. Most of these documents focus on intentions, rather than being specific in terms of real activities, resources or responsibilities. More focused, targeted and harmonized actions would be much desirable under the present demographic and employment conditions in Hungary.

Macro-level changes in the last two decades pushed Hungary into an increasingly difficult situation regarding the economy and governmental resources. In terms of the welfare state classification, Hungary, like all the former Communist states, used to have a quasi social-democratic orientation. This political approach ceased to exist together with the Communist system, leading to growing marketization. Currently, Hungary is closer to the Continental, corporatist welfare type, combined with other features. Comparative analysis of the micro data on formal adult education revealed that participation rates in LLL are lower in the corporatist or Mediterranean societies, as it is in Hungary (Hefler et al. 2011). Of course this is a fragile placement of the country in the welfare system in accordance with the arguments on the large variety of classifications in the introductory chapter of this book.

Reference to the well-known occupational labour market (OLM) versus internal labour market (ILM) concept can be helpful to understand the present situation of the institutional level. Due to its historical traditions, Hungary used to be closer to the OLM-type linkage between the school system and the labour market. However, the country moved to the ILM direction after the collapse of Communism in 1990, which resulted in a decline in vocational specificity or the signalling function of the educational programmes. Consequently, as the research on SMEs proved, employers started to increasingly distrust the formal educational system. The labour market side expressed negative attitudes toward the usefulness of the formal school programmes. Interestingly enough, the growing marketization in the world of schooling, and the financial dependence of educational institutions, among others, on adult learners, did not make the school system more responsive to the needs of the labour market. Educational programmes, regardless of their level, in most cases continue to offer general training without much practical focus. Apparently, this strategy of more academically oriented adult learner courses could be useful under the conditions of the rapidly changing situation in the labour market, even though only a minority of employers are pleased with these school programmes. Hungary has the potential to drastically change the relationship between the employer-type learning-type institutions. Undoubtedly, more research is required to create policies efficient and productive enough in enforcing cooperation between these institutions.

The analysis at the level of the individual led to three important conclusions on the comparison of learners and non-learners. From a multivariate perspective, old age and having a small child in the family turned out to be significant barriers among demographic factors. Both indicators are crucial from a life course perspective, underlining the connection between the phase one occupies in their individual life cycle and the decision of returning to school. Longer time spent out of the school system decreases the likelihood of participating in adult education. Furthermore, in Hungary, both the self-employed and the unemployed participate in LLL to a lesser extent. Weak labour market integration, however, increases the chances of studying, which can also easily mean a reversed causality. Weakly integrated workers might try to accumulate further human capital in order to stabilize their labour market situation. Weak integration to the labour force could also be a consequence, not a cause, of the learning activity. Studies show that positive attitudes towards LLL increase the probability of returning to school, while people with negative experiences or opinions on schooling are less likely to take up studying again.

Conclusions about the motivators, attitudes and satisfaction for the targeted analysis of those participating in formal adult education are more difficult to draw. However, the majority of adult learners have labour-related goals when returning to school. An even larger majority have positive attitudes towards their studies and enjoy learning. Obviously, there is a selection effect behind these results. As mentioned above, those with negative attitudes do not tend to return to adult learning and, consequently, could not be respondents of the targeted survey investigating them either. This fact makes it difficult to interpret how they are satisfied with the system of adult education in Hungary: those who were not satisfied with their decision have probably left the school they may have signed up to and, consequently, could not be in the sample of the survey. Nevertheless, both initial education and the level of participation have an impact on satisfaction: those studying at tertiary level are less satisfied and express more criticism about adult learning in Hungary. Some findings at the individual level, for example attitudes towards the missing practical focus of the adult education programmes or doubts about the usefulness of attending formal adult education, are in accordance with the negative opinion of the employers on formal adult education.

At the end of the chapter, we want to draw attention to some policy recommendations emanating from our discussion:

1. Enhanced cooperation between government authorities and more targeted and precise goal settings would be required in the LLL policy.
2. Policy measures should particularly aim to strengthen the cooperation between employers and schools. Adult education programmes should put more emphasis on courses with stronger practical orientation and vocational specificity.
3. A life cycle perspective should be central to some jointly developed policy measures by the appropriate ministries, related to education and family policy. On the one hand, targeted messages should be put out to show that there is no age limit to improving skills and knowledge. On the other hand, childcare institutions should be more available and accessible to ease the difficulties of reconciling childcare duties and adult learning. Learning institutions, third-sector organizations or even community initiatives can develop flexible solutions for childcare. Learning institutions can be more proactive in helping parents as only a few respondents (about 3 per cent) mentioned that childcare is available in the institute they are studying at.
4. Learning trajectories need to be developed for school drop-outs and those with a low level of initial schooling (ISCED 1–2) to acquire qualifications and learning.

The public policy of adult skills and education looks quite complex in Hungary, with the structure of incentives also being fragmented. The role of employers' involvement is crucial to increase the participation rates in adult learning. Policies on labour market progression and skill development should be linked together and, for example, learning and education advice needs to be included in the unemployment services offered to those looking for work.

NOTES

1. This chapter benefits from previous country reports throughout the running time of the project. I thank the co-authors of those reports: Éva Tót (SP1), Matild Sági (SP2), Anikó Balogh (SP2, SP3, SP5), Janka Salát (SP3), Saida Ayupova (SP4), Ágnes Szölősi and

Anna Józan (SP5). Saida Ayupova and Szilvia Altorjai contributed to the writing of this chapter.
2. This section is based on the LLL2010 Hungarian national report in SP1 (Tót et al. 2007) and a recent update by Saida Ayupova.
3. The term is mainly used by economists and indicates how much education or, more precisely, the curriculum of various school programmes provides information to employers on the content of the skills potentially obtained by students (Spence 1974).
4. This section is based on the LLL2010 Hungarian national report in SP4 (Ayupova and Róbert 2010) and in SP5 (Balogh et al. 2010). A draft summary of the reports was prepared by Saida Ayupova.
5. This section is based on the LLL2010 Hungarian national report in SP2 (Róbert 2010) and in SP3 (Róbert et al. 2009). A draft summary of the reports was prepared by Szilvia Altorjai.
6. Szilvia Altorjai also contributed to this part of the chapter.

REFERENCES

A 2001 évi CI törvény a felnőtt képzésről (2001), (Act CI on Adult Education).

A Magyar Köztársaság kormányának stratégiája az egész életen át tartó tanulásról (2005), (National Lifelong Learning Strategy Paper).

Aypova, Saida and Péter Róbert (2010), 'Formal Adult Education in Small- and Medium-Sized Enterprises: The Case of Hungary', *LLL 2010 SP4 National Report*, Budapest: TARKI Social Research Center.

Balogh, Anikó, Anna Józan, Ágnes Szöllősi and Péter Róbert (2010), *The Institutional Aspects of Adult Education in Hungary*, Budapest: TÁRKI Social Research Centre.

Bukodi, Erzsébet and Péter Róbert (2008), 'Hungary', in Irena Kogan, Michael Gebel and Clemens Noelke (eds), *Europe Enlarged: A Handbook of Education, Labour and Welfare Regimes in Central and Eastern Europe*, Abingdon: Policy Press, pp. 183–212.

Emberi erőforrások fejlesztése operatív program 2007–2013 (2006), (Human Resources Development Operative Programme).

Hefler, Günter, Péter Róbert, Paul Ringler, Matild Sági, Stephanie Rammel, Anikó Balogh and Jörg Markowitsch (2011), 'Formal Adult Education in Context – The View of European Statistics', *SP 2 – Synthesis Report*, Budapest – Krems: TÁRKI – DUK.

Kertesi, Gábor (2010), 'Roma Employment at the Turn of the Millenium: An Analysis of the Nationwide Representative Roma survey of 2003', in Károly Fazekas, Anna Lovász and Álmos Telegdy (eds), *The Hungarian Labour Market 2010*, Budapest: Institute of Economics, HAS, pp. 135–150.

Kolosi, Tamás and Péter Róbert (1985), 'Die Rolle des Abend- und Fernstudiums bei der gesellschaftlichen Mobilität', in Manfred Kaiser, Reinhard Nuthman and Heinz Stegmann (eds), *Berufliche Verbleibsforschung in der Diskussion*, Nürnberg: IAB, pp. 335–365.

Nemzeti Cselekvési Terv a társadalmi összetartozásért (2004), (National Action Plan on Social Inclusion 2004–2006).

Róbert, Péter (2010), 'Predicting the Probabilities of Participation in Formal Adult Education', *LLL 2010 SP2 National Report*, Budapest: TARKI Social Research Institute.

Róbert, Péter, Janka Salát, Anikó Balogh and Éva Tót (2009), *LLL2010 SP3 National Report*, Budapest: TARKI Social Research Institute.
Spence, Michael A. (1974), *Market Signaling: Informational Transfer in Hiring and Related Screening Processes*, Cambridge, MA: Harvard University Press.
Tót, Éva, Péter Róbert, Matild Sági and Anikó Balogh (2007), 'Lifelong Learning Policies in Hungary. LLL2010 SP1 National Report', LLL2010 Working Paper No 6, Budapest: TARKI Social Research Institute.

12. The lifelong learning hybrid: the case of Bulgaria

Pepka Boyadjieva, Valentina Milenkova, Galin Gornev, Kristina Petkova and Diana Nenkova

INTRODUCTION

The Bulgarian tradition in adult education originated in 1870s when the first Sunday schools were organized. Following liberation from the Ottoman Empire (1878), Sunday and evening schools for adult education became widespread. Although the education system during the Communist regime (1944–1989) was subjected to enormous ideological pressure and constant politically motivated reforms, it was mostly successful in widening access to education and achieving priority status for continuous vocational education. After the 'Gentle Revolution' of 1989 there has been a clear tendency of an increasing number and diversification of the institutions offering adult continuous education. A significant part of this increase is due to efforts by the state to support the vocational education and the requalification of people over 16 years of age as well as to spread programmes targeting specific social groups (such as Roma, low-literate and long-term unemployed people). The post-totalitarian educational dynamics has culminated in the years prior to the accession of Bulgaria to the European Union (EU) and, ultimately, after the accession when the country took part in the EU lifelong learning (LLL) policies.

This historical dynamics of the Bulgarian educational system, however, is still not systematized and convincingly understood in theoretical terms. That is why our chapter aims, first of all, to propose a theoretical perspective for better understanding both the tension-provoking presence of the LLL concept in scientific debate and the (national) specificity of the development of LLL in Bulgaria. We argue that the LLL paradigm is essentially generated by the societies and cultures of late modernity and – in the conditions of global openness – transmitted across borders to less developed societies. As far as the dependent – that is, directed by external models – modernization of national societies is by its very nature hybrid or 'bricolage', the resulting impact does not adhere to a strictly universal historical trajectory, but to a variety of more or less parallel paths dependent on the national contexts.

Then we proceed with discussing three different manifestations of LLL hybridity in contemporary Bulgarian society, namely: the 'shifting sands' of the concept of LLL in the Bulgarian educational policies; the 'bricolage institutional context of LLL' and the zigzag movements in implementing LLL in Bulgaria. Following this line of analysis, we outline the specifically Bulgarian form of LLL hybridity.

LLL AS A HYBRID: TOWARDS A THEORETICAL FRAMEWORK

LLL as an Educational Concept of the Societies of Late Modernity

'Lifelong learning' is certainly one of the most fashionable concepts in contemporary social-political discourse. But even as the term becomes central to European policies and programmes, increasingly sharp critiques are levelled at it from academic circles. The critical emphasis is in two main directions: (1) the epistemological status of the notion of 'lifelong learning' (Grace 2004; Boshier 2001; Duke 2001); and (2) the aims and functions of the policies and practices of lifelong learning (Borg and Mayo 2005; Crowther 2004; Preston 1999; Wain 2000; Field 2001; Jarvis 2001).

Isn't there something paradoxical in the situation described above? How are we to explain this important and yet tension-provoking presence of the concept both in scientific debate and in the sphere of politics?

We share the thesis that the revival of the notion of lifelong learning during the 1990s and the way in which it has been understood can be explained only when viewed in the context of the changing socio-structural characteristics and the globalization processes of late modernity. In attempting to find a synthetic characteristic of the late modern world, Ulrich Beck refers to Wassily Kandinsky's article, remarkably entitled 'And'. In it, Kandinsky looks for the right word to characterize the twentieth as opposed to the nineteenth century. According to Beck, Kandinsky's answer is surprising: 'whereas the 19th century was subordinated to the logic of either-or, for the 20th century the logic of *and* is in effect. In the first case we have division, specialization, a search for the unambiguous, for predictability of the world; in the latter, there is togetherness, multiplicity, insecurity' (Beck 1993, p. 9). In other words, while early modernity was dominated by differentiation processes, late modernity was predominantly characterized by reverse ones of obliteration of social boundaries, of crossing them and of interpenetration between the social spheres.

To this synthetic definition of the basic principle of late modernity we need to add several more specific characteristics in order to better understand the social context of its working (Giddens 1990, pp. 36–53; Bauman 2002, pp. 431–435):

1. the constant 'fluidity' of the social structures;
2. the changing institutional order;
3. the related development of disembedding mechanisms, which tends to free social activity from localized constraints;
4. the emergence of politics as an integral, more important than ever, part of the habitat;
5. the displacement of the self-organization of human agents in their life project resulting in perpetual self-constituting with no visible end to it;
6. the changing status of knowledge and its reflexive appropriation, where 'to know' is no longer synonymous with 'to be certain'.

The concept of lifelong learning is a basic reflection of the described context. Just as mass-scale school education was a response to the needs of societies of early modernity, the concept, practices and policies of lifelong learning can only be possible and explicable in the context of late modernity. Lifelong learning is connected with the increasing 'permeability' between the social spheres as well as with the processes of individualization and growing reflexivity.

Lifelong learning (LLL) is a sort of 'manifestation of the dedifferentiation process', which is 'a breakdown of clear and settled demarcations between different sectors of education and between education and the lifeworld' (Usher 2001, p. 165). It is both a manifestation of this interpenetration and a factor of its acceleration. That is why it may be defined as 'a metaphor that highlights both the fact that education is without boundaries, i.e. that it is not reducible to previously envisaged results or formal instructions, *and* its post-modern quality, that is its non-systematicity, signifying power and socio-cultural contextuality' (Usher 2001, p. 166). It is a question of acknowledging the hybrid character of LLL, of acknowledging the fact that:

1. LLL is a principle of education which leads to the emergence of an assembly of different practices (institutionalized and informal, organized and sporadic, purposeful and unintended) effecting a series of both official and hidden lessons.

2. LLL includes different kinds of knowledge and skills within different perspectives (personal and social; employment and citizenship; leisure and work).
3. LLL is not always a cumulative process; it could include not only upgrading but also disruptions and new starts.
4. Providing counseling services is an intrinsic element of LLL.
5. Policy and ethical dimensions are an inseparable part of LLL's theory and practice.

The Other Meaning of Hybridity and the Specificity of the Bulgarian Case

There is another meaning of hybridity that plays a central role when we outline the national characteristics of the historical development of LLL. In order to better understand it, we need to recall that etymologically 'hybrid' and 'hybridization' designates the processes of mixing; of crossing various races and various animal or vegetable breeds. This is a mixing of living systems that have different natures and different rhythms, and it also denotes the tensions arising thereby, including the arrhythmic and chaotic states that occur when a common modus vivendi is sought.

When examined at the level of modern national societies, the term points to the processes of modelling and change of societies in the image of other societies, that is under their 'modernizing pressure'; obviously, such processes are ridden with tension, social disruptions and conflicts. In such cases societies usually go through long and painful processes of mutual adjustment of exogenous and endogenous patterns of social activity. These patterns, which were initially stabilized elements of different and often alien historical contexts, usually manage to surmount their mutual strangeness and to produce hybrid forms that gradually evolve towards synthesis.

One of the important dimensions of their initial strangeness is the empirically observable differences in the degree of development of these national societies as measured on the modernity scale. Here it is important to take into consideration that, despite the later influential criticism (Eisenstadt 2000; Kaya 2004) of what we may call the 'linear view' on modernization processes (Lerner 1963; Inkeles and Smith 1974; Inkeles 1983), the notion it implies that there is a commensurability across different national developments has found a stable place in most political and social-scientific discourse. This explains why both in 'highly developed' and in 'less developed' societies there is a widespread view regarding the common logic of development along the stages of modernity and hence the possibility and need for a didactic approach with regard to the lagging national societies (including a common plan and methods, a single control centre, etc.).

However let us go back to the idea – central to our analysis – of the tension between the endogenous and exogenous components of the modernization dynamics in the recipient societies and the hybridity resulting from the transnational irradiation of modern forms. One important ramification of this line of analysis is the notion of the bricolage character of the processes of renewal occurring in these societies, meaning that renewal is effectuated with any materials that happen to be at hand. Figuratively speaking, social renewal in such cases is built not on the ruins but with the ruins from the past. Despite its fundamental character, transition, for instance, from a communist regime to a democratic society 'is not the passage from one order to another but rearrangements in the patterns of how multiple orders are interwoven' (Stark 1996, p. 995). In this sense, post-communist social reality – with its typical tense co-existence and complex interweaving of old and new forms of social organization – is a characteristic example both of hybridity and of bricolage. What is more, in the life of the recipient society these two phenomena are effectuated by means of the same mechanisms; the latter include, according to Dale, borrowing (imitation, copying), learning, harmonization, dissemination, standardization, installing interdependence, imposition (Dale 1999). The mechanisms differ in several dimensions, which are of decisive importance for the effect they have: in their source (a national institution, a supranational one), in the nature of the relations (voluntary, formally voluntary, coercive), and in the character of the process (borrowing, learning, convincing, collective agreement).

We may generalize that, even though based on differing metaphors, these two analytic orientations, which are centred, respectively, on the hybrid and on bricolage, prove very similar both in their meaning and mechanisms of materialization and in their effectiveness in the study of externally induced regenerating ideas, practices, and organizational patterns. Both hybridity and bricolage imply the highly problematic character of what we may call the 'domestication' or assimilation of externally induced renewal processes, and they put a special stress on the (re)groupings – specific to each recipient society – of old and new elements.

On the basis of the above discussion it is clear, for instance, that the prescriptive transmission of patterns of thought and behaviour from national societies with a high 'modernization index', to those with a lower one, inevitably has – along with the very desirable effects – some very undesirable ones for the recipient society. On one hand, it is capable of accelerating the autopoietic process and helping to reduce the 'historical lag'. On the other hand, such a transfer inevitably produces noise disturbance in the field of social communication between the sender and receiver society. This distortion is evident by the speed and degree of dissemination among the addressees and also in the semantic precision of the messages and their structural 'fit' with the other elements of the system. A logical theoretical expectation is that, among the empirical manifestations of a society functioning in the hybrid (or bricolage) mode, an important role would be played by several variables. These variables would include: unclear definitions of the imported concepts with a resulting discrepancy between different interpretations of those concepts; the connecting of concepts with nation-specific meanings; resistance to (and inertia in), the assimilation of different activity contexts (interpersonal, group, institutional, etc.); hence, some typical imitativeness and formalism of use, as well as a very limited actual employment of these concepts.

Remaining within the delineated theoretical perspective, in the following paragraphs we will discuss three different manifestations of LLL hybridity in contemporary Bulgarian society:

1. the 'shifting sands' of the concept of LLL in the Bulgarian educational policies;
2. the bricolage institutional context of LLL, including inherited 'old rigid' institutions and newly established 'flexible' ones;
3. the zigzag movements in implementing LLL in Bulgaria.

THE 'SHIFTING SANDS' OF THE CONCEPT OF LLL IN THE BULGARIAN EDUCATIONAL POLICIES

We believe that the institutional perspective provides the most adequate framework for understanding the policies and practices of LLL in the Bulgarian social context. Institutionalism, especially the new institutionalism, emphasizes the dependence of the local social institutions on a broader social environment. This refers to the fact that 'the environments *constitute* local situations – establishing and defining their core entities, purposes, and relations' (Meyer et al. 2007, p. 188). Viewed in this perspective, the way of perceiving the concept of LLL, the policies and practices in this sphere appear as an embodiment of the predominating social (both national and supra-national) 'myths'. In the analysis below we will trace how these processes take place under the conditions before and after the Bulgarian 'Gentle Revolution'.

Continuing Education in a Vocational and Ideological Trap

During the years of the Communist regime, all social spheres were more or less controlled by communist ideology and subordinated to its goals. This was entirely true for education, which was supposed to be a tool for the communist rebirth of society. The policies in the field of continuing education and education for adults, which were the archetypes of lifelong learning, were also meant to fully serve the objective of 'communist building'. These policies were oriented in two directions: vocational education and communist rearing. Continuing education was closely connected with the development and demands of the socialist economy and was conducted in the form of qualification, requalification and specialization, organized in enterprises, and mostly by the trade unions. A key political document in this connection was the law 'for closer connection between school and life', passed in 1959, which introduced a system of post-diploma qualification in higher schools.

A specific form of continuing education was the preparatory courses for enrolment in higher schools, organized for young people of working class and rural origin. The graduates of these courses had the right to be enrolled as students without a competitive entry exam or by competing for a guaranteed number of openings (quotas). The courses were first created in 1950, abolished in the mid-1950s, then re-established in the early 1970s, and continued until 1989. The preparatory courses for young people of working class and rural origin were among the most effective mechanisms of social engineering, purposefully created and entirely controlled by the Party authorities. The goal was to 'create an intelligentsia from the working class circles that would be loyal to the People's Republic of Bulgaria and to the people's government' (Committee for Science, Art and Culture 1950, pp. 1, 3). Such courses for workers were organized in nearly all the socialist bloc countries, but comparative analysis shows that in Bulgaria their social engineering role was particularly prominent, inasmuch as they existed until the very end of the Communist regime and very obviously asserted the priority of social-class criteria over academic considerations (Boyadjieva 2010).

The educational practices in the sphere of non-formal education were in the form of cultural-mass and propaganda activities, where participation was mandatory for all the employed. These activities were conducted in enterprises, cultural centres and the mass political organizations (such as the Fatherland Front and the Communist Youth Organization), practically reducing education to ideological indoctrination in the cannons of Communist propaganda.

The Difficult Road Towards a Holistic Vision of LLL

In striving to quickly regain its place among the democratic states after the 'Gentle Revolution' of 1989, Bulgaria invariably demonstrated a clear willingness to assimilate European initiatives in the field of education. Due to the legacy of the past and the lack of sufficient institutional capacity, LLL remained for a long time an attractive slogan rather than a deeply understood and grounded orientation of education. This shortcoming was evident from the following:

1. the legitimation of LLL mostly by continuous reference to European initiatives;
2. the assimilation of the concept of LLL but not of the ideas that make it substantial: that is, the concepts of learning organizations, learning regions, learning citizens, and so on;
3. the marginal place given to LLL with respect to the basic educational normative acts and practices relevant to education;
4. the development of LLL policies not simply as tied to policies in other sectors – especially economic policies – but as entirely subordinated to them.

The economic concerns dominate completely the development of LLL policy in Bulgaria. This fact can be associated with the following:

1. Recent tendencies in the socio-economic development:
    a. The adverse demographic situation within the labour market, especially the long-term trends of decreasing active population and of an aging labour force.
    b. Instability of the labour market: a relatively high level of unemployment at the beginning of the twenty-first century (13.7 per cent in 2003), followed by a decline in unemployment (5.6 per cent in 2008) and a subsequent increase (10 per cent in 2010). An additional problem stems from the fact that the unemployment is unevenly distributed in social-demographic terms (the highest unemployment rate being among low-educated and Roma people) and geographic terms (big regional differences).
    c. A high level of poverty – 14 per cent of the population is defined as poor (National Statistical Institute 2005, p. 7).
2. The quality of professional skills of human resources:
    a. 22 per cent of the labour force has basic and lower education (National Statistical Institute 2010);
    b. there are deficits in the training of modern basic skills in the new professions;
    c. dequalification among the long-term unemployed, particularly the elderly.

Under these conditions, the need for a longer and more intense involvement of people of working age in economic life emerges as a crucial challenge for Bulgaria. Understandably, LLL is considered a major tool for coping with the problem. Most probably, that is why the LLL national policy rests on a relatively narrow understanding of the personal perspective on LLL: human capital and human resources are confined to people's professional qualifications and personal development is basically related to the person's employability.

Indicative in this respect is the fact that the integral National Strategy for LLL was adopted as late as 2008 and that the first national normative document entirely oriented to LLL was the National Strategy on Further Vocational Training 2005–2010 (Ministry of Education, Youth and Science 2004). Even when the role of LLL for personal development is taken into account, it proves to be ultimately tied, once again, to economic considerations. The national strategy for LLL succeeds to a considerable degree in encompassing all the various aspects of LLL. However, even within the national strategy the holistic understanding of LLL sounds mostly declarative, for the issue is in fact tied only to the development of the economy. The aim of the strategy is defined as:

> the creation of conditions for every citizen of the Republic of Bulgaria to develop his personal and professional knowledge, skills, and capacities for the improvement of his own prosperity and of the competitive capacity of the national economy by: 1) increasing the adaptability of every individual to the economic and social changes; 2) encouraging participation in all forms of LLL for professional and personal development. (Ministry of Education, Youth and Science 2008, p. 7)

It is evident that both the personal and the social purpose of LLL are defined here from an economic perspective. There is no mention of the role of LLL for the development of civil society and the formation of individuals capable of creative self-fulfillment and an independent civic standpoint. The stress is on the passive aspect of personal realization, that is, on adjustment to changing conditions of life.

The other predominant perspective of Bulgarian LLL policy is the social inclusion: LLL is regarded as a means for reducing poverty and overcoming social exclusion of groups at risk:

1. Different LLL policies are included in the National Strategy for Combating Poverty and Social Exclusion 2003–2007 (Ministry of Labour and Social Policy 2003). For their realization, the two National Action Plans envisaged measures for guaranteeing equal access to quality education for groups at risk (long-term unemployed,

disadvantaged people and people with low levels of education or qualifications).

2. According to the Employment Promotion Law, the employees receive funds for organizing:
   a. training for acquiring professional qualification for unemployed people below 29 years old;
   b. vocational training for the unemployed and former prisoners.
3. Within the framework of the project 'Social Inclusion', Roma Cultural Centres were established. They provide literacy training and professional guidance to people from this minority group.
4. In Bulgaria there are significant and long-lasting regional differences in economic development. One of the aims of the Employment Strategy 2004–2010 is to overcome the existing disproportion by means of various initiatives, including LLL practices. In addition, vocational training centres and non-governmental organizations (NGOs) devoted to meeting the specific needs of a given region have been established. Together with the community centers these (vocational training centres and NGOs) are particularly important for less developed and less populated regions as some regions do not even have any schools.
5. Under the National Programme 'Overcoming Poverty', in the 13 poorest municipalities, unemployed people are offered literacy courses, vocational training, subsidized employment and self-employment.

The 'Shifting Sands' as Persistent Bias

The radical change of the social conditions in Bulgaria after 1989 defines the social purpose of LLL and puts it in the service of various goals. Both before and after this turning point in history there has been an obvious vocational bias and, connected to this, a neglect for the 'self-directed learning' and 'promoting active citizenship' dimensions of LLL. Lifelong learning is mainly viewed as a factor for encouraging people's active participation in economic life, which is evident by the fact that LLL is viewed predominantly in the context of vocational education and training. Due to the persistence of this vocational bias, the existing liberating and enabling potential of new concepts such as 'learning citizens', 'knowledge society', 'learning cities/regions' and 'learning organizations' has been overlooked to a considerable extent in the contemporary policy documents and practices of LLL in Bulgaria.

Despite the undoubtedly positive impact of LLL for the adoption of a national strategy in this area, the attainment of a holistic vision for LLL is yet to come. Such a vision would imply an understanding that the implementation of LLL requires a radical change in the understanding of education and learning (including their non-formal and informal components) and a re-evaluation of all elements of the traditional educational practice – elements ranging from what knowledge and curriculum are, to the methods of assessment, organization, and management of the teaching process. This means that instead of realizing the LLL conception through separate policy documents or as additional policy elements in other social spheres, the conception should serve as a general inspiration. It should also be an organizing principle for the basic normative acts in the sphere of education, for instance, the School Education Act and the Higher Education Act.

THE BRICOLAGE INSTITUTIONAL CONTEXT OF LLL

The next paragraphs analyse the institutional context of LLL in contemporary Bulgaria. The LLL institutions functioning today in Bulgaria can be classified into several groups according to the historical periods of their appearance:

1. institutions created in capitalist Bulgaria (at the end of the nineteenth and first decades of the twentieth century), including evening schools and educational classes in prisons;
2. institutions created during the Communist regime, including societies for the dissemination of knowledge and centres for continuous education in universities;
3. institutions created in the years of post-Communist society: professional centres.

Especially important to an understanding of the contemporary institutional context of LLL in Bulgaria is the fact that the social development in all three historical periods of emergence of LLL institutions corresponded to different modernization models: (1) the National Revival model, which began with the establishment of a Bulgarian state in 1878 and continued until 1944; (2) the socialist modernization model, implemented during the Communist regime, 1944–1989;[1] and (3) the liberal, market-oriented modernization project, which developed after the 'Gentle Revolution' of 1989 (see Kabakchieva and Boyadjieva 2010). In addition to universal modernization features, each of these models had its own logic and underlying motive forces. Each should be the object of a separate analysis to show how the different logics underlying these modernization projects impacted on the formation and functioning of LLL institutions. Such a study would show which of the LLL institutions existing today are of a hybrid kind, combining elements of differing natures in their organization and way of functioning. In the present chapter we will confine ourselves to emphasizing the bricolage character of the general institutional environment of LLL in Bulgaria. For this purpose the following analysis will outline the institutional context of LLL as made up of institutions created in different historical periods, and we will show how each one of the LLL institutions changed over time.

Evening Secondary Schools

Evening secondary schools were the first institutional form of LLL in the history of Bulgaria. Their archetype was the evening schools and courses that date from the end of the nineteenth century. The National Education Act of 1891 introduced evening and Sunday schools for adults without primary education. In 1896 the publication of the journal *Evening School* began, and in 1896 the Bulgarian Teachers' Union adopted a teaching programme for evening schools. The National Education Act of 1909 made it obligatory for all municipalities to open two-year additional courses, which were day, evening or holiday courses (Atanasov 1977; Ilieva 2007).

Under the conditions of intensified modernization in the 1920s and 1930s, the number of such courses increased. The creation of evening schools was one of the mechanisms for raising the educational level of Bulgarians and, especially, of reducing the large percentage of people with no education or with uncompleted primary education. Evening schools in which general educational training was emphasized continued to develop throughout the years of the Communist regime as well. One of the main causes for their growth was the fact that, after the Communist revolution in Bulgaria in 1944 and the end of World War II, it was felt that the country had a shortage of specialists. This was connected to the fact that a large part of the previous bourgeois intelligentsia had been eliminated or removed from its social position.

Socialist modernization required qualified cadres, and in accordance with Communist ideology, these had to be created from working-class circles. The teaching methods whereby people could pursue studies while working were a good opportunity to meet this requirement. The first evening secondary schools (11 in all) were created in the autumn of 1946. The National Education Act of 1948 provided a legal basis, in addition to evening schools, for extramural education as well. At the end of the 1950s the first shift classes were created as the number of people desiring to get an education was growing. Especially important for the development of evening secondary schools was the Law for Closer Tie between School and

Life and for Further Development of the People's Education (1959), which established the legal equality of evening and extramural education to that of regular (day) education. The 1960s and 1970s was the time of largest growth in the proportion of adult students attending evening schools.

During the post-Communist years the situation of evening secondary schools changed substantially. Their number decreased mainly (but not only) as a result of decreased state funding for education. Only one evening school remained in most large cities and by the 2005–2006 year there were 25 evening schools with a total of 2618 students in Bulgaria. Evening secondary schools provided education for people aged over 16, and classes in primary and secondary education. Some of these schools, in addition to evening training, conducted training of adults in two shifts. There were two other forms in evening schools: extramural and individual. The individually trained students were generally people with specific educational needs.

As the first and oldest institutional form of LLL, evening secondary schools certainly played a positive role in providing an opportunity for adults to obtain knowledge and skills that would help their social adaptation and realization. Created in the course of the first modernization model in Bulgaria and continuing into the years of the Communist regime, they were a particularly important 'second-chance' institution, and demonstrated the commitment of the state to educating adults. In the years of post-Communist society, the individual inclinations and priorities became the leading consideration for people enrolling in evening secondary schools. Under present-day conditions, marked by shortage of funds, meagre state support and demographic crisis, the leadership of evening schools has introduced various mobile forms in order to keep adult learners in school. An important facilitation is the presence of school psychologists, while in some of the evening schools children's areas are provided where mothers, attending classes, can leave their children. Thus, in post-Communist social reality the stress was shifted to individual and institutional initiative and commitment, in order to compensate for the decreased state support.

Schools in Prisons

The first educational and training activities in Bulgarian prisons began in the 1930s, before the Communist era. These first proto-forms of LLL may be regarded, like evening schools, as elements of the modernization process that developed in Bulgarian bourgeois conditions before 1944. The first school in the penitentiary system was opened in 1956 (Ilieva 2007). During the Communist era there were 12 prisons in Bulgaria and, as each prison had a school, the number of students attending them was considerable.

In the post-Communist period, only six of the 12 prison schools have been preserved; the main cause of this decrease was financial. These remaining schools are designed to cover the basic types of prisons: (1) those for repeat offenders; (2) for first-time offenders; (3) for women and girls; (4) preventive prisons for juveniles. The qualification of the students and the certificates issued for completed degree of education are no different from those obtained in civil schools, which certainly increases the motivation of the inmates to take part in the teaching process. The reforms that have taken place in the prison system are aimed at affirming models and practices of treatment of inmates that guarantee their human rights and create conditions whereby they will benefit by their time spent in prison. In this connection, prison schools are actively contributing to making prisons a place in which prisoners will not merely be isolated, but will be prepared for social inclusion after serving their sentences.

The emphasis of training activities is on vocational training; the choice of qualification depends on the available production facilities. The choices include: food industry, metal processing, car repairs, plumbing, tailoring and sewing. Conditions are provided in penitentiaries for production activities in which students can apply what they have learned. A positive practice in the training of inmates is the use of all possible methods. In addition to day training the independent form of training is also applied; brief literacy courses are organized, and classes are held outside the school framework in the prison dormitories for the purpose of active communication between teachers and students.

From the viewpoint of our history, prison schools are institutional forms of LLL, which have been influenced by the three different modernization models. The main distinguishing feature of prison schools as a form of LLL stems from their purpose, which is to teach literacy and skills to people serving prison sentences. It is not coincidental that in Bulgaria these prison schools are under dual control. The prisons are under the Ministry of Justice but the training and curriculum are under the control of the Ministry of Education. This dual status, and the double inspection they are subject to, indicates their lesser inclination to changes and their structural inertia.

'Knowledge Societies'

'Knowledge Societies' are a non-governmental form of training and qualification of children and adults, which was introduced after 1989. They are the direct successors of the Georgi Kirkov Society for Dissemination of

Scientific Knowledge, founded in 1972 as part of the so-called Communist Party education, which was subordinated to the top level of the Communist Party. From an ideological perspective, the Georgi Kirkov Societies followed the strict canon of Communist ideas and values. Their main purpose was to help in rearing the Bulgarian population of all ages in the spirit of devotion to the communist ideal. Numerous local societies were founded as part of their network, conducting activities that included lectures, publishing and education.

Today's 'Knowledge Societies' inherited the structure and staff of the Georgi Kirkov Societies. The teaching is done by school teachers and lecturers from the higher and secondary schools throughout the country and the aim is to provide additional out-of-school training for all who want it, regardless of previous education, qualification or skills. The 'Knowledge Societies' offer a large number of specialized courses on foreign language training and computer skills, and a wide range of counselling services. Since 1992, as participants in European educational programmes, and in collaboration with Bulgarian and foreign educational institutions, the Societies have developed and implemented various international projects.

Compared with other institutional forms of LLL, the 'Knowledge Societies' working in the sphere of non-formal education underwent the greatest degree of development and change. From being a highly ideological institution, politically committed to the Communist Party and funded by the state, they turned into independently funded NGOs with a markedly pragmatic orientation and active international contacts. An in-depth and empirically based analysis would show whether, and to what degree, the elements and practices established under the conditions of the Communist regime are being reproduced (overtly or covertly) in the way the 'Knowledge Societies' function today.

Centres for Continuing Education in Universities

This institutional form of LLL first appeared in Bulgaria during the Communist era. The Law for Closer Links between School and Life and for Further Development of the People's Education (1959) was the legislative basis for the creation of requalification centres at higher schools. Today such centres exist in all universities and function in accordance with the respective statutes of the universities. Although the various centres differ in organization and specific objectives, their general characteristic is to organize and conduct teaching for obtaining additional professional qualification in a given field. The trainees are adults who want to increase their qualification on the basis of a specialized curriculum and obtain a higher educational degree or a new professional specialty.

Since their establishment the centres for continuing education at higher schools have undergone restructuring and changes. The main differences between the 'old' and 'new' institutional form is in the content and character of the training offered, but also in the way of funding, introducing new market mechanisms into the sphere of education. Today they emphasize initiative and innovation for continuous education and the search for new market niches of education services. The forms and kinds of training offered are also increasing in variety, and the number of courses and specialties is growing.

Vocational Training Centres

Vocational training centres are a typically new institutional form of LLL, created in the years of post-Communist social reality. The development of these centres has been influenced by European policies and is closely linked with the implementation of the National Strategy on Further Vocational Training 2005–2010.

Vocational training centres are part of the formal education system: 678 such centres had been licensed by the end of 2008. Vocational training centres are open to students aged over 16 and function in accordance with the Vocational Education and Training Law. The training centres issue certificates for vocational qualification in four different degrees of growing complexity, variability and personal responsibility in accordance with state educational requirements. Vocational training centres are licensed and coordinated by the National Agency for Vocational Education and Training (NAVET), established with the Vocational Education and Training Act in 1999 as a body under the authority of the Council of Ministers.

Vocational training centres are a new institutional form of LLL created as a result of political decision making at the highest level, being a body of the Council of Ministers. This indicates the commitment of the state to the development of vocationally oriented LLL. Most generally, vocational training for adults is under pressure from various factors: (1) the processes of globalization and the opening of the national labour market; (2) structural changes in Bulgarian enterprises after 1989; (3) international competition; (4) changes in the nature of work at the workplace and in the responsibilities of the individual employee. This mix of internal and external factors shows the complex influences that were interwoven in the creation of vocational centres.

The different forms of LLL in Bulgaria are marked by uneven intensity of change and, over time, they have undergone different kinds of influence. Some of them, such as the 'Knowledge Societies', changed deeply'; others such as prison schools have largely preserved the features of the old forms; while others such as evening schools and centres for continuing education at universities combine the 'old' forms of organization and practices with new ones. Some of the LLL institutions in Bulgaria initially appeared during the first decades of the twentieth century in the context of the first modernization model implemented in Bulgaria. Others were created in the years of the socialist modernization to directly serve its purposes, and ceased to exist after the 'Gentle Revolution'. The changed social environment after 1989 was favourable to the development of new LLL forms such as the vocational training centres for qualification and requalification. This variety of forms demonstrates the dynamic change of LLL over time but also the continuity in its development, as evidenced by the preservation of structural elements and concrete practices. This is how the bricolage institutional context of LLL was shaped in contemporary Bulgaria and came to include inherited 'rigid old' institutions and newly established 'flexible' ones.

THE ZIGZAG MOVEMENTS IN MAKING LLL A REALITY IN BULGARIA

A recently published document of the EU Commission examines performance and progress of the European countries under the Education and Training 2010 Work Programme. The main conclusion of the report with regard to lifelong learning participation of adults is that there is 'vast difference between countries as concerns both performance levels and progress'. There are countries (for instance, Sweden, the United Kingdom, Denmark, Norway and Iceland) in which 'participation in lifelong learning is becoming a reality'; at the same time, other countries (such as Belgium, Bulgaria, Greece, Italy, Latvia, Poland and Portugal) are 'falling further behind' (DG Education and Culture 2008, pp. 8, 13–14). While in the first group of countries there is evident consistency and systematic efforts to developing LLL practices, in countries such as Bulgaria the picture is varied and the consolidation of LLL is not pursued through building upon past achievements and practices but mostly by zigzag movements, which in some cases are not even sideways but backwards.

For instance, international comparative studies on LLL have shown that in the Bulgarian society positive and negative trends are often simultaneous. According to the data from the Labour Force Survey of 2009, only 1.4 per cent of Bulgarians aged 25–64 participated in formal or non-formal education and training[2] and, thus, the country lags far behind both the EU average (9.3 per cent) and the EU benchmark (set at 15 per cent to be reached by 2020) (Eurydice 2011, p. 13).

At the same time, the findings of the Adult Education Survey of 2007 show, somewhat surprisingly, that the participation of Bulgarian citizens in LLL forms[3] surpassed the average level for all European countries included in the survey: 36.4 per cent to 34.9 per cent (Eurydice 2011, p. 14). A more careful examination of the data reveals, however, that the prevalent LLL practices in Bulgaria had clear specificity.

The data show that there is an increase in the rate of participation of Bulgarian adults in formal education – from 1.2 per cent to 2.1 per cent. However, in a comparative perspective this percentage is still very small (see Figure A.1 in the Appendix to this volume). In addition, participation in formal education is still not a reality for the people aged above 36 years (see Figure A.3). Even more alerting is the fact that Bulgaria is among the countries with the highest social inequality. Demographic obstacles to participation in formal adult education, such as being a woman, older than 45 years, having a small child or living in the countryside, are among the most pronounced. Bulgaria is also among the 'leading' countries with regard to the existence of social barriers (low level of education, insecure or manual job, low salary) to participation in formal adult education (Róbert et al. 2011).

At the same time, Bulgarians seem to be much more inclined to participate in different types of non-formal education. Their participation, however, was entirely dominated by job-related activities as illustrated by the observation that Bulgaria and Hungary are the two countries in which participation in non-job-related LLL activities is remarkably low (Boateng 2009, p. 3).

Bulgaria also stands out significantly among the European countries with regard to the role of the employers as providers of non-formal education and training. In Bulgaria, employer-provided activities account for almost 70 per cent of all non-formal activities, whereas the weighted EU average is about 40 per cent (Boateng 2009, p. 8). The second most important provider of non-formal education – that is, the non-formal education and training institutions – is significantly lagging behind and provides 12.6 per cent of all learning activities. The Bulgarian formal education system is not active enough in initiating non-formal education activities, with only 2.54 per cent of the respondents indicating that a formal education institution had provided for their participation in non-formal education.

Equally interesting are the data indicating which categories of employment are least included in LLL activities. The unemployed and inactive categories account for the largest proportion of non-participation in all the countries, but Bulgaria, once again together with Hungary, holds a leading position and here the trend reaches excessive proportions: 92.9 per cent of the unemployed are not included in education or training, which is considerably higher than the average for Europe (75.7 per cent). As for participation in LLL activities of employed persons, Bulgaria has better than the average values for Europe (Boateng 2009, p. 4).

If we trace the trends over the years, we once again see a contradictory picture. The data from Continuing Vocational Training Survey (CVTS)-2 and CVTS-3 (Eurostat 1999, 2005) reveal few positive changes and even deterioration in some indicators related to continuing vocational training. For 1999–2005, the percentage of training enterprises increased negligibly, from 28 to 29. There was an increase in participation in continuing vocational training (CVT) courses and in the percentage of enterprises providing them. However, the percentage of enterprises with a training plan decreased from 22 to 9 per cent; and of enterprises having a special training budget, from 15 to 6 per cent.

Moreover, the Bulgarian companies in general do not feel a great need to raise the qualifications of their employees: 71 per cent of the enterprises in 1999, and 50 per cent of them in 2005, indicated as a reason for the unavailability of vocational training the fact that they did not feel a need for additional training of their employees (Eurostat, CVTS-2 and CVTS-3).

The cited data lead us to several basic conclusions regarding the process of making LLL a reality in Bulgaria:

1. LLL develops above all in the field of job-related activities. The person-formative and social aspects of LLL are very restricted and practically not displayed in any significant way.
2. The variety of the institutional context of LLL is mostly formal. In fact, enterprises are the basic LLL providers, while the institutions of formal education have not become significant and effective institutions as regards LLL.
3. Most of the Bulgarian enterprises have yet to build a culture of training; for them, becoming 'educating institutions' still remains a challenge and an important direction for future development.

Last but not least, since Bulgaria has been extremely responsive and eager to compromise with all the initiatives coming from European organizations, their assimilation has often assumed the character not of authentic learning and harmonization, but of conformist borrowing, imitation or copying. Thus, certain elements quite alien to Bulgarian realities of today were artificially implanted, thereby generating alienated and ineffective social practices.

For instance, Bulgaria was among the first to join the consultation process for the European Memorandum on Lifelong Learning, but the impact of EU policies on Bulgarian LLL policy works foremost through borrowing and copying as a rule, without serious enough critical assessment. As stated in the National Report on Education and Training 2010: 'Bulgaria has accepted in entirety the basic formulations and ideas of the Memorandum, and has begun to implement them' (European Commission 2005, p. 8). However, due to the general socio-cultural state of our society, including the inadequate administrative capacity, some of them have remained at the level of policy declarations and documents, or have been only formally accepted.

So, our analysis indicates that making LLL a reality in Bulgaria can be expected only in the long run and only through coordinated efforts on the part of all the interested institutions, including purposeful changes of public mentality patterns. Despite existing positive elements the national policy and practices in the area of LLL as a whole still lack order and continuity. Making LLL a reality amounts to a radical change in the very understanding of education and learning (including their non-formal and informal components) and a re-evaluation of all elements of the traditional educational practices ranging from what knowledge and curriculum are, to methods of assessment, organization and management of the teaching process. However, we should bear in mind that, as a policy and practice, LLL is deeply embedded in the general socio-economic and cultural context. That is why our progress towards making LLL a reality will largely reflect the socio-economic and cultural situation in the country, the character of its labour market, and the changing characteristics of the economic culture of enterprises.

CONCLUSION

Let us sum up the main results of the overall analysis. First of all we have to underline that the dependent – which is directed by external models – modernization of national societies is by its very nature hybrid or bricolage. In its empirical diversity it does not adhere to a universal historical trajectory, but to a variety of more or less parallel paths dependent on the national contexts. It is in this sense that we can consider as natural the conflicts between the social agents of the external modernizing influence on the one hand, and of the traditional, endogenous way of life on the other. The outcomes of these conflicts depend on the national self-esteem and the integrity of the recipient societies. As a whole, the societies characterized by stronger integrity and self-esteem are more likely to follow a creative pattern of modernization, while those with weaker integrity or self-esteem tend to follow, vice versa, a pattern of passive imitation and (self-)alienation.

The moral of the story is to be seen in two respects, theoretical and practical. The theoretical one refers to the significance of focusing our research interest on the creative, non-conformist dimensions of the LLL ideas and practices emerging in the different national contexts. The practical respect points to the necessity for more refined guidance by the EU, especially using instruments of LLL policy better adapted to the highly specific national realities of the member states.

NOTES

1. Without going into the intense debates on the nature of the socialist modernization model, and especially on how successful it was, we will mention that socialism has been defined as a modernization project for lagging societies, as a form of development designed for catching up with the more advanced countries on the basis of accelerated industrialization, the formation of cooperatives, and urbanization (Daskalov 2009, pp. 695–696).
2. The reference period for participation in learning activities was four weeks prior to the survey.
3. The reference period for participation in learning activities was 12 months prior to the survey.

REFERENCES

Atanasov, Zheko (1977), *Istorija na Balgarskoto Obrazovanie* (History of Bulgarian Education), Sofia: Sofia University St Kliment Ohridski Publishers.

Bauman, Zygmunt (2002), 'A Sociological Theory of Postmodernity', in Craig Calhoun, Joseph Gerteis, James Moody, Steven Pfaff and Indermohan Virk (eds), *Contemporary Sociological Theory*, London: Blackwell Publishing, pp. 429–440.

Beck, Ulrich (1993), *Die Erfindung des Politischen. Zu einer Theorie reflexiver Modernisierung*, Frankfurt am Main: Suhrkamp.

Boateng, Sadiq K. (2009), 'Population and social conditions', *Eurostat, Statistics in Focus*, **44**, 1–10.

Borg, Carmel and Peter Mayo (2005), 'The EU Memorandum on Lifelong Learning: Old Wine in New Bottles?' *Globalisation, Societies and Education*, **3** (2), 257–278.

Boshier, Roger (2001), 'Lifelong Learning as Bungy Jumping: In New Zealand What Goes Down Doesn't Always Come Up', *International Journal of Lifelong Education*, **20** (5), 361–377.

Boyadjieva, Pepka (2010), *Socialnoto Inzhenerstvo. Politiki na Priem vav Vissheto Obrazovanie prez Komunisticheskija Rezhim v Bulgaria* (Social Engineering. Admission Policies in Higher Education during the Communist Regime in Bulgaria), Sofia: CIELA.

Committee for Science, Art and Culture (1950), *Postanovlenie* (Ordinance), Centralen Darzhaven Arhiv (Central State Archives), F. 136, op. 5, a.e. 381.

Crowther, Jim (2004), '"In and Against" Lifelong Learning: Flexibility and Corrosion of Character', *International Journal of Lifelong Education*, **23** (2), 125–136.
Dale, Roger (1999), 'Specifying Globalization Effects on National Policy: A Focus on the Mechanisms', *Journal of Educational Policy*, **14** (1), 1–17.
Daskalov, Rumen (2009), 'Balgarskijat Komunizam v Historiografijata' (Bulgarian Communism in Historiography), in Ivajlo Znepolski (ed.), *Istorija na Narodna Republika Balgaria* (History of the People's Republic of Bulgaria), Sofia: CIELA, pp. 661–707.
DG Education and Culture (2008), *Progress towards the Lisbon Objectives in Education and Training. Indicators and Benchmarkers*, Brussels. Available at http://ec.europa.eu/education/policies/2010/doc/progress08/report_en.pdf (accessed 12 May 2011).
Duke, Chris (2001), 'Lifelong Learning and Tertiary Education: The Learning University Revisited', in David Aspin, Judith Chapman, Michael Hatton and Yukiko Sawano (eds), *International Handbook of Lifelong Learning*, Dordrecht: Kluwer Academic Publishers, pp. 501–528.
Eisenstadt, Samuel N. (2000), 'Multiple Modernities', Daedalus, **129** (1), 1–29.
European Commission (2005), *Education and Training 2010. Bulgarian Contributions to 2006 Joint Report of the Council and Commission*, available at http://ec.europa.eu/education/lifelong-learning-policy/doc/nationalreport08/bg_en.pdf (accessed 20 January 2011).
Eurostat (1999), *CVTS-2*. Available at http://epp.eurostat.ec.europa.eu/portal/page/portal/education/data/database (accessed 10 January 2011).
Eurostat (2005), *CVTS-3*. Available at http://epp.eurostat.ec.europa.eu/portal/page/portal/education/data/database (accessed 10 January 2011).
Eurydice (2011), *Adults in Formal Education: Policies and Practice in Europe*, Brussels: EACEA.
Field, John (2001), 'Lifelong Education', *International Journal of Lifelong Education*, **20** (1–2), 3–15.
Giddens, Anthony (1990), *The Consequences of Modernity*, Stanford, CA: Stanford University Press.
Grace, Andre P. (2004), 'Lifelong Learning as a Chameleonic Concept and Versatile Practice: Y2K Perspectives and Trends', *International Journal of Lifelong Education*, **23** (4), 385–405.
Ilieva, Kornelia (2007), *Obrazovanieto na Vazrastnite v Bulgaria i Obrazovatelnata* Politika (Education of Adults in Bulgaria and Educational Policy), Sofia: IZZ/DVV.
Inkeles, Alex (1983), *Exploring Individual Modernity*, New York: Columbia University Press.
Inkeles, Alex and David Smith (1974), *Becoming Modern: Individual Change in Six Developing Countries*, London: Heinemann.
Jarvis, Peter (2001), 'Questioning the Learning Society', in Peter Jarvis (ed.), *The Age of Learning. Education in the Knowledge Society*, London: Kogan Page, pp. 195–204.
Kabakchieva, Petya and Pepka Boyadjieva (2010), 'Conceptualizing Overlapping Modernities: A View from Post-Communist Eastern Europe', paper presented at the XVII ISA World Congress of Sociology, Gothenburg, July.
Kaya, Ibrahim (2004), 'Modernity, Openness, Interpretation: A Perspective on Multiple Modernities', *Social Science Information*, **43** (1), 35–57.

Lerner, David (1963), *The Passing of Traditional Society: Modernizing the Middle East*, Glencoe, IL: Free Press.
Meyer, John W., Francisco O. Ramirez, David J. Frank, and Evan Schofer (2007), 'Higher Education as an Institution', in Patricia J. Gumport (ed.), *Sociology of Higher Education: Contributions and Their Contexts*, Baltimore, MD: John Hopkins University Press, pp. 187–221.
Ministry of Education, Youth and Science (2004), *Nacionalna Strategija za Prodalzhavashto Profesionalno Obrazovanie 2005–2010* (National Strategy on Further Vocational Training 2005–2010), Sofia, available at http://www.minedu.government.bg/opencms/export/sites/mon/left_menu/documents/strategies/strategy_prof_edu-2005-10.pdf (accessed 5 February 2011).
Ministry of Education, Youth and Science (2008), *Nacionalna Strategija za Uchene prez Celija Zhivot za Perioda 2008–2013* (National Strategy for Lifelong Learning for the Period 2008–2013), Sofia, available at http://www.minedu.government.bg/opencms/export/sites/mon/left_menu/documents/strategies/LLL_strategy_01-10-2008.pdf (accessed 12 March 2011).
Ministry of Labour and Social Policy (2003), *Nacionalna Strategija za Borba s Bednostta i Socialnoto Izkljuchvane 2003–2007* (National Strategy for Combating Poverty and Social Exclusion 2003–2007), available at http://www.mlsp.government.bg/bg/docs/indexstr.htm (accessed 10 April 2008).
National Statistical Institute (2005), *Bulgaria: Predizvikatelstvata na Bednostta* (Bulgaria: The Challenges of Poverty), Sofia: Nacionalen Statisticheski Institut, available at http://www.nsi.bg/publications/Poverty_regio.pdf (accessed 7 February 2011).
National Statistical Institute (2010), *Obrazovanieto v Republika Bulgaria* (Education in the Republic of Bulgaria), Sofia: Nacionalen Statisticheski Institut.
Preston, Rosemary (1999), 'Critical Approaches to Lifelong Learning', *International Review of Education*, **45** (5/6), 561–574.
Róbert, Péter, Matild Sági and Anikó Balogh (2011), 'Formal Adult Education in the Context. The View of European Statistics: The AES Data SP 2', Comparative Report (TARKI).
Stark, David (1996), 'Recombinant Property in East European Capitalism', *American Journal of Sociology*, **101** (4), 993–1027.
Usher, Robin (2001), 'Lifelong Learning in the Postmodern', in David Aspin, Judith Chapman, Michael Hatton and Yukiko Sawano (eds), *International Handbook of Lifelong Learning*, Boston, MA: Kluwer Academic Publishers, pp. 165–182.
Wain, Kenneth (2000), 'The Learning Society: Postmodern Politics', *International Journal of Lifelong Education*, **19** (1), 36–53.

13. Formal adult education in the context of the transforming labour market in Russia

Anisya Khokhlova, Vladimir Kozlovskiy and Maria Veits

INTRODUCTION

Severe socio-economic and political changes after the collapse of the Soviet Union had a great impact on the transformation of the Russian labour market. In the late 1980s and early 1990s a sharp and chaotic transition began from a state-planned economy to liberal capitalism. Since this transition was rather destructive for most spheres of the newly forming Russian society it also caused a severe crisis in the labour market, which resulted in growing rates of unemployment and the inability of the system of formal education to meet the requirements of employers and learners. Starting from the 2000s a slow but stable economic growth began which had a positive effect on the development of the labour market. However, the recession of 2008 again caused transition period problems (stagnation of a number of industries, unemployment) and formed preventative governmental policy. According to this policy, formal education was supposed to fill the gap between the requirements of the labour market and the offers of the system of education by retraining the newly unemployed and those on the verge of cutbacks, as well as suspend the exit of young graduates to the labour market. However, those measures not only proved to be ineffective but also demonstrated the inflexibility of the system of formal education under changing socio-economic conditions as well as promoting the non-formal sector as a serious competitor in the education services market.

In this chapter we will focus on the transformations of formal education in Russia over the last decades and the reasons for its low ability to meet the requirements of employers, learners and international education standards. Our main argument is that despite the official rhetoric, the dynamics of post-Soviet education in Russia can be described as a way from, rather than towards, the creation of a coherent system of lifelong learning that would be responsive to the demands of the changing labour market. The chapter is based on analysis of the Russian legislative framework and official statistics relating to the education of adults as well as data obtained during our empirical research, namely a survey of adults who participated in formal education programmes in north-west Russia (1002 respondents) and in-depth interviews with representatives of the government, education institutions for adults, Russian experts on lifelong learning, managers of small and medium-sized enterprises (SMEs) and their learning employees.

HISTORICAL BACKGROUND OF THE CURRENT SYSTEM OF FORMAL ADULT EDUCATION IN RUSSIA

Formal Adult Education in the Soviet Era: Overview of Key Features

Even though it has been over 20 years since the collapse of the USSR, contemporary Russian adult education is still very similar to the Soviet system. In the 1990s a severe crisis in most social institutions, including education, had a serious impact on the system of lifelong learning, so today it still faces the consequences of those transformations and represents a range of various programmes rather than a complex and well-connected structure, as it was during the Soviet era. Therefore, provision of the background of the Soviet education system is crucial for understanding the operation of, and transformation in, the system of adult education in contemporary Russia (Shlenov, Mosicheva and Shestak 2005; Lomakina 2005).

During the Soviet era, the state paid much attention to adult education. The development of adult education was a very important component of the education system of the USSR in general (Vladislavlev 1978). In the 1920s and 1930s a programme was conducted promoting overall literacy at the national level, which also presumed the creation of a network of free and equally accessible education institutions at all levels. Later on, they became quite well developed in both large cities and remote areas. (Most small town schools would provide primary and basic secondary education, International Standard Classification of Education – ISCED – levels 1–2, and school graduates from provincial regions could easily enter institutions of higher education in the city because the system of education was largely standardized all over the country.)

Formal adult education reached out to broad strata of the population. For example, in the academic year of 1975–1976, out of 46 million adults involved in various forms of education, 10 million obtained basic education, 6.2 million of whom went to evening schools or learned by correspondence (Tonkonogaya 2000). The system of evening schools was highly popular in the Soviet era due to a large amount of people with very low or no education and was therefore quite well developed. Students had state financial support that allowed them to live moderately, but self-sufficiently. There was also a range of privileges and payments for working mothers. For people with disabilities there was a system of factories where they could work and this would give them a certain level of financial independence. Those factories had vocational schools attached to them, where people with disabilities could obtain a specialization guaranteeing them employment at the enterprises. However, overall, access to education for disadvantaged groups was a rather ambivalent and contradictory aspect of the Soviet education system: there were some quotas and reserved places for ethnic minorities, military persons, workers, and so on, which would make receiving education easier for them. On the other hand, there were also barriers for particular categories of the population, such as Jews or people labelled 'enemy of the people' and their families. Therefore, even though the proclaimed idea of the Soviet system of education was to provide equal opportunities to learn for all citizens, there were some hidden – and sometimes even quite openly demonstrated – ways of giving priority and better access to education to some specific groups.

The system of non-formal adult education also played a significant role in the USSR, although in the last years before the collapse of the Soviet Union it was increasingly seen as secondary in comparison with formal education (Osipov 1998). The system of non-formal education developed in two major directions.

Firstly, an expanded network of the so-called 'peoples' universities' was created all over the country. These organizations functioned under the umbrella of the All-Soviet Union society 'Knowledge' and would offer a wide range of generally accessible free courses, seminars, conferences and public lectures, thus providing numerous possibilities for adult learners to develop or update their professional and social knowledge and skills. Education programmes and curricula were developed with the active participation of the learners (Vladislavlev 1978). Although very popular and widespread in the 1970s, with the loss of financial and organizational support from the state in the 1990s this kind of non-formal education was doomed to disappear.

Secondly, in the USSR there was a comprehensive system of advanced training and skills improvement. In the late 1960s and early 1970s a network of postgraduate adult education was created that included: (1) institutions of advanced training and their affiliated branches; (2) faculties of advanced training and skills improvement; and (3) various courses of advanced training attached to higher schools and enterprises. In the 1970s, around 1.5 million adults were involved in these forms of education annually (Vladislavlev 1978). The number of institutions providing advanced training and skills improvement increased rapidly; however, this mode of non-formal education also suffered from the socio-economic changes of the 1980s and especially the 1990s.

Generally, between 1960 and 1985 the number of adults who enjoyed additional education services increased from 42.6 per cent to 60.4 per cent (Tonkonogaya 2000). The very status of education during the Soviet era was much higher, and possession of a degree generally guaranteed its holder a job placement. The state elaborated an entire scheme to allocate graduates among employers so that after graduation they would be given an assigned workplace. The system of patronage of enterprises over educational institutions was also beneficial both for education and for employers. Therefore, effective bridges existed between education offers and the demands of the employment system that turned education into a significant vehicle for social improvement. Employees had a wide range of opportunities to obtain a higher level of formal education or upgrade their professional skills while working.

Conditions of Adult Education Development during Perestroika and the Post-Perestroika Period

In the late 1980s and early 1990s, the Soviet system of education began to decay due to major financial difficulties, which were typical for all social institutions in the new Russia. The economic and social transformations of the 1990s led to a situation in which adult education reduced dramatically. For instance, according to a survey conducted in St Petersburg and the Leningrad region between 1990 and 1995, only 1.9 per cent (or 2.1 million people) of the total adult population were involved in various forms of education in Russia (Onushkin and Litke 1996). The sharp crisis in the system of adult education during Perestroika and afterwards was basically determined by the fact that education had been a hostage of the state's financial support, which very soon became insufficient. It was also not flexible enough to adapt to the rapidly changing external conditions, namely the collapse of the USSR and the failure of coordination between education and employment, as well as the crises at, and often closure of, various plants, science intensive enterprises and research institutions that formerly played an important role as mediators between education and labour. The new labour market and the conservative system of education developed in different conditions and at different speeds and thus moved in different directions. As a result, education (or at least its formal sector) and the labour market turned into almost isolated fields of the Russian socio-economic system.

One of the most negative changes of the system of education in this period was severe shrinkage of the system of vocational education, which started to lose its status and turned from an important mediator between learners and the labour market into a shelter for those who failed to enter higher education institutions. The portrait of their learners started to change and currently contains mainly representatives of the so-called 'disadvantaged categories', such as current and former prisoners, children from dysfunctional families, young criminals, early school leavers, orphans, people with disabilities, etc. Such transformation can be explained by general and higher professional education becoming more widespread and required due to the decline of education standards. In order to secure itself from complete destruction, the system of vocational education undertook a range of attempts to protect itself and partially update its education programmes, often making the paid ones most popular.

Another problem is the decreasing access to more flexible evening programs at different ISCED levels. According to the Russian State Committee for Statistics, after the collapse of the USSR, the number of evening schools decreased from 2100 in 1990–91 to 1300 in 2010–11 (see Figure 13.1 below). In 1970–71, when the system of evening schools was yet widespread and rather developed, there were 6900 evening schools in the country. In addition to this, the proportion of evening schools within the total number of education institutions is rather low: 1533 out of 55 786 (2008). In the 2007–2008 academic year, a total of 594 000 students (see Figure 13.2) were enrolled in evening, part-time and external general education programmes, which constituted only 2.88 per cent of the total number of students attending general schools. Unfortunately, statistics concerning the age structure of students enrolled in general education programmes in Russia is unavailable, so it is impossible to estimate the proportion of adult learners to the overall number of students.

Both the official statistics and representatives from vocational and evening schools state that the number of learners in these education institutions has steadily decreased over the last few years. As shown in Figure 13.2, the number of learners in evening schools, which was stable at the beginning of the 2000s, began to decrease in 2005. According to our respondents, even though the decline has not been sharp, it is quite stable and disruptive because most vocational schools are experiencing a growing lack of learners on an annual basis.

The continuous decrease of learners in vocational schools could be explained by the demographic decline of the Russian population in general and the implementation of per capita budgeting in the education system.

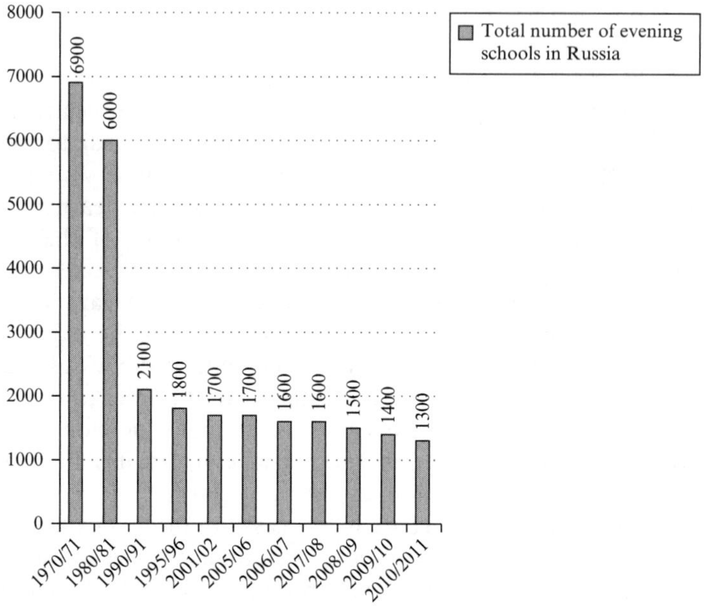

Source: Russian State Committee for Statistics (2010).

Figure 13.1 Number of evening schools in Russia

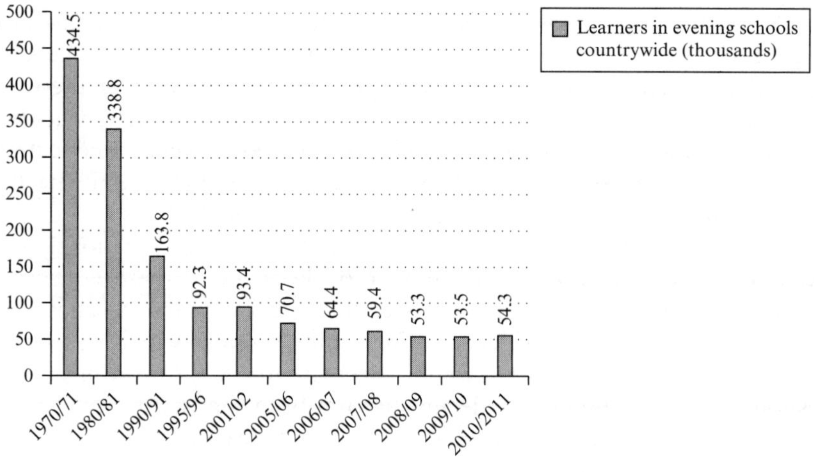

Source: Russian State Committee for Statistics (2010).

Figure 13.2 Number of learners at evening schools in Russia

Over the last 20 years, the population of Russia decreased from 148.3 million people in 1989 to 142.9 million people in 2010, and the decline continues (All-Russian Census 2010). Such a decrease affects the number of graduates in secondary general schools. Starting from 2007 there has been a noticeably sharp decline in secondary school graduates: from 958 900 in 2008 to 822 000 in 2010 (Russian State Committee for Statistics). This decrease in the number of secondary school graduates (9th and 11th grades) has led to a decline in the numbers of students in vocational schools and institutions of higher education. By the end of 2010, the number of vocational school students at ISCED levels 3 and 4 decreased by 36 per cent and 26 per cent respectively in comparison with the numbers from 2006 (Russian State Committee for Statistics).

Implementation of the per capita financing system of education may also serve as a reason for the decline of learners in vocational and evening schools. The budget of each education organization is now based on the number of enrolled students. This regulation puts the education institutions in a situation of competition for potential learners, and vocational and evening schools lose this contest to secondary schools, which try their best to make their learners remain at school and continue their education instead of attending an evening or vocational school. For the latter, this appears to be a serious challenge and a reason for concern, with regard to ensuring both a reasonable number of students and sufficient financial support on the part of the state. Therefore, both vocational and evening schools now have to rethink their outreach strategies and education programmes in order to attract potential learners, as well as lower the standards of their entrance examinations. The vice-principal of one of the vocational schools in St Petersburg, interviewed for the project, commented:

> We do experience difficulties enrolling new students. You know, we are now in the so-called 'saving mode' of learners because of per capita budgeting. They [general education secondary schools] do not want to let their pupils leave, so now we take anyone. We enrol all who come to us.

Vocational schools are also currently experiencing hard times due to the obsolescence of their range of specializations, teaching methodologies and equipment. Formal programmes offered by vocational schools are not competitive in the education and labour market and lose out to non-formal education courses that are usually paid for, but supply up-to-date specializations and short-term learning programmes. This makes non-formal programmes quite attractive for people more interested in learning a profession in a short period of time than in receiving a diploma from a formal education institution. However, vocational schools also cooperate with evening shift schools to deliver secondary education diploma provision, so students of vocational schools with an incomplete secondary school diploma may complete their education while learning a profession. Non-formal institutions are allegedly unable to provide a complete secondary school education and a diploma that would allow their holders to ascend the educational ladder of the formal education system.

Research carried out by various institutions and research teams in Russia shows that (potential) adult learners are fully aware of the transformations that the education system has undergone in the recent past and consider them to negatively affect the quality of education services, their relevance for future careers and the access of adults to education. For example, in the framework of an all-Russian longitudinal study by the Institute of Integrated Social Research at the Russian Academy of Science, respondents were asked whether they succeeded in obtaining a 'good education', with their answers reflecting the negative trend in such evaluations. The share of those respondents who claimed that they had obtained the desired 'good education' decreased from 54 per cent in 1997 to 39.3 per cent in 2003. The respondents also showed more doubt about their future possibilities to obtain the 'good education' that they had failed to get in the past (27.1 per cent in 1997 and 29.7 per cent in 2003). More people even started to argue that obtaining a 'good education' was not one of the priorities in their life plans (12.9 per cent in 1997 and 14.7 per cent in 2003) (Klyucharev 2005).

For the purpose of the study, in 2003 this research team divided the sample into three groups depending on the respondent's income. Predictably, respondents with higher income turned out to be more satisfied with the obtained education: 71.6 per cent claimed that they had obtained a 'good education' in contrast to 26.9 per cent of respondents with the lowest income. Forty per cent of the latter expressed doubt about their chances of remedying the unfavourable situation in the future, whereas only 3.6 per cent of the richest respondents said they would not be able to obtain the 'good education' that they had failed to get in the past. Finally, 22.6 per cent of low-income respondents confided that they did not see a 'good education' as one of the priorities in their life plans, whereas only 3 per cent from the high-income group said so. This shows that during the rapid development of the paid education services market, and given the generally low quality of life, the problem of equal access to tertiary education in Russia no longer remains a topical problem only for traditionally disadvantaged groups but rather turns into a systemic economic and social problem.

Older respondents (age group 40–49) showed more satisfaction with their education than younger ones (age group 20–39): 39.2 per cent of the former and 30 per cent of the latter said they had obtained the desired 'good education'. However, they turned out to be less optimistic about their future education paths: 39.2 per cent of them admitted they would like to obtain a 'good education' but they would not be able to do so. Among young respondents this share was 18.4 per cent. Young respondents excluded a 'good education' from the priorities in their life plans more rarely than older respondents: 4.3 per cent and 16.4 respectively (Klyucharev 2005).

According to another survey carried out in 2003–2004 by the Institute of Integrated Social Research, 75.1 per cent of adult Russians consider a 'good education' to be the major factor of success in the contemporary world. Only 25 per cent of respondents to that survey described their possibilities of obtaining the desired education as 'good', 47.4 per cent as 'satisfactory' and 21.8 per cent as 'bad' (Klyucharev 2005). Moreover, 64.8 per cent argued that in the last decade it has become more difficult to participate in education programmes, whereas only 20.4 per cent took the opposite view.

The Russian citizens were obviously unsatisfied with the changes that the education system experienced after the collapse of the Soviet Union. 27.5 per cent of respondents evaluated the situation in the education policy and education institutions of Russia in the period investigated as 'disastrous'; 28.7 per cent as 'recessionary' and 22.9 per cent as 'bearable'. When asked to evaluate education conditions in a historical context, over 50 per cent of respondents admitted to the success of the education system during the reign of Brezhnev; 18.4 per cent during the reign of Stalin; and only 9.4 per cent in contemporary Russia (Klyucharev 2005).

FORMAL ADULT EDUCATION IN TODAY'S RUSSIA: ACTUAL EDUCATIONAL OFFERS AND THE DEMANDS OF THE LABOUR MARKET

Transforming the Education System in the 2000s: Blending Old and New Principles

The relative stabilization of the Russian economy in the 2000s was marked by the development of an intricate conglomerate of traditions, innovations and possibilities in the education market. As a result, within the system of formal education, a range of learning opportunities is currently foreseen for adult learners. Some general secondary schools offer evening classes. Formally, studies in such evening schools have to be internal, although they presuppose lower learning loads than common secondary school programmes. However, in practice, learning often takes the form of instruction by correspondence: for example, pupils can pass examinations without attending lessons. Some institutions also offer part-time classes. However, as mentioned above, the proportion of students participating in evening, part-time and external programmes is currently very low and does not exceed 3 per cent of the total number of enrolees.

Adult education at other ISCED levels is organized in a similar way. In other words, officially the curricula for adult learners and younger learners do not differ, although the quantity of working hours within the evening education and correspondence course programmes (designed for adult learners) is significantly lower. In 2008, 375 initial vocational schools (out of 2644) offered evening and part-time programmes; 2.27 per cent of the total number of students attending secondary vocational schools were enrolled to evening classes; 20.4 per cent chose education by correspondence whereas 0.5 per cent chose external studies (Russian State Committee for Statistics).

Universities and other institutions of higher education (ISCED levels 5–6) offer a wide range of BA (four-year), specialist (five-year) and MA (six-year) programmes including those that presuppose evening, part-time or external studies. In 2008, there were 1134 institutions of higher education in Russia including 474 in private ownership. Four per cent of the students in public tertiary education institutions and 5.7 per cent in private institutions took evening courses; 42 per cent of students in public institutions and 69.6 per cent in private institutions chose correspondence courses; 2.5 per cent of students in public institutions and 1.2 per cent of students in private institutions chose external studies.

Interestingly, although evening education and correspondence course programmes at ISCED levels 2–6 were initially intended mainly for employed adult learners, young students who do not yet work – and in fact have never left full-time education – still constitute a significant proportion of the learners participating in these programmes. The basic reasons for such attractiveness of evening education programmes and correspondence courses for younger learners are the comparatively low level of competition and lower entry requirements.

Unfortunately, there are no official statistics regarding the participation of adult learners in formal education, either generally or by ISCED level. Correspondingly, there are no statistics on the participation of employed adult learners in formal education. Therefore, it appears quite hard to track the numbers of adult learners, and particularly employed adult learners, involved in the system of formal education and the changes in these numbers over recent years. However, according to the findings of our survey where adult learners in formal education were investigated,

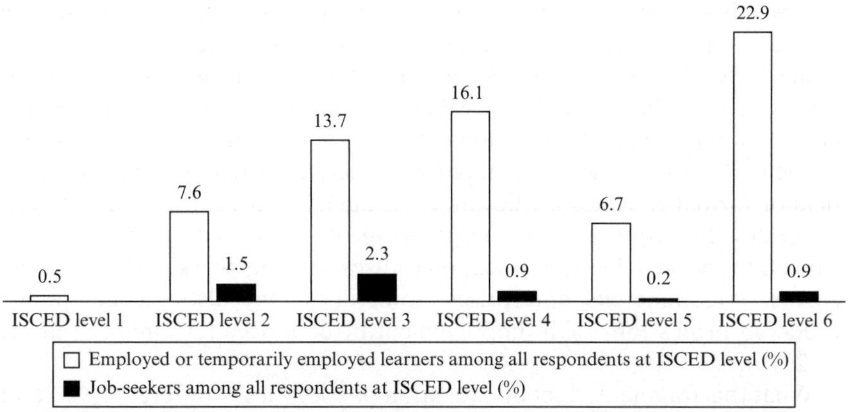

Source: Survey of adult learners in formal education (ALiFE) and formal education institutions (Subproject 3), LLL2010 – ALiFE 2007.

Figure 13.3 Involvement of employed and job-seeking learners in formal education

employed learners were generally involved in education programmes at ISCED levels 4 and 6 (see Figure 13.3).

The fact that the sample was not representative, since quotas were constructed to collect a sufficient number of answers from learners at all ISCED levels, must be considered. However, despite this, these findings are generally in line with the conclusions of the experts according to which employed participants in formal education in Russia predominantly enrol in programmes of higher education. It could also be concluded that the Russian system of adult education in its current form does not provide favourable conditions for adult learners to combine work and studies.

The sphere of non-formal education for adults in Russia includes additional professional training programmes, personnel retraining courses and professional skills improvement programmes as well as numerous other – mostly chargeable – education offers. Non-formal education in today's Russia is almost completely isolated from formal education. Mechanisms of recognition of prior non-formal learning and work experience by the formal sector do not exist in Russia as such. The system of formal education recognizes only prior formal educational experience: in order to enrol in any education institution one must hold a certificate or a diploma demonstrating the completion of a previous step on the education ladder. Many representatives of formal education clearly see the institutions of non-formal education as a potential competitor and often perceive cooperation with them as unacceptable and senseless.

Nevertheless, paradoxically, both private and public education service providers in the field of continuous non-formal education are often attached to existing institutions of general and vocational formal education. Such symbioses make possible the use of material resources disposable for the formal educational sector, such as buildings, equipment, curricula, and so on, and enlisting the services of teachers occupied in the field of formal education, who can consequently earn extra money. It also facilitates the acquisition of the government licence for the provision of education services. Private education centres not only work with individual clients or commercial enterprises; sometimes they also execute public orders in professional skill improvement or employee retraining (Veits et al. 2010).

What this fragmented set of education possibilities at different levels and qualities lacks, of course, is strict orientation to the target group – adults as actual and potential employees. The demands of the employers are also taken into consideration only rarely, and the policy of convergence of education and the labour market remains declarative rather than implemented.

Institutional Regulation of the Interaction between Education and the Labour Market

In recent years, policy-making in the sphere of adult education in Russia has been rather controversial and lacked consequent and coherent steps and measures to make lifelong learning programmes more accessible and widespread throughout the country. The fact that the system of adult education is insufficiently developed is to a great extent caused by the lack of government policy aimed at building a unified fully functional structure that would be able to satisfy both learners' needs and labour market demands.

Overall, the interviewed experts state that the issues of lifelong learning in contemporary Russia are not discussed to the necessary extent and that few processes aimed at the promotion and development of access to adult education are being conducted. Relying on the information gathered, we have outlined barriers that complicate access to education for (potential) adult learners, especially the employed, which are as follows.

The absence of lifelong learning as a coherent and structured education system that prevents formal adult education from stable and regulated development

According to the experts on adult education who we interviewed, the sphere of adult education appears to have been thrown upon its own resources – state officials are not engaged in the process of making adult education in Russia a separate but integrated part of the system of formal education. If some professionals have initiatives for the promotion of adult education, they must implement them themselves because the government is not so active in expanding the sphere of adult education, even though the pronounced strategy for development of the education system states the opposite. Existing adult education programmes require profound modernization and enhancement, experts say.

The lack of official practical initiatives to establish lifelong learning (LLL) as a coherent system

Hardly any initiatives come from government structures, either at the national level or at the mid-level of municipality or city administration. When they do, they normally use established and non-innovative adult education teaching methodologies: the module system is not widespread. However, when initiatives do take place, they all relate to the sphere of formal education – the systems of non-formal and especially informal learning are not stimulated, developed or regulated by the government.

The concept of LLL, which is rarely used and poorly understood by all actors

The lack of clear and mutual understanding shown by learners, education institutions, employers, government officials and other actors involved in the sphere of lifelong learning about all aspects of the term and the forms that adult learning can have prevents learners from clearly articulating the needs they have from a specific education programme and, consequently, deprives them from the ability to make a better choice in the education market. At the same time the services providers' lack of understanding of what lifelong learning is and how it should be approached prevents them from providing relevant education programmes that could be beneficial for learners.

The lack of programmes or a coherent system of privileges aimed at disadvantaged groups of adult learners (the unemployed, early school leavers, migrants, former military personnel, etc.)

The interests of most representatives of disadvantaged groups are hardly protected when it comes to enhancing their access to education; this is especially so in relation to adult learners. Reserved places for members of disadvantaged groups in vocational education institutions are lacking, although they exist in non-formal professional retraining programmes as well as reserved working places. Some privileges for learners with disabilities are available at ISCED levels 5–6, such as lower acceptance requirements. Sadly, this prerequisite has created a high level of corruption in higher education institutions, where graduates present fake documents stating a disability in order to enrol on more favourable terms. Generally, privileges aimed at representatives of disadvantaged groups are again very fragmentary and do not appear to be of a systematic and structured nature. For instance, there is no reduction in daycare fees for single mothers who both work and study.

There are also no specific programmes aimed specifically at the constantly growing number of labour migrants, many of whom do not have good professional knowledge or skills, including the ability to speak Russian at a moderate level. This group receives no professional training support, either formal or non-formal, from the government or employers. Meanwhile, the number of officially registered labour migrants to Russia from former Soviet republics has grown, especially a few years before the recession when the economic situation in Russia had improved and become quite stable. In 2004 there were 119 100 migrants, while in 2005 and 2006 their number increased to 177 200 and 186 400 respectively. A large leap of about 100 000 came in 2007 and 2008, when officially registered migrants numbered 287 690 and 281 600 respectively (Russian State Committee for Statistics). Needless to say, the number of unregistered migrants in Russian is much higher. In today's Russia the share of migrants in the country's labour force is quite essential, with natives of former Soviet republics coming to large Russian cities for employment as construction and road workers, cleaning staff and street market traders; that is, they take up jobs that require everyday communication and (at least) a basic professional knowledge. However, their chances of obtaining this knowledge are rather low and many employers suffer from poor communication with their foreign employees.

The sharp decrease in vocational education institutions at ISCED levels 3–4

The barriers described above somewhat correlate with the almost complete destruction of the system of vocational education, which can only with difficulty be restored in the coming years. The lack of vocational schools, where learners could acquire professional skills in a short period and be certain of future job placement (arranged either by a potential enterpriser or the vocational school) surely prevents people from engaging in lifelong learning.

The rapid commercialization of formal learning

According to Russian legislation, obtaining general and vocational education at ISCED levels 1–4 is free of charge and is expected to be financed from the consolidated budget. Russian citizens also have the right to obtain their initial higher education free of charge (assuming they meet the entry

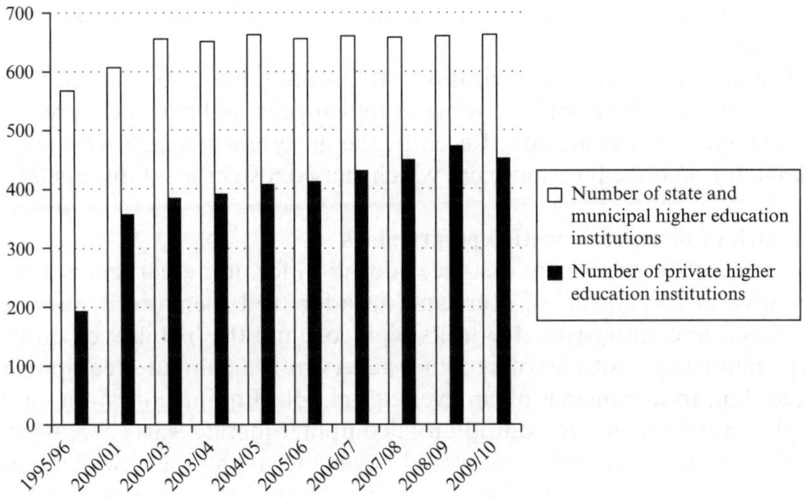

Source: Russian State Committee for Statistics.

Figure 13.4 Number of state and private higher education institutions, 1996–2010

requirements). However, subsequent higher education requires payment. In reality, most universities offer both paid and unpaid programmes. There are special quotas for free and paid places in every institution of higher education.

The commercialization of formal education is especially rapid at ISCED levels 5–6. Generally, the number of free (state-financed) places in the higher education system is gradually decreasing and in their place the number of paid full-time programmes is constantly increasing. In 1993, the share of students holding state-financed positions amounted to 93 per cent; as early as 2003 it had already reduced to 50 per cent (Sokolin et al. 2003). The number of private higher education institutions where education programmes are also paid increased each year and by the end of 2010 constituted 452, as opposed to 662 state or municipal institutions at ISCED levels 4–6 (Figure 13.4).

The latest tendency of the government to reduce expenditure on education (for instance, per capita budgeting) makes evening classes and learning by correspondence at university unprofitable, which results in a decrease in the two learning modes that have always presented a good opportunity for adults to obtain a higher education. The newly introduced range of higher schools in Russia is also expected to lead to insufficient financial support for those education institutions at ISCED levels 5–6 not included on the list of privileged institutions, forcing them into further commercialization in order to survive.

The increasing commercialization of education has also touched vocational schools, where paid-for programmes appear, and may also spread to secondary school education. Recently, the government suggested making secondary school education paid, which caused a significant discussion.

The lack of distance education programmes

The attempt to implement distance education for adult learners is a new initiative in the system of Russian education and therefore it does not yet function countrywide due to its high cost and the inability of quite a large number of both learners and teachers to use computer equipment. According to a principal of an evening school: 'Equipment is not easily implemented because in addition to a computer literate learner we need a computer literate teacher who would be able to use all the new technologies. However, such teachers are quite few.' Nevertheless, it must be noted that formal education institutions show interest in developing the system of distance education, which they see as especially important to learners from disadvantaged groups or employed students. A principal of an evening school insists on implementing such a system in her school because:

> there are students who really need it. For example, students with disabilities or those who have to make business trips often. There are not so many of these students, of course, but I understand how up-to-date and necessary it is nowadays. Moreover, we would like to be able to offer distance education to young mothers who cannot attend school because they have to babysit their children.

Nevertheless, even though distance education is being promoted as an alternative for adult learners and has started to be a solution for some learners (for example, prisoners), plans for the development of a network of distance education programmes throughout the country will not be realized soon due both to financial and human resources shortages.

The absence of legislative regulations covering adult education

Currently, there are no specific official regulations structuring the system of adult education in terms of legislation aimed at adult learners. There are, however, fragmentary regulations and laws targeted at some representatives of socially vulnerable groups, which operate at various ISCED levels. Additionally, the government does not encourage adults to participate in education, either by elaborating outreach strategies aimed specifically at various potential adult learners and especially those from underrepresented categories (early school leavers, people with disabilities, migrants, etc.), or by providing them with conditions that would enhance their ability to become involved in the education processes (free daycare centres for young working mothers, facilities for people with disabilities, etc.).

Formal Adult Education and its Relevance for Enterprises and Employees

Our interviews with managers of small and medium-sized enterprises show that today employers are sceptical about the quality and accessibility of formal adult education in contemporary Russia and are not eager to actively invest in their employees' formal education (Khokhlova et al. 2010). They generally see the expense of formal education programmes in comparison to short-term non-formal courses, and the lack of correspondence between the goals of education and the needs of the company, as two major problems of the contemporary education market. However, there are also some systemic obstacles in such cooperation of education institutions and enterprises such as the instability of the economic situation (particularly high inflation rates), which complicates long-term planning and investments; the incoherent character of Russian legislation (frequent changes in fiscal policy, certification rules, structure and function of the Ministry of Health and Social Development and the Ministry of Industry and Commerce), which makes cooperation even more unpredictable; and insufficient support from the state (for example in the form of tax concessions).

At the same time, many enterprises still see the high level of completed formal education as an imprescriptible condition of employment. Instead of educating existing staff, they prefer to play safe by taking on highly educated specialists or students. As a result, the staff are often overqualified and, in many cases, the working responsibilities of the employees do not correspond with their educational backgrounds. A high education level is seen by the management as the employee's private concern rather than an issue to be considered, both bottom-up and top-down.

On the other hand, employees see formal education as an important but labour-intensive and time-consuming means of gaining cultural capital and consider formal diplomas and certificates as a necessary pass to the labour market. However, they also criticize formal education programmes for their weak connections to common working duties, and describe a wide range of institutional, social, financial and personal barriers in their access to education (financial problems and limitations; the insufficient social capital of the learners; the lack of support provided for adult students by education institutions; difficulties in combining learning with work and household chores; problems with keeping up and competing with younger students, etc.). Under these conditions of uncertainty (especially at a time of global recession) many employees see education as a means of decreasing the risk of dismissal, whereas for potential employees education becomes a 'check-room' (Beck 1992) where they can wait until the unfavourable period is over and postpone their entrance to the inhospitable labour market.

LATEST INITIATIVES OF THE GOVERNMENT TO MODERNIZE THE SYSTEM OF FORMAL EDUCATION: EVALUATION AND PROGNOSIS

The current state of formal education in Russia in the context of the major political, social and economic transformations in the country over the last two decades shows a high necessity for reforms aimed at renovation and improvement of the entire system of education in Russia. Those changes should be aimed at decreasing the existing gaps between the requirements of the labour market, the possibilities of education system, and the motivation and abilities of learners to improve their qualifications.

Therefore, reformation and modernization of the education system appeared among the top development priorities of Russian government policy, starting in the early 2000s when the socio-economic and political situation in Russia began developing towards stability. Then in 2002, the Concept of Modernization of the Education System was suggested as part of the education development plan up to 2020. The Concept relies on four main principles: the provision of high-quality education and focus on the effectiveness of education institution management; the creation of an education system that corresponds to the requirements of the innovative development of the country's economy; provision of access to quality education regardless of citizen income or habitation; and a centralized system of work with talented children and young people.

Among other initiatives aimed at the modernization of education at all ISCED levels, the Concept presumes complex reformation and renovation of the system of vocational training, which would return ISCED level 3 education to its former positive status and subsequently generate interest in it on the part of potential learners. This is indeed an important aspect because, as has been mentioned earlier, vocational training programmes are in crisis now and require the government to undertake effective measures to allow the system of vocational education to function properly.

Special attention is paid in the Concept to the development of a lifelong learning system. The range of measures proposed by the authorities include: an increase in the number of lifelong learning programmes; the creation of a national system of education quality assessment (of both citizens and suggested education programmes); the provision of conditions for education mobility for learners; the implementation of developed education infrastructure that would allow a person to obtain new qualifications (electronic education resources, and a wide range of innovative lifelong learning programmes, including online programmes); the encouragement of citizens to improve their education, and so on. An ambition on the part of the government to take into consideration the development of lifelong learning as a system is a positive aspect of the overall education transformation programme. The example of the mid-1990s, when during the harsh economic crisis most industries collapsed and millions of employees lost their jobs and were unable to adapt to the new labour market situation, shows how important it is to develop a system of lifelong learning. In addition to that it is required to provide people with the necessary conditions for participation in lifelong learning programmes and increase their motivation for doing so. The development of a range of financial and other encouragement for employers investing in the education of their employees should also be included in the plan for the increase of lifelong learning at the national level. Lifelong learning programmes should be both formal and non-formal, and correspondent with each other: a bridge between the two is a prerequisite for a coherent system of adult education.

Currently, it is crucial for the education system to be closely connected with the needs of the labour market; the changes within the education system should start from lower levels, such as secondary school and even pre-school programmes. The problem of equal access to education, in terms of the regional, social and financial situation of potential learners of all ages, is also extremely relevant. Therefore, the fact that the state modernization strategy for the education system pays much attention to the problem of access to education and equalization of opportunities for children of pre-school age is a positive aspect of this government initiative. However, with social differences increasing, this measure is obviously not enough to combat inequality of access to education at all levels, especially at ISCED levels 4 and 5.

The Concept was rather harshly criticized by some education officials for its vagueness, inability to be realized within the set timeframe and some reforms that appear to be mainly negative, such as per capita budgeting (Smolin 2008). This financial system presumes that the budget of each education institution is not fixed and depends on the number of students. This transformation has a severe impact on the education system in general. On the one hand it causes a situation in which education institutions compete for students in order to get better funding, while for secondary schools it serves as a reason to encourage students to stay on at school.

However, for regional education the new provision is also having a major negative effect: most provincial schools are small and the number of pupils is constantly decreasing. Therefore, after the implementation of per capita financing, their budgets have been sharply decreasing. This leads to the closure of small schools and creation of large regional or district education centres, to which pupils of small schools get transferred. Thus, instead of building a network of small secondary schools located in small towns and villages that are located close to potential pupils, a network of large education centres located in larger towns is being created. Hence, those who live in small towns appear to be distant or even excluded from the secondary education system because of being remote to the new education centres. This may lead to a situation in which provincial learners appear to be totally uncompetitive, both in entry exams to vocational and higher education institutions, and in the labour markets in larger cities, to where most of them relocate to pursue career and job placements.

Other incentives relating to improvements in the Russian education system include two major projects: a national project entitled Obrazovanie ('Education') and the law entitled On Compulsory Full General School Education (in force since 1 September 2007). The Obrazovanie project was launched in 2006 as one of the main implementation instruments for the goals set out in the Concept. The project is based on four main principles:

1. Determination of so-called 'points of development'. The state aims to encourage institutions and entire regions in the implementation of innovative education practices and support of teachers and talented learners. The most effective practices and initiatives receive financial and other support from the state.
2. Provision of access to education and equal enrolment possibilities. This principle presumes measures aimed at the improvement of infrastructure in education institutions countrywide.
3. Introduction of new management strategies and mechanisms. There is a plan to implement new management schemes in education institutions that would provide closer connection between the education system and the labour market.
4. Major financial supply transformations for education institutions. Financing will be budgeted to provide realization of education institution development programmes, which will increase their financial independence. Finance distribution within the education system will be based on per capita budgeting, with the special demands of learners in each region considered separately. Bonus programmes for teachers will also be implemented.

In order to enhance education opportunities and provide better self-realization in education and careers, a law entitled On Compulsory Full

General School Education was implemented. The law presumes implementation of a countrywide obligation for citizens to complete three stages of general education: primary (ISCED level 1), non-full secondary education (ISCED level 2), and full secondary education (ISCED level 4).

The law, implemented in 2007, may be seen as a rather positive step towards including early school leavers and people with incomplete secondary school diplomas in the lifelong learning system and, consequently, giving them a chance to improve their career paths. According to this law, all Russian citizens are obliged to obtain a complete secondary school education (ISCED level 4), which may encourage those with incomplete secondary school diplomas to turn to evening school in order to increase their level of education, allowing them to apply to higher education institutions. The same reason may attract learners to the vocational schools, which have also been significantly affected by the new socio-economic conditions.

This short overview of current reforms shows that the education system reforms are of a rather chaotic nature, which makes their implementation and development within the overall educational sphere quite complex. In addition, the planned intentions and measures being undertaken often contradict each other: on the one hand, the strategy of education modernization promotes enhancement of equal access to education; while on the other hand we face a rather clear tendency to increase commercialization within education at all levels.

CONCLUSION

Russia today lacks a coherent system of lifelong learning, the importance of which for the sustainable development of the national economy and the coordinated functioning of the education sector and the labour market has long been recognized in Europe and North America and is widely discussed in both political and scientific discourse (Dave 1976; Dohmen 1996; Jarvis et al. 1999; Jarvis 2004; Field 2004). Even though there are numerous programmes for adult learners at all ISCED levels, a system of adult education does not really exist as such in Russia. The education programmes available for adult learners are rather fragmentary and are not embraced by a single unified structure. Adult education programmes are scattered within the system of education (evening schools, advanced training, etc.) and do not represent a separate sector with its own rules, conditions, content and specific teaching methodologies. Adult education in Russia does not constitute a separate branch within the system of formal education, with the exception of postgraduate programmes and doctoral studies. Adults have the opportunity to bridge gaps in their education at any ISCED level, but in most cases the available education possibilities are integrated into the general system of elementary, secondary (general and vocational) and higher education and are accessible both to adult learners and to younger learners who have never left full-time education. The fragmentary attempts to develop education programmes for adult learners are complicated by such factors as the lack of a legislative basis that would regulate such education activities, and the lack of teaching methods and methodologies targeted directly at adults. The major principle of adult education provision is the opportunity of learners to combine education with full-time work. In practice, this principle is realized through the system of evening classes and correspondence learning. The curricula designed for this system also presuppose greater emphasis on self-instruction.

Generally, formal education remains a product of the Soviet plan system and is unable to adapt to and meet the demands of the nascent capitalist labour market. The newly undertaken policy measures aimed at conducting systemic modernization reforms of formal education have proven to touch mainly upon its formal aspect; meanwhile core problems such as a lack of financing result in an absence of modernized education programmes and updated equipment, and a deficiency of qualified and motivated teaching staff, especially at the level of vocational education. Other problems including a high level of bureaucracy preventing innovative developments within the education system, and a lack of any form of connection between education and the labour market (graduates' allocation to enterprises, patronage of enterprises over education institutions, a system of internship, etc.) are not being taken into consideration by the government. These factors and an inability to effectively use the positive heritage of the Soviet education system have become the largest obstacles to bridging the gap between the formal education system and the labour market.

REFERENCES

ALiFE (2007), Survey of adult learners in formal education (ALiFE) and formal education institutions (Subproject 3), LLL2010 – ALiFE 2007.
All-Russian Census (2010), available at: http://www.perepis-2010.ru/results_of_the_census/results-inform.php.
Beck, Ulrich (1992), *Risk Society: Towards a New Modernity*, New Delhi: Sage.
Dave, Ravindrakumar H. (ed.) (1976), *Foundations of Lifelong Education*, Oxford: UNESCO Institute for Education and Pergamon Press.
Dohmen, Guenter (1996), *Lifelong Learning: Guidelines for a Modern Education Policy*, Bonn: Federal Ministry of Education, Science, Research and Technology.
Field, John (2004), *Lifelong Learning and the New Social Order*, Stoke on Trent: Trentham Books.

Jarvis, Peter (2004), *Adult Education and Lifelong Learning: Theory and Practice*, London, New York: Routledge Falmer.

Jarvis, Peter, John Holford and Colin Griffin (1999), *Theory and Practice of Learning*, London: Kogan Page.

Khokhlova, Anisya, Maria Veits and Vladimir Kozlovskiy (2010), *Patterns of Formal Education Support in Russian Small and Medium-Sized Enterprises*, SP 4 Country Report, Lifelong Learning 2010: Towards a Lifelong Learning Society in Europe: The Contribution of the Education System. Available at: http://lll2010.tlu.ee/folder.2006-02-22.7534376022/subproject-4-survey-of-enterprises/sp4-national-reports-adult-formal-education-and-sme-s/sp4_report_rus.doc/view.

Klyucharev, Gennadiy (ed.) (2005), *Непрерывное образование и потребность в нем* (Continuing Education and Demand for It), Moscow: Наука.

Lomakina, Tatyana (2005), *Концепция непрерывного профессионального образования* (The Concept of Continuing Vocational Education), Moscow: ИТИП РАО.

Onushkin, Viktor and Fyodor Litke (1996), *Развитие образования взрослых в России, Северо-Западном регионе, Санкт-Петербурге и Ленинградской области 1990–1995 гг.* (The Development of Adult Education in Russia, Northwest Region, St. Petersburg and Leningrad Region in 1990–1995), Saint Petersburg: Статистика.

Osipov, Alexandr (1998), *Общество и образование* (Society and Education), Novgorod: НовГУ.

Russian State Committee for Statistics (2010), available at: http://www.gks.ru/.

Shlenov, Yuriy, Irina Mosicheva and Valeriy Shestak (2005), 'Непрерывное образование в России' (Continuing Education in Russia), *Высшее образование в России* (Higher Education in Russia), **3**, 36–49.

Smolin, Boris (2008), *Альтернативы, Российское образование в 2020-м: программа для долгожителей?* (Alternatives, Russian Education in 2012: A Program for Long-Livers?) Available at: http://alternativy.ru/ru/node/678.

Sokolin, Vladimir et al. (eds) (2003), Россия в цифрах (Russia in Figures), *Крат. стат. сб.* (Brief Collection of Statistics), Moscow: Russian State Committee for Statistics.

Tonkonogaya, Evgeniya (ed.) (2000), *Образование взрослых на рубеже веков: вопросы методологии, теории и практики. Том I. Социально-экономические и правовые предпосылки развития образования взрослых. Книга 1. История развития образования взрослых в России* (Adult Education at the Turn of the Century: The Issues of Methodology, Theory and Practice. Vol. I. Social, Economic and Legal Preconditions of Adult Education Development. Book 1: The History of Adult Education Development in Russia), Saint Petersburg: ИОВ РАО.

Veits, Maria, Anisya Khokhlova and Vladimir Kozlovskiy (2010), 'Participation of Adults in Lifelong Learning in Russia: Possibilities and Barriers', *Lifelong Learning 2010: Towards a Lifelong Learning Society in Europe: The Contribution of the Education System*, St Petersburg: Nauka, pp. 126–156.

Vladislavlev, Alexey (1978), *Непрерывное образование: проблемы и перспективы* (Continuing Education: Problems and Prospects), Moscow: Мол. Гвардия.

14. Adult education in Lithuania: towards increasing employability and social cohesion, or neither?

Meilutė Taljūnaitė, Leta Dromantienė, Irena Žemaitaitytė and Liutauras Labanauskas

INTRODUCTION

To paraphrase Cervero and Wilson (2005, p. 4), it can be said that European Union (EU) and member-state policies (not only the literature) have always promoted optimistic views about adult education. However, Jarvis (2004, p. 19) explains that 'despite the rhetoric about learning enriching our humanity, even our spirituality and the democratic society, the main emphasis of planning in all of these documents is that the end-result of learning will be employability'. We add 'social cohesion' to Jarvis's statement, as in this chapter we seek to explore whether lifelong learning policies and practices in Lithuania have something in common with employability and social cohesion goals. Our chapter draws on data from a 6th Framework project entitled 'Towards a Lifelong Learning Society in Europe: the Contribution of the Education System' (LLL2010). The first section presents an overview of the new trends of the policy context of lifelong learning in Lithuania. The next section provides a brief review of literature on employability and social cohesion. In the subsequent three sections we focus on employability and social cohesion as essential in maintaining and securing full employment. A brief discussion of the complexities of these two concepts and how they are operationalized in relation to the politics of adult education in Lithuania is presented. The chapter ends with a conclusion where key points of our discussion are summarized.

GENERAL POLICY CONTEXT OF ADULT EDUCATION IN LITHUANIA

The Lithuanian education system was inherited from the legacy of the former Soviet Union. As the state sovereignty and legitimacy issues easily spill over into the education, citizenship or justice domains, the most immediate tasks of the government after the restoration of Lithuania's independence in 1990 were:

- restructuring education systems in policy, financial management, standards, and centralization;
- the expansion of opportunities for learning choices by establishing the principles of humanity and democracy;
- improvements in education assessment and quality assurance.

Here we offer a brief chronological and historical explanation of the changes that took place in the education policy domain in the period of 1990–2010. Three rather distinct periods in the Lithuanian lifelong learning trajectory during these 20 years can be traced (Taljūnaitė and Labanauskas 2010). In the first period, starting in the early 1990s and coinciding with Lithuania's 'Singing Revolution' movement for independence, education reform became a focus of public debate. In the *Concept of National School* (1988–1991) education was first and foremost viewed as an important vehicle of nation-building and fostering economic and political stability. The Law on Education was adopted in 1991 (with subsequent amendments in 1993, 1994, 1995 and 2011). The second period began in mid-1992, when the Lithuanian government published a document entitled *The General Concept of Education in Lithuania* (1992), which stated that 'the education system is based on European cultural values'. This document is by far the most important and influential document, and turned from the education process to 'the result of education' as the main goal. It set out fundamental guidelines for the reform of the education system, and following its approval by the government it has been the basis for the implementation of education reforms since then.

The country's burning ambition to join the EU (which happened in spring 2004) was a precondition for the main stakeholders in education (ministries, universities, academics, etc.) to engage in discussions on the European Commission (EC) Memorandum on Lifelong Learning in May–June 2001. This marked the third period in Lithuania's trajectory towards lifelong learning. As a result of the discussions in mid-2001 new terms and concepts appeared in policy documents and entered general academic discourse on education. The new concepts – such as adult education, learner's competences and involvement in the labour market – have been introduced into Lithuanian education policy.

In 'post-Lisbon' Lithuania, the development of policy, process and the system of adult education has gained particular importance and adult education was further shaped in line with laws and strategies on education. In the light of national goals – the democratization of society, a strengthening of the market economy and accession to the European Union – three documents set up new strategic trends in the development of education. In the first of them, *The Republic of Lithuania Law on Education* (2003), the goal of education was stated as being to ensure conditions enabling a person to acquire the basics of civic and political culture that embody democratic traditions, and to develop the abilities and experience needed by a person for competence as a citizen of Lithuania and a member of the European and global community as well as of a multicultural society. *The National Education Strategy Guidelines for 2003–2012* highlighted the mission of education: to assist a person in the acquisition of professional qualifications which meet the standards of modern technologies, culture and individual abilities, and to provide for lifelong learning, to seek new competencies and qualifications instrumental for the person's career advancement and for giving meaning to their life.

Since 2004 Lithuania has had an explicit Lifelong Learning Implementation Strategy (with amendments in 2008) which aims to foresee and define areas for lifelong learning development and measures for implementing these goals, with particular emphasis on professional training and adult continuous learning. In April 2009 the Lithuanian Parliament (Seimas) passed a new Law on Higher Education and Research, which aims towards a rather radical restructuring of the higher education system. The declared objective of the 2009 law is to improve higher education and training through:

1. a new funding model for higher education ('student's basket');
2. internationalization and marketization of higher education; and
3. optimization of the network of higher education institutions (state-owned universities, colleges and research institutes).

The reform directly responded to the key aims of the National Education Strategy 2003–2012: lifelong learning and social justice in education, rational use of resources, quality of education and responsible management. The 2009 reform of higher education implemented a new higher education institution management model and determined their wider social responsibilities, encouraged the merger of higher education institutions and competition between universities and colleges for quality of education. Although all three reform objectives stated above were interrelated, the first objective, i.e. a new funding model for higher education (the so-called 'student's basket'), had some direct potential implications for adult education. The 'student's basket' consisted of funds allocated to secondary school leavers who achieved the best academic results. In other words, the best-performing secondary school leavers were guaranteed tuition fee-free studies at any higher education institution in Lithuania at which they enrolled. The secondary school leavers who had lower academic achievements were supposed to pay full tuition fees. Despite the fact that all students in higher education were offered the possibility to receive state-guaranteed and nationally administered bank loans to cover tuition fees, living expenses and so on, the 2009 reform sparked heated debates in the academic, political and wider milieus about the overall purpose of education. These debates were centred on two views: education as a cost and education as a social investment. Moreover, the reform was introduced in times of sharp economic recession, and consequently was regarded by many students, academics and even some stakeholders in education as central in perpetuating more inequality. As far as adult education was concerned, since 2009 analysis and evaluation of the consequences of the reform was centred on two issues: the loss of human capital and access to adult education.

Our short overview reveals that since 1990, the Lithuanian education system evolved from a highly ideological and domestic one, to a more open, 'internationalized' (or 'internationalizing') one, and – at least at the policy level – an education system for all. As a result of the gradual implementation of education policies and strategies, a system of formal and non-formal adult education providers was formed with shared responsibilities by the main organizers such as government bodies, local institutions and non-governmental organization (NGOs), including adult learning centres, the Lithuanian Association of Adult Education, centres of vocational training, municipalities, the Labour Exchange Office, employers' associations, and the Lithuanian Labour Federation among many others. All in all, Lithuanian education policy reforms were highly significant for creating the possibility (and challenge) of turning from social capital formation to human capital development goals in adult education.

THE LINKS BETWEEN EDUCATION, EMPLOYMENT AND SOCIAL COHESION

Durkheim provided the first systematic theorization of the historical role and social function of mass education in terms of social integration, leaving a legacy that links education with social cohesion: social cohesion was seen as the glue that kept members of a social system together (Durkheim 1956, quoted in Jupp et al. 2007, p. 142). Education is directly linked with the situation of being employed. This is an axiom of the modern world, as learning enables people to play a full part in their community, family, neighbourhood, workplace and public space (Conceição et al. 2003). In the Durkheimian perspective of organic solidarity, working together fosters social cohesion (Guibet Lafaye 2009).

The literature on social cohesion suggests two dimensions of enquiry: the inequality dimension and the social capital dimension (Fontainha 2005). These dimensions are interrelated in our analysis: we regard education as an 'opportunity' for employment and thus, belonging to society. Lifelong learning in contemporary Europe has been identified as the means by which states can both retain their competitive economic edge and achieve social cohesion and stability. Employee skills must be constantly renewed to enable them to meet the challenges of evolving technology, increasing internationalization and local and global territorial redistribution of demographic resources. Demographic factors (e.g. the preponderance of older people) have caused people to stay in the labour market longer, and rapid technological change requires and necessitates continuous learning.

As a member of the European Union, Lithuanian society faces these global as well as national challenges. The development of adult education opportunities and non-formal training has become very important in order to help learners stay in the labour market and successfully pursue a career. The interests of the state, employers and individuals coincide in this sphere, as it is widely understood that neither the individual without adequate qualifications, nor employers without a qualified workforce, will be able to compete in the labour market, be it national or globalized. The competitive enterprise acts as a link between the employer and the individual in the competition by the state in the European and world markets (Žemaitaitytė 2007). Thus the interplay of learning individual, learning organization and learning society is an essential condition not only for employment, but also for economic development (see Figure 14.1).

PARTICIPATION IN LIFELONG LEARNING

Adult participation in lifelong learning varies greatly in Europe and the failure to reach the Lisbon target of 12.5 per cent participation in lifelong learning proves to be imminent for many countries, Lithuania being no exception. Only 4.5 per cent of Lithuanians aged 25–64 years participated in lifelong learning in 2009 (see Figure 14.2). According to the survey of

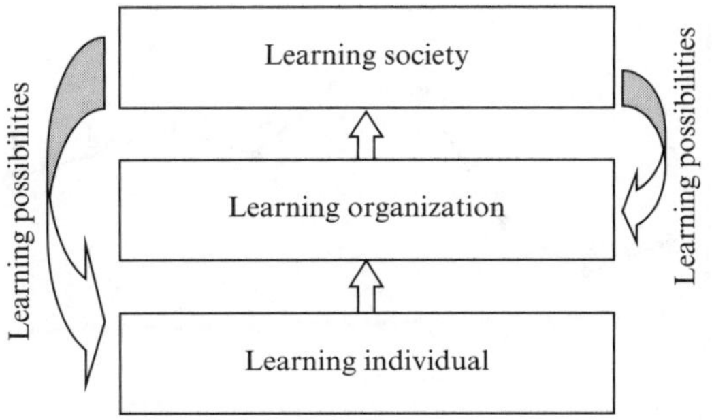

Source: Žemaitaitytė (2007).

Figure 14.1 Interplay of learning individual, learning organization and learning society

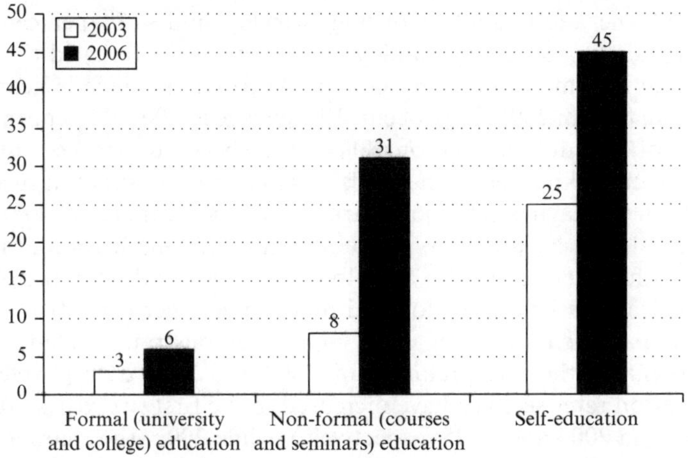

Figure 14.2 Adult learners by forms of learning in Lithuania, %, one year reference

adult education carried out by Statistics Lithuania in 2006 (see Statistics Lithuania 2007), within one year 55 per cent of the adult learners participated in formal, non-formal and informal learning. This is twice more than in 2003 (28 per cent; EU average in 2003: 42 per cent). There were more women than men (58 and 52 per cent respectively) and there were more participants residing in urban than in rural areas (61 and 42 per cent respectively). Various courses, seminars, conferences were attended by 31 per cent of the adult population. This is four times more than in 2003: 8 per cent (see Figure 14.2).

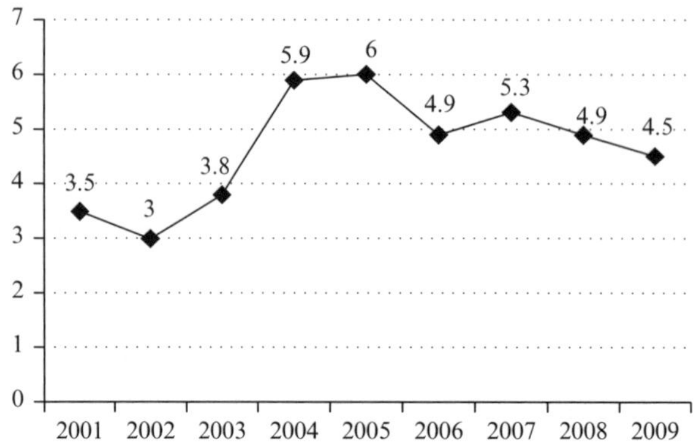

Figure 14.3 Participation in lifelong learning in Lithuania, aged 25–54, %

Half of the adults studied during working hours, 74 per cent were paid for training courses by employers. Survey results revealed that those involved in informal education made up 45 per cent, which is nearly two times more than in 2003: 25 per cent (EU average in 2003: 33 per cent). The majority of the adult population (80 per cent) believed that the continuing improvement of knowledge and skills was more important for a successful career than for staying in the job market (Statistics Lithuania 2007).

As revealed in Figure 14.3, participation in lifelong learning rates for Lithuania have tended to ebb and flow since 2001, although the number of adult learners has never totalled more than 6 per cent. It is evident that the participation rates have never demonstrated steady trends and this makes the interpretation of 2003 and 2006 data problematic. Participation rates seem to have increased in the first two years after EU accession (in 2004 and 2005 respectively), while 2007 (the characteristics of which were unprecedented economic boom, followed by sharp recession at the end of 2008) marks the beginning of a gradual decrease in participation rates.

The recession seems to have influenced participation in lifelong learning, as 2008 and 2009 (characterized by deep economic decline and increased unemployment) saw further drops.

THE SOCIAL PROFILES OF ADULT LEARNERS

Investigations into the social profiles of Lithuanian adult learners reveal significant differences in demographic variables. Firstly, there is a gender gap. Women are engaged in learning activities to a higher extent than

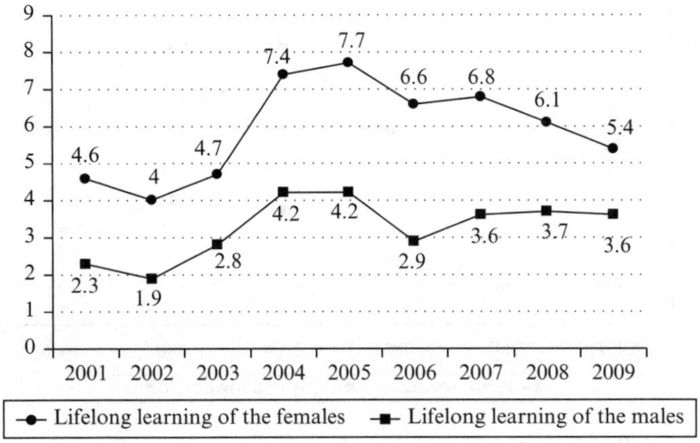

Figure 14.4 Participation in lifelong learning in Lithuania by gender (aged 25–54), %

men (Figure 14.4). Consequently the unemployment level of women has almost always been lower than that of men, yet despite women being more educated, average gross hourly earnings for women in 2009 were 86.5 per cent compared to those of men (Statistics Lithuania 2010a, 2010b). These data signal possible (cultural or structural) barriers to equal treatment of both genders in the Lithuanian labour market that undermine the power of education to remove these barriers.

In Lithuania urban residents accounted for 50 to 80 per cent of training participants, because many more training services are available in urban areas and the participation in training by residents of rural areas is not increasing (see Table 14.1 and Figure 14.5). If we look at unemployment rates we see evidence that there was more unemployment amongst urban

Table 14.1 Adult learners in Lithuania by sex and residence, %, one year reference, 2007

	Total	Men	Women	Urban	Rural
Participated in some kind of learning, including short courses and informal learning, %	55.0	51.6	58.1	60.7	42.0
Did not participate in any kind of learning, %	45.0	48.4	41.9	39.3	58.0
Total, thousands	1795.1	851.8	943.3	1248.5	546.6

Source: Statistics Lithuania (2007).

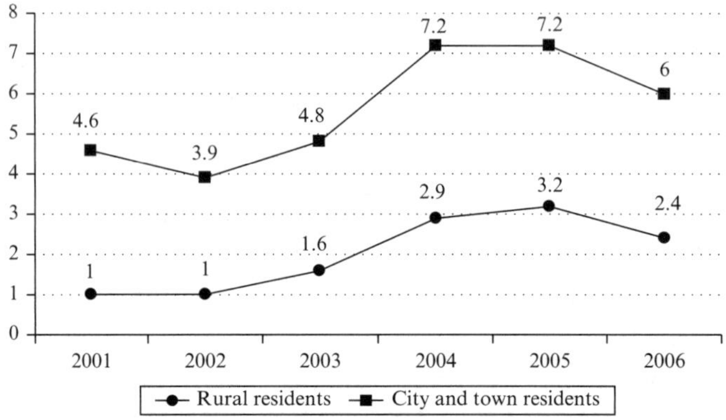

Figure 14.5 Participation in lifelong learning by place of residence (aged 25–64), %

residents until 2005. Since 2006 there have been more people out of work in rural areas. The implications are rather clear: disparities in access to education and jobs remain considerable between rural and urban areas in the country.

Hence, there is mutual dependency between education and employment variables: access to education enables access to the labour market, whereas participation in the labour market generates willingness to enrol in education in order maximize the chances to stay in the labour market.

The data on participation in formal adult education confirm the fact that participation in learning declines with age: formal education activity is the most intense among people aged 25–34. The participation of cohorts between 55 and 64 is extremely low in Lithuania (LFS ad hoc module on LLL 2003). The type of employment contract was also an important factor affecting participation in adult learning for employed persons. People employed part-time participated in education less frequently than those employed full-time. The employed adults were more likely to have participated in formal learning than non-employed adults, and the divide between the employed and unemployed population participating in formal education remains rather distinct.

To sum up our overview of descriptive quantitative data it is evident that demographic, social, cultural and technological trends are stimulating an increasing need for learning opportunities in Lithuania. However, adult participation rates remain quite socially determined. Structurally and individually based barriers, such as gender, place of residence, age, type of (un)employment or migration, limit the potential and the social diversity of adult learners in Lithuania.

PARTICIPATION OF ADULTS IN FORMAL EDUCATION

Formal education encompasses general secondary schools (including secondary schools for adults), vocational education, and higher education including universities and colleges (i.e. universities of applied sciences). Formal adult education is regulated and controlled by the state, which results in approved certification. Formal education institutions can provide non-formal courses. Any adult (a person not younger than 18 years old) can be a participant in the adult education system in Lithuania (Ministry of Education and Science 2003).

The numbers of adults in formal higher education have been small and rather steadily decreasing (see Table 14.2). The formal education system in Lithuania is individualized and diversified in respect to learners' ambitions and skills. Wide opportunities are provided to plan one's professional career, and choose disciplines and courses in relation to personal study needs and interests. In this respect, the learner who has completed secondary school takes a maturity examination and can later continue at college, university or vocational school. There are no entrance exams to enter vocational or higher education (except for art or military-related studies in which artistic skills or aptitude tests are required). Successful application to formal vocational or higher education schools is determined by academic achievements at secondary school. In cases where secondary school achievement is low, the application is predetermined by the learner's ability to pay study fees, as colleges and universities have the right to accept an unlimited number of students who are able to pay tuition themselves. In absolute numbers the proportion of students who pay full study fees has

Table 14.2 Formal higher education (college and university) students by age

Age (year)	2003	2004	2005	2006	2007	2008	2009
25 and older at colleges, %	35.3	36.1	35.2	32.8	30.1	29.3	27
25 and older at universities, %	31.5	32.9	32.3	32.5	30.1	30.6	29.6
Total number of college students	40472	52185	55949	56297	60096	61383	56704
Total number of university students	130245	138516	141771	143204	144336	149017	144301

Source: Statistics Lithuania (2010c); % of total – author calculations.

been increasing gradually since the 2009 higher education reform (in 2010 there were 17 500 first-year students who studied for free and 12 500 who paid full tuition fees; in 2009, 20 800 and 15 500 respectively). However, the data on learners by age who pay full formal study fees are impossible to find in official data sources.

Learners aged 30–34 in formal higher education make up the largest part of all adult students. This data reveals the need for special policy and institutional emphasis on this group of learners for the following reasons. Individuals aged 30–44 or younger are supposed to stay in the labour market for at least 20–25 years, according to current Lithuanian retirement legislation. Thus, investment in these individuals is of particular relevance as this cohort is made up of the most economically active people who make up the second largest group of east-to-west Lithuanian emigrants. Moreover, the cost of higher education is increasing and the measures of the reform of higher education in 2009 might prevent some secondary school leavers both from entering higher education and finding work thereafter. According to Daujotis (2010), the 'student basket' system created two 'classes' of student in higher education, that is, those who study for free and those who pay full study fees. Consequently, this may add to social inequality, if not result in a separate social 'class' of adults lacking education and qualifications and consequently having fewer chances for employment. Thus, the goals of lifelong learning remain at stake in this respect.

Because of the loss of domestic human capital, it is likely that immigrants will gradually reshape the Lithuanian labour market as well as the education system. Some immigrant integration measures are already in place (better access to the labour market than most Baltic states) (see MIPEX III index 2011 for details). The data on adult immigrant learners are not available as the number of immigrants is very small. However, an increase in the immigrant population might be expected in the long run (taking the possible impact of active recruitment measures by employers and formal higher education providers in the future into account). Thus, taking immigrant learners into consideration when preparing labour market and education policies, or strategies at national or institutional level, will become a necessity. Newcomers can receive language support (MIPEX III index 2011), however intercultural education is only part of official aims (Pilinkaitė-Sotirovič 2011).

A qualitative study of 45 adult newcomers – 28 having permanent or temporary resident status – has revealed that adult newcomers restriction or non-participation in Lithuanian society through the target language was mainly related to the lack of educational language learning resources targeted at this specific group, considering that the materials currently in use locally had been devised before Lithuania became an EU member state

(Zygmantas 2011). Furthermore, apart from study purposes, the willingness of these learners to do business in Lithuania (and not for citizenship purposes) was among the most significant reasons to learn the local language (Zygmantas 2011).

Moreover, in recent years, web or media formal higher education institution rankings have been promoted as a tool to demonstrate study quality and attract more learners. The high employability of graduates is one (of the many) important criteria for getting 'bonus' points and climbing up the rankings. However, manipulation of the (un)employment figures that are used by higher education institutions in such rankings is highly questionable, if not unethical. The employability data in national university and college rankings reflects only the number of unemployed graduates who registered themselves with the Labour Exchange (a state organization that registers job seekers to find jobs for them and administers unemployment benefits). The data on types of jobs, the mismatch between qualification and a type of job or structural indicators, such as emigration or overqualification, are not collected and therefore not analysed. As a result of such unemployment data manipulation, the employment figures for university and college graduates increased dramatically to 99–100 per cent. Despite the fact that higher education institutions explicitly state how they calculate employability chances for the graduates of their study programmes, such practice may mislead learners in deciding about their future careers and depreciate the value of higher education itself.

MOTIVES OF ADULT LEARNERS IN FORMAL EDUCATION

Adults participating in training have different goals and motives, the understanding of which allows the whole training process to be made more effective (Vöörmann 2010). The Lithuanian results of the LLL 2010 international survey (undertaken in 2007) show that the main motives for participation in adult formal education are to 'learn more on the subject of my interest', to 'gain awareness of myself and others' and to gain 'knowledge/skills useful in my daily life'. An employer's requirement to enrol was mentioned very seldom as the motive to start a study programme. Among the surveyed adult learners some reported that their reason to take up learning was job related, while others reported that they returned to the education system because of personal reasons (Mikulionienė and Žemaitaitytė 2009). There are quite clear differences between people learning at lower ISCED levels and those who are on higher-level study programmes. Personal and non-job-related reasons dominate among people on study programmes of ISCED levels 1, 2 and 3, whereas adults on higher ISCED study programme levels (4, 5 and 6) indicate mainly job-related reasons for studying (Mikulionienė and Žemaitaitytė 2009). Such results might be influenced by individuals' goals and by the fact that the survey was carried out in 2007, when Lithuania was in a phase of economic growth and adults began to spend more time learning for personal development reasons. Today the results of the research would no doubt be different, because during the business depression more and more people learn in order to keep themselves in the labour market.

Unlike 'traditional' students who continue their education without a break, the majority of adults returning to education after a break face the issue of reconciling a number of different roles. They may have to harmonize the learner's role with the roles of husband/wife and/or mother/father (Mikulionienė and Žemaitaitytė 2009). Moreover, according to the LLL2010 survey, quite a significant proportion of adult learners are confronted with different problems when participating in formal education: 41 per cent feel that there is too little time for study; the same percentage, on average, spends 5–14 hours on domestic tasks (washing, ironing, cleaning, preparing meals, shopping) every week; every third learner reported experiencing financial problems; and every fourth learner faces difficulties arranging childcare (Dromantienė et al. 2009). Thus, adult learners are quite a specific target group for education providers. Since the majority of adult learners are trying to reconcile several social roles in their daily lives, provision of educational services must be flexible enough (in terms of training schedules and payment); in addition, they should be combined with other services supporting and facilitating the study process (for example, financial support, short-term childcare arrangements, etc.).

Learners' study motives differ according to ISCED level. Those who study at ISCED levels 1 and 2 want 'to learn knowledge/skills useful in my daily life', 'gain awareness of myself and others' and 'get a break from the routine of home and work'. Whereas those at ISCED level 4 (post-secondary and non-tertiary education), want to do their job better. The motives 'to start up my own business', 'participate in group activities' and 'meet new people' were expressed more strongly by the learners of ISCED level 3. While analysing the difficulties the learners face, the results of the survey show that the main issues are lack of time and financial problems.

Learning, creativity and education are essential and intimately connected features of an individual living in modern society. For adult learners in Lithuania, education first of all helps to increase self-esteem, and stimulates self-respect and self-reliance. Secondly, a very important factor is engagement of meaningful activity and opportunities for personality development. Thirdly, adult learning is also notably related to a close relationship with family, friends and others who provide support. To a lesser extent, education affects one's reflections on career opportunities. Moreover, for more than one-third of learners, learning is an enjoyable pastime (Monkevičius 2010). The results of the survey show that the vast majority of those surveyed were confident of successfully completing the course, and were satisfied with lifelong learning and its benefits.

EMPLOYERS AND ADULT FORMAL EDUCATION

Study of the relationship between lifelong learning and the workplace is quite rare (Kanopiene and Mikulioniene 2010). Case studies on formal learning practices in small and medium-sized enterprises (SMEs) were among the first attempts to investigate the implications of lifelong learning in the workplace. The survey data show the positive attitude of employers towards LLL and specifically to formal education. The surveyed employers admit that institutions of formal education provide knowledge that is important in respect of the learner's general skills. However, they consider this knowledge as theoretical and inadequate to the demands of practice. Therefore, depending on the size and financial capacities of the company, different strategies are applied in order to fill this gap. Small enterprises that base their activities on highly skilled labour focus on the promotion of very active self-education for employees and the use of specific forms of informal internal education (seminars, individual consultations, supervision). Medium-sized companies with a prevalence of routine labour focus on promotion of informal training in order to develop the specific skills required at work. They introduce informal training schemes to their human resources management (HRM) and human resources development (HRD) strategies, paying primary attention to internal training. Medium-sized enterprises that base their activities on highly skilled labour pay primary attention to formal training (external, distance learning, etc.) as means to increase the specific qualifications of employees. The best results in respect of LLL promotion are achieved in those enterprises that integrate the personnel training strategy into the business strategy of a company, for example in the companies that base their development on participation in public procurement operations. In small companies the employers' individual perceptions of formal education can be a decisive factor in the training culture of the enterprise (Kanopiene and Mikulioniene 2010).

We have to note that there are obstacles with regard to implementation of employment policy measures as well as recommendations to overcome them: the development of career guidance and counselling systems, lack of employer attention to the education of employees, and poor motivation of adults to participate in lifelong learning are among the most significant (Ministry of Social Security and Labour 2008). Another obstacle is the mismatch between qualifications and labour market demands, which is reflected in structural and territorial unemployment data (Pocius 2005). Structural unemployment in Lithuania is determined by three main factors: the age structure of the unemployed, inappropriate qualifications and the emigration of highly skilled employees.

BRIDGE BETWEEN FORMAL AND NON-FORMAL EDUCATION

Non-formal education has an implicit goal alongside the formal education system to act as an option to stimulate the labour market to provide greater chances of employability, and thus ensure the diversity of forms and modes of human capital development. The need for an educational focus on diversity also emerges from the interviews with education stakeholders presented in the Lithuanian national report on adult access to education: 'Lithuania struggles to become an open and diverse society, but in education this is slowed down by a small number of study programmes offered in English or other foreign languages' (Taljūnaitė et al. 2010).

Non-formal education is a key bridge to those experiencing social exclusion (as well as ethnic minorities or immigrants) to participation in the labour market. The predominant non-formal education and training providers still remain employers. The following strengths of non-formal education in Lithuania can be highlighted: 'Independence from many formal procedures in comparison with the formal education system. The flexibility and orientation towards personal needs of the participants as well as labour market needs' (Taljūnaitė et al. 2010).

The weaknesses of the non-formal education system relate to strategic and structural reform to give better expression to non-formal education: 'there is no non-formal education system strategy, there is no funding and quality assurance system, no monitoring mechanisms as well as no recognition of the competences of non-formal learning' (Taljūnaitė et al. 2010).

The significant feature of the non-formal education sector in Lithuania is rather fierce competition and the abundance of services that exceed market demand, especially in the private sector. The number of privately owned non-formal education providers almost doubled in 2009 and 2010 (see Table 14.3) as a result of securing the EU structural funding aimed at human capital development objectives through non-formal training. However, there is a lack of inter-institutional cooperation and there is a

Table 14.3 Economic entities in operation at the beginning of the year by activity type, ownership type and year

	2007	2008	2009	2010
Non-formal adult education				
Public and private ownership	628	699	1097	1145
Public ownership	128	142	155	148
Private ownership	500	557	942	997

Source: Statistics Lithuania (2011).

need to introduce a common system of monitoring formal and non-formal education quality (Taljūnaitė et al. 2010).

DISADVANTAGED GROUPS IN ADULT FORMAL EDUCATION

In Lithuania there is a growing awareness of the need to invest in human capital and develop its potential, however the institutional focus of education providers on target groups is rather chaotic and there are limiting factors to the development of this potential. We highlight some of these limiting factors by using qualitative research findings from LLL2010 that discuss the social profiles of Lithuanian adult formal learners. For example, the diversity of adult learners and the multiplicity of forms, modes and means of learning are seen as a barrier and as a 'dilution' rather than an enrichment of the learning environment in formal higher education institutions, where there is the division of 'work' between the management and teaching personnel. For the management, widening access and attracting new target groups primarily means improving the infrastructure for people with disabilities and securing more funding. People with disabilities are the only clear category of learners identified by the higher education institution management. The members of other disadvantaged groups are not 'visible' at university and colleges as there is no data management system and information on the social profiles of learners is not collected. The 'statistical invisibility' of students from risk groups other than disabled people persists. The promotion and implementation of the 'soft' agenda for increased access is considered rather additional work that is put on teachers' shoulders.

It is evident that there is no system of reserved places for disadvantaged groups, which is based on a formalist assumption of equality that does not recognize indirect discrimination; in other words, discriminatory effects and impacts (Downes 2011). Traditionally disadvantaged groups are somehow not distinguished: 'For socially disadvantaged groups the admission policies are the same as those provided by the state. There are no special screening criteria because we just have an admission policy and the university has to follow it' (Taljūnaitė et al. 2010).

Admission to all public and almost all private colleges and universities in Lithuania is centralized and is organized by the Association of Lithuanian Higher Education Institutions. However, any schemes provided for reserved places for traditionally disadvantaged groups at university are discussed neither by teaching staff, nor by managing staff (Taljūnaitė et al. 2010). The rules for admission are decided by the school. No priorities or privileges are given to students from the at-risk social groups. For people with a disability, or orphans, priority is given if they collect the same number of points as someone else (Taljūnaitė et al. 2010). Both formal and non-formal institutions acknowledge the usefulness of the recognition and validation of prior learning, but they recall different reasons why there are issues to resolve in this area. For formal institutions (especially colleges and universities) the context is firstly legal: there is no legal framework that would facilitate recognition of prior learning. Moreover, validation of non-formal and prior learning remains a methodological challenge, despite the fact that some initial internal institutional procedures and practices exist. However, these procedures of validation of prior learning have been so far applied unequally. Non-formal education providers recall the lack of inter-institutional cooperation. Another important reason might be the flexibility of the curriculum and abundance of courses for which there is no uniform quality assessment. The fierce competition between non-formal education providers might be used to enhance their interest in quality assessment and inter-institutional cooperation with formal education providers. However, with regard to competition between state and private non-formal education institutions, the former are likely to take an advantageous position.

Interviews with stakeholders in adult education demonstrate that education institutions seem to find it hard to organize childcare for adult learners. Childcare is not part of their core activities and funding possibilities are limited or only available from project funding by EU structural funds. Both formal and non-formal education providers recognize the need for childcare facilities.

Reductions on tuition fees or exemptions of tuition are regulated by law and are usually category-based in formal tertiary state-funded institutions. Some means-tested reductions of tuition fees and/or single payments are available for adults in state-funded institutions, but these funds are usually limited. Moreover, in tertiary education measures are taken to keep the tuition fees as low as possible. Private tertiary and non-formal institutions have more flexibility in this respect; fee reductions are usually means-tested, but they tend to be smaller than at state-funded colleges or universities and are available to only a small number of learners. Private formal higher education students have more flexibility in the ways they can pay tuition fees, which for them can be postponed, or regular (monthly, quarterly) payments can be made over an extended period of time.

An education institution cannot be assumed to be a unitary space (Downes 2011). However, access issues are treated as a peripheral feature of higher education providers in Lithuania. The research findings show that reaching out to those coming from a disadvantaged background is not the primary or the only concern of education providers. The interest in adult learners (and other target groups) lies mainly in concerns for recruiting a sufficient number of students, and the goals of lifelong learning are a secondary concern (especially in higher formal and non-formal education). In most cases, education providers do not have specific measures aimed at attracting adults or members of other target groups. This shows that there is still some room for improvement in promoting increased access.

CONCLUSIONS

There are evidently three levels within lifelong learning policy: conceptual, legislative and strategic (measures of implementation). National programmes for ongoing adult learning are in place and implemented. The system of information and consultation about learning opportunities is being developed and improved. Education policy reformers seem to be aware of the need to invest in human capital and this awareness manifests very clearly in the goals and objectives of strategies and reforms. It can be said that for adults some aspects of participation in the lifelong learning process are improving: ministries, government institutions, regional administration and municipalities cooperate to address certain issues. Lifelong learning depends on the following statements of principle: new key competencies for all; more investment in human resources and the prevention of social exclusion; implementation of innovations in learning and teaching; the valuing of learning and teaching. The education reforms in Lithuania of the past 20 years have aimed to change some of the rules of the game in education. New initiatives undertaken by Lithuanian education policy reformers in 2009 are expected to yield results in the future; however our data on adult education show that the efforts to improve participation in lifelong learning are not sufficient. This raises a fundamental debate about the overall purpose of education, a debate that is based on two views: education as a cost, which the state cannot bear; or education as an investment, which contributes to building social capital and fostering social cohesion. We can also conclude that adult education has been a secondary concern of education system reformers, as they tended to give more prominence to 'mainstream' education while underestimating the importance of adult access to higher education as well as lifelong learning goals.

In this chapter we also looked at the issues of employability and social determinism in adult education and we conclude that despite policies promoting positive views on adult education, participation in lifelong learning (both formal and non-formal programmes) is highly selective. Our qualitative and quantitative data clearly demonstrate that the education system favours advantaged groups and this has a number of side-effects for the social and economic development of the country and social cohesion. For example, training and education is more easily available in urban areas where the average population and labour force is better educated and the chances for employment are higher. Our analysis also shows explicitly that gender, age and labour market statuses exist as well as institutional and organizational barriers to the development of lifelong learning in Lithuania. Adult learning in Lithuania is characterized by low participation and rather sharp social divides. With regard to non-formal adult education institutions, the evidence confirms the primacy of the private market. However, private non-formal education is usually sought by employed learners unless they are provided with company training. Thus, the increasing number of private non-formal education providers seemingly does not signal widening access to education for those in need. The social profiles of those enrolled in adult education might be characterized by demographic and economic variables. Women are more likely to be enrolled in both formal and non-formal education whereas men are more privileged in the labour market. Urban and employed residents are more likely to be involved in both formal and non-formal study. The majority of adults aged 25–64 in formal higher study are most likely to be 30 to 39 years old. It is important to note that they are supposed to stay in the labour market for 20–30 years according to existing retirement legislation; however this age group is most susceptible to East–West emigration. Thus, one of the future challenges relates to the capacity to develop adult education policy in coordination with employment and migration policies.

Demographic, social, cultural and technological trends stimulate the increasing demand for learning opportunities in Lithuania. However, adult participation rates are quite socially determined. Structurally and individually based barriers limit the potential and the social diversity of adult learners in Lithuania. Thus, when examining the behaviour of adults in relation to participation it is important not only to take into account the immediate social situation of individuals (such as family and work dynamics), but also to consider the institutional context and its influence upon the individual, because the objective and subjective factors are interrelated. In other words, 'people are making their worlds at the same time as their worlds are making them' (Watson 2001 quoted in Webber 2004). Thus more focus on human capital building (not only social capital) through lifelong learning is an essential tool in maintaining and securing full employment and cohesion in Lithuanian society.

REFERENCES

Cervero, Ronald M. and Arthur L. Wilson (2005), 'At the Heart of Practice: The Struggle for Knowledge and Power', in R.M. Cervero and A.L. Wilson (eds), *Power in Practice: Adult Education and the Struggle for Knowledge and Power in Societsy*, San Francisco, CA: Jossey-Bass, pp. 1–21.

Conceição, Pedro, Manuel V. Heitor and Bengt-Åke Lundval (2003), *Innovation, Competence Building, and Social Cohesion in Europe: Towards a Learning Society*, Cheltenham, UK and Northampton, MA, USA: Edward Elgar.

Daujotis, Vytautas (2010), 'Inteviu' (Interview with Vytautas Daujotis), *Lietuvos rytas* (Lietuvos Rytas Daily), 12 April.

Downes, Paul (2011), 'A Systems Level Focus on Access to Education for Traditionally Marginalized Groups in Europe: Comparing Strategies, Policy and Practice in Twelve European Countries', in *Comparative Report: Subproject 5, LLL2010 (draft of 2011 March 25)*, Dublin: St Patrick's College of Dublin City University, Educational Disadvantage Centre.

Dromantienė, Leta, Vida Kanopienė, Sarmitė Mikulionienė, Natalija Norvilė and Irena Žemaitaitytė (2009), *The Survey of Lithuanian Adult Learner's Participation in Formal Education: Standard Tabulations and Main Data*, Vilnius: MRU.

Durkheim, Emile (1956), *Education and Sociology*, Glencoe, IL: Free Press.

Fontainha, Elsa (2005), 'Social Cohesion Across Europe: Does Time Allocation Matter?' *European Review of Labour and Research*, **11** (1), 1–15.

Guibet Lafaye, Caroline (2009), 'Modèles de la cohésion sociale', *European Journal of Sociology*, **50**, 389–427.

Jarvis, Peter (2004), *Adult Education and Lifelong Learning: Theory and Practice (3rd edition)*, Oxford: Routledge.

Kanopiene, Vida and Sarmite Mikulioniene (2010), 'Attitude of Employers towards LLL of Employees: Case of SME in Lithuania', in V. Kozlovskiy, R. Voormann and T. Roosalu (eds), *Learning in Transition: Policies and Practices of Lifelong Learning in Post-Socialist Countries*, St Petersburg: Nauka, pp. 107–125.

LLL (2010), *Lifelong Learning 2010. Towards a Lifelong Learning Society in Europe: The Contribution of the Education System*, EU 6th Framework project website. Available at: http://lll2010.tlu.ee/.

Mikulionienė, Sarmitė and Irena Žemaitaitytė (2009), 'Lietuvos besimokančiųjų suaugusiųjų demografinis protretas: LLL2010 tyrimo rezultatai' (Demographic Portrait of Adult Learners in Lithuania: LLL2010 Survey), *Socialinis darbas* (Social Work), **8** (2), 5–15.

Ministry of Education and Science (2003), 'Lietuvos Respublikos švietimo įstatymas' (Law on Higher Education and Research), *Valstybės žinios* (State Gazette), No. 38-1804.

Ministry of Social Security and Labour (2008), 'Mokymosi visą gyvenimą užtikrinimo strategija' (Lifelong Learning Implementation Strategy), *Valstybės žinios* (State Gazette), No. 122-4647.

MIPEX III index (2011), 'Lithuania'. Available at http://www.mipex.eu/lithuania (accessed 10 June 2011).

Monkevičius, Algirdas (2010), 'Lifelong Learning: Aspects of Creativity and Happiness', *Socialinis darbas* (Social Work), **9** (2), 39.

Pilinkaitė-Sotirovič, Vilana (2011), 'Įvairovei atvira mokykla: multikultūrinio pažinimo praktikos' (Opening Doors to Diversity at Schools: Practices of Multicultural Education), presentation at Pranešimas konferencijoje 'Migrantų integracijos politikos indeksas' (Migrant Integration Index Presentation Conference), Vilnius, 2 June.

Pocius, Arunas (2005), 'Struktūrinis nedarbas Lietuvoje' (Structural Unemployment in Lithuania), in Statistikos departmentas (Statistics Lithuania), *Demografinė situacija, Socialinė būklė* (Demographic and Social Trends), pp. 1–23.

Statistics Lithuania (2007), 'Suaugusiųjų švietimo tyrimas' (Adult Education Survey), available at http://www.stat.gov.lt/lt/news/view/?id=1885 (accessed 16 August 2010).

Statistics Lithuania (2010a), *Statistical Yearbook of Lithuania 2009*, Vilnius: Statistics Lithuania.

Statistics Lithuania (2010b), *Vyrai ir moterys Lietuvoje 2010* (Men and Women in Lithuania), Vilnius: Statistics Lithuania.

Statistics Lithuania (2010c), 'Students by Age'. Available at: http://db1.stat.gov.lt/statbank/SelectVarVal/Define.asp?Maintable=M3110105andPLanguage=1 (accessed: 2 September 2010).

Statistics Lithuania (2011), 'Economic entities in operation that general activity is non-formal adult education or pupils and youth additional education at the beginning of the year by type of ownership', Vilnius: Statistics Lithuania Database of Indicators. Available at: http://bit.ly/W4RbAv (accessed 11 November 2011).

Taljūnaitė, Meilutė and Liutauras Labanauskas (2010), 'Improving Policy and Evolving Practices of Social Cohesion ir Formal Education: The Case of Lithuania', in Vladimir Kozlovskiy, Rein Voormann and Triin Roosalu (eds), *Learning in Transition: Policies and Practices of Lifelong Learning in Post-Socialist Countries*, St Petersburg: Nauka, pp. 107–125.

Taljūnaitė, Meilutė, Liutauras Labanauskas and Juratė Terepaitė-Butvilienė (2010), *The Access of Adults to Formal and Non-Formal Adult Education. Country Report: Lithuania*, Vilnius: LLL2010/Lithuanian Social Research Centre.

Vöörman, Rein (2010), 'The Impact of Ascriptive Characteristics on Motives for Participation in Training: Estonia on the Backdrop of Selected European Countries', in Vladimir Kozlovskiy, Rein Vöörmann and Triin Roosalu (eds), *Learning in Transition: Policies and Practices of Lifelong Learning in Post-Socialist Countries*, St Petersburg: Nauka, pp. 107–125.

Watson, Tony J. (2001), 'The Emergent Manager and Processes of Management Pre-Learning', *Management Learning*, **32** (2), 221–235.
Webber, Trix (2004), 'Orientations to Learning in Mid-Career Management Students', *Studies in Higher Education*, **29** (2), 259–277.
Žemaitaitytė, Irena (2007), *Non-Formal Adult Education: Development Tendencies in the Contemporary Europe*, Vilnius: Mykolas Romeris University.
Zygmantas, Janete (2011), 'Adult Newcomers' Difficulties in Learning Lithuanian: An Ethnographic Case Study', Doctoral thesis, Vilnius University.

15. Developing human capital in post-socialist capitalism: Estonian experience

Ellu Saar, Triin Roosalu, Eve-Liis Roosmaa, Auni Tamm and Rein Vöörmann

LIFELONG LEARNING IN ESTONIA: SETTING THE SCENE

This chapter introduces the developments in adult education in Estonia, one of the post-socialist European Union (EU) member states, during the post-socialist period. We suggest that Estonia's post-colonial setting (Bunce 1999, 2003) has contributed to the extent to which the advancements in the sphere of education and lifelong learning (LLL) during the socialist project have been partly reversed since the beginning of the social transformation. Our analysis also contributes to the formulation of substantive conclusions regarding the conditions and results in the (de-)development (Meurs and Ranasinghe 2003) of human capital in post-socialist society.

Fragoulis et al. (2004) indicate that in most transition countries in Europe reform initiatives in the 1990s and in the 2000s were mainly limited to the initial formal education system. While the system of initial education seems to operate quite efficiently (at least in quantitative terms) and reveal superior (to EU-15) performance, there is a lack of education and training provisions for adults in Estonia. All in all, in Estonia, just as in other transition economies, the low educational level of the population was not the problem. Rather, it is the orientation towards preparing the workforce which often specialized in a narrow technical field and was employed in contracting sectors and professions (Eamets 2008) that makes the availability of further education of great importance.

We argue that these developments have historical roots due to path-dependent development. However, in addition to path-dependence the specific character of transformation in transition countries is also important.

Different authors (see for example Ashton et al. 2000; Brown et al. 2001) assume that the relationships central to an understanding of the process of skill formation and lifelong learning are those between the state, the education and training systems which deliver skills, capital in the form of employers through which the demand for skills arise, and workers in the form of employees and their organizations, which influence the supply of skills. These provide the basic groups which, in specific cultural contexts, form the institutions through which skills are formed. In Estonia the skill formation system is rather 'under construction', being rearranged from the Soviet-influenced system. Thus, the current stage of its development is highly dependent on the peculiarities of the Soviet system and the whole process of societal change (and especially market reforms) that has occurred over the last two decades. The Estonian case is special in terms of the radical character of market reform, which has been deep, profound and swift in nature. Thus, Estonia might be recognized as advanced in terms of marketization. However, given the high speed and the fact that institutional solutions have often been 'imported',[1] it would be very important to study how these solutions work and what impact they have on adult participation in lifelong learning.

Previous analysis (see Roosmaa and Saar 2010) has shown that in post-socialist countries a different logic of institutional impact shapes participation in adult learning compared to the EU-15. In our evaluation, while there is a lack, or neglect, of the search in scientific literature for an understanding of how the post-Soviet post-socialist societies in Europe differ from other post-socialist societies in Europe, we expect that our conclusions will also serve as new ground to extend the distinction between post-socialist and post-Soviet European societies when studying and comparing different social processes. The inevitable need to accommodate the heritage of the socialist regime when developing new institutions characterizes all post-socialist countries in Europe. In addition to this, the previous Soviet republics also have to get by with their experience of belonging to the Soviet Union, which in most cases – and certainly in the case of the Baltic republics – was not fully legitimized in society. As Valerie Bunce (1999) explains, while the institutional development of the Soviet Union made this socialism a self-destructive system, 'nationalism was as much about regime destruction and regime construction . . . as it was about . . . state subtraction and state building' (Bunce 1999, p. 101). Specifically it is this aspect of 'state subtraction' with which other post-socialist countries did not necessarily have to deal. However, for countries such as Estonia it meant that not only was there a need to find new ways to continue as a society and construct institutions fit for the new regime, but also that any traces of the old system were likely to be denied and destroyed as being part of the colonial Soviet state, as much as being part of the previous regime itself. The major difference stemming from this in relation to the development of the education systems lies in the fact that in Estonia, the previously well-established institutionalized systems, including those for adult education and lifelong learning, were discontinued. When, at the beginning of the societal transformation, there was a lack of resources, attention was paid to other aspects of regime construction and state building.

Development of institutions such as those of adult education took more time and was dependent on the economic growth and opportunities that were opened up with the EU accession process, which was completed in 2004. During the transformation years, it is argued (Meurs and Ranasinghe 2003), many post-socialist countries actually did undergo de-development of their stock of human capital, despite the lack of socially sensitive investments in the healthcare and education systems.

Our theoretical perspective is the bounded agency model, which is premised in the assumption that the nature of institutional arrangements and broad structural conditions can affect a person's capability to participate through the way these institutional arrangements construct structural conditions and help individuals overcome both structurally and individually based barriers (Rubenson and Desjardins 2009). Our attention in this chapter is focused on providing an overview of those regulatory processes, norms, meaning systems and behavioural patterns that emerge from the data collected and analysed within the research project 'Towards a Lifelong Learning Society in Europe: The Contribution of the Education System' (LLL2010).

In order to put our results in context and enable evaluation of whether or not these account for positive or negative developments in a society, we start with an explanation of institutional and ideological changes on the way from the Soviet to the European Union. Thereafter, we give an overview of educational provision and the providers' views on lifelong learning based on our original research. We then contextualize further by outlining the more general policy goals, employer practices and the views of individual learners. Our conclusions are on practices in the formal education system in the wider social context of, firstly, changes compared to the Soviet period, and secondly, the interrelated effects and outcomes at the different institutional levels of the individual, the enterprise and policy-makers.

ECONOMIC CONTEXT, INSTITUTIONAL ARRANGEMENT AND IDEOLOGIES DURING THE SOVIET PERIOD AND AFTER: FROM HUMAN INTERESTS TO HUMAN CAPITAL?

Ideologies and Values Pertaining to Education during the Soviet Era and the Twenty Years of Transition

The goal of communist education was formulated by Marx and Engels: education is the comprehensive harmonious development of all the spiritual and physical resources of every member of society. This goal derived from the suggestion that in communism, motivation to work is something inherent in people, who just want and need to contribute to the advancement of society (Whitmarsh and Ritter 2007). Marxism's founders substantiated the guiding principle of education in communist society – the combination of education and labour (Roberts 2001). These ideas were formalized and further developed in the USSR.

In practical terms this meant that in 1958, the Supreme Soviet of the USSR passed a law 'Strengthening of the Connections between School and Life and the Development of the Educational System in the Soviet Union'. On 24 April 1959, the corresponding law for the Estonian SSR followed. Connecting study and work had to guarantee the growth of work efficiency. Theoretical and practical production training of 10–12 lessons a week together with work in an enterprise were added to the curricula of secondary schools.

Educative work also presupposes self-education. Exactingness toward oneself and one's behaviour, the capacity for self-discipline and self-organization, and the ability, as Lenin discussed, to work out communist views for oneself – this is an aspect of the greatest importance in the creation of the new, socialist person (Byford and Jones 2006; Zajda 2003). In a mature socialist society, attention to matters of self-education is supposed to increase. Socialism poses very sharply the question of the internal responsibility of a person, personal civic conscience, the assimilation of spiritual and moral values, and the perfecting and self-perfecting of the human personality (see Gerber and Hout 1995). We can even witness how such factors came to play out in terms of learner motivation in Estonia during the late Soviet era. According to human capital theory (Becker 1964), people invest in education first of all because more educated people earn more, but in the former socialist countries this logic did not work: the less educated often earned more than people with a higher education (see Helemäe et al. 2000). However, the motive to move from blue collar to white collar was quite strong even though it was only due to the attraction of white collar social status. Above this, equality at the level of material well-being favoured evaluation of cultural self-development. Analysis of value orientations of Estonian youth during the Soviet period indicated that value hierarchies were stable and no big inter-cohort changes could be identified (Saarniit 1998). The typical value hierarchy was the following: the highest place was given to self-development; the second place to the group of altruistic values; and the last position to material values and social status.

In the beginning of the 1990s, a new value system was formed characterized by a dramatic increase in materialist values and a decrease in post-materialist values. Sociological research has pointed out three main dimensions to the process: an increasing prevalence of: (1) personal interests over social interests; (2) material and status values over intellectual values; (3) the professional aspect of education over the general cultural aspect (Saarniit 1998). The general appreciation of education also changed: education as such was no longer the aim, it became a tool, for example with which to get a higher salary.

The collapse of the communist regime in Estonia was reflected in the strong liberal discourse in education curricula, with neoliberalism being explicit in the attempts to introduce the notion of decentralization, deregulation, market rules and values, the rhetoric of choice, and an ideology of service provision (Aava 2009). This shift has been accelerated by implementing the *acquis communautaire* as part of the accession to the European Union. 'Lifelong learning' is now a key term in the EU lexicon, and in recent years, it has in some respects displaced and come to stand for 'education and training', although drawing attention to the wider role of learning in a 'learning society' (see Holford et al. 2007). According to this analysis, EU policy in education has been constrained by its vocational orientation, having the needs of the economy and employers in mind. Although an economic orientation was reinforced by the Maastricht Treaty, which also itemized certain other issues (e.g., quality) and certainly did not prohibit developments in other directions, it did set EU education policy on this particular economic and vocational course, which was further strengthened by the economic framing of the discourse on lifelong learning in the 1990s. Therefore, the authors conclude that the lifelong learning policy at the EU level has been shaped by the demands of competitiveness and the requirements of subsidarity, while lifelong learning is seen as a key way of addressing social exclusion as well as being a key to economic competitiveness and employability.

Estonia, as other post-communist countries, tends to see lifelong learning as a way to enhance economic development (see Holford et al. 2007). The neoliberal policy choices, incorporating an instrumental approach to schooling, narrowed the aim of schooling to work-related goals and self-actualization through increased labour market competitiveness. This shift is also reflected in the views and practices of adult learners themselves. A comparison of data from 1997 and 2007 indicates that among working adults, the discursive space has decreased enormously with regard to learning for reasons other than labour market competitiveness in general or one's current job in particular. When looking at Estonian adults' reflections on their own learning experiences we see that employed people who participated in any type of training were much less likely to study for personal reasons in 2007 than in 1997 (Tamm and Kazjulja 2010). This indicates a major shift in society in either reasoning or understanding of the nature of lifelong learning as solely a tool for managing labour market success. This result seems to say that working adults in 2007 believed that participation in lifelong learning was more likely to solve mainly work-related insecurities or aspirations than a decade ago, or that individual goals were not set or seen as worthy of being set in comparison with work-related goals. Work-related motives and the wish to bring more benefit to the society were accepted in 2007 among the dominant legitimate reasons for enrolling in formal education (Roosalu and Roosmaa 2010). The ranking of motives for attending adult formal education in Estonia also differed from Western countries in 2007: in Estonia more than three-quarters of people held that training helps one to do one's job better and increases one's career prospects, while in Western countries this figure was 57 per cent (Vöörmann 2010). While intrinsic aims were also present, they were expressed substantially less often than in Western countries.

On one hand, the discourses of competitiveness and labour market integration are central in discussing the role of education and lifelong learning in society. On the other hand, a discussion of the more intrinsic aims of the learning processes is present, even if only weakly in the relevance attributed to self-realization and self-advancement in popular beliefs. The presence of such views, currently quite eagerly accommodated by the dominant discourse of self-advancement because of workplace needs, can be noted in a fifth of students; while for more than a third study is not necessarily exclusively connected to the strict 'competitiveness and financial remuneration' thesis (Roosalu and Roosmaa 2010), which does sound as if perhaps this is among the more helpful ruins of the previous era that continues to benefit adult education in Estonia.

It has been noted earlier that the full toolbox of key terms and institutionalized EU lifelong learning policies have been implemented in post-socialist countries, although sometimes without due national discussion of their suitability (Holford et al. 2007). It is likely that, as Bunce (1999, 2003) explains, Estonia was more apt to take those 'new' aspects over without questioning them, given the nature of Estonian democratization as being part of the destruction of the Soviet state. But is there a reason to suggest that EU developments could be not that applicable for the new member states, such as Estonia, and that other choices would have been accepted had there been such a discussion? We claim that the education system in Soviet Estonia really was even more advanced compared to current EU policies and development in the more developed countries, and in ways had reached a level where the immediate instrumentalist labour-market-related aims of education were seconded by the more general aims of education as a value in itself. Let us therefore, in what follows, study the skill formation systems in two eras more closely.

(DIS)CONTINUITIES IN FORMAL ADULT EDUCATION: PROVISION, PARTICIPATION, BARRIERS

The Skill Formation System and Adult Education during the Soviet Period and during the Transition

The peculiarities of the Soviet system of skill formation are still important in Estonia both at the institutional level (as still influencing the scale of possible development choices) and at the individual level (in 2007 half of the population aged 15–64 had obtained their highest level of education before 1991, i.e. during the Soviet period). Under Soviet rule, skill formation was a part of the party-state institutional structure. In socialist Estonia, schools and curricula in general were modelled on the so-called German system, providing clear division between general and vocational education and emphasizing specificity of occupational skill in vocational education. However, the Estonian education system worked differently, as it was embedded in a totally different socio-economic-political context compared with Germany.

Firstly, the Estonian pre-transition economy had been characterized as 'soviet-style low production quality and extensive development-oriented economic structure' (Ennuste et al. 2004). The Estonian economy, as part of the former Soviet economy, was not driven by market logic but was centrally administrated. The pressure on the skill formation system to secure flexible upgrading of skills was rather weak.

Secondly, in a command economy the logic of coordination between economic actors is bureaucratic, rather than of the market or corporate type. In a closed economy and under centralized planning there was no need for such coordination of this complex system, which would effectively respond to market-based changes in demand for labour. The state was so profoundly involved with the formation of skills that there was no need for proactive training policies managed by enterprises.

Thirdly, the command economy operated under a chronic shortage of primarily blue-collar labour. Changing jobs entailed almost no risk to the future prospects of the mover. In this sense there was no need to provide additional social security guarantees (income and employment protection) for workers obtaining specific (as opposed to general) skills, as is the case in Western countries. Because of stable demand for blue-collar workers with different levels of qualification, it was not workers but rather management of enterprise who needed to adapt to rare (e.g., bureaucratically imposed) changes in the enterprise environment. Given this situation, authorities did not push too much with the centralized requirements to upgrade the qualification of blue-collar workers. Thus, there was neither pressure on, nor strong motive for, blue-collar workers to continue their education. Enterprises preferred a 'get ready-for-consumption' workforce to the upgrading of blue-collar qualifications. But white-collar workers were obliged to upgrade their qualifications after normatively defined periods (e.g., once in five years).

Fourthly, not only was the system of education highly stratified, highly centralized and highly segmented across the bureaucratic lines,[2] but the labour market was also bureaucratically segmented. The division between so-called all-union enterprises, which were ruled by the all-union (branch) ministries, and the so-called local enterprises, ruled by the Estonian ministry, was of great importance. This division coincided with the ethnic background of workers as well as their educational background (many workers from the all-union segment migrated to Estonia after completion of their education). As a result, segmentation in the labour market occurred along bureaucratic rather than purely occupational or industrial lines. Skills possessed by those educated and trained in the Former Soviet Union (FSU) were applicable in bureaucratically determined segments of the economy. In this sense, the distinction between the occupational and organizational types of social space is relevant to the Estonian case.

Fifthly, non-job-related adult education for personal development was relatively well developed. It was promoted and subsidized by the state due to its connection with socialist ideology. Courses were provided free of charge or very cheaply.

As to market reforms, while the first steps towards market economy were taken at the end of the Soviet period (from 1987, when Estonia was part of the Soviet Union) the process that is often called the 'return to the market economy' started after the restoration of independence in 1991. The difficult economic situation of enterprises pushed employee training and development aside and priority was given to short-term goals related to survival in the market. The move towards the market economy in the first half of the 1990s was characterized by significant change in the sectoral structure of the economy (the contribution of industry declined both in relative and absolute values, while the significance of services increased) as well as the geographical structure of foreign trade (from Eastern to Western markets) (Terk 1999). Estonia experienced a 'passive' structural change towards a service economy that was less borne by real growth in service industries than by an enormous shrinkage of the primary and secondary sectors.

However, these changes were frequently accompanied by a transition from more complex production to less complicated work, usually involving subcontracting to foreign companies, mainly from Scandinavia. A substantial part of the labour force works in low-wage export industries or in enterprises whose business models exist to benefit from low wages (Eamets 2008). Estonia has a significantly higher proportion of unqualified workers in the workforce, while the proportion of white-collar workers is notably lower compared with most European countries (Saar 2008) – even with a generally above-average share of higher-educated people. Unlike in most developed EU countries, the Estonian economic structure is characterized by a low level of industrial and technological innovation (Paas and Sepp 2008). The shift from industry towards relatively low-innovation 'trading' has been more dominant than the shift towards the modern post-industrial service economy.

This means that Estonia integrated into the global economy mainly through labour-intensive traditional industries controlled by highly mobile transnational corporations, and through resource-based exports and related services (Paas and Sepp 2008), which have high diversity in their human resource development strategies and practices.

According to Nölke and Vliegenthart (2009) in Hungary, Poland, the Czech Republic and the Slovak Republic a special type of capitalism is emerging – a dependent market economy (DME). Estonia seems to be a drastic and liberal example of DME because its export is based on labour-intensive traditional industries and services which are controlled by highly mobile transnational corporations. Some of these corporations, rather than significantly investing in local facilities, usually subcontract production with no need to train employees. However, some corporations entered the market with direct investments, and by offering higher wage levels hired the best-qualified workforce, to whom the international training was provided in order to ensure stable high production quality; by doing so the goal of training became higher efficiency. In cases where local executive management was trained abroad the aim was also to train the local managers to improve and become more convenient business partners for the multinational corporations.

In the private sector the proportion of employer-financed training is agreed in individual contracts or collective agreements. Due to low coverage by collective agreements the majority of employees in Estonia rely on individual employment contracts. We also found indications that the role of collective bargaining in continuing vocational training is low (Nurmela and Roosaar 2009). During the cycles of shortage of labour, the issue of skill formation has been constantly tackled by the employers' association. Despite this, just as with management in the command economy, there are employers who do not consider themselves responsible for skill formation, while also feeling free to follow a poaching strategy, hiring employees of other companies who have already received the relevant training.[3] They take for granted the proactive role of the state: according to their claims, the education system should be reoriented towards better provision of vocational education. Until 2012 the costs for all kinds of personnel education and training by the employer were taxed in Estonia to the same extent as wages, as if they were to be regarded as direct income support to the employee, and this has clearly discouraged employers from training their employees. In conclusion, in the competitive sector, pressure to upgrade skills is rather low; moreover, this low pressure does not motivate employers to invest in human capital. The transition to the market economy did not bring about an increase in the demand for qualified labour, nor a demand for the flexible upgrading of skills.

As to the public sector, compared to the pre-transition period, the responsibilities of the state have decreased. Ongoing training financed by the state is currently mainly for civil servants and teachers in state and municipal schools (previously this was in the fixed amount of 2–4 per cent of the payroll for people in public service, although this has been now preserved only for teachers to the extent of 2 per cent), as well as for the unemployed. In addition, the state budget includes a small budget to support the activities of the Adult Education Council as well as the 'hobby education' institutions. The state also remains the main actor in the system of skill formation. In Western countries the peculiarities of the skill formation system were dependent first of all on the activities of employers' associations, on the way they coordinate these activities and negotiate them with trade unions.

Given the monopoly of the former socialist state and its institutions over the provision and financing of the whole range of institutionalized education activities, and a stable economic structure and secure material conditions for the population, the patterns of participation in LLL during the transition were and are primarily dependent on how the state abandons this monopoly; these patterns depend on what the new institutional settings were when replacing the previous one, and how (in which way, to what extent, at what speed) market mechanisms were allowed to work. It is nevertheless worth noting that while in the previous era workplaces were a major driver of adult learning, the emerging private ownership of small enterprises did not take up this role, further individualizing care for human capital so as to convince the individual that their learning is labour-market-related (see also Roosalu and Roosmaa 2010).

Provision of Formal Adult Education: From More To Less Support for Adult Learning?

In the Soviet period, one can separate different phases in the development of the education system according to adult involvement. At the end of the 1950s and beginning of the 1960s, the reforms undertaken during Khrushchev's period had an important impact on education. There was an aim to encourage evening and part-time study at the level of secondary and higher education. The number of graduates from these departments increased (Helemäe et al. 2000). At the start of the 1960s, quotas were determined for admission to higher education institutions, which favoured people who were already working. Enterprises could send their workers to study as scholarship holders and they had the opportunity to enter outside general competition. It was a period in which the quite widespread strategies were: (1) work and evening or part-time study; and (2) commencing learning after some working period. This means that the number of people who studied in the formal education system in their late twenties or thirties was quite high.

In 1964 (after the fall of Khrushchev) there was a change of course: the benefits were reduced and there was preferential development of day study at the higher education level. There was then an annual reduction in the proportions in favour of day study. At the end of the 1960s special preparatory departments were opened in the higher education institutions for those who were already working. The role of the preparatory departments, however, remained modest, because in 1972–1975, graduates of the preparatory departments formed under 10 per cent of admissions to university (Helemäe and Saar 1999). At the beginning of the 1970s restrictions were imposed on entry to day studies: people older than 35 could not enter. This meant that the number of people who continued their studies at university after some working period decreased.

In the second half of the 1960s, universal secondary education was proclaimed a goal. The result was that in the 1970s the share of graduates from correspondence and evening secondary schools reached its maximum.

Enterprises were obliged to send their workers without secondary education to so-called working youth secondary schools. Therefore in the 1970s the development of correspondence studies at the level of secondary education facilitated the increase of the number of adults in the formal education system.

In the 1980s the proportion of secondary school graduates attending correspondence and evening schools decreased steadily. The same tendency is pronounced for higher education. The result was that the number of adults studying in the formal education system decreased and the more widespread learning strategy was to start working after graduation. However, during the Soviet period education (including adult formal education) was free of charge. Additionally, there was a general state-guaranteed study allowance, to enable students to stay out of labour market during their initial studies. It was still quite common for the (potential) employer to pay the (prospective) employee a quite substantial study allowance while they studied, with the view that the student at graduation would start (or return) to work for the employer. The structural change in the economy and society seriously affected the life plans of that generation, who were graduating from such programmes at the beginning of the transition.

With the structural change from the Soviet Union to independence, the previous institutional setting was destroyed as something potentially resembling continuity with the Soviet system, or Russia. As the argument of post-colonialism goes (see Bunce 1999, 2003), we witness reluctance to preserve any of the institutional or formal settings, or at least denounce these as needing severe reform. Therefore, the notion used by Stark (1996) about building the society not on the ruins, but with the ruins of the socialist system heritage becomes a symbolic statement in itself. So, what are the turnarounds we can see the adult education system to have taken, and what are the ruins we can still witness as becoming the cornerstone of the new, post-1990s system of adult education in Estonia?

According to typology of diversity in educational supply for adults (Hefler 2011), the formal adult education system in Estonia has a low level of diversification because the variety of institutions providing formal adult education is restricted to the very same institutions that also provide initial education. However, compared to the time immediately after the social change, the educational offer during the transition period has already become more flexible and diverse, for example by introduction of special shorter formal training programmes, or programmes designed in cooperation with certain enterprise or regional industrial clusters, which was also reflected in our interviews within this project (Tamm and Roosmaa 2010). Special schools for adults have been spared only at the general education level: those who have acquired basic education (grade

9) or gone beyond the age of compulsory school attendance at 17 may acquire basic and general upper secondary education in adult 'gymnasiums', and study is free of charge for students. However, adult secondary school students receive no study allowance, which means that they either have to work or are supported by family members. The number of adolescents without basic education increased in Estonia during the 1990s (Eurostat), therefore, the continuation of studies in adult gymnasiums is becoming more popular among younger age groups. In 2008 most of the students (67 per cent) were aged 20 years, the normal age for completing upper secondary education. A significant proportion (24 per cent) of students enrolled part-time were aged 21 to 25. A large share of students at adult secondary schools come from disadvantaged backgrounds, for either family or social reasons.

Based on a 2006 amendment to the law, vocational education institutions, which were previously engaged in formal education only, may now offer several flexible opportunities to participate in vocational training: vocational orientation courses within the framework of preliminary vocational training to basic school and upper secondary school students; vocational training in basic school and upper secondary school, giving basic vocational skills; vocational secondary education; vocational training on the basis of basic education; vocational training on the basis of secondary education; vocational training without the requirement for basic education.[4] Vocational education is provided free of charge except for some post-secondary programmes which are not included in state-commissioned education. Vocational schools pay a study allowance if the student's academic achievement and behaviour are satisfactory. Some vocational schools receive support from local governments to cover the accommodation and catering costs of students from economically disadvantaged backgrounds. In vocational schools, the share of older learners has somewhat increased in recent years. In the academic year 2009–2010 the share of students aged 25 years and older was 15 per cent. Compared with general secondary schools, vocational schools have more students who have problems or are at risk of dropping out.

In addition, universities and professional higher education institutions enable adults to study part-time. Obtaining higher education via part-time study is mostly payable, with the exception of, for instance, teachers' training. In the 2008–2009 academic year 71 per cent of adult students paid for their studies themselves. Study allowances and study loans are granted only to students who study full-time, which means that these allowances are not available to most adult learners. Adults studying part-time do not have student health insurance.

The training programmes available for adults in these sectors of education do not in general differ from the normal full-time courses in terms of objectives, structure, main content or the awarded qualifications which are all state-recognized. In acquiring higher education, no difference is made between learners in full- and part-time study. In the middle of the 1990s, 79 per cent of those participating in part-time higher education were under 30. Now the age distribution of students has changed: 40 per cent of part-time students and 33 per cent of full-time students are older than 30. The percentage of older students is higher in professional higher education institutions, studying business management, law, teaching and healthcare.

Barriers to Adult Participation in Formal Learning

So far, only some institutions have actively advertised learning opportunities for adults. Private education institutions as newcomers in the education market have to compete for students and thus have found new students mainly among adults. Public universities have the advantage of being able to choose among the best candidates. However, due to the decreasing number of school leavers at secondary school stage, universities now think more about attracting adult learners. The most widespread means for attracting representatives of disadvantaged groups consist of reducing the enrolment fee and/or other costs. Only a small proportion of education institutions organize preparatory courses to level out the inequalities in preparing for entrance exams, but there are rarely any courses to specifically encourage adults and make them more comfortable in their decision to take up study. However, to that end, any previous experience in non-formal education, especially those offered in the university setting by university lectures, may prove helpful, and this is sometimes the route to further studies in higher education.

Two reasons for the increase in older age groups in formal education can be mentioned: firstly, new qualification requirements imposed for some occupations (e.g. nursing, pre-school teaching); secondly, postponing graduation, or only choosing to acquire tertiary education at a later age after having already entered the labour market.[5] According to Adult Education Survey (AES) 2007 data, 5 per cent of 25–64-year-old respondents participate in formal adult education in Estonia. This percentage is slightly lower than the EU average. There is a clear relationship between age group and formal adult education activity: the younger the adult, the more likely that they participate in formal education. Approximately eight times more respondents participate in formal learning in the 25–39 age group than in the 40-and-over age group (16 per cent in contrast with 2 per cent). In the 'leading countries' (Sweden, Norway, Belgium and the Netherlands) the participation rate in the oldest cohort varies from 4 to 8 per cent, while in Estonia it is only 1.5 per cent. Income and social group have a very strong impact on participation in formal adult education in Estonia. For example, manual workers have a ten times lower probability of participation compared with non-manual workers.

A comparison of European countries indicated that Estonia with other Baltic countries and the Slovak Republic represent an average situation in unequal access of demographic groups to formal adult education (see Hefler et al. 2011). Regional differences in access to formal adult learning are not generally relevant, but being of an age over 45 seems to be a barrier. However, it seems that the social barriers – such as being an early school drop-out, being weakly integrated into the labour market, or having a low level of income – play an important role in Estonia. Since demographic obstacles – such as gender or age, living in rural areas or having small children – are less important, social disadvantages play a more crucial role when people decide to return to school.

In what follows, we address the following types of barriers: access barriers to the learning programme – adults may experience specific barriers, for example situational, dispositional or institutional – and barriers to staying in the learning programme and completing it.

Adult access to basic, secondary and vocational education in Estonia is more flexible compared with higher education. A survey of adult learners indicated that more than half of adult basic and secondary schools and 90 per cent of vocational schools are actively recruiting students from disadvantaged groups. Compared with ordinary schools the adult secondary school offers more support to students who belong to risk groups or are at risk of dropping out. Adult gymnasiums enrol young people who have dropped out of the initial education system. The majority of those who have dropped out of or left their previous school are lower secondary students. They had conflicts with teachers or other problems and could not continue in their old school. Some vocational schools offer people who are older than the compulsory school attendance age (17 years) and have not finished lower secondary education initial vocational education and the possibility of finishing lower secondary education. An interviewed representative of a vocational school, who was the author of the idea, explained that:

> When visiting general educational institutions and talking to people from local governments we discovered that there are many adults who have not finished lower secondary education. We discussed the problem with the Ministry of Education and Research and found a solution: such people are offered an opportunity to acquire lower secondary education at the local secondary school by distance learning and at the same time they can live in our dormitory and acquire initial vocational education.

The Ministry has implemented this policy in two other vocational schools. However, the attitude to risk groups is not as positive at all vocational schools.

It seems, then, that the role of adult gymnasiums and in some way also vocational schools offering adult formal education is to 'save' pupils who have not fared so well in the initial education system and to give them opportunity to get an education.[6] The situation in higher education is more complicated. More than half the students pay tuition fees (Saar and Lindemann 2008). In higher education, reserving places for certain groups is not very widely adopted – only very few free study places are reserved for people with special needs or for athletes. The issue has only begun to be discussed in the context of the decreasing number of school leavers, the precarious economic situation and the apprehensions of potential students about drawing a study loan on the one hand, and the insufficient state funding of higher education on the other. It is hoped that because the number of school leavers is decreasing the current level of funding will enable more free study places to be offered to adults and under-represented target groups. The situation worsened during the post-2008 economic depression; representatives of higher educational institutions (interviewed in 2009) noted that an increasing number of students are struggling to pay their study fees.

One barrier to starting higher education is the current skill level of students. Universities apply thresholds for admitting students. Applicants who have graduated from the best schools and come from economically well-off families have a much better chance of being admitted than those who come from weaker schools or have special needs because, as a rule, they achieve better results in state examinations. Thus they are more likely to be admitted to state-commissioned study places. The knowledge (both general and of specific subjects) of school leavers was considered to be rather uneven. This means that candidates from schools where the level of teaching is lower are less likely to be admitted to day courses. Although universities offer preparatory courses to those who wish to better their knowledge, these courses are provided for a fee and are not available in all regions.

A representative of the Ministry of Education and Research admitted when interviewed (Tamm and Saar 2010) that:

> The current system of state commissioned education is considered normal – people believe that if you have graduated from a so-called elite school (one of the best schools in Tallinn or Tartu, which accept 7-year-olds to year one on the basis of entrance tests) then you have the right to a state funded study place because you are better than others. Nobody seems to realise that the advantages of an elite school graduate may be the result of his/her better starting position

> compared with a graduate from a secondary school in the countryside or a small town. Our society does not recognize that social fairness is a problem. People do not want to see it.

To some extent, higher education has become somewhat more accessible due to colleges opened in the regions, allowing the student to decrease transport and accommodation costs. Local colleges are also perceived as more student friendly, as they are in general smaller in student numbers.

The recognition of earlier studies and work experience in admitting students (as is widespread in several Nordic countries) is absent in Estonia. Earlier studies can be used (to obtain credit points) only after admittance. Cooperation between formal and non-formal educational institutions has been limited. In particular this applies to recognition of previous studies and work experience. The representative of one non-formal education institution complained that: 'Unfortunately knowledge acquired in informal education is not recognized by formal education . . . Efforts have been made but it does not seem to function properly. Non-formal education is seen as a hobby club – it is not taken very seriously'. On the other hand, universities also offer an opportunity to enrol for courses through the Open University. Such learners are not officially students and can study one or two subjects by paying only for the credit points received. This provides adult learners with an opportunity to test their ability and willingness to study and to assess the quality of the course. Later, they can transfer to formal education. Although several universities have Open University departments, their focuses are different.

Situational barriers are those closely tied to a person's life situation. A survey of adults learning in the formal education system indicated that the most important problem for adults turned out to be time, as almost half of all adults admitted having too little time to study. Quite a significant problem is related to stress at work. Family-related barriers tended to be mentioned less frequently. Childcare may also be a problem: even though in general there is high coverage with public childcare, adult students have to attend classes in the evenings or at weekends, and sometimes sessions last through the entire week, so childcare at night becomes a problem. Larger secondary schools have classes both during the day and in the evenings, and then more students prefer daytime classes, while others have to rely on help from their families or friends. Schools however consider organizing childcare on school premises too complicated because of strict state requirements.

Almost a third of students experience problems with transport. The travel fare concessions granted to pupils of general educational institutions are decided by local governments. Although students can use travel fare concessions, transport costs may be significant for those who live away from schools, and since buses stop running early students may have problems returning home from county centres after classes. Adult secondary schools do not have dormitories where students from economically disadvantaged backgrounds or distant regions can stay during the week. Since even those studying evening or distance courses have to attend classes several times a week, the distance to school or lack of transportation may prevent people from starting or continuing learning.

Among institutional barriers, financial reasons are the most prevalent, particularly for adults studying in higher education institutions because many adult students must pay tuition fees. Paying for one's studies assumes that students earn a decent income or have the possibility to repay a study loan. Those studying part-time cannot draw a loan. More than a third of adult secondary school students and vocational school students experience financial problems. One of the main reasons for dropping out of vocational school is finding a job – because of their financial problems many students are ready to change school for even the lowest paid jobs.

Dispositional barriers, such as difficulties competing with younger students, are reported by less than one-fifth of students. Many adults, in particular those who have lower education and who have been away from school for a longer period, are unable to perceive themselves as learners; in addition, public opinion (including family, co-workers, employers) does not always encourage adults to return to education. Those who return to education after a number of years need preparatory courses and counselling before as well as during study.

Strategies of Educational Institutions to Support their Adult Students

Representatives of adult gymnasiums indicated (Tamm and Saar 2010) that ordinary schools (the initial education system) are oriented towards average pupils with no problems at school. This means that pupils with learning and behaviour problems are not getting sufficient attention. Big classes in general secondary school also hamper dealing with these problems. One head teacher compared teaching in the initial education system with a conveyor belt. In adult gymnasiums due to the nature of the target group both the head teacher and the staff have to support students more than those in the initial education system. Teachers in adult gymnasiums must work individually (individual tutoring, extra classes) with students to prevent them dropping out and to improve their progress. The adult secondary school has a different attitude towards students: they are treated as responsible adults. The learning environment is supportive.

Employer Practices to Support their Working Students

The interviews conducted with representatives of schools and employers indicated that employers' attitudes towards studying vary significantly; some employers fully support their employees, others believe that coping with work and study is the learner's problem. Although most employers admit that education is important there is room for development at the single enterprise level. This concerns in particular general education.

The main support provided by employers to learners (see Roosalu and Tamm 2010) is allowing them flexible working hours: either they can choose when they do their work without change in overall hours, or they can opt for part-time schemes. Only some enterprises offer indirect financial support by continuing to pay the learner's salary for the time spent at lectures or on study leave. Paying the fees or other costs related to study is limited because this was (during the time of interviews) taxable by the fringe benefit tax. However, some companies are ready to provide financial support if necessary.

In the past, financial support was also offered by enterprises whose employees were studying at evening school. However, during the transition period, the schools have received no financial or moral support from enterprises. Because of the current economic situation students have faced difficulties, for example many do not take study leave because they are afraid of losing their jobs. The representative of one adult gymnasium admitted that:

> Some people do not dare to ask their employer to allow them to leave early two or three times a week; they are afraid of losing their job and being replaced by someone who can work full time. Very few employers – mainly state agencies – support employees who are acquiring general education. Other companies are less supportive. For example chain stores where secondary education is a must. If people can agree with their colleagues and they have a work schedule that allows them to attend classes, they can study. Employers make no allowances. Students say that they are not able to continue. Despite the fact that the law requires employers to give study leave to their employees.

The economic situation of the learner is further complicated by their loss of job, and also the unemployment of a family member may make them more likely to discontinue study. Sometimes working students migrate abroad to find a (better) job, which again increases their chances of discontinuing their studies. The result of this, combined with the greater impact of barriers during economic crises – such as transport and other related costs – is that the number of drop-outs from adult gymnasiums has increased.

CONCLUSIONS AND DISCUSSION

Stenning and Hörschelmann (2008) indicate that differences between post-socialist countries and Western countries are often reduced to their relative backwardness. These states are perpetually deemed to be 'catching up' in both material and institutional terms (see also Masson 2004). Despite this, the Estonian population arrived at the transition with high educational level and labour market experience, and these assets were quite evenly distributed among the population. Our comparisons with the Soviet period highlight some benefits of the previous enlightenment project. The educational system was highly standardized and stratified. The transition to universal secondary education was forced. Nevertheless, the education system and policies were predisposed toward formal adult learning and the participation of disadvantaged social groups. From whatever angle the production-regime-centred ideology might be regarded, it has its logic in a different argumentation than the current European mainstream and its lifelong learning policies. While EU policies stress individual competitiveness in the labour market as a tool to secure economic growth and raise the level of individual remuneration, the Soviet education system in its later stages was more prone to support and encourage people to find a purpose in contributing to – not necessarily materialistic – common social goals. In so doing, education could and did become a tool to achieve social integration and development, rather than only economic progress. The mental, but also structural and institutional, shift towards a neoliberal market-oriented paradigm took place in Estonian society during the 1990s.

As a consequence, we argue, the transformation brought about, in general terms, realignment from the more notorious goals of learning as enlightenment per se and the instrumentalization of education and knowledge as something relevant only for the productive sphere. Such orientation towards providing the population with labour market-relevant skills was the reason for the Soviet system's development of vocational education, and one can therefore consider Soviet policies as similar to current EU development towards the knowledge-for-economic-growth paradigm.

This development was coupled in Estonia with the abolition of the otherwise perfectly functional institutional arrangements that had been developed by the end of the socialist period. This was especially so in adult education, because of choices made within the newly independent country to oppose anything connected to the previous system because it was imposed from outside. A lack of resources, first and foremost financial but also those capable of legitimizing the possible strengths of the previous system, eventually led to the weakness of the new decentralized and market-based system, which has a clear tendency – and good reasons –

to follow market logics in education. Hence the outcome of increased inequalities in participation and the role of the formal education system in catering for the 'weak', or those of disadvantaged backgrounds, because the 'strong' more easily find their own way in the system.

Estonia inherited from the Soviet period a poorly diversified formal adult education system which worked quite well when the role of the state was crucial in the process of lifelong learning. Later, this low diversification combined with marketization and liberalization in education brought about a sharp increase in inequality of participation because individuals are mainly responsible for their own education.

After ten years with societal transformation, the Organisation for Economic Co-operation and Development (OECD) (2000) report on Estonia's education policy stated that employers should play an increasing role in the demand for accessible training opportunities. Other providers – primarily non-public institutions – respond to the need, although these programmes tend to be in areas where the demand and potential for economic gain are greatest and are available primarily in the urban areas. Today, state policies for regulating quality continue to be weak and the cost of non-public programmes makes them inaccessible to large segments of the adult population.

Coordination, linkages and pathways between formal and non-formal learning are still not very well developed, as can be seen in the difficulties in promoting cooperation between the different networks of schools and other stakeholders, and the quite slow progress in the recognition of prior learning.

We conclude that while formal education provides participation opportunities for adults at all educational levels, different levels are seen to have different aims in the overall framework of lifelong learning. Provision at the basic, secondary and also vocational levels is targeted to a greater extent at groups with special educational needs, since the general (compulsory) education system is not able to effectively involve and provide for all groups but can mainly manage the mystical 'average' student, complying with the norms and requirements. Provision of higher education has been characterized by more flexibility in order to attract diverse adult learners with needs that are different to those of traditional students; however, this practice has been more widespread in private universities since the beginning of the transformation period, while in public universities the respective views have been emerging only recently and therefore are still quite new. However, public support for implementation of these practices has been low and state financing has not quite caught up with the need to become a flexible learning space for lifelong learning.

During the socialist period adults, and employees in particular, enjoyed a learning-supportive environment within both the workplace and the education system. The Soviet period in Estonia was followed by destruction of institutions from that system, including those that could have supported the provision of education to the adult population, such as the national qualification framework which encouraged further training and human resources development (HRD)-supportive management practices, all with a view to secure the continuous development of human capital. As a result, in the sphere of education, increased inequality of access together with the neoliberalizing of society, workplaces and education system has meant that human capital did not enjoy continuous development. In addition, in some cases this viewed the meaning of education from a much more instrumentalist and labour-market-driven perspective. The question of further postmaterializing of the value system, which would direct attention towards other aspects of the functions of education in society and would enable definition and measurement of education efficiency in different terms, remains somewhat open as yet.

However, it is worth thinking of the changes in Estonian education and lifelong learning as reflecting the special nature of its state formation. As discussed by Valeri Bunce, these changes come within the framework of the dissolution of not only the socialist system but also the Soviet state. Therefore we suggest a clearer differentiation between post-Soviet and post-socialist European countries. In addition, we suggest it would be useful to think of Estonian society – and perhaps also the societies of other post-socialist countries – as currently undergoing a phase of de-development of their human capital, as suggested by Meurs and Ranasinghe. This, we claim, poses some unique problems for these societies and their education and lifelong learning systems.

NOTES

1. Bohle et al. (2007) emphasize the role of international political, as well as economic, bodies in the establishment of different transition strategies. The impact of neoliberal ideology through external advisors and the conditionality of the internal financial institutions were considered very important (see Wedel 2001; Kennedy 2002).
2. The system was highly stratified: the scope of choices (and length of educational path) was strongly determined by school, where general education was obtained. Estonian general (not vocational) education was highly standardized. Credential signals were addressed rather to institutions of higher education to facilitate their selection process, not to employers.
3. The mentality prevalent in business circles is oriented only toward an individualist competition ideology. Research showed that the idea of cooperation with competitors is strongly rejected (Terk 1999, p. 62).
4. As the drop-out rate from basic schools increased in the 1990s, parliament adopted an amendment to the Vocational Educational Institutions Act, providing for preliminary

vocational training for young people up to 25 years of age who have not completed basic education. These young people can now acquire basic education parallel to vocational education.

5. While in 1999, 64 per cent of university graduates were 24 years old or younger, in 2003 this age group accounted for approximately half of all graduates. In 2003 only 63 per cent of all students graduated within the standard period of study (Eesmets 2004).
6. According to an OECD (2000) report the subject content of basic school can be mastered by only the top 15 per cent of students.

REFERENCES

Aava, Katrin (2009), 'Haridusalaste tekstide võrdlev diskursusanalüüs' (Comparative discourse analysis of educational texts), *Eesti Rakenduslingvistika Ühingu* Aastaraamat (Estonian Papers in Applied Linguistics), **5**, 7–17; in Estonian.

Ashton, David, Johnny Sung and Jill Turbin (2000), 'Towards a framework for the comparative analysis of national systems of skill formation', *International Journal of Training and Development*, **4** (1), 8–25.

Becker, Gary (1964), *Human Capital. A Theoretical and Empirical Analysis with Special Reference to Education*, Chicago, IL: University of Chicago Press.

Bohle, Dorothee, Hugo Radice and Stuart Shields (2007), 'Introduction', *Competition and Change*, **11** (2), 81–87.

Brown, Philip, Andy Green and Hugh Lauder (2001), *High Skills: Globalisation, Competitiveness and Skill Formation*, Oxford: Oxford University Press.

Bunce, Valerie (1999), *Subversive Institutions: The Design and the Destruction of Socialism and the State*, Cambridge: Cambridge University Press.

Bunce, Valerie (2003), 'Rethinking Recent Democratization: Lessons from the Postcommunist Experience', *World Politics*, **55** (2), 167–192.

Byford, Andy and Polly Jones (2006), 'Policies and Practices of Transition in Soviet Education from the Revolution to the End of Stalinism', *History of Education*, **35** (4–5), 419–426.

Eamets, Raul (2008), 'Economic Structure, Labour Market and Education', in Mati Heidmets (ed.), *Estonian Human Development Report 2007*, Tallinn: Eesti Koostöö Kogu, pp. 97–101.

Eesmets, Kersti (2004), 'Education and Well-Being', in Alari Purju (ed.), *Social Trends 3*, Tallinn: Statistical Office of Estonia, pp. 19–35.

Ennuste, Ulo, Kalev Kukk, Tiia Pyss and Mare Viies (2004), 'Political Economy Narrative Analysis of Estonian 1987–2006 Capitalist Market Reform Process'. Available at: http://www.gdnet.org/pdf2/gdn_library/global_research_projects/understanding_reform/Estonia_third_draft.pdf (accessed 03.05.2011).

Fragoulis, Haralabos, Jean-Raymond Masson and Vaclav Klehna (2004), 'Improving opportunities for Adult Learning in the Ascending and Candidate Countries of Central and Eastern Europe', *European Journal of Education*, **39**, 9–30.

Gerber, Theodore P. and Michael Hout (1995), 'Educational Stratification in Russia during the Soviet Period', *American Journal of Sociology*, **101**, 611–660.

Hefler, Günter (2011), *The Qualification-Supporting Company – The Significance of Formal Adult Education in Small and Medium Organizations*, LLL2010 SP4 comparative report, working paper. Available at: http://LLL2010.tlu.ee.

Hefler, Günter, Péter Róbert, Paul Ringler, Matild Sági, Stefanie Rammel, Anikó Balogh and Jörg Markowitsch (2011), *Formal Adult Education in Context – The View of European Statistics*, SP 2 – Synthesis Report.

Helemäe, Jelena and Ellu Saar (1999), 'The Estonian Education System in the Second Half of the 20th Century: Opportunities and Choices for the Cohorts', in Raivo Vetik (ed.), *Estonian Human Development Report 1999*, Tallinn: UNDP, pp. 84–92.

Helemäe, Jelena, Ellu Saar and Rein Vöörmann (2000), *Kas haridusse tasus investeerida? Hariduse selekteerivast ja stratifitseerivast rollist kahe põlvkonna kogemuse alusel* (Returns to Education. On the Selective and Stratifying Role of Education: the Example of Two Cohorts), Tallinn: Teaduste Akadeemia Kirjastus.

Holford, John, Sheila Riddell, Elisabet Weedon, Judit Litjens, Guy Hannan, Vida A. Mohorčič Špolar, Peter Beltram, Angela Ivančič and Jasmina Mirečeva (2007), 'Lifelong Learning: Patterns of Policy in Thirteen European Countries LLL2010 SP 1 Comparative Report', *LLL2010 Project Reports*, **1**. Available at: http://www.gdnet.org/pdf2/gdn_library/global_research_projects/understanding_reform/Estonia_first_draft.pdf.

Kennedy, Michael D. (2002), *Cultural Formations of Post-Communism: Emancipation, Transition, Nation and War*, Minneapolis, MN, USA and London, UK: University of Minnesota Press.

Masson, Jean-Raymond (2004), 'Implementation of the Lisbon Objectives by the Acceding and Candidate Countries', *Vocational Training*, **33** (3), 6–22.

Meurs, Mieke and Rasika Ranasinghe (2003), 'De-Development in Post-Socialism: Conceptual and Measurement Issues', *Politics and Society*, **31** (1), 31–53.

Nölke, Andreas and Arjan Vliegenthart (2009), 'Enlarging the Varieties of Capitalism. The Emergence of Dependent Market Economies in east Central Europe', *World Politics*, **61** (4), 670–702.

Nurmela, Kristi and Liis Roosaar (2009), 'Estonia: Collective Bargaining and Continuous Vocational Training'. Available at: http://www.eurofound.europa.eu/eiro/studies/tn0804048s/ee0804049q.htm (accessed 30.04.2011).

OECD (2000), *Reviews of National Policies for Education – Estonia*. Paris: OECD.

Paas, Tiiu and Jüri Sepp (2008), 'Structure of the Estonian economy', in Mati Heidmets and Erik Terk (eds), *Estonian Human Development Report 2007*, Tallinn: Eesti Koostöö Kogu, pp. 92–97.

Roberts, Ken (2001), 'The New East European Model of Education, Training and Youth Employment', *Journal of Education and Work*, **14** (3), 215–230.

Roosalu, Triin and Eve-Liis Roosmaa (2010), 'Back At School: Do They Really Have Nothing Else To Do? Lifelong Learning Ideologies', in Vladimir Kozlovskiy, Rein Vöörmann and Triin Roosalu (eds), *Learning in Transistion: Policies and Practicies of Liflong Learning in Post Socialist Countries*, St Petersburg: Nauka, pp. 41–65.

Roosalu, Triin and Auni Tamm (2010), 'Human Resource Managers as Agencies of Lifelong Learning: The Case of Estonia', in Vladimir Kozlovskiy, Rein Vöörmann and Triin Roosalu (eds), *Learning in Transistion: Policies and Practicies of Liflong Learning in Post Socialist Countries*, St Petersburg: Nauka, pp. 221–233.

Roosmaa, Eve-Liis and Ellu Saar (2010), 'Participating in Non-Formal Learning: Patterns of Inequality in EU-15 and the New EU-8 Member Countries', *Journal of Education and Work*, **23** (3), 179–206.

Rubenson, Kjell and Richard Desjardins (2009), 'The Impact of Welfare State Regimes on Barriers to Participation in Adult Education. A Bounded Agency Model', *Adult Education Quarterly*, **59** (3), 187–207.

Saar, Ellu (2008), 'Expansion of Higher Education and Opportunities in the Labour Market', in Mati Heidmets (ed.), *Estonian Human Development Report 2007*, Tallinn: Eesti Koostöö Kogu, pp. 20–27.

Saar, Ellu and Kristina Lindemann (2008), 'Estonia', in Irena Kogan, Michael Gebel and Clemens Noelke (eds), *Europe Enlarged: a Handbook of Education, Labour and Welfare Regimes in Central and Eastern Europe*, Bristol: Policy Press, pp. 151–181.

Saarniit, Jüri (1998), 'Value Change and Value Marginality of a Generation: Ethnic Differences in Communist and Post-Communist Estonia', in Helena Helve (ed.), *Unification and Marginalization of Young People*, Helsinki: The Finnish Youth Research Society, pp. 43–68.

Stark, David (1996), 'Recombinant Property in East European Capitalism', *American Journal of Sociology*, **101** (4), 993–1027.

Stenning, Alison and Kathrin Hörschelmann (2008), 'History, Geography and Difference in the Post-Socialist World: Or, Do We Still Need Post-Socialism?' *Antipode*, **40** (2), 313–335.

Tamm, Auni and Margarita Kazjulja (2010), 'Who Learns What: The Different Experiences of Professional Groups in Further education in Estonia', in Vladimir Kozlovskiy, Rein Vöörmann and Triin Roosalu (eds), *Learning in Transistion: Policies and Practicies of Liflong Learning in Post Socialist Countries*, St Petersburg: Nauka, pp. 155–170.

Tamm, Auni and Eve-Liis Roosmaa (2010), *A Review on the Formal Education Participation of SME Employees*, SP4 National Report – Estonia.

Tamm, Auni and Ellu Saar (2010), *SP5 Estonia country report*.

Terk, Erik (1999), 'Estonia's Economic Development: Achievements, Conflicts. Prospects', in Raivo Vetik (ed.), *Estonian Human Development Report 1999*, Tallinn: UNDP, pp. 60–66.

Vöörmann, Rein (2010), 'The Impact of Ascriptive Characteristics on Motives for Participation in Training: Estonia on the Backdrop of Selected European Countries', in Vladimir Kozlovskiy, Rein Vöörmann and Triin Roosalu (eds), *Learning in Transition: Policies and Practicies of Lifelong Learning in Post-Socialist Countries*, St Petersburg: Nauka, pp. 135–153.

Wedel, Janine R. (2001), *Collision and Collusion: The Strange Case of Western Aid to Eastern Europe*, London: Palgrave Macmillan.

Whitmarsh, Lona and Ruxandra Ritter (2007), 'The Influence of Communism on Career Development and Education in Romania', *The Career Development Quarterly*, **56**, 85–95.

Zajda, Joseph (2003), 'Educational Reform and Transformation in Russia', *European Education*, **35** (1), 58–88.

Conclusion: lifelong learning as a social field and entrance point to policy-making for education and training

Ellu Saar, John Holford and Odd Bjørn Ure

The importance attached to adult education institutions throughout this book leads to a discussion of structures and institutional agency. The analyses of lifelong learning (LLL) at a micro, meso and macro level emphasize both institutional and socio-personal processes, including their implications for policy-making. By treating LLL as a social field, institutional perspectives on social change and path-dependency are displayed. This necessitates looking further into the social science perspectives, and our concluding remarks start with a retrospective of them.

TYPOLOGIES AND SOCIAL MECHANISMS

The previous chapters have dealt with how formal adult education is positioned within national education systems, the LLL discourse and in the framework of social sciences' contribution to LLL. As to the latter, we have demonstrated that typologizations of formal education within the landscape of adult education research are confronted with the classical challenge for social sciences of explaining how bits and pieces function, as against only categorizing them.

In spite of the literature on mechanism-based explanations in social societies (Elster 1989; Machamer et al. 2000), it may be easier to dissect all these elements than to explain how they function together and why they behave as they do. The act of carefully dissecting complex social processes, to determine their most important constituent components, has been one principle in the so-called analytical sociology (Hedström 2005). An alternative view of social mechanisms includes relational or structural and environmental mechanisms (Bunge 2004; Pickel 2006), while Elster tends to view social mechanisms as basically psychological mechanisms (Elster 1989 cited in Mayntz 2004).

MULTILEVEL ANALYSIS OF LLL AS A FIELD

Making use of theoretical elements from the sources mentioned in the Introduction, a social field has been investigated by lining up in sequence: its historical origin, the underlying power structures, its institutions and individuals pushing or moving these institutions. This may be referred to as the agency exercised along more or less path-dependent trajectories used to explain complex social phenomena.

This perspective allowed the authors of the chapters to position adult education within the broader LLL discourse. Adult education is considered a social and institutional field. As shown in Chapter 9 on Austria, by introducing a typology, a country's total participation in formal adult education results from seven independent organizational fields. Karen Myers, Natalie Conte and Kjell Rubenson (2012) propose five broader types of learning, in which adults participate according to how adult education and training is organized in practice. The broadness of these types comes from the inclusion of non-formal learning in the typology. Types of adult learning can be further described in terms of who provides the programme or course; who pays for it; the learner's purpose in taking it; the programme duration and other design and delivery features (Myers et al. 2012, p. 12).

Throughout our book, cross-country comparisons and studies of participation of social groups within one country have turned out to be fruitful for policy purposes because they respond to the existence of rather independent fields of educational provision. Austria has for example an adult education community that is experiencing an overall expansion of formal adult education along three lines: new provisions, increasing student population and transformation of existing provisions. Although traditional adult education is becoming an active player in formal adult education, the provision of formal education to adults – with the exception of second-chance programmes – remains outside the sphere of adult education and is not targeted by policy instruments in this sphere.

The main political goals concerning LLL revealed in the country chapters centre on widening access to, and participation in, adult education. For this reason, factors that hinder and promote came to the fore and were subject to multilevel analysis in line with the combined micro-, meso- and macro-level perspective underlying this book. Hungary (Chapter 11) can illustrate this perspective, which seeks to explain the low participation in formal adult learning in terms of policy deficits, institutional deficits and deficits at the individual level. On the governmental or policy level, the lack of cooperation between ministries hampers the required interdepartmental coordination of an LLL policy. This is exacerbated by strong competition for limited financial resources at intra- as well as interministerial level, and further diminishes the motivation to cooperate.

Macro-level changes in the last two decades pushed Hungary into an increasingly difficult economic situation with implications for the welfare state classification; thus changing the country from a quasi social-democratic orientation to growing marketization, at the point of resembling corporatist or Mediterranean societies. At an individual level, learners' dissatisfaction with the missing practical focus of the adult education programmes and doubts about the usefulness of attending formal adult education comply with employers' negative opinions of formal adult education.

INSTITUTIONAL AND SOCIO-PERSONAL PROCESSES

The attempt throughout this book to combine multilevel analyses and institutional perspectives on LLL is certainly a theoretical challenge. This is however not a purely academic exercise because it boosts the understanding of barriers to adult education, with potential implications for policy-making. Furthermore, by analysing multilevel barriers to adult education we demonstrate the interaction between structural factors and individuals' dispositions. Rubenson and Desjardins explain this point succinctly:

> broad structural conditions and targeted policy measures are seen to directly affect the extent and impact of institutional and situational (job and family related) barriers. Structural conditions play a substantial role in forming the circumstances faced by individuals and limit the feasible alternatives to choose from, and therefore they can bound individual agency. (Rubenson and Desjardins 2009, 195–196)

We will add that the act of positioning adult education in a broader context of LLL, understood as a social field composed of subsystems of which adult education is one, has potential repercussions on how participation barriers are dismantled. Chapter 6 on Ireland demonstrates how policies for local community LLL can cope with the integration of socio-personal and institutional processes. This refers back to an older discussion of the distinction between lifelong learning and lifelong education, to which Stephen Billett (2010, p.405) has contributed by stating that LLL does not consist of courses to be organized (for specific institutional purposes), enacted and regulated: 'The balance and reconciliation between the needs and the imperatives of individuals, their communities, workplaces and country . . . is central to considerations of what constitute the purposes, accesses and outcomes of individuals' lifelong learning'.

The research underpinning our book confirms the importance of personal motivation for embarking on and completing adult education. Our use of data from the EU Adult Education Survey, combined with our own surveys, show that access to job positions and securing job prospects are a strong motivating factor for adults attending education and training courses. This employability dimension has been a cornerstone in national and EU policies on LLL, although with shifting emphasis on employability as opposed to active citizenship (see Chapter 1).

Policy-making for LLL has also centred on the inclusion of informal and non-formal learning, perhaps to the extent of relegating formal education to a number of 'capital sins', which are often ascribed to Paolo Freire's 'highly influential prototype' (Hefler 2012, p. 39). By scrutinizing LLL from a formal education perspective, this book has followed another path. When the reader turns the last page of this book, the properties of 'formal' or 'non-formal' education may therefore no longer be classified as being either the 'bad' or the 'good' side of education but as variations of instruction that coexist and take on different functions, while following different institutional logics (ibid., p. 39).

In summary, formal adult education can be perceived as a double process: firstly, providing a (second) chance for adults who receive from education what educational institutions gradually have been able to deliver; and secondly, pushing learners to take steps on institutionalized ladders of social and career mobility (ibid., p. 166). One implication for policy would be that employers on a collective basis become ready to systemically reward qualifications acquired by adults.

We presume that future debates on adult education and lifelong learning can include non-formal and informal learning in policy-making, without playing down the role of formal education. Moreover, lifelong learning research could redefine the employability dimension of LLL through sharper analysis of the socio-personal and institutional processes behind adult learners' wish to access job positions and secure their job prospects. In this landscape, we believe that comparative research on types of formal adult education and their social fields will continue to explain cross-country and intra-country differences as well as the inherent dynamics.

REFERENCES

Billett, Stephen (2010), 'The Perils of Confusing LLL with LLE', *International Journal of Lifelong Education*, **29** (4), 401–413.

Bunge, Mario (2004), 'How Does It Work? The Search for Explanatory Mechanisms', *Philosophy of the Social Sciences*, **34** (2), 182–210.

Elster, Jon (1989), *Nuts and Bolts for the Social Sciences*, Cambridge: Cambridge University Press.

Hedström, Peter (2005), *Dissecting the Social: on the Principles of Analytical Sociology*, Cambridge: Cambridge University Press.

Hefler, Günter (2012), *Taking Steps – Formal Adult Education in Private and Organisational Life*, Vienna: LIT.

Machamer, Peter, Lindlay Darden and Carl F. Craver (2000), 'Thinking about Mechanisms', *Philosophy of Science*, **67** (1), 1–25.

Mayntz, Renate (2004), 'Mechanisms in the Analysis of Social Macro-Phenomena', *Philosophy of the Social Sciences*, **34** (2), 237–259.

Myers, Karen, Natalie Conte and Kjell Rubenson (2012), *Adult Learning Typology. Adult Learning and Returns to Training Project*, Ottawa: Social Research and Demonstration Corporation.

Pickel, Andreas (2006), *The Problem of Order in the Global Age: Systems and Mechanisms*, New York: Palgrave.

Rubenson, Kjell and Richard Desjardins (2009), 'The Impact of Welfare State Regimes on Barriers to Participation in Adult Education: A Bounded Agency Model', *Adult Education Quarterly*, **59** (3), 187–207.

Appendix

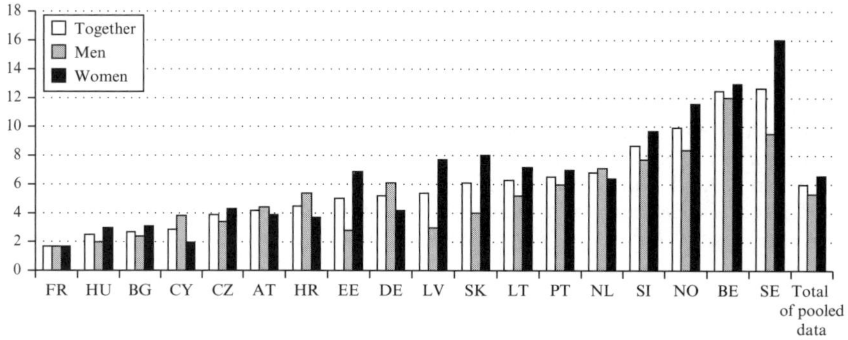

Figure A.1 Participation in formal adult education by country and gender, %

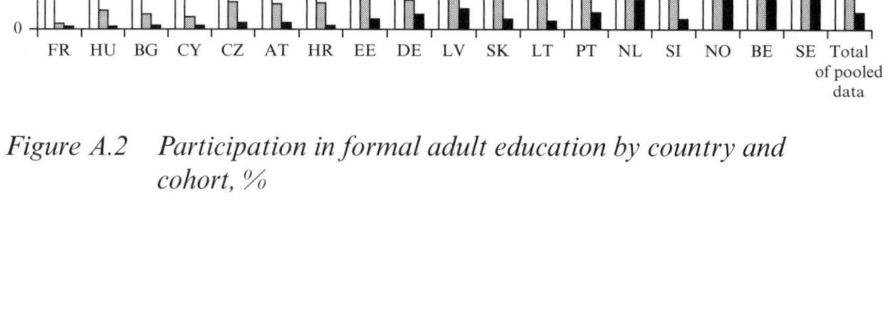

Figure A.2 Participation in formal adult education by country and cohort, %

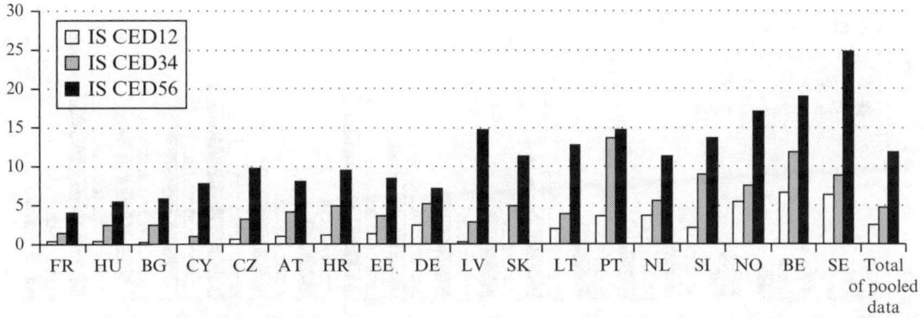

Figure A.3 *Participation in formal adult education by country and initial level of education, %*

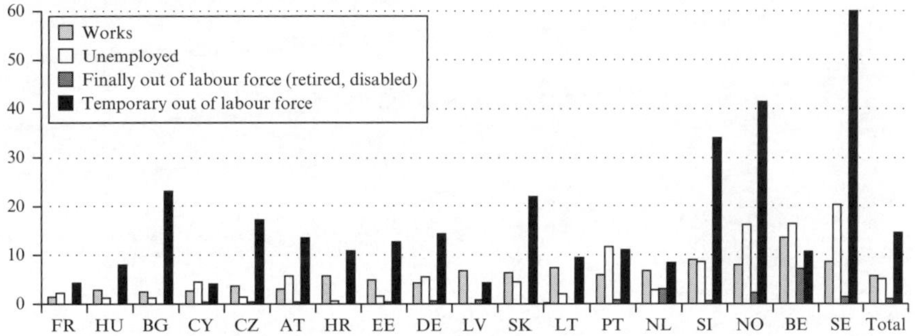

Figure A.4 *Participation in formal adult education by country and participation in labour force, %*

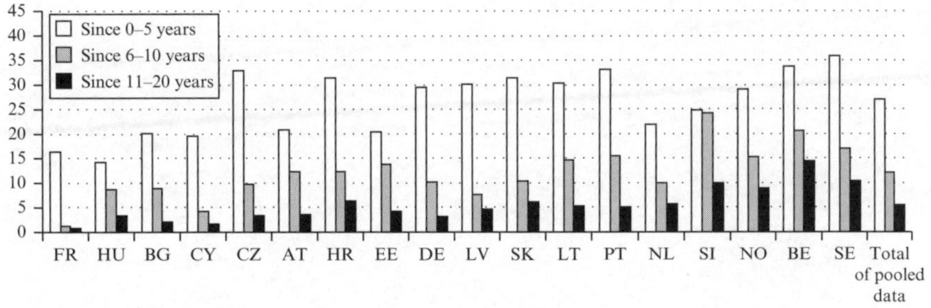

Figure A.5 *Participation in formal adult education by country and duration of time since individual obtained their highest education level, %*

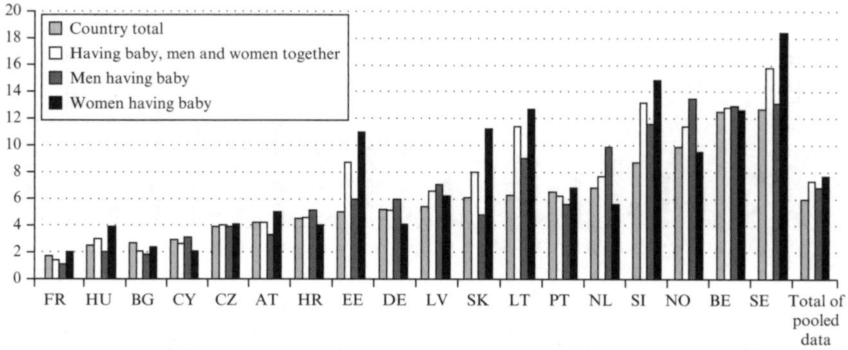

Figure A.6 Formal education participation by having 0–3-year-old child in family by gender and country, %

Index